Violence and R

Media coverage of civil wars often focuses on the most gruesome atrocities and the most extreme conflicts, which might lead one to think that all civil wars involve massive violence against civilians. In truth, many governments and rebel groups exercise restraint in their fighting, largely avoiding violence against civilians in compliance with international law. Governments and rebel groups make strategic calculations about whether to target civilians by evaluating how domestic and international audiences are likely to respond to violence. Restraint is also a deliberate strategic choice: governments and rebel groups often avoid targeting civilians and abide by international legal standards to appeal to domestic and international audiences for diplomatic support. This book presents a wide range of evidence of the strategic use of violence and restraint, using original data on violence against civilians in civil wars from 1989 to 2010 as well as in-depth analyses of conflicts in Azerbaijan, El Salvador, Indonesia, Sudan, Turkey, and Uganda.

JESSICA A. STANTON is an assistant professor of Political Science at the University of Pennsylvania. Previously, she held fellowships at the Center for International Security and Cooperation at Stanford University, the John M. Olin Institute for Strategic Studies at Harvard University, and the Christopher H. Browne Center for International Politics at the University of Pennsylvania. Her research has been published in the Journal of Politics and the Journal of Conflict Resolution.

Violence and Restraint in Civil War

Civilian Targeting in the Shadow of International Law

JESSICA A. STANTON

University of Pennsylvania

CAMBRIDGE
UNIVERSITY PRESS

University Printing House, Cambridge CB2 8BS, United Kingdom

One Liberty Plaza, 20th Floor, New York, NY 10006, USA

477 Williamstown Road, Port Melbourne, VIC 3207, Australia

4843/24, 2nd Floor, Ansari Road, Daryaganj, Delhi - 110002, India

79 Anson Road, #06-04/06, Singapore 079906

Cambridge University Press is part of the University of Cambridge.

It furthers the University's mission by disseminating knowledge in the pursuit of education, learning and research at the highest international levels of excellence.

www.cambridge.org
Information on this title: www.cambridge.org/9781107670945

First published 2016

A catalogue record for this publication is available from the British Library

Library of Congress Cataloging in Publication data
Names: Stanton, Jessica A., 1978– author.
Title: Violence and restraint in civil war : civilian targeting in the shadow of international law / Jessica A. Stanton, University of Pennsylvania.
Description: New York, NY : Cambridge University Press, 2016. | Partially based on author's thesis (doctoral - Columbia University, 2009) under the title: Strategies of violence and restraint in civil war. | Includes bibliographical references and index.
Identifiers: LCCN 2016010209| ISBN 9781107069107 (Hardback) | ISBN 9781107670945 (Paperback)
Subjects: LCSH: Civilians in war. | Civilians in war–Case studies. | Civil war–Protection of civilians. | Civil war–Protection of civilians–Case studies.
Classification: LCC JZ6385 .S78 2016 | DDC 341.6/3–dc23 LC record available at https://lccn.loc.gov/2016010209

ISBN 978-1-107-06910-7 Hardback
ISBN 978-1-107-67094-5 Paperback

For Emery and Teodor

Contents

Figures

Tables

Acknowledgments

This book began as two seminar papers, written in 2002 during my first year of graduate school at Columbia University. In those papers, I set out to explore whether and how international law influences the behavior of belligerents during wartime – in particular, during civil wars. Most research on international law had focused on its role in international economic relations, but I was interested in whether international law could have any impact on the behavior of actors whose security was threatened during wartime, and, if so, why some actors might be more susceptible to the influence of international law than others. The project changed considerably over the years – becoming a broader exploration of the dynamics of civil war violence – as it morphed from seminar papers into dissertation research, and ultimately into this book. But driving the project has always been a curiosity about the impact of international legal standards on wartime behavior and the conditions under which actors are willing and able to limit their use of violence.

More than a decade has passed since I wrote those first seminar papers, and in that time, many people and institutions have provided valuable guidance and support. My advisors at Columbia, Jack Snyder and Page Fortna, were incredibly generous with their time and advice. Jack's enthusiasm for the project from its first incarnation as a seminar paper through to its conclusion was an important source of encouragement, especially at moments when I was most unsure about how to proceed with the project. His probing questions and seemingly encyclopedic knowledge of cases of civil war challenged me to develop a more compelling argument, backed by more extensive evidence. Page offered detailed feedback at every stage of the process. I am particularly grateful for her patient willingness to help me work through problems as they arose in the course of research and writing – offering suggestions for how to refine the logic of an argument, reorganize a chapter, and conduct field interviews. Her mentorship while I was in graduate school and in the years since not only has strengthened my scholarship, but also has guided me through the transition from graduate student to professor.

A number of other faculty members at Columbia also deserve thanks. Tanisha Fazal provided valuable feedback on my dissertation research at multiple stages of the project, as well as practical advice for establishing an academic career. Three other faculty members – Séverine Autesserre, Michael Doyle, and Macartan Humphreys – joined Jack Snyder and Page Fortna on my dissertation defense committee. They each read my dissertation in its entirety and gave me extensive comments, which significantly influenced the changes I made in writing this book.

My friends and colleagues in graduate school were – and in many cases, continue to be – my most trusted sounding board for new ideas. Many of them, including Brianna Avery, Josh Baron, Christina Greer, Leila Kazemi, Thania Sanchez, and Alex Weisiger, gave me crucial feedback at the earliest stages of this project.

During my dissertation research and writing, I received generous fellowship support from the Center for International Security and Cooperation (CISAC) at Stanford University, the John M. Olin Institute for Strategic Studies at Harvard University, and the Christopher H. Browne Center for International Politics at the University of Pennsylvania. Each of these places, and the community of scholars they brought together, greatly enriched my research, exposing me to new ways of thinking about my project and about political science more broadly. I am especially grateful to my colleagues at each of these institutions, and to the participants in each institution's research seminar, for their valuable comments on this project. Jeremy Weinstein and David Cunningham deserve special mention for the careful, detailed critiques and suggestions they provided as discussants in these seminars. Conversations with David, as well as with Kathleen Cunningham and Dara Cohen, have been important sources of ideas and encouragement throughout the last ten years. I am grateful for their friendship.

While I was at CISAC in 2005–2006, I had the good fortune to reconnect with my undergraduate advisor at Stanford, David Abernethy. He was the first to spark my interest in political science with his courses on African politics, foreign aid, and human rights. His teaching and mentoring shaped my intellectual interests, and he patiently guided me through my first major attempts at academic research as an undergraduate. He was and continues to be a role model for me of how to be a thoughtful and caring scholar and teacher.

Conducting field research in Uganda and Indonesia, in 2005 and 2006, respectively, was both the most challenging and the most rewarding part of this project. I am grateful to the many people in Indonesia and Uganda who shared their time, their insights, and their personal experiences with me; who guided me to new sources of information; and who helped me to understand the nuances and complexities of the civil wars in each of these countries. Before I left for Uganda, Adam Branch, Zachary Mampilly, and Jennifer

Tappan offered helpful advice on both practical matters and research; once I arrived, Russell Schiebel did much the same. For sharing their expertise on conducting research in Indonesia and providing guidance at a critical point in my field research, I thank Harold Crouch, Mirjam Künkler, and Kumiko Mizuno. Special thanks go to Neda Farzan and my partner, Ayodeji Perrin, who traveled with me during my field research, offering friendship and moral support. They encouraged me to remain optimistic, even on my most frustrating days of research. For providing the financial support that allowed me to carry out this field research, I thank the Graduate School of Arts and Sciences, the Arnold A. Saltzman Institute of War and Peace Studies, and the Weatherhead East Asian Institute, all at Columbia University.

Since arriving at Penn, I have benefited from the advice and support of a wonderful community of colleagues. I am especially grateful to my colleagues in international relations – Avery Goldstein, Julia Gray, Mike Horowitz, Ed Mansfield, and Alex Weisiger – who have read much of my work over the years, and have offered thoughtful advice and support. The Christopher H. Browne Center for International Politics at Penn generously funded a book conference to discuss a draft of this book manuscript. Alex Downes and Stathis Kalyvas served as discussants at this conference, and provided extensive, detailed commentary on every chapter of the manuscript. Many of my colleagues at Penn participated as well, offering helpful comments and suggestions for revisions, including Eileen Doherty-Sil, Daniel Gillion, Jeff Green, Nancy Hirschmann, Matt Levendusky, John Lapinski, Marc Meredith, Rudy Sil, and David Steinberg, as well as my international relations colleagues. A number of undergraduate and graduate students at Penn provided valuable research assistance, including Joseph Cloward, Marissa Dwyer, Megha Jain, Andrew Levin, Katie McCarthy, Laura Resnick, and Basak Taraktas.

At Cambridge University Press, my editor, Robert Dreesen, patiently guided this project through its evolution from a manuscript to a book; I am grateful to him for his support and advice throughout this process. Two anonymous reviewers provided careful feedback on the full book manuscript. Their suggestions greatly improved the final version of the book.

Finally, words are insufficient to express how deeply appreciative I am for the love and support of my family. It is not possible to catalogue the lifetime of debts I have accumulated to my parents, Joan and Michael; however, I am most grateful to them for their unwavering confidence in me, and their unending encouragement. My brother, Michael, is a loyal friend and supporter, always optimistic about the prospects for this book. Over many years of research and writing, my partner, Ayodeji, has been a sounding board for many of the ideas and arguments that make up this book. He pushed me to sharpen my arguments and my prose, with his incisive questions and his meticulous editing. His friendship has been a source of strength and reassurance for more than a decade now. This book is dedicated to our children, Emery and Teodor, who have brought such immense joy into our lives.

Abbreviations

AGAM	Forces of the Free Aceh Movement (Angkatan Gerakan Aceh Merdeka)
CNRM	National Council of Maubere Resistance (Conselho Nacional da Resistência Maubere)
COHA	Cessation of Hostilities Agreement
DEP	Democratic Party (Demokrasi Partisi)
FMLN	Farabundo Martí National Liberation Front (Frente Farabundo Martí para la Liberación Nacional)
Fretilin	Revolutionary Front for an Independent East Timor (Frente Revolucionária do Timor Leste Independente)
GAM	Free Aceh Movement (Gerakan Aceh Merdeka)
HEP	People's Labor Party (Halkın Emek Partisi)
HSM	Holy Spirit Movement
ICC	International Criminal Court
IGAD	Intergovernmental Authority on Development
JEM	Justice and Equality Movement
LRA	Lord's Resistance Army
NIF	National Islamic Front
NRM/A	National Resistance Movement/Army
NTC	National Transitional Council
PKK	Kurdistan Workers' Party (Partiya Karkerên Kurdistan)
SIRA	Aceh Referendum Information Centre (Sentral Informasi Referendum Aceh)
SLA	Sudan Liberation Army
SPLA	Sudan People's Liberation Army

UDT	Timorese Democratic Union (União Democrática Timorense)
UNAMET	UN Mission in East Timor
UNPO	Unrepresented Nations and Peoples Organization
UPDA	Ugandan People's Democratic Army

Introduction

In January 2005, the International Commission of Inquiry on Darfur issued a report to the United Nations detailing crimes committed by Sudanese government forces during the ongoing conflict in Darfur. The Commission found that "government forces and militias conducted indiscriminate attacks, including killing of civilians, torture, enforced disappearances, destruction of villages, rape and other forms of sexual violence, pillaging and forced displacement, throughout Darfur."[1] Sudanese government officials interviewed for the report claimed that their actions in Darfur were "conducted on the basis of military imperatives"; the Commission, however, disputed this contention, stating that "most attacks were deliberately and indiscriminately directed against civilians."[2]

Referring specifically to evidence from the Commission's report, the UN Security Council in March 2005 referred the situation in Darfur to the International Criminal Court (ICC). After several years of investigation, on March 4, 2009, the ICC issued an arrest warrant for Sudan's president, Omar al-Bashir, charging him with war crimes and crimes against humanity committed during the conflict in Darfur. According to the arrest warrant, "a core component" of the Sudanese government's counterinsurgency campaign involved attacks on civilians from the Fur, Masalit, and Zaghawa ethnic groups believed to be supporting the insurgency.[3] These attacks, including murder, extermination, forcible transfer, pillage, rape, and torture, were widespread and systematic, affecting "hundreds of thousands of individuals ... across large swathes of the territory of the Darfur region."[4] In July 2010, the ICC issued a second arrest warrant for Bashir, adding genocide to the list of his alleged crimes in Darfur and accusing Sudanese government forces of deliberately targeting Fur, Masalit, and

---

[1] United Nations 2005, 3.   [2] Ibid.   [3] International Criminal Court 2009, 4.   [4] Ibid., 5.

Zaghawa individuals on the basis of their ethnicity.[5] In addition to Bashir, the ICC also accused two other high-level officials of war crimes and crimes against humanity, issuing arrest warrants for Ahmad Harun, the former Minister of State for the Interior of the Government of Sudan, and Ali Kushayb, a leader of the Janjaweed – a pro-government militia that collaborated closely with regular Sudanese government forces in carrying out attacks against civilians.[6]

At the same time that the Commission of Inquiry was warning of escalating government atrocities in Darfur, another long-running civil war was coming to a conclusion. At the end of January 2005, Indonesian government representatives met in Helsinki with members of the Free Aceh Movement (Gerakan Aceh Merdeka, GAM) for renewed peace negotiations to end the conflict in Indonesia's northernmost province of Aceh. When the Acehnese rebellion began in 1989, the Indonesian government under General Suharto responded by launching a campaign that has been described as the "institutionalization of terror."[7] Indonesian government forces regularly killed Acehnese civilians – shooting them at close range in face-to-face encounters and deliberately leaving their dead bodies in public places as a warning to others sympathetic to the GAM rebellion. This counterinsurgency strategy, however, changed dramatically with Indonesia's transition to democracy following the fall of Suharto's military dictatorship in 1998. Indonesia's new civilian leadership sought to rein in military operations in Aceh, reduce human rights abuses, and pursue a negotiated resolution to the conflict.

During this same period of time, in the 1990s, the Kurdistan Workers' Party (Partiya Karkerên Kurdistanê, PKK) was fighting to gain autonomy for Turkey's Kurdish minority. The Turkish government's counterinsurgency strategy differed significantly from the Sudanese and Indonesian strategies. Although the Turkish government attempted to undermine civilian support for the insurgency, the government endeavored to limit civilian casualties. A central component of the government's strategy, for example, involved the destruction of Kurdish villages believed to be aiding the insurgency. Before destroying villages, however, security forces evacuated civilians.[8] Torture and other forms of mistreatment were common during evacuations, but civilian casualties remained low.

Rebel groups in these three conflicts also differed in their behavior toward civilians. In its Darfur investigation, the International Commission of Inquiry found no evidence that either of the two main rebel groups, the Sudan Liberation Army (SLA) or the Justice and Equality Movement (JEM), had carried out "a 'systematic' or 'widespread' attack against the civilian population."[9] While noting several incidents involving the killing of civilians by rebel forces, the Commission observed: "the incidents and number of deaths

[5] International Criminal Court 2010.
[6] International Criminal Court 2007a; International Criminal Court 2007b.
[7] Robinson 1998, 140.   [8] Amnesty International 1993b.
[9] United Nations 2005, 80. See also Jumbert and Lanz 2013.

have been few"; rebel group attacks were "in most cases against military targets, police or security forces."[10]

Likewise, GAM did not use large-scale violence against civilians in Aceh. The group did punish suspected government informants – for example, arresting and detaining a Bireuen man they believed to be aiding the Indonesian military before releasing him with a warning. When GAM members discovered that he was still collaborating with the government, they burned down his house.[11] GAM also maintained a court system to prosecute individuals suspected of aiding the government; although it was not uncommon for GAM to punish collaborators with death, GAM targeted individuals for punishment, rather than whole families or villages.

The PKK in Turkey, however, explicitly targeted civilians for attack, a strategy it brazenly announced at a press conference on June 8, 1993. PKK leader Abdullah Öcalan warned, "We are going to wage an all-out war against [the Turkish state] until it agrees to negotiate. The Turkish state must understand once and for all it cannot annihilate us and that the only solution is to negotiate. Turkey will have a bloody summer if the army continues its campaign against us. We will hit economic and tourist interests throughout Turkey."[12] The PKK subsequently launched a series of attacks on public places in major cities across Turkey. The first of these attacks came just weeks after the press conference, on Sunday, June 27, when a bomb exploded in the garden of a hotel in Antalya, a popular tourist destination along Turkey's Mediterranean coast. That same night, not far from the first hotel, a second bomb went off in front of the Sheraton hotel, and a third exploded in a shopping area nearby.[13] The bombings wounded 26 civilians, 12 of whom were foreign tourists.[14] Over the next several years, the PKK continued bombing public civilian targets – shopping areas, bus stations, restaurants, and tourist attractions in a number of different coastal cities as well as in Istanbul. Bombing public places was not the only form of violence that the PKK directed against civilians; the PKK also killed individual civilians it suspected of collaborating with the Turkish government and destroyed homes in villages believed to be supporting the government.

The armed conflicts in Sudan, Indonesia, and Turkey are civil wars. All three cases involve a government confronting organized, armed opposition originating within the country's borders, with significant military confrontations between government and rebel group forces. As these three cases illustrate, however, civil wars vary in the extent to which governments and rebel groups direct violence against civilians. But how much does wartime violence against civilians vary across cases of civil war?

---

[10] United Nations 2005, 77, 69.   [11] Human Rights Watch 2001.

[12] "Turkish Separatists End Ceasefire, Threaten All-Out War, Tourism," *Agence France-Presse*, 8 June 1993.

[13] "26 Injured in Bomb Blast at Turkish Resort," *Reuters News*, 28 June 1993.   [14] Ibid.

Media coverage of civil wars tends to focus on the most gruesome atrocities and the most extreme conflicts – genocide in Rwanda or ethnic cleansing in Bosnia. One might think, therefore, that most civil wars involve massive violence against civilians. In this view, most governments and rebel groups deliberately attack the opponent's civilian supporters, as the Bashir regime did in Darfur and the PKK did in Turkey. Is this true? Do most governments and rebel groups engaged in civil war commit heinous atrocities against civilians?

No study has looked systematically across cases of civil war at *forms* of government and rebel group violence against civilians. Although certain types of violence, such as ethnic cleansing and genocide, have been the subject of extensive research, these studies focus on one particular type of violence and, as such, do not address the full variation in scale and forms of violence against civilians during civil war.[15] Similarly, studies of variation in violence against civilians across conflicts that measure violence by estimating the number of civilians killed by each side in the conflict ignore violence against civilians that inflicts severe suffering without killing large numbers of civilians.[16] Even when civilians are killed, lethal violence can take many forms, as the Sudanese, Indonesian, and Turkish conflicts demonstrate.

The first aim of this book is to fill these gaps in our understanding of civil war violence. Using original data on government and rebel group violence against civilians in all civil wars from 1989 to 2010, this book provides a comprehensive study of violence against civilians. The focus is on four of the most severe forms of violence directed against civilians: massacres – the killing of a group of civilians during a single face-to-face encounter; scorched earth policies – the destruction or burning of civilian homes or crops; deliberate bombing or shelling of civilian targets; and forced expulsion – the permanent removal of civilians from a territory under threat or use of force. All of these forms of violence are violations of international humanitarian law, which is the body of law governing belligerent behavior during wartime. Under international humanitarian law, all belligerents – governments as well as rebel groups – are prohibited from attacking civilians and civilian targets.[17]

These data show that among 103 rebel groups fighting in civil wars between 1989 and 2010, 30.1 percent massacred civilians, 27.2 percent burned civilian homes and crops, 29.1 percent exploded bombs in populated public places (e.g., bus stations, hotels, shopping centers), and 10.8 percent forcibly expelled civilians from territory. However, 41.8 percent of rebel groups did not engage in *any* of these forms of violence, largely abiding by the principles of civilian immunity laid out in international humanitarian law.

---

[15] See, for example, Valentino 2000; Harff 2003; Valentino 2004; Straus 2006.

[16] Valentino, Huth, and Balch-Lindsay 2004; Eck and Hultman 2007; Hultman 2007; Weinstein 2007; Wood 2010; Hultman 2012; Wood, Kathman, and Gent 2012; Salehyan, Siroky, and Wood 2014; Wood 2014b.

[17] Best 1994.

Among governments involved in civil wars from 1989 to 2010, the patterns of violence are similar: 24.5 percent of governments massacred civilians, 47.1 percent burned civilian homes and crops, 21.6 percent deliberately bombed or shelled civilian targets, and 13.7 percent forcibly expelled civilians from territory. Yet, forty-nine percent of governments refrained from using *any* of these four forms of violence.

This overview of the data indicates that while violence against civilians is common in civil war, it is not universal. More than 40 percent of all governments and rebel groups fighting in civil wars from 1989 to 2010 did not engage in any of the most severe forms of violence against civilians. This does not mean that these governments and rebel groups never attacked a single civilian during the course of their fighting; some degree of violence against civilians is present in all civil wars. What the data show is that it is possible to distinguish a spectrum of civil war violence: some governments and rebel groups engage in extreme atrocities, such as massacres and deliberate bombing of civilian areas; other governments and rebel groups employ forms of violence that inflict significant suffering on civilians, but fewer casualties; and still other governments and rebel groups rarely use violence against civilians.

Throughout this book, I refer to intentional efforts to avoid violence against civilians as efforts at restraint. Governments and rebel groups engaged in civil war often face strong incentives to target civilians; limiting violence against civilians thus requires significant effort by the parties – planning military operations that minimize harm to civilians, training soldiers to differentiate between military and civilian targets, and disciplining soldiers who abuse civilians. Restraint is a deliberate choice in civil war. Surprisingly, this phenomenon of restraint has received little attention in research on civil war.

The second aim of this book, therefore, is to explain this wide variation in civil war violence. Why do some governments and rebel groups deliberately attack civilians, while others refrain from targeting civilians, largely complying with the norms of civilian immunity codified in international humanitarian law? Why did the SLA and JEM in Darfur and GAM in Aceh exercise restraint in their dealings with civilians, while the PKK carried out deliberate bombings of civilian targets throughout Turkey? Why did the Sudanese government use extreme violence against civilians in Darfur, while the Turkish government sought to limit civilian casualties during its counterinsurgency operations? And what can explain the change over time in the Indonesian government's response to insurgency in Aceh?

In addition to explaining why some belligerents use high levels of violence against civilians and others choose not to use *any* form of violence against civilians, this book examines cases in the middle of this spectrum of violence, where the parties deliberately attack civilians and impose significant damage and suffering, but inflict fewer civilian casualties. In examining the full spectrum of violence in civil war, this book also seeks to understand why governments and rebel groups chose the particular forms of violence they did – why the Sudanese government massacred civilians believed to support the insurgency and used aerial bombardment to destroy civilian homes and crops, while the Turkish government destroyed villages suspected of sympathizing with the insurgency without inflicting high civilian casualties. Why did GAM use targeted arrests and killings to eliminate suspected government collaborators while the PKK exploded bombs in public places?

Answering both questions – the question about violence versus restraint and the question about forms of violence – is essential to understanding patterns of violence against civilians during civil war. Looking only at the dichotomy between violence and restraint would ignore much of the variation in government and rebel group violence against civilians. And examining only the variation in forms of violence would miss the fact that governments and rebel groups do not simply choose between different types of violence against civilians; they often choose not to use *any* of the most severe forms of violence against civilians. The choice to avoid violence against civilians is surprising in light of the common wisdom, which tends to view all civil wars as involving significant atrocities against civilians. Explaining restraint is thus crucial both for scholars interested in gaining a complete understanding of belligerent behavior during civil war, and for policymakers interested in minimizing the impact that civil war has on civilians, strengthening norms against civilian targeting, and increasing compliance with international humanitarian law.

STRATEGIES OF VIOLENCE AND RESTRAINT TOWARD CIVILIANS

It is not surprising that some governments and rebel groups deliberately attack civilians during civil war. Civilians are often intimately involved in civil war: they provide supplies, shelter, and financing. They are also sources of intelligence, offering information about local conditions and geography, about the movement of opposing troops, and about the individuals or villages collaborating with the opponent. Perhaps most importantly, they are political constituents, on whose behalf the belligerents fight. Undermining the opposition's base of civilian support can be a fatal blow.

Government and rebel group decisions about whether to target civilians, while based on strategic calculations about the extent to which civilian targeting will help to accomplish their political goals, take place in the shadow of international law. The earliest attempt to use international law to regulate warfare – the 1864 Geneva Convention – established protections for individuals wounded in combat and envisioned wars as international or interstate wars (wars between two or more states). As international humanitarian law evolved, however, it expanded to include protections for a wider set of noncombatants – not only wounded soldiers, but also civilians – and to apply to a wider set of armed conflicts – not only interstate wars, but also non-international or civil wars (wars occurring within a state).[18] The atrocities committed against civilians during World War II urged states to further elaborate this body of international humanitarian law with the signing of the 1949 Geneva Conventions and, later, the 1977 First and Second Additional Protocols to the Geneva Conventions. The main objective of these agreements is to prohibit deliberate attacks against noncombatants, including civilians. Following World War II, states also negotiated a series of international human rights agreements, protecting individuals from mistreatment during peacetime as well as during wartime.

With the shift away from a bipolar distribution of power at the end of the Cold War came a growth in international humanitarian and human rights norms as well as a more prominent role for international institutions in enforcing these norms.[19] The United Nations initiated sanctions against abusive governments, such as Milosevic's government in Yugoslavia; established international or hybrid tribunals to punish individuals responsible for committing war crimes during civil wars in the former Yugoslavia, Rwanda, Sierra Leone, and Cambodia; and contributed to the establishment of the ICC.[20] Certain protections for civilians during interstate and civil wars are now considered part of customary international law, meaning that all actors engaged in a conflict – both governments and rebel groups – are bound by these rules, regardless of whether they have ratified the relevant treaties. The enforcement of international humanitarian law remains inconsistent; international actors respond more forcefully to some cases of civilian abuse than others. But the prevalence of humanitarian norms has grown to the point that belligerents who target civilians will almost certainly draw domestic and international criticism. Violation is not without cost.

Within this international context, restraint is often a deliberate strategic choice by governments and rebel groups, who avoid direct attacks on civilian populations and abide by international legal standards of behavior in an effort to win support from domestic and international audiences.[21] During the Cold War, governments and rebel groups vied for support from the superpowers by articulating a communist or anticommunist political agenda. Now, belligerents often seek assistance from Western governments and Western-led intergovernmental organizations, such as the North Atlantic Treaty Organization (NATO) and the United Nations, by demonstrating a commitment to democracy and human rights. Foreign governments may lobby for terms of settlement

---

[18] Ibid.; Robertson 1999.

[19] Hafner-Burton and Tsutsui 2005; Hafner-Burton and Tsutsui 2007; Sikkink 2011; Teitel 2011.

[20] On the history and politics of international efforts to hold states and individuals accountable for crimes committed during wartime, see, for example, Bass 2000; Teitel 2011.

[21] Jo and Thomson 2014 similarly argue that rebel groups comply with international norms regarding access to detainees out of a desire for greater legitimacy; Jo 2015 argues that a desire for legitimacy drives rebel group compliance with other aspects of international law as well, including international humanitarian law prohibiting attacks on civilians.

favorable to their preferred side, mobilize international public opinion against the opposing side, and even mediate a resolution to the conflict. Support from foreign governments can be a powerful advantage during civil war and a good reason to exercise restraint.

Although it may seem as if all belligerents fighting in civil wars would benefit from increased domestic and international support, in fact, the need for domestic and international support varies depending on the nature of the belligerent's political constituency. Some governments and rebel groups need support from broad domestic and international constituencies; these governments and rebel groups are likely to exercise restraint rather than risk domestic and international backlash by engaging in brutal violence against civilians. The domestic and international costs of violence are high for these belligerents. Governments and rebel groups with *narrower* domestic and international constituencies are *less* likely to exercise restraint; these governments and rebel groups have fewer constraints on their behavior, and the costs of engaging in violence are lower.

Variation in the Domestic and International Costs of Violence

The need for support from domestic audiences – and thus the *domestic* costs of violence – depends on the government or rebel group's relationship with its *domestic* constituents. Three key factors shape this relationship: (1) the degree to which institutions compel leaders to be responsive to their constituents, (2) the inclusiveness of the political system, and (3) the consolidation of political power.

First, domestic political institutions can constrain leaders – for example, through the holding of regular elections and the establishment of checks on the power of the executive – forcing leaders to behave in ways consistent with public demands. When these political constraints are robust, as in democratic regimes, leaders are likely to be more sensitive to widespread public criticism and, therefore, less willing to engage in violence against civilians. When constraints on leaders are weak, as in autocratic regimes, the domestic costs to engaging in violence are lower. Similarly, the more developed a rebel group's political institutional structure – for example, the more complex the rebel group's local governance institutions in territories under its control – the greater the incentives for rebel group leaders to respond to the demands of their civilian constituents and the greater the likelihood of restraint.

Second, the inclusiveness of the political system shapes the composition of the belligerent's domestic constituency: the broader the domestic audience to whom a government or rebel group must appeal, the higher the domestic costs of violence and the greater the likelihood of restraint. The domestic costs of violence thus not only depend on *whether* a government or rebel group has institutional incentives to be responsive to its domestic constituents, but also depend on *who* the belligerent's constituents are. Governments and rebel groups with exclusionary political systems seek to exclude certain groups from access to political power; these governments and rebel groups have narrow civilian constituencies, drawing support from a particular ethnic or religious group or a particular region of the country. Belligerents with more inclusive political systems seek a broader base of domestic support, and are more likely to exercise restraint.

Third, the degree to which a government or rebel group's political power is consolidated influences the urgency of the need to build support from domestic constituents. By definition, all rebel groups engaged in civil war lack consolidated political power and thus face some domestic costs to the use of violence against civilians. While all governments facing internal rebellions in some sense lack consolidated political power as well, governments vary more widely in the stability of their regimes. Leaders of unstable regimes – regimes recently established through a process of political transition or the creation of a new state – have a more urgent need to build support from domestic constituents and, therefore, face higher domestic costs to violence.

Similarly, governments and rebel groups weigh the *international* costs of violence by evaluating their need for support from *international* constituencies. Governments and rebel groups that believe they will have difficulty achieving their political objectives without international support perceive high costs to targeting civilians. Governments with unstable regimes have an acute need for international support: a loss of international support may be devastating, undermining already weak political institutions and prompting domestic actors to question the government's viability. In stable regimes, leaders can better endure criticism from international actors. The international costs of engaging in violence, therefore, are higher for governments with unstable regimes, increasing the likelihood that such governments will use restraint as a means of appealing to international actors for support.

The domestic political setting also influences the extent to which rebel groups need to build support from international constituencies; rebel groups fighting autocratic opponents have a particularly pressing need for international support, turning to international actors in the hopes that increased international pressure will urge the government to negotiate. Most rebel groups achieve their political objectives by coercing the government into making concessions, and the opportunities a rebel group has for pressuring the government into making concessions depend on the nature of the government's political institutions. Even if rebel group violence generates public demands for an end to the conflict, the political institutions in autocracies insulate the government from public pressure and the need to be responsive to these demands. Unable to use violence to generate domestic pressure for government concessions, rebel groups facing autocratic opponents exercise restraint to appeal to international actors for support.

Ultimately, these arguments about restraint during civil war are arguments about how belligerents garner support from domestic and international constituencies. Governments and rebel groups that seek to build and maintain broad domestic and international constituencies face high costs to using violence against civilians. In deciding whether to use violence or to exercise restraint toward civilians, governments and rebel groups consider how their constituents will respond. When governments and rebel groups anticipate that violence will bring condemnation and a loss of support from domestic and international constituents, they are likely to seek to limit violence against civilians. Governments and rebel groups with narrow domestic and international constituencies tend to be more isolated from domestic and international criticism, thus reducing the costs of violence and the incentives for restraint.

Variation in the Incentives for Violence

This is not only a book about the conditions under which restraint is most likely. Violence against civilians is not identical across all conflicts; it varies both in scale and in form. This is therefore also a book about *variation* in violence. What can explain the character of violence against civilians in civil wars? Why do belligerents choose particular strategies of violence over other available alternatives?

In the second part of this book, I explore variation in civil war violence, focusing on three different strategies of violence: control, cleansing, and terrorism. Governments and rebel groups may use violence (1) to control civilians and thereby control territory; (2) to cleanse territory of a particular religious or ethnic group; or (3) to terrorize the opponent's civilian constituents, in an effort to coerce the opponent into making concessions. Within each of these three strategies, violence ranges from low- to high-casualty variants of control, cleansing, and terrorism.

A belligerent's choice among these strategies of violence depends on how the belligerent weighs the benefits of violence. While belligerents weigh the *costs* of violence considering their relationship with *their own* domestic and international constituents, belligerents evaluate the *benefits* of violence based on an assessment of *their opponent's* relationship to its constituents. The greater the civilian support for the opponent (and the lower the civilian support for the belligerent) in the disputed territory, the greater the threat these civilians pose, and the greater the benefit a belligerent is likely to obtain by using violence to control or eliminate these individuals. Whether a government or rebel group adopts a strategy of control or cleansing depends on the size and geographic concentration of the opponent's civilian constituency. The smaller and more geographically concentrated the opponent's civilian constituency, the more feasible it is to employ a strategy of cleansing to eliminate this constituency entirely. Governments and rebel groups also consider the extent to which the opponent's political institutions compel leaders to be responsive to the demands of their domestic civilian constituents, including constituent demands to make concessions to alleviate violence against civilians. Thus, a strategy of terrorism will be more appealing to a belligerent the greater its opponent's sensitivity to losses among its civilian constituents.

CONTRIBUTIONS

This book makes four major contributions to research on civil war violence and research on international human rights and humanitarian law. First, it provides a cross-national study of forms of government and rebel group violence against civilians in all civil wars from 1989 to 2010; all of these forms of violence are prohibited under major international humanitarian legal treaties. To date, no such study exists. Second, in examining both government and rebel group behavior, this book illuminates the interaction between belligerents in civil war; belligerents evaluate the *costs* of violence based on an assessment of their relationship with *their own* domestic and international constituents, and belligerents weigh the *benefits* of violence based on an assessment of *their opponent's* relationship to its constituents. Third, the book's focus on restraint as a distinct phenomenon permits a more complete analysis of the strategic calculations governments and rebel groups make – particularly how the standards set by international humanitarian law shape these calculations. Finally, as the evidence in the statistical analyses and case studies shows, governments and rebel groups comply with international legal standards as a means of winning both domestic and international favor, considering not only how domestic constituencies will respond to their behavior, but also how international actors will respond.

Research on International Human Rights and Humanitarian Law

The argument of this book contends that relationships with domestic and international constituencies shape government and rebel group incentives to abide by international humanitarian legal standards. International humanitarian law provides a framework that all actors involved in a conflict – governments, rebel groups, domestic constituencies, and international constituencies – reference in making judgments about appropriate wartime behavior. Although the impact of international law is indirect, law constrains behavior by establishing standards that governments and rebel groups use when positioning themselves to make appeals for support from domestic and international constituencies. In addition, domestic and international constituencies enforce these standards when they respond by extending or withholding their support.

The argument of this book thus speaks directly to two major strands of research regarding compliance with international human right norms and law. First, scholars analyzing the process through which governments internalize international human rights norms have emphasized that governments often initially abide by international legal obligations for instrumental reasons[22] – what Thomas

---

[22] Keck and Sikkink 1998; Risse and Sikkink 1999; Goodman and Jinks 2004; Risse, Ropp, and Sikkink 2013. On the internalization of international legal norms more generally, see, for example, Koh 1997; Finnemore and Sikkink 1998; Koh 1998.

Risse and Kathryn Sikkink term "tactical concessions."[23] As these scholars show, however, even when governments behave strategically, international norms and law can shape the contours of this strategic calculation, constraining the options available to governments and forcing governments to engage with international standards of appropriate conduct. Domestic and international actors also influence the strategic or instrumental adoption of international norms. Margaret Keck and Kathryn Sikkink, for example, present persuasive evidence demonstrating that pressure from domestic and international actors – networks of domestic and international human rights NGOs, foreign governments, and intergovernmental organizations – influences government calculations about whether to abide by international human rights norms.[24] Although the initial decision to abide by international humanitarian norms may be instrumental, socialization processes can lead to greater internalization of international human rights norms over time. This book does not explicitly examine the internalization of international humanitarian law; it is likely, however, that such processes of socialization are taking place, as governments and rebel groups engage with their domestic and international constituencies over issues of compliance.[25]

Second, this book shares with a large body of recent research on international human rights law an emphasis on how the domestic institutional context affects states' willingness and ability to commit to international human rights instruments and to comply with their obligations under international human rights law.[26] Beth Simmons, for example, argues that international legal commitments often have serious implications for domestic politics – placing questions of implementation onto the national political agenda, facilitating litigation in domestic courts to challenge government violations of international human rights law, and contributing to political mobilization to press for improvements in government human rights practices.[27] Whereas Simmons and others within this strand of scholarship focus on the processes through which actors within domestic society can induce greater state compliance with international law, this book analyzes leader decision making, arguing that

---

[23] Risse and Sikkink 1999, 25.   [24] Keck and Sikkink 1998.

[25] Scholars examining norm internalization have focused on processes of government socialization, but it is possible to conceive of rebel groups as subject to similar processes of socialization. For example, many rebel group leaders interact frequently with domestic and international human rights organizations, and these interactions might contribute to the internalization of international human rights norms. See, for example, Jo and Thomson 2014; Jo 2015.

[26] See, for example, Moravcsik 2000; Neumayer 2005; Hafner-Burton and Tsutsui 2007; Hathaway 2007; Hafner-Burton, Tsutsui, and Meyer 2008; Vreeland 2008; Keith, Tate, and Poe 2009; Powell and Staton 2009; Simmons 2009; Lupu 2013; Grewal and Voeten 2015. Many argue that domestic institutions shape compliance with other types of international legal commitments as well (see, for example, Burley 1992; Slaughter 1995; Dai 2005; Slaughter and Burke-White 2006).

[27] Simmons 2009.

governments and rebel groups comply with international law when they believe that doing so will help them to maintain the support of key domestic and international constituencies.

Much of the research specifically addressing international humanitarian law has focused on how perpetrators of wartime atrocities ought to be punished. Yet international humanitarian law was created with the aim of preventing brutality against civilians. Preventing wartime atrocities requires a better understanding of the conditions under which governments and rebel groups are likely to direct violence at civilians as well as the conditions favoring restraint. By examining the dynamics of civil war, this book improves understanding of the multiple ways in which civil wars are fought so that violence against civilians can be anticipated and even averted.

Research on Civilian Targeting

In recent years, scholars have begun to fill this gap in our understanding of civil war with research on the dynamics of violence at the local level – what some have called the microdynamics of conflict.[28] These studies examine variation in violence within a single case of civil war, analyzing, for example, the interaction taking place between belligerents at the local level as they compete for territory[29] or the ways in which armed groups control the use of violence among their members.[30] These micro-level studies have improved our understanding of why violence might vary across regions or across time *within* a single conflict. In many cases, however, these arguments cannot easily be extended to the cross-national level to account for variation in violence *across* cases of civil war. In addition, because the unit of study is a single civil war, domestic variables, such as government regime type, and international variables, such as foreign diplomatic support, often remain constant.

By largely ignoring the ways in which domestic and international variables might influence government and rebel group behavior, micro-level studies have focused on struggles for power and control at the local level, overlooking struggles for power and control – over resources, territory, and institutions – at the national level. How this struggle plays out at the national level depends on the domestic and international context of the war, which influences calculations about the consequences of using violence against civilians and thus, shapes government and rebel group decision making. An analysis of the ways in which the domestic and international context varies is essential to explaining why civil war violence against civilians varies so widely.

---

[28] Examples include Verwimp 2003; Verwimp 2005; Humphreys and Weinstein 2006; Kalyvas 2006; Straus 2006; Kalyvas and Kocher 2007; Weinstein 2007; Lyall 2009; Balcells 2010; Lyall 2010; Balcells 2011; Wood 2014a. For a general discussion of micro-level research, see Kalyvas 2008; Cederman and Gleditsch 2009.

[29] Kalyvas 2006.   [30] Humphreys and Weinstein 2006; Weinstein 2007.

Moreover, studies that have examined cross-national variation in civil war violence have focused on explaining *either* the behavior of governments or the behavior of rebel groups;[31] this book is one of the first efforts to examine *both* government and rebel group behavior and compare the factors driving each. And while a number of cross-national studies of civilian targeting in *interstate* wars have looked at the influence of international variables on belligerent behavior,[32] very few studies of *civil* war violence have done so.[33]

THREE STRANDS OF ARGUMENT IN THE LITERATURE ON CIVILIAN TARGETING

The findings in this book challenge several broad strands of argument that dominate the literature on civilian targeting – the first focusing on the organizational structure of armed groups, the second focusing on the military context, and the third focusing on international factors. These existing arguments fall short in that they tend to focus on particular costs or particular benefits of violence; this book seeks to improve upon existing work by examining a wider range of costs and benefits of violence in a comprehensive study, uncovering important differences between civilian targeting in interstate wars and civilian targeting in civil wars.

The Organizational Structure of Armed Groups

Several influential arguments emphasizing the organizational structure of armed groups view restraint as the preferred strategy of belligerents, arguing that violence against civilians occurs when armed groups lack the organizational capacity to control the use of violence among their soldiers.[34] Belligerents need support from the civilian population and fear that violence may alienate potential supporters; the domestic costs of engaging in violence are high. Some groups possess organizational structures that tie them closely to the communities within which they operate; these groups are both more dependent on civilians for support, thus facing particularly high domestic costs of violence, and better able to use their organizational resources to ensure that their members exercise restraint toward civilians.

---

[31] Azam and Hoeffler 2002; Harff 2003; Valentino, Huth, and Balch-Lindsay 2004; Eck and Hultman 2007; Hultman 2007; Weinstein 2007, chapter 8; Wood 2010; Salehyan, Siroky, and Wood 2014; Wood 2014b.

[32] Downes 2006; Morrow and Jo 2006; Valentino, Huth, and Croco 2006; Morrow 2007; Downes 2008; Morrow 2014.

[33] Exceptions include Harff 2003; Wood, Kathman, and Gent 2012; Salehyan, Siroky, and Wood 2014.

[34] Weinstein 2005; Humphreys and Weinstein 2006; Weinstein 2007.

Some have argued that problems of organizational control are particularly severe among groups with access to external sources of funding who use short-term rewards to recruit members, attracting individuals who lack a strong commitment to the group's political cause. Lack of discipline among these low-commitment recruits can lead to looting and opportunistic violence against civilians.[35] While these arguments acknowledge that groups may face different domestic costs for the use of violence, they do not weigh the international costs of violence, nor do they acknowledge perceived benefits of intentionally directing violence against civilians. Governments and rebel groups often incorporate civilian targeting into their strategy for waging war; in these cases, strong organizational control can lead to *increased*, rather than decreased, violence against civilians.[36]

More recent work on the organizational dynamics of armed groups recognizes that violence against civilians is often strategically motivated, but emphasizes that nonstrategically motivated violence, or opportunistic violence, is also common in civil war and can plague even those armed groups that seek to restrain levels of violence against civilians.[37] An armed group's organizational characteristics – effective command structure[38] or the presence of systems emphasizing discipline and political education[39] – can help to reduce opportunistic violence. Also within the organizational strand of argument, some have posited that particular organizational imperatives can increase incentives for group members to use violence against civilians; for example, armed groups may use group-perpetrated violence, such as rape, as a means of strengthening group bonds and manufacturing social cohesion.[40] Because both strategic violence and nonstrategic violence occur during civil war, these more recent studies of the impact of organizational characteristics on group behavior advance arguments that can coexist with the strategic arguments put forth in this book.

The Military Context

The second strand of argument focuses on the way in which the military context shapes belligerent behavior. The three factors most commonly cited as influencing incentives for civilian targeting are the costs of the conflict, the relative strength of the belligerents, and the degree of contestation over territory. Arguments emphasizing the costs of the conflict originated within the literature on civilian targeting in interstate war, positing that

---

[35] Weinstein 2005; Weinstein 2007; Salehyan, Siroky, and Wood 2014. See also Azam 2002; Azam 2006. Although Azam does not make explicit arguments about organizational control, he argues that violence against civilians is tied to looting.

[36] For a discussion of this point, see Wood 2009.

[37] Wood 2006; Wood 2009; Hoover Green 2011; Manekin 2013.   [38] Manekin 2013.

[39] Hoover Green 2011.   [40] Cohen 2013.

governments are only willing to carry out large-scale attacks on an opponent's civilian constituency when conflicts become too costly to bear.[41] Likewise, in civil wars, governments and rebel groups may become desperate to win concessions from their opponent as the costs of the conflict rise, and may see attacks on civilians as a more efficient use of waning resources. In an interstate war, however, targeting the opponent's constituents involves attacking *foreign* civilians. In a civil war, targeting the opponent's constituents involves attacking *citizens of one's own country*; in attacking the opponent's supporters, a belligerent, competing for support within the domestic population, risks losing its own civilian support. The domestic costs of violence against civilians, therefore, may be higher in civil wars than in interstate wars.

A second military context argument focuses on the relative strength of the belligerents, arguing that violence against civilians is a weapon of the weak. Drawing on insights from the study of terrorism, scholars have posited that a government or rebel group that is weak in comparison to its opponent or that has suffered significant military losses may attack the opponent's *civilian* population as a substitute for fighting direct *military* engagements.[42] In contrast, belligerents that are strong in comparison to their opponents can attain victory through direct military engagements, without attacking civilians. Others have suggested an alternate mechanism: weak rebel groups and rebel groups depleted by military losses have difficulty eliciting voluntary civilian cooperation and thus have incentives to obtain resources through looting or coercion, leading to increased violence against civilians.[43]

A third major argument emphasizing the military context focuses on the degree of contestation over territory, positing that when contestation over territory is high, governments and rebel groups have strong incentives to use violence against civilians to coerce civilian cooperation, and thereby consolidate control over territory.[44] When one side possesses complete control over territory, its pervasive presence and the threat of violence is enough to prompt "voluntary" collaboration. But in areas of partial control, belligerents may use violence against civilians selectively, targeting suspected enemy collaborators; violence against civilians may escalate as parties attempt to convince civilians that aiding the other side will be costly. As control over territory declines, a belligerent's access to reliable sources of information also declines, making it more difficult to identify suspected enemy collaborators and increasing the likelihood that the belligerent will use indiscriminate rather than selective violence.

---

[41] Downes 2006; Downes 2008.
[42] Valentino, Huth, and Balch-Lindsay 2004; Hultman 2007. See also research on terrorism, such as Crenshaw 1981; Pape 2003.
[43] Wood 2010; Wood, Kathman, and Gent 2012; Wood 2014a; Wood 2014b.
[44] Kalyvas 2006.

Scholars have pointed to other aspects of the military context that may influence behavior as well. Some have argued, for example, that because rebel groups using guerrilla warfare rely heavily on civilians for support, governments have stronger incentives to attack civilians in conflicts against rebel groups employing guerrilla warfare than in conflicts against rebel groups using conventional warfare.[45] Others have argued that groups use terrorist violence as a means of outbidding rival factions for support from civilian constituencies,[46] meaning that conflicts involving multiple rebel groups are associated with a greater likelihood of terrorism.

Arguments emphasizing the military context are right to point out that belligerents may perceive benefits to violence under certain circumstances, and that military factors influence these calculations, but the military context – including the costs of the conflict, the relative strength of the belligerents, the degree of contestation over territory, the use of guerrilla tactics, and the number of insurgent groups – is only one component of the larger strategic context that belligerents face. In weighing the benefits of violence, belligerents also consider the nature of their opponent and the likelihood that their opponent will make concessions in response to attacks on its civilian constituents. Furthermore, arguments emphasizing the military context pay less attention to variation in the costs of engaging in violence. It may be true that the military context can create incentives for belligerents to engage in violence against civilians, but this is only part of the story. A more complete analysis of belligerent behavior requires an understanding of how belligerents weigh these incentives in favor of violence against the potential costs of directing violence against civilians.

International Factors

The third strand of argument, focusing on international factors, recognizes that civilian targeting can be costly internationally. Governments that have ratified relevant international humanitarian treaties or governments that participate extensively in international organizations may incur reputational costs if they fail to uphold international legal standards; governments that rely heavily on international trade for the functioning of their economy may be concerned that civilian targeting will offend key trading partners.[47] Similarly, rebel groups receiving backing from democracies may be less likely to target civilians, as democracies are likely to withhold aid from abusive groups and to pressure groups they support to comply with international human rights standards.[48] As the empirical findings in this book show, however, the domestic context of the

---

[45] Valentino, Huth, and Balch-Lindsay 2004. But see Balcells 2010, who argues that even in civil wars fought conventionally belligerents may have incentives to target civilians, if they believe that civilians loyal to the opponent are present behind the frontlines.

[46] Bloom 2005; Kydd and Walter 2006; Chenoweth 2010.   [47] Harff 2003.

[48] Salehyan, Siroky, and Wood 2014.

civil war influences how governments and rebel groups respond to these international costs of targeting civilians, making some governments and rebel groups more vulnerable to the international costs of violence and thus more likely to exercise restraint. Other scholars have argued that in interstate wars, reciprocity can motivate compliance: governments may be more likely to abide by their international legal commitments when they believe that their opponent will do so as well.[49] However, reciprocity may be weaker with regard to violence against civilians because even if the other side retaliates by attacking civilians, soldiers are not directly harmed.[50] In addition, in civil wars, governments might not trust their rebel opponents to abide by international law, particularly as rebel groups cannot commit themselves formally by ratifying international agreements.

RESEARCH DESIGN AND ORGANIZATION OF THE BOOK

Chapter 1 presents the book's theoretical argument. The first part of the chapter details the domestic and international costs to engaging in violence against civilians, arguing that these costs vary depending on the belligerent's relationship with its *own* domestic and international constituents. The broader the domestic and international constituencies from which a belligerent draws support, the higher the domestic and international costs of violence. When the costs of violence are high, belligerents are likely to make deliberate efforts to avoid violence against civilians, using restraint to appeal for international and domestic support. When the costs of violence are low, however, belligerents might use violence strategically as a means of pursuing their political objectives. The second part of the chapter explores this strategic use of violence, outlining the conditions under which belligerents are likely to adopt three different strategies of violence against civilians: control, cleansing, and terrorism. In choosing whether to adopt any one of these strategies of violence, belligerents weigh the benefits of violence, and do so largely based on an assessment of their opponent's relationship with its constituents.

In assessing these arguments about violence and restraint, this book examines a variety of evidence, drawing on both quantitative and qualitative methodologies. Chapter 2 introduces an original data set on government and rebel group violence against civilians in all civil wars from 1989 to 2010, providing a detailed discussion of the measures of violence against civilians and presenting an overview of the data. Chapter 3 uses this new data set to conduct statistical tests of the book's main theoretical arguments. This quantitative evidence offers several advantages. First, rather than examining prominent civil wars and assuming that violence in these cases is representative, a data set that includes all civil wars provides a means of conceptualizing the full spectrum of violence

---

[49] Morrow and Jo 2006; Morrow 2007; Morrow 2014.   [50] Morrow 2014.

occurring in civil war. The data thus answer important questions about how many governments and rebel groups target civilians, how many governments and rebel groups limit violence against civilians, and which forms of violence are most and least common during civil war. Second, the statistical analyses in Chapter 3 identify patterns in government and rebel group violence, pointing to particular factors that are correlated with civilian targeting across cases of civil war and helping to determine whether the arguments presented in the book are generalizable arguments that can account for violence across cases. The statistical findings lend support to the claim that strategic considerations drive government and rebel group behavior – the need for support from domestic and international constituencies motivates restraint and the characteristics of the opponent's civilian constituency influence which strategy of violence a government or rebel group is likely to employ.

The quantitative analyses presented in Chapters 2 and 3 offer strong evidence that relationships with domestic and international constituencies influence belligerent calculations regarding violence. Nevertheless, qualitative case studies allow for a more nuanced evaluation of the book's arguments and compensate for weaknesses in the quantitative analyses in several key ways.

Four considerations were central to the case selection in this book. First, the quantitative analyses point to correlations that hold across cases of civil war, but limits on the availability of data make it difficult to use the quantitative analyses to identify the causal mechanisms driving these correlations. Through case studies, it is possible to trace causal mechanisms – to better understand *why* particular factors might be linked to government and rebel group violence or restraint. Second, one of the challenges of using the quantitative analyses to evaluate causal mechanisms is that the data set is not a time series data set; each of the variables is measured only once for each conflict. Thus, the data set cannot analyze changes over time in government and rebel group strategies of violence, nor examine shifts over time in key variables, such as government regime type or regime stability. For most cases, the fact that these variables are measured only once is not problematic; for example, in nearly 80 percent of the civil wars that took place from 1989 to 2010, the government's regime type did not change during the conflict, and in most cases, government and rebel group strategies of violence remain relatively consistent over time. Still, cases in which these key variables of interest do change over time are particularly useful in evaluating the hypotheses put forth in this book. Third, although the statistical analyses show that particular types of governments and rebel groups – those with broad domestic and international constituencies – are more likely to exercise restraint, they provide less information about how governments and rebel groups behave when faced with conflicting incentives. The case studies provide an opportunity to explore this question. Fourth, while the statistical analyses highlight patterns that hold across cases, not all cases fit these patterns. The case studies thus also allow for the study of outliers, as a means of exploring the limits of the theoretical arguments, as well as possible extensions of the theoretical arguments. The qualitative case studies are thus an essential component of the analysis in this book.

The case studies draw on a variety of primary and secondary sources, as well as on field research I conducted in Uganda in summer 2005 and Indonesia in summer 2006, where I interviewed 45 people with direct knowledge of the conflicts in these countries: local-level and national-level government officials, including individuals directly involved in peace negotiations; military officials; former rebel group members; journalists; scholars; representatives from Ugandan, Indonesian, and international human rights organizations; aid workers; and diplomats. In addition, the Ugandan case study, which examines the conflict between the Lord's Resistance Army (LRA) and the Ugandan government, introduces a second original event-level data set on all reported incidents of violence involving either the Ugandan government or the LRA, from 1988 to 2003, as well as all major reported political events relevant to the conflict. The event-level data allow for an examination of patterns and shifts in LRA behavior over time.

As a group, the cases reflect the wide spectrum of government and rebel group violence against civilians in civil war, as shown in Figure I.1.[51]

Chapters 4 and 5 examine cases of government (Chapter 4) and rebel group (Chapter 5) restraint – the Indonesian government's conflicts with GAM in Aceh and the Revolutionary Front for an Independent East Timor (Frente Revolucionária do Timor Leste Independente, Fretilin) in East Timor. These Indonesia cases offer a valuable opportunity to explore the impact of government regime change on government and rebel group behavior during civil war. After 1989, only two governments transitioned from autocracy to democracy during an ongoing civil war: Indonesia and Nepal. In Nepal, the regime transition took place, in large part, because of political pressure resulting from the ongoing conflict with Maoists.[52] In Indonesia, however, the regime transition was caused by factors unrelated to the ongoing Acehnese and East Timorese conflicts, making this a particularly useful case for examining arguments regarding the impact of regime type and regime transition on government and rebel group strategies. Indonesia was an autocracy, led by General Suharto, at the start of both conflicts and did not begin its transition to democracy until many years later, when the Asian financial crisis contributed to the collapse of the Indonesian economy, precipitating widespread popular protests that ultimately brought down the autocratic regime in 1998.

Chapter 4 traces government counterinsurgency operations in Aceh and East Timor before, during, and after democratic transition. Under Suharto, the Indonesian government pursued strategies of high-casualty control and

---

[51] Because others have written extensively about strategies of control in the context of civil war (Kalyvas 2006), the case studies are weighted more heavily toward analyzing government and rebel group strategies of restraint, terrorism, and cleansing.

[52] Shah 2008.

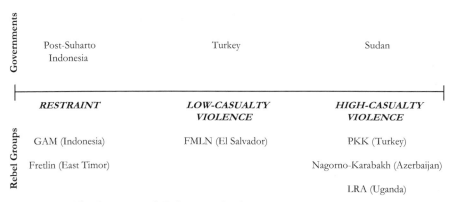

FIGURE 1.1: The Spectrum of Violence in Civil War.

cleansing in Aceh and East Timor. As the government transitioned to democracy, the new civilian leadership made efforts to restrain the military's use of violence against civilians in Aceh and East Timor. The shift was not immediate, as the government struggled to minimize the military's role in Indonesian politics.

Chapter 5 examines restraint by the rebel groups in these conflicts. Within the domestic political context of autocratic rule by Suharto, the insurgencies had little hope of generating domestic pressure on the government to make concessions. Instead, both GAM in Aceh and Fretilin in East Timor appealed to the international community for support. Restraint was a response to the high international costs of using violence. As the comparison of these two cases shows, however, not all rebel groups that make international appeals achieve the support of international actors. GAM miscalculated its ability to draw a parallel between the conflicts in Aceh and East Timor because it failed to appreciate that the different circumstances under which the two regions were incorporated into Indonesia would lead foreign governments and the United Nations to view the two conflicts differently.

Chapters 6, 7, and 8 turn to the question of variation in violence. Chapter 6 looks at government counterinsurgency strategies across the spectrum of violence: Sudan's use of high-casualty cleansing in its fight against insurgents in Darfur and Turkey's use of low-casualty cleansing and terrorism in its struggle to defeat the PKK. Chapter 7 examines the causal mechanisms driving variation in rebel group strategies of violence through a comparison of the PKK in Turkey and the Farabundo Martí National Liberation Front (Frente Farabundo Martí para la Liberación Nacional, FMLN) in El Salvador. Chapter 8 analyzes the extreme violence of the LRA in Uganda, a theoretical and empirical outlier that provides an opportunity to consider extensions of this book's theoretical arguments.

The Sudan case, examined in Chapter 6, is important to consider for a number of reasons. First, understanding the causes of the Sudanese government's use of extreme violence against civilians in the context of civil war, one of the most recent cases of such a strategy, is of interest to both scholars and policy makers. Second, a strong theoretical argument about the causes of wartime violence against civilians must account for major cases, such as the conflict in Darfur. This chapter demonstrates that the Sudanese government's behavior in Darfur is, in fact, consistent with the argument of this book. The Sudanese government had strong incentives to use extreme violence against civilians: as a long-standing autocratic government already unpopular with international actors, the Sudanese government had little sensitivity to domestic and international criticism. Additionally, the insurgency's civilian support base consisted predominately of ethnic groups concentrated in the western region of Darfur. Under these conditions, the Sudanese government calculated that the costs of violence against civilians would be low. As the argument of this book would predict, the Sudanese government adopted a strategy of high-casualty cleansing.

The other case study in Chapter 6 focuses on the Turkish government's counterinsurgency operations against the PKK, arguing that although the government faced incentives for cleansing and terrorism, it had to weigh these incentives for violence against the pressure from domestic and international constituencies to exercise restraint. First, the Turkish government confronted an insurgent group with significant support among Kurdish civilians living in Southeastern Turkey, creating strong incentives for the government to target this base of support. Second, the Turkish government relied on a narrow domestic constituency to remain in power – ethnic Turks; the domestic costs of violence against civilians outside of that constituency – in this case, Kurdish civilians – were to some extent limited. At the same time, Turkey faced significant domestic and international constraints on its counterinsurgency operations, possessing well-established democratic institutions and eager to be admitted to the European Union (EU). Turkey adopted a strategy of terrorism that imposed high costs on Kurdish civilians – evacuating them from their homes and destroying their villages – while making explicit efforts to limit civilian casualties.

In Chapter 7, I examine the causal mechanisms driving variation in rebel group strategies of violence – low- and high-casualty terrorism and high-casualty cleansing. In the section on terrorism, I compare two rebel groups fighting against democratic governments: the PKK in Turkey, an exclusionary insurgency fighting for the autonomy of the Kurdish ethnic group, and the FMLN in El Salvador, an inclusive insurgency fighting for control of the central government. The PKK and FMLN are representative cases: all but one of the 16 exclusionary rebel groups that have fought against democratic governments since 1989 are separatist groups, like the PKK; all but one of the six inclusive rebel groups fighting against democratic governments are leftist groups that launched their insurgencies during the Cold War, like the FMLN in El Salvador.

Recall that the theoretical logic posited in this book may not apply to Cold War-era conflicts, as the international context during this period encouraged governments and rebel groups to make ideological appeals for domestic and international support, rather than appeals based on claims of compliance with international human rights standards. Nevertheless, the El Salvador case allows for an exploration of the ways in which incentives for violence and restraint differed during the Cold War period. In addition, because the Salvadoran government began its transition to democracy in the mid-1980s while the conflict was ongoing, the case permits an examination of changes in FMLN strategy as the government democratized.

Chapter 7 argues that both the PKK and the FMLN adopted a strategy of terrorism because they believed their government opponents would be sensitive to civilian losses. The two insurgencies differed, however, in the forms of terrorism they used. The FMLN restricted its attacks to infrastructure targets such as power lines and roadways, imposing high economic costs on the government without inflicting many civilian casualties, because it was concerned with maintaining support from a broad national constituency. Conversely, the PKK had a narrow domestic constituency, concentrated among Kurds in the eastern and southeastern regions of the country; it was thus able to engage in a higher casualty strategy of terrorism, exploding bombs in public places such as tourist sites and bus stations outside the separatist region. This chapter also notes that the PKK used a strategy of high-casualty control to attack Kurdish villages that mobilized pro-government militias, but backed away from this strategy when it became clear that attacking Kurdish civilians was unpopular among the group's civilian constituents.

The last section of this chapter turns from terrorism to cleansing, briefly examining Nagorno-Karabakh's struggle for autonomy from Azerbaijan. With a small, geographically concentrated population of Azeri civilians living inside the separatist region, the Karabakh Armenian rebels had strong incentives to cleanse the region of these government supporters as a means of asserting the Armenian claim to the contested territory. It is rare for rebel groups to use high-casualty cleansing; only 10 rebel groups fighting in civil wars since 1989 have adopted this strategy, and four of these 10 cases of rebel group cleansing occurred in the Balkans, which many studies extensively document and analyze. Examining the Nagorno-Karabakh conflict in Azerbaijan thus offers an opportunity to expand our understanding of civil war dynamics beyond the few cases that have received the most intense media and scholarly attention.

Chapter 8 analyzes the extreme violence of the LRA in Uganda and challenges the common wisdom about the LRA, which asserts that the group's violence has no discernible logic. The LRA case is an outlier both theoretically and empirically: while many of the rebel groups examined in this book have narrow civilian constituencies, the LRA is unusual in that it lacks a domestic civilian constituency all together. The LRA did receive some support from civilians in Northern Uganda at the start of its rebellion, and in these early years, the LRA pursued a strategy similar to that of the PKK – attacking government and military targets, but also using a strategy of high-casualty control to target villages where local pro-government militias were active, in an attempt to deter civilians from collaborating with the government. The LRA's civilian constituency withered away, however, as the LRA failed to clearly articulate its political agenda, leading the group to turn to abduction to fill its ranks.

The theoretical argument of this book does not anticipate a case such as this, in which the rebel group lacks a civilian constituency; studying this case provides an opportunity to consider whether and how the theoretical argument of this book might be extended. At its core, this book argues that the relationships governments and rebel groups have with domestic and international constituencies influence incentives and disincentives for violence. And in fact, as the Uganda case study demonstrates, the LRA's behavior toward civilians is in many ways consistent with this claim. Without a domestic base of support and backed by the unpopular Sudanese government, the LRA was unable to build international support, leaving the group with almost no domestic or international constraints on its use of violence. The LRA thus adopted an extreme strategy of terrorism, targeting civilians in Northern Uganda as a means of dramatically increasing the costs of the conflict. The evidence in this chapter shows that the LRA has used violence strategically throughout the conflict in an effort to force greater government concessions.

The Conclusion returns to one of the book's core arguments – the idea that international norms emphasizing respect for human rights and humanitarian law significantly influence the dynamics of violence in civil war. If international human rights and humanitarian norms continue to grow in strength, governments and rebel groups in need of domestic and international support are likely to face even greater pressure to comply with international legal standards for wartime conduct. Even so, governments and rebel groups that are insulated from domestic and international pressure will continue to deliberately target civilians in violation of international standards. The book ends with a discussion of the recent civil war in Libya, using this case as a means of exploring the applicability of the book's arguments to a new case of civil war and considering whether the book's arguments can shed light on the policies most likely to halt wartime atrocities against civilians.

Strategies of Violence and Restraint

Governments and rebel groups vary considerably in the extent to which they use violence against civilians. At one end of the spectrum of violence, some governments and rebel groups use almost no deliberate violence against civilians; some even actively restrain their soldiers from committing acts of violence against civilians. At the other end of the spectrum of violence, some governments and rebel groups perpetrate severe atrocities against civilians, committing grave breaches of international humanitarian law while devastating civilian targets and imposing high civilian casualties. Many governments and rebel groups fall somewhere along the middle of this spectrum, deliberately attacking civilian targets and causing considerable destruction without killing large numbers of civilians.

This chapter thus addresses two questions. First, why do some governments and rebel groups attack civilians deliberately during civil war, while others do not? And second, why do governments and rebel groups who attack civilians use the particular forms of violence they do?

Governments and rebel groups carefully weigh the costs and benefits of engaging in violence against civilians, making strategic calculations about whether to engage in violence as well as about which strategy of violence to adopt. This strategic calculation takes place in the shadow of international law, with international human rights and humanitarian norms setting standards of appropriate conduct during wartime – in particular, prohibiting deliberate attacks on civilians. Belligerents who abide by these standards can use their good behavior to lobby domestic and international actors for support. Thus, restraint is often a deliberate strategic choice in civil war, with governments and rebel groups abiding by international legal standards and eschewing direct attacks on civilians to win support from domestic and international audiences. Violence against civilians, too, is strategic. Governments and rebel groups calculate the extent to which violence against civilians will help them to accomplish their political goals, but belligerents make these calculations with the knowledge that violence can cost them the support of both domestic and international constituencies.

How a belligerent weighs these domestic and international costs of violence varies depending on the belligerent's relationship with its own domestic and international constituencies. Some governments and rebel groups need support from broad domestic and international constituencies; these governments and rebel groups are likely to exercise restraint rather than risk domestic and international backlash by engaging in brutal violence against civilians. Governments and rebel groups with *narrower* domestic and international constituencies are *less* likely to exercise restraint; these governments and rebel groups have fewer constraints on their behavior, and the costs of engaging in violence are lower.

Among belligerents that target civilians, strategies of violence vary considerably, with some belligerents using violence (1) to control civilians and thereby control territory, (2) to cleanse territory of a particular ethnic or religious group, or (3) to terrorize the opponent's civilian constituents and thereby coerce the opponent into making concessions. A belligerent's choice among these strategies of violence depends on how the belligerent weighs the benefits of violence. While belligerents weigh the *costs* of violence considering their relationship with *their own* domestic and international constituents, belligerents evaluate the *benefits* of violence based on an assessment of *their opponent's* relationship to its constituents. The greater the civilian support for the opponent in the disputed territory, the greater the incentive to use violence to control these hostile civilians. The smaller and more geographically concentrated the opponent's civilian constituency, the more feasible it is to eliminate this constituency entirely, through cleansing. And the greater the opponent's sensitivity to losses among its civilian constituents, the more appealing a strategy of terrorism becomes, given the likelihood that the opponent will respond to violence by making concessions.

This chapter proceeds in five sections. The first section, The Character of Violence in Civil Wars, makes the case that much of the violence that belligerents direct against civilians during civil war is strategically motivated. I also argue that restraint is often a deliberate strategy in civil war. The second section, The Costs of Violence and the Incentives for Restraint, focuses on the distinction between strategies of violence and strategies of restraint, asking why some governments and rebel groups do *not* engage in deliberate attacks on civilians, instead directing their violence primarily at the opponent's military. The third section, How Does Violence Vary?, develops a conceptual framework for understanding how violence varies across cases of civil war. I distinguish between three strategies of violence: (1) violence to control territory, (2) violence to cleanse territory, and (3) violence to terrorize the opponent's civilian constituents and force concessions from the opponent. The fourth section, The Benefits of Violence, focuses on this variation in violence, asking why belligerents choose strategies of control, cleansing, or terrorism. Finally, Alternative Explanations for Violence and Restraint examines alternative explanations for variation in wartime violence against civilians.

THE CHARACTER OF VIOLENCE IN CIVIL WARS

All civil wars, by definition, involve violence directed at the opponent's military forces.[1] Attacks on the opponent's military may serve as a form of military denial: military casualties, damage to military equipment, and destruction of military bases or supply lines directly reduce the opponent's ability to prosecute the war. Attacks on the opponent's military may also serve as a form of coercion: as losses of soldiers, equipment, and supplies mount, the military costs of the conflict rise, which may induce the opponent to make concessions that it otherwise would not. Whether for purposes of denial or coercion, rebel groups routinely attack government soldiers, weapons, supply lines, and military bases. When police or paramilitary forces are involved in counterinsurgency operations, rebel groups often target them as well. In targeting government forces, rebel groups may use conventional tactics; for example, in Sudan, the Sudan People's Liberation Army (SPLA) used large armed units and heavy artillery to engage government forces in battles for strategically located towns and positions. Alternatively, rebel groups may adopt unconventional or guerrilla tactics, using hit-and-run attacks to weaken the government's military capacity over time; Assamese insurgents fighting for autonomy in Northeast India, for example, launched frequent bomb attacks against police stations.

In confronting an insurgency, governments, too, direct much of their violence against rebel group military forces. Governments attack rebel group bases and lines of supply or communication, as the Turkish government did in bombing Kurdistan Workers' Party (Partiya Karkerên Kurdistanê, PKK) bases located in the mountains of neighboring Iraq. Governments often attempt to engage the rebel group directly, much like the battles to secure key strategic positions during the conflict in Southern Sudan. In addition, governments use traditional policing methods such as arrest, detention, and interrogation to deplete rebel forces and to obtain intelligence. When the Maoist insurgency broke out in Nepal in 1996, for example, the government responded with mass detentions of individuals suspected of aiding the insurgency.[2]

---

[1] By most definitions, for a conflict to qualify as a civil war, both the government and the rebel group must possess organized military forces and must inflict a minimum number of military casualties on their opponent. See, for example, and Fearon and Laitin 2003; Doyle and Sambanis 2006.

[2] Amnesty International Annual Report 1997, 241.

Violence against Civilians

In a civil war, civilian casualties are practically inevitable. Civilians are mistakenly detained, interrogated, even killed during government sweep operations; civilians are hit by the fragments of bombs exploded near rebel bases or government troop installations; civilians are caught in the crossfire as opposing militaries battle for control of settled areas. While these civilian casualties may be anticipated, they are *unintentional*. This kind of unintentional violence against civilians is not the focus of this book. Alternatively, individual soldiers may carry out *intentional* acts of violence against civilians, taking advantage of the weak rule of law that pervades conflict zones to settle personal feuds, loot civilian property, or otherwise profit; in doing so, soldiers may intentionally injure, rape, and kill civilians. Such violence against civilians, while intentional on the part of the individual, may not be intentional on the part of the group; frequently, soldiers act without the consent of group leadership.[3] This kind of individually motivated violence against civilians is also not the focus of this book.

This book examines *intentional* violence against civilians in civil war that is directed or encouraged by government and rebel group leadership. In many cases, leaders of an armed group instruct their members to deliberately attack civilian targets to achieve particular strategic objectives in the conflict. For example, during military training or when giving instructions regarding military operations, leaders may depict civilians as complicit in the activities of the opposing side – providing intelligence, supplies, and other forms of support to the opponent. In some cases, leaders may imply that these forms of support render civilians "the enemy" and thus legitimate targets for attack. In other cases, leaders may explicitly designate civilians as "the enemy" or state that the war has eliminated any possibility of civilian immunity.

Three patterns emerge from the evidence, indicating that much of the violence against civilians that occurs during civil war is intentional violence sanctioned by group leadership. First, in a number of cases, government or rebel group leaders have made public statements indicating that they explicitly commanded group members to direct violence against civilians. Abdullah Öcalan, the leader of the PKK in Turkey, for example, announced publicly in 1993 that he had ordered the members of his group to begin launching attacks against tourist sites throughout Turkey.[4]

Second, in many cases the ways in which attacks were carried out suggest that leaders commanded their troops to target civilians. Although direct evidence of superior orders is often unavailable, many attacks on civilians involve

---

[3] Weinstein 2005; Weinstein 2007.

[4] Salim Yassine, "Turkish separatists end ceasefire, threaten all-out war, tourism," Agence France-Presse, 8 June 1993; Nadim Ladki, "Kurdish guerrillas declare all-out war on Turkey," Reuters, 8 June 1993.

a level of coordination that would be difficult to achieve without some degree of organization and planning on the part of higher level officials. During the conflict in Chechnya, for example, the Russian air force bombarded the capital of Grozny for months;[5] in Darfur, the Sudanese government's air and ground attacks on civilian targets were often coordinated, with similar patterns of attack repeated throughout the conflict.[6] Among rebel groups, too, the level of coordination involved in attacks on civilians is often high. The Farabundo Martí National Liberation Front (Frente Farabundo Martí para la Liberación Nacional, FMLN) in El Salvador, for example, launched thousands of attacks on power lines and power stations during its insurgency;[7] the Moro Islamic Liberation Front (MILF), which is fighting for an autonomous Muslim region in the Southern Philippines, has focused its violence on towns and cities with majority-Christian populations. It is unlikely that individual soldiers, acting on their own, would produce such consistent patterns of attack over time.

Third, in many civil wars, abuses of civilians are not merely isolated incidents, but take place on a large scale, with violence spread throughout a region or country. In Darfur, the number of civilians killed in violent incidents, most of which were perpetrated by Sudanese government troops working with Janjaweed militias, is estimated at between 220,000 and 270,000 during the first three years of the conflict.[8] Approximately 200,000 civilians perished during the conflict in East Timor, most killed by the Indonesian government.[9] In such cases, it is nearly impossible to sustain the claim that violence is unintentional on the part of the group; killing civilians in such large numbers would be incredibly difficult to achieve without coordination.

Defining Restraint

While violence against civilians is common in civil war, in many cases, governments and rebel groups seek to limit attacks on civilian populations and civilian targets, such as residential areas of cities and towns, crops and livestock, and civilian infrastructure. I conceptualize violence as a spectrum, with high levels of deliberate violence against civilians, such as the Sudanese government's attacks on civilians in Darfur, marking one end of the spectrum, and low levels of violence against civilians marking the other end

---

[5] Smith 1998; Blandy 2003.
[6] Amnesty International 2004b; International Crisis Group 2004a; Human Rights Watch 2004a; Human Rights Watch 2004b; U.S. Department of State, the Bureau of Democracy, Human Rights, and Labor and the Bureau of Intelligence and Research 2004; Prunier 2005; United Nations 2005.
[7] U.S. Department of State 1992; Byrne 1996.   [8] Reeves 2006.
[9] Amnesty International 1985.

of the spectrum. I refer to extremely low levels of violence as restraint. Many levels and forms of violence fill in the middle of this spectrum of violence, as I illustrate through the data analysis and case studies in this book.

To be clear, the category of restraint is not intended to represent a complete absence of violence against civilians. Data on the targeted killing of individual civilians during civil war – what some would term selective violence – shows that nearly every single government and rebel group killed some civilians they believed to be aiding the opponent. For this reason, some might argue that using the term "restraint" is misleading and that it would be more accurate to refer to these cases simply as cases of low violence. My use of the term "restraint," however, is intended to capture a set of behaviors that indicate a deliberate attempt to limit violence.

The extent of restraint required varies across cases, depending on the strength of incentives to engage in violence against civilians, but limiting violence against civilians – or minimizing civilian casualties – requires some degree of restraint. Governments and rebel groups must train their soldiers to differentiate between military and civilian targets and must develop specific rules of engagement to govern the use of force against the opponent's civilian constituents. Further, armed groups must encourage or enforce compliance with these procedures and rules by monitoring the behavior of their members, rewarding rule-consistent behavior and punishing violations. As scholars studying the internal, organizational dynamics of armed groups have demonstrated, a variety of social, psychological, and organizational factors make it challenging for leaders to implement this kind of control over the use of violence among members of the armed group, particularly when soldiers are encouraged to use violence in pursuit of the war effort more generally.[10] Thus, even among governments and rebel groups that adopt strategies of restraint, the resulting behavior may vary, with some governments and rebel groups better able than others to implement strategies of restraint to control the use of violence among their members.

 As the case studies in this book demonstrate, governments and rebel groups often *do* have strong incentives to direct violence against civilians, yet they choose military operations that limit civilian casualties, and they publicly express their respect for international norms of noncombatant immunity. Restraint is often a deliberate strategic choice in civil war. To look only at violence, without also considering restraint, would ignore much of the variation in government and rebel group strategies.[11]

---

[10] Wood 2006; Weinstein 2007; Wood 2009; Hoover Green 2011; Cohen 2013; Manekin 2013.

[11] In her examination of variation in wartime sexual violence, Wood 2006 also emphasizes the importance of understanding deliberate policies of restraint, or the absence of sexual violence. Straus 2012 makes a similar argument in his study of genocide, advocating analysis of negative cases in which genocide or other forms of political violence were possible, but did not occur.

THE COSTS OF VIOLENCE AND
THE INCENTIVES FOR RESTRAINT

What, then, can explain strategies of restraint in civil war? Prior research has focused primarily on the strength of incentives encouraging governments and rebel groups to use violence; however, governments and rebel groups make strategic calculations about the extent to which violence *or restraint* will aid them in achieving their political objectives and thus also carefully weigh the costs of engaging in violence against civilians and the benefits of restraint.

International human rights and humanitarian norms have become more widely accepted in the years since the end of the Cold War.[12] Both domestic and international audiences often make reference to these norms in expressing their opposition to wartime abuses of civilians. This does not mean, however, that governments and rebel groups will always respond by exercising restraint. For some governments and rebel groups, the prospect of losing domestic and international support may be devastating, raising the costs of engaging in violence against civilians. But for other governments and rebel groups – those better positioned to endure domestic and international criticism – the costs of civilian targeting are lower. The likelihood that a belligerent will exercise restraint depends significantly on the costs of civilian targeting, which depend, in turn, on the belligerent's relationship with its own constituents – how vulnerable the belligerent is to pressure from its domestic and international constituents.[13]

Governments and rebel groups that need to build support from broad domestic and international constituencies often use their good behavior to do so, appealing to international standards of appropriate conduct, highlighting the restrained nature of their military operations, and claiming to behave in accordance with international laws of war. Such belligerents position themselves as legitimate international actors, worthy of material aid or diplomatic assistance.[14] Having the public support of key domestic and international actors can be an important advantage, as these actors lobby on behalf of their preferred group, pressure the opponent to make concessions, and propose favorable settlements during peace negotiations.[15]

---

[12] Hafner-Burton and Tsutsui 2005; Hafner-Burton and Tsutsui 2007; Sikkink 2011; Teitel 2011.

[13] Research on international human rights law has shown that government relationships with their domestic constituents influence incentives for ratification of international human rights treaties (Hafner-Burton, Tsutsui, and Meyer 2008) and incentives for compliance with international human rights obligations (Simmons 2009).

[14] Jo and Thomson 2014 similarly argue that a desire for greater legitimacy motivates rebel group compliance with international standards regarding the treatment of detainees; Jo 2015 argues that a desire for greater legitimacy drives rebel group compliance with other aspects of international law as well, including international humanitarian law prohibiting attacks on civilians.

[15] Moral hazard arguments claim that rebel groups may initiate conflict intentionally to provoke a harsh government response, in the hopes that this will prompt international intervention

The Domestic Costs of Violence

Governments and rebel groups weigh the *domestic costs* of violence based on their relationship with their *domestic constituents*. All governments and rebel groups need some degree of political support from domestic constituents to remain in power and maintain the political status quo (in the case of governments) or to gain power and alter the political status quo (in the case of rebel groups). Civil war is, after all, a struggle for political power at the domestic level. *Whose* support specifically the belligerent needs and how urgently it needs this support, however, varies. Three characteristics of a belligerent's political system shape the belligerent's relationship with its domestic constituents: (1) the degree to which institutions compel leaders to respond to constituents, (2) the inclusiveness of the political system, and (3) the consolidation of political power.

For governments, this translates to three key regime characteristics: (1) regime type, which impacts incentives for responsiveness; (2) regime inclusiveness – whether the political system includes multiple groups in decision making; and (3) regime stability, which influences the government's sense of urgency in securing its base of support. Scholars of international relations have long argued that government regime type influences behavior, focusing on the ways in which regime type creates institutional incentives for leaders to be responsive to public demands. Drawing on Immanuel Kant's work,[16] proponents of democratic peace arguments claim that democratic leaders have strong incentives to behave in accordance with the preferences of their citizens. Democratic leaders avoid entering into costly wars because the domestic public must bear the costs of war – mobilization of human and material resources, damage to civilian infrastructure, civilian and military casualties – and because political institutions allow the domestic public to influence decision making in a democratic system.[17] Others have argued that these institutional constraints may also influence how democratic governments fight wars: democratic leaders are likely to be sensitive to widespread public criticism because democratic institutions hold leaders accountable to the public, constraining the ability of leaders to take actions that would contradict public preferences. Consequently, democratic governments are more likely to have difficulty tolerating long and costly wars, to fight only those wars they are likely to win, and to adopt policies that minimize the costs of war.[18] Democratic governments also face normative

---

(Crawford 2006; Kuperman 2006). Regardless of whether rebel groups intend to provoke government repression with their initial rebellion, I argue that once a conflict has begun, some governments and rebel groups have incentives to exercise restraint as a means of encouraging favorable international involvement in the conflict.

[16] Kant 2003.   [17] See, for example, Doyle 1986; Russett 1994; Oneal and Russett 2001.

[18] See, for example, Bueno de Mesquita et al. 1999; Reiter and Stam 2002; Bueno de Mesquita et al. 2003; Valentino, Huth, and Croco 2010. On public sensitivity to wartime casualties in democracies, see Mueller 1973; Gartner and Segura 1998.

constraints on their behavior: ideals emphasizing respect for individual rights may encourage democratic governments to value the lives of their citizens more highly, making them more sensitive to military and civilian casualties incurred during conflict.[19]

Although these arguments are referring, for the most part, to the constraints democratic leaders face in fighting *interstate* wars, the domestic constraints on government behavior might weigh even more heavily during *civil* war. Most interstate wars are fought at least in part on foreign territory, creating some separation between a government's domestic civilian constituents and wartime violence; civil wars are fought primarily on domestic territory, allowing civilians to witness wartime violence directly. The domestic public may be willing to tolerate the killing of foreign civilians during interstate wars,[20] but domestic backlash is likely to be more severe in response to the killing of civilians during domestic counterinsurgency operations. Leaders of democratic regimes are thus less likely to engage in violence against civilians in civil war.

Although leaders of autocratic regimes also have political constituencies whose support they must maintain in order to remain in power,[21] in comparison with democracies, autocratic governments face fewer domestic constraints on their behavior. Criticizing government policies is difficult for the domestic public in autocratic states, which tend to place restrictions on individual freedoms and the media. Additionally, even when criticism is possible, autocratic leaders face little pressure to respond to public criticism in the absence of an institutionalized political mechanism, such as elections, through which the public can hold them accountable. Less constrained by domestic political institutions, autocratic governments are thus less likely than their democratic counterparts to exercise restraint.

It is possible to similarly conceive of rebel group political institutions as falling along a spectrum in terms of the degree to which they constrain the decisions of rebel group leaders; many rebel groups do establish sophisticated political organizations that significantly influence rebel group behavior.[22] Existing research has posited a number of factors that shape the structure of rebel governance, including the goals of the insurgent organization, the insurgent group's political ideology, the strength and character of existing institutions, the degree of competition with other armed groups, and the existence of periods of peace.[23] These studies demonstrate that rebel group political institutions range in complexity, and variation in the structure of these institutions shapes interactions between civilians and rebels.

---

[19] Valentino, Huth, and Croco 2010. Some have relied on similar reasoning to argue that democracies are less likely to kill their own citizens; see Rummel 1994; Rummel 1997.

[20] Downes 2006; Downes 2008.

[21] Bueno de Mesquita et al. 1999; Bueno de Mesquita et al. 2003; Weeks 2008.

[22] Mampilly 2011; Arjona 2014.

[23] Mampilly 2011; Arjona 2014; Gutiérrez Sanín and Wood 2014.

I focus on the ways in which a rebel group's political structure affects its incentives to be responsive to domestic constituents. In some rebel groups, the political structure is little more than a single individual representing the group's interests at the United Nations, while in other rebel groups, the political structure consists of an executive branch with representatives responsible for mobilizing popular support, lobbying foreign governments, and representing the group in peace negotiations. Some rebel groups even maintain complex local governance structures in regions under their control, offering services such as policing, the adjudication of disputes, and the certification of marriage.

Although the means of holding rebel group political leaders accountable rarely parallels means of government accountability – for example, through the holding of regular elections – the more developed a rebel group's political institutional structure, the greater the opportunities available for civilians to convey their preferences to rebel group leaders and the greater the incentives for these leaders to respond. Rebel groups that do not establish any governance structures, while they may have a complex military organizational structure, likely have the fewest constraints on leaders. Rebel groups with multifaceted governance structures – groups that provide services to their constituents at the local level and designate political representatives to conduct the group's affairs at the national and international level – likely have the greatest constraints on leader decision making. Popular backlash in response to violence against civilians is costly for such groups, increasing incentives for restraint.

H1:   *The stronger the institutional incentives for government and rebel group leaders to be responsive to public demands, the greater the likelihood of restraint.*

The domestic costs of violence depend not only on *whether* a government or rebel group has institutional incentives to be responsive to its domestic constituents, but also on *who* these constituents are. The more inclusive a government or rebel group's political system, the broader the domestic base of civilian support it will need in order to achieve its political objectives. Belligerents that need to maintain a broad base of civilian support cannot afford to use violence in ways that might lead to significant popular backlash. Thus, the broader the domestic audience to whom a government or rebel group must appeal, the higher the costs of violence and the greater the likelihood of restraint.

Even in democratic countries where institutions compel responsiveness to the domestic public, these institutions may be designed in such a way that small but significant minority groups are not well represented in government. In majoritarian electoral systems, for example, although small minority groups may not be excluded formally from voting in elections or holding political office, in practice, a country's demographic make-up, in combination with its electoral system, may result in several larger parties dominating the political system to the exclusion of smaller parties unable to garner a majority or plurality of votes in most districts.[24] Political leaders in these circumstances may thus have few incentives to appeal to minority groups or to take seriously their criticisms of government policies. Although democratic regimes, in general, are likely to be more inclusive than autocratic regimes, some autocratic regimes may seek to appeal to a broad domestic audience, even though they might lack formal institutional mechanisms to enforce government accountability to the domestic public.

Rebel groups, too, vary in the degree to which they are inclusive of individuals from diverse societal groups. Revolutionary groups seeking power in the central government sometimes derive legitimacy by claiming a commitment to establishing a government that will include many different groups in public policy making. Other revolutionary groups are more exclusionary, fighting primarily to install a particular ethnic or religious group in power. Separatist groups fighting for autonomy for a particular region of the country also vary in their inclusiveness. Some separatist groups espouse a particular ethnic or religious group's right to rule the disputed territory to the exclusion of others, while other separatist groups would allow for greater inclusion in government.

H2:   *The more inclusive a government or rebel group's political system, the greater the likelihood of restraint.*

It is important to note the role that ideology plays in influencing the political institutions that governments and rebel groups create to structure their relationships with their political constituents.[25] In fashioning the first two hypotheses, I have treated the degree to which a government or rebel group's institutions encourage responsiveness to constituents and the inclusiveness of a belligerent's political system as given attributes, sidestepping the question of *why* governments and rebel groups construct particular types of political institutions. Some governments, however, may be motivated by an ideology that emphasizes individual rights and freedoms, such as the right of individuals to participate in their system of government, which may, in turn, motivate the government to build and maintain a set of democratic political institutions. Similarly, a government motivated by an ideology that conceives of citizenship as requiring equal and legitimate access in the political process for all individuals in the country may develop inclusive political institutions, placing few restrictions on political participation and ensuring the representation of even small minority groups in the governance structure. Other governments may possess more exclusionary ideologies, perhaps based in nationalism or belief in the privileged position of a particular religion; such governments might construct political institutions that entrench the power of particular ethnic, religious, or national groups and restrict the participation of other groups.

---

[24] Scholars of power sharing have written extensively about these issues; see, for example, Lijphart 2007.

[25] Gutiérrez Sanín and Wood 2014.

For rebel groups, ideology may play an equally important role in the development of political structures and institutions.[26] Some rebel groups, for example, possess ideologies that view a particular ethnic group or religious sect as inferior; these rebel groups are likely to develop political systems that exclude these "inferior" ethnic and religious groups from access to power and representation. Other rebel groups hold beliefs that criticize past histories of discrimination and emphasize the need for greater equality; these groups are likely to devise political structures that prioritize broad participation in governance. Groups motivated by Marxist ideologies offer another example; ideas about the centrality of revolution to the achievement of societal transformation may lead Marxist groups to articulate inclusive political agendas and to build political institutions that allow for broad participation in governance.[27] I briefly discuss ideology in the case study chapters, noting its influence on a government or rebel group's political system, but leave a more nuanced treatment of this issue to future research. This discussion suggests that a deeper analysis of the role that ideology plays in civil war – and in particular, the role that ideology plays in structuring government and rebel group organizations – is warranted, as Francisco Gutiérrez Sanín and Elisabeth Wood convincingly argue.[28]

Thus far, I have argued that two factors influence how belligerents weigh the domestic costs of violence: (1) the degree to which political institutions encourage responsiveness to constituents and (2) the inclusiveness of the political system, which together determine the government or rebel group's domestic constituency. In addition, the domestic costs of violence depend on the urgency of the government or rebel group's need to secure support from this constituency. The third characteristic of a government or rebel group's political system that influences the domestic costs of violence, therefore, is the degree to which a government or rebel group's political power is stable and consolidated. All rebel groups lack consolidated political power in that they are not the official governing authority; all rebel groups thus face some domestic costs to the use of violence against civilians. Similarly, all governments confronting domestic rebellions to some extent lack consolidated political power in that they are facing a violent challenge to their rule. Among governments, however, the degree to which political power is consolidated varies more widely, depending on the stability of the regime. A stable regime that has been in power for many years is likely to be able to survive some loss of domestic support and, therefore, have greater leeway to use violence against civilians; rebellion may force the government to make political concessions, but is unlikely to lead to the collapse of the regime. In unstable regimes that have recently been established, either through a process of political transition or through the creation of a new state, a loss of domestic support could be devastating. One way that leaders of

[26] Mampilly 2011.   [27] Gutiérrez Sanín and Wood 2014.   [28] Ibid.

unstable regimes can seek greater domestic support is by refraining from attacks on civilians and appealing to domestic audiences through their compliance with international humanitarian law.[29] Governments with unstable regimes also may use restraint to appeal to international audiences.

The International Costs of Violence

Belligerents weigh the *international costs* of violence based on their relationship with *international constituents*. Again, two factors are important: who the belligerent's international constituents are and the strength of incentives to be responsive to these constituents. Belligerent international constituencies vary considerably. In many cases, foreign governments provide financing, weapons, supplies, or even military personnel to governments and rebel groups without concern for the belligerent's degree of respect for international humanitarian norms.[30] Foreign governments may provide military assistance to support their coethnics in a neighboring state,[31] to undermine a rival government, or to quash rebellions generating instability in the region. Western governments and Western-led intergovernmental organizations, however, have taken the lead in strengthening international human rights and humanitarian norms and, in doing so, have also become more willing to respond to violations of these norms. Governments and rebel groups that behave in accordance with international norms can use their good behavior to appeal for support from this Western international constituency.

Since the end of World War II, international humanitarian law has grown in strength, with the signing of the 1949 Geneva Conventions, the 1977 First and Second Additional Protocols to the Geneva Conventions, and the 1998 Rome Statute of the International Criminal Court.[32] These treaties outlaw a range of different types of violence against noncombatants during interstate and civil wars, including murder, mutilation, torture, rape, and the forced relocation of civilians.[33] Protections for civilians are also part of customary international

---

[29] I am not challenging the link between democratization and the likelihood of war (Mansfield and Snyder 1995; Snyder 2000; Mansfield and Snyder 2005). Instead, I am arguing that once transitional governments become engaged in civil war, they are likely to limit their use of violence against civilians.

[30] Salehyan, Siroky, and Wood 2014.   [31] See, for example, Saideman 2001.

[32] On the history of international humanitarian law, see Best 1994; Robertson 1999.

[33] The four 1949 Geneva Conventions share the same Article 3, which applies to "armed conflict not of an international character occurring in the territory of one of the High Contracting Parties." Article 3 maintains that parties to noninternational conflicts must adhere to the most basic provisions of the Geneva Conventions, namely that "persons taking no active part in the hostilities" are to be "treated humanely." See Geneva Convention Relative to the Protection of Civilian Persons in Time of War, 75 UNTS 287, Entered Into Force 21 October 1950. The Second Additional Protocol and the Rome Statute develop more detailed guidelines for behavior in noninternational conflicts (civil wars). See Protocol Additional to the Geneva Conventions of 12 August 1949, and Relating to the Protection of Victims of Non-International Armed Conflicts

law; all governments and rebel groups are thus obligated to avoid targeting civilians regardless of whether they have ratified the relevant treaties.[34] While rebel groups cannot join international treaties, rebel groups often make explicit reference to international law and, in some cases, even publicly commit to abide by the terms of international agreements. Karenni rebels fighting against the Burmese government, for example, issued a statement in 1997 indicating that their insurgent government had incorporated "all international treaties and Geneva Conventions" into its charter.[35]

The post–Cold War shift away from a bipolar distribution of power created a renewed role for international institutions such as the United Nations and an acceleration in the growth of international human rights and humanitarian norms.[36] In addition, technological developments have made it easier for journalists and nongovernmental organizations(NGOs) such as Amnesty International, Human Rights Watch, and their local partners throughout the world to research human rights abuses, to investigate and report on violations of international humanitarian law, and to publish their findings widely through press releases and in-depth reports.[37] In this international context, Western international actors have become both more aware of wartime atrocities and more willing to take action against these violations of international standards. Foreign governments and the United Nations have often called for an end to atrocities, threatening to implement sanctions or to cut off diplomatic relations with offending governments. The UN Security Council, for example, issued resolutions calling for a halt to fighting in more than half of the civil wars that took place from 1989 to 2010; in many of these resolutions, the Security Council also demanded an end to violations of humanitarian law.[38] The United Nations initiated peacekeeping missions in one-third of the civil wars that took place from 1989 to 2010.[39] The international community has held leaders accountable for atrocities committed during civil war through UN-sponsored war crimes tribunals in Cambodia, Rwanda, Sierra Leone, and the former Yugoslavia,

---

(Protocol II), 1125 UNTS 609, Entered into Force 7 December 1978; Rome Statute of the International Criminal Court, 2187 UNTS 90, Entered Into Force 1 July 2002.

[34] Henckaerts and Doswald-Beck 2005. The Statute of the International Court of Justice defines customary international law as rules that have become "a general practice accepted as law." Statute of the International Court of Justice, Article 38(1)(b), 26 June 1945.

[35] Unrepresented Nations and Peoples Organization 1997, 98. An NGO, Geneva Call, collects similar statements of intended adherence to international law on its website: www.genevacall.org.

[36] For a broader discussion of how the end of the Cold War impacted civil wars, see Kalyvas and Balcells 2010.

[37] Mathews 1997; Keck and Sikkink 1998; Hafner-Burton 2008.

[38] I calculated the statistic on UN Security Council Resolutions using data from the UN Security Council. Available online at http://www.un.org/en/sc/documents/resolutions/.

[39] I calculated the statistic on UN peacekeeping using data from the UN Department of Peacekeeping Operations. Available online at http://www.un.org/en/peacekeeping/operations/. On the effectiveness of peacekeeping operations, see Doyle and Sambanis 2006; Fortna 2008.

and through the creation of the International Criminal Court (ICC), which had opened investigations into nine cases of internal conflict through 2015.[40]

The enforcement of international humanitarian law is by no means consistent, but belligerents likely have some expectation that civilian targeting will bring criticism from Western actors. In addition, belligerents who behave in accordance with international norms can use their good behavior to appeal for support from Western international constituencies. International humanitarian norms thus provide a framework that both international actors and belligerents reference in setting expectations about appropriate behavior. Although the impact of international law is indirect, law constrains behavior by establishing standards that belligerents use when positioning themselves to make international appeals and that international actors enforce in extending or withholding support.[41]

What exactly do belligerents hope to obtain from Western governments and intergovernmental organizations? Diplomatic assistance. A foreign government, for example, may advocate for its preferred side in the conflict, seeking to shift international public opinion by utilizing media and other public forums that a belligerent may have difficulty reaching. A foreign government may also lobby other governments directly to lend their support to the cause. Together, these governments may propose sanctions cutting off financial or military assistance to the disfavored opponent. Foreign governments may also push for terms of settlement favorable to their preferred side, may coerce the opposing side to make political concessions, or may even offer to serve as a mediator in peace negotiations or participate as a member of a contact group of concerned states. Foreign governments or multilateral organizations, such as the United Nations, threatened to impose or imposed economic sanctions against one or both actors in about half of the civil wars that took place from 1989 to 2010,[42] and along with international NGOs, were involved in mediating settlements in more than 60 percent of civil wars during that period.[43] Having a powerful Western government or intergovernmental organization on one's side during a civil war can thus be an important advantage.

---

[40] Postwar justice strategies have become both more common and more internationalized in recent decades (Vinjamuri and Boesenecker 2007). On the history of international war crimes tribunals, see Bass 2000; Teitel 2011.

[41] Although governments and rebel groups may initially abide by international humanitarian standards for instrumental reasons – to obtain support – a socialization process may occur over time (e.g., Koh 1997; Goodman and Jinks 2004).

[42] I calculated this statistic using data from the UN Security Council Sanctions Committees (available online at https://www.un.org/sc/suborg/en/sanctions/information), the U.S. Department of the Treasury (available online at https://www.treasury.gov/resource-center/sanctions/Programs/Pages/Programs.aspx), and the Threat and Imposition of Sanctions (TIES) Data (Morgan, Bapat, and Krustev 2009).

[43] I calculated this statistic using mediation data from Svensson 2007; Regan, Frank, and Aydin 2009.

Diplomatic backing from Western states can also have important economic consequences – particularly for governments. Most civil wars take place in developing countries, where governments are often heavily reliant on foreign aid to finance basic services such as healthcare and education, as well as to finance the government bureaucracy. Diplomatic backing from Western donor countries, therefore, can mean that crucial sources of aid will continue to flow; conversely, drawing condemnation from these donor countries can mean cuts in aid. Many donor governments concerned about the Sudanese government's human rights record in Southern Sudan and Darfur, for example, continued to channel aid to multilateral organizations and NGOs active in these regions, but provided almost no direct assistance to the Sudanese government. In 2008, Canada disbursed US$55.2 million in aid to multilateral organizations working in Sudan, supporting activities of the United Nations Children's Fund (UNICEF) among other UN agencies, and sent another US$13.6 million to NGOs such as Médecins Sans Frontières; but Canada provided only US$4,300 of aid directly to the Sudanese government.[44]

Although governments and rebel groups that abide by international humanitarian law primarily seek diplomatic assistance, in rare cases, belligerents have been able to draw international military intervention on their behalf – often by drawing a sharp contrast between their own good behavior and the abuses of their opponent. NATO conducted air strikes against the Yugoslav government during the civil war in Kosovo in the late 1990s; more recently, international forces aided the Afghan government in its fight against the Taliban insurgency and backed rebels fighting against Col. Muammar el-Qaddafi's government in Libya.

Governments and rebel groups vary in the extent to which they seek support from Western international actors; the greater the incentives to appeal to this Western international constituency, the higher the international costs of violence, and the stronger the incentives to exercise restraint. Governments whose regimes are unstable have a particular need to secure the backing of international actors.[45] These governments, as discussed in the previous section, seek to build their authority and legitimacy in part by gaining support from domestic constituencies, but international support can also be critical for these regimes. A loss of international diplomatic support could lead the domestic public to question the government's viability. Stable regimes, in contrast, are likely to be able to weather international criticism, even if it comes from important international backers; for these governments, a loss of international diplomatic support or a reduction in foreign aid may bring hardship, but is unlikely to threaten the government's survival. Because stable governments are less

---

[44] These statistics are from the Organization for Economic Co-operation and Development (OECD) Creditor Reporting System database; the data are reported in 2009 constant US$. Available online at www.oecd.org.

[45] Note that the argument here is about regime instability, not military weakness.

vulnerable to international criticism, they are less constrained in their ability to direct violence against civilians.

While all governments with unstable regimes may need international support, some of these governments are better positioned to make appeals to Western international constituencies. As international norms favoring democracy have grown stronger, the legitimacy of a government has increasingly become associated with the character of the government's political institutions and, in particular, the degree to which institutions allow for broad participation in the political system. Thus, governments that came to power by overthrowing a democratically elected government are unlikely to win sympathy from Western international audiences.

H3:   Governments in need of building domestic and international support – in particular, governments with unstable regimes – are more likely to adopt strategies of restraint.

A rebel group's incentives to appeal to Western international constituencies depend in large part on the government opponent – in particular, on the government's willingness to make political concessions. Rebel groups fighting in civil wars have two means of achieving their objectives: they can defeat the government outright or they can use violence to impose costs on the government, thus forcing government concessions. Military victories in civil war, however, have become much less common over time; while 75 percent of civil wars from 1944 to 1989 ended in military victory, only 30 percent of civil wars from 1990 to 1997 ended in military victory.[46] Most rebel groups in the contemporary period, thus, are likely to evaluate carefully their prospects for eliciting government concessions.

One of the primary factors rebel groups consider in evaluating the likelihood of government concessions is the regime type of their government opponent. As discussed earlier, political institutions and norms in democratic countries create incentives for leaders to adopt policies that accord with the preferences of their citizens.[47] In democracies, regular elections, in combination with broad political participation, allow citizens to express their policy preferences as well as to hold democratic leaders accountable for their decisions; while institutional checks on the executive's power further constrain leader decision making. In autocracies, in contrast, public debate and criticism is limited by restrictions on freedom of speech and association,[48] while the lack of political institutions demanding government accountability means that even as violence mounts,

---

[46] DeRouen and Sobek 2004. Civil war termination statistics from Toft (2009) show a similar pattern.

[47] Doyle 1986; Russett 1994; Oneal and Russett 2001.

[48] A number of scholars have examined variation in autocratic institutions (e.g., Geddes 1999; Gandhi 2008). The argument of this book emphasizes commonalities among autocratic governments and the ways in which autocratic governments differ from democratic governments.

autocratic governments have few institutional incentives to respond to public demands for a resolution to the conflict.[49] Although autocratic leaders may depend on the support of particular political constituencies in order to maintain power, these constituencies tend to be narrow in comparison to the constituencies supporting democratic leaders.[50] The more autocratic a government's institutions, therefore, the more likely it is that the government will be able to hold out against any military or civilian losses the insurgency might impose. For these reasons, rebel groups likely perceive autocratic governments as less willing than democratic governments to make political concessions in response to domestic public pressure. Unable to leverage domestic pressure to force government concessions, rebel groups facing autocratic governments, instead, seek to attract international attention, in the hope that international pressure will force government concessions.[51] Refraining from violence against civilians is one way in which rebel groups can seek international support.

In addition to having greater need for international support, rebel groups facing autocratic opponents are better positioned to make international appeals. In an age in which international norms heavily favor democratic forms of government, rebel groups facing democratic opponents are likely to have difficulty proving the legitimacy of their grievances; their democratic opponents are already likely to be considered legitimate by Western international actors. Rebel groups facing autocratic governments, however, tend to be able to win international sympathy more easily, particularly if the government abuses civilians; these rebel groups can contrast their respect for international humanitarian law with the government's brutality against civilians.[52]

 H4:   *Rebel groups in need of building international support – in particular, rebel groups facing more autocratic opponents – are more likely to adopt strategies of restraint.*

While each of the factors laid out here on its own should influence the need for domestic and international support and, thus, also should influence behavior, it is when these factors operate in combination with one another that incentives for restraint will be strongest.

HOW DOES VIOLENCE VARY?

Thus far I have referred to civilian targeting as a single strategy; in fact, civilian targeting is a varied strategy. Strategies of civilian targeting vary in

---

[49] Although some autocratic governments hold elections, these elections do not threaten the power of the government and do not hold the government accountable in the same way as elections in a democracy (Gandhi and Lust-Okar 2009).

[50] Bueno de Mesquita et al. 1999; Bueno de Mesquita et al. 2003; Weeks 2008.

[51] This pattern bears similarity to the boomerang pattern described by Keck and Sikkink 1998.

[52] On how rebel groups market themselves to the international community, see Bob 2005. See, also, Jumbert and Lanz 2013, on the internationalization of the conflict in Darfur.

two key ways: first, in terms of the *target audience for violence*, and second, in terms of the *target of violence*.

The target audience for violence refers to the group whose behavior a government or rebel group aims to change through the use of violence. In directing violence against civilians, governments and rebel groups, perhaps most obviously, may seek to change the behavior of civilians themselves. To successfully maintain and extend physical control over territory, governments and rebel groups must defend the territory militarily as well as secure civilian cooperation. Violence may serve, therefore, as a means of forcing civilians to cooperate and deterring civilians from providing aid to the opponent.[53] In some conflicts, rather than seeking civilian cooperation, governments and rebel groups may aim to rid a particular territory of its civilian population. Here, civilians are often still the target audience for violence, with governments and rebel groups using violence against small groups of civilians as a means of inducing the wider civilian population to abandon the territory. In more extreme cases, however, governments and rebel groups may seek to eliminate a particular civilian population. When violence is aimed at *eliminating* civilians rather than *coercing* civilians, no target audience for violence exists. Finally, governments and rebel groups may use violence in an effort to alter the behavior of a third party actor – the opponent. By attacking an opponent's civilian constituents, a government or rebel group can ratchet up the costs of the conflict for the opponent, in the hope that the opponent will choose to make concessions rather than endure continuing civilian losses.

Violence against civilians varies not only in terms of the target audience for violence, but also in terms of the target of violence.[54] Some governments and rebel groups use violence in a limited way, minimizing civilian casualties by attacking only those individuals believed to be actively aiding the opponent – what Stathis Kalyvas refers to as selective violence, involving attempts to "ascertain individual guilt."[55] Other examples of limited or low-casualty violence include attacks on targets such as power stations or oil pipelines, which will produce economic hardship, but few civilian casualties. Other governments and rebel groups, rather than limiting their targets of attack, target all civilians belonging to a particular ethnic, religious, or national group – what is often termed "collective targeting."[56]

Using these two dimensions of variation – the target audience for violence and the target of violence – it is possible to differentiate between six different strategies of violence against civilians, as shown in Figure 1.1: low- and high-casualty control, low- and high-casualty cleansing, and low- and high-casualty terrorism. These strategies of violence are not mutually exclusive. Governments

---

[53] Kalyvas 2006.
[54] Note that the target of violence may also be military. Here, I focus on violence directed against civilians.
[55] Kalyvas 2006, 142.   [56] Ibid.

Target Audience for Violence	Target of Violence	
	Limited	Broad
Civilians *aim is to coerce civilians*	Low-casualty control	High-casualty control
No audience *aim is to eliminate civilians*	Low-casualty cleansing; forced displacement	High-casualty cleansing; genocide
Opponent *aim is to coerce opponent*	Low-casualty terrorism	High-casualty terrorism

FIGURE 1.1 Types of Violence Against Civilians.

and rebel groups may use multiple strategies of violence during a civil war. The next section details these six strategies of violence.

Control

During civil war, rebel groups and governments depend heavily on the civilian population for food, shelter, and perhaps most importantly, information about the opponent's troop movements, sources of supply, and civilian sympathizers.[57] Cutting off the opponent's access to its civilian base can severely restrict the opponent's ability to carry out military operations, and, therefore, is often central to a strategy of military denial during civil war. Severing the ties between an opponent and its civilian base is not, however, an easy task. Many civilians will not easily be deterred from aiding their preferred side. Belligerents thus have strong incentives to use violence as a means of coercing civilians into cooperating and deterring civilians from providing aid to the opponent; by controlling civilians, belligerents can thereby extend their control over territory.[58]

Low-casualty forms of control involve limited violence; troops identify, interrogate, and then often kill specific individuals believed to be assisting the enemy. The aim is to draw a clear connection between the undesired behavior – aiding the opponent – and the punishment – torture or death.[59] In drawing this connection, such violence seeks to punish or eliminate those individuals who are aiding the opponent, as well as to deter the wider civilian population from future collaboration with the opponent. Civilians are, therefore, both the

[57] Lawrence 1929; Mao 1961. More recently, see Valentino, Huth, and Balch-Lindsay 2004; Kalyvas 2006. Some argue that governments do not rely as heavily on civilians for support as do rebel groups and, therefore, are less likely than rebel groups to use large-scale violence against civilians (Valentino, Huth, and Balch-Lindsay 2004, 385). Kalyvas 2006 disputes this, arguing that governments and rebel groups both must secure civilian cooperation in order to control territory.

[58] Kalyvas 2006.   [59] Kalyvas 2004.

target of violence and the target audience for violence. Not *all* civilians, however, are targeted with violence; instead, violence is directed only at those civilians believed to be enemy collaborators.

While low-casualty control imposes individual punishments, targeting only those individuals who are actively collaborating with the opponent, high-casualty control imposes collective punishments, expanding attacks to individuals or groups who are associated with collaborators, but are not collaborators themselves. In strategies of high-casualty control, civilians are still both the target of violence and the target audience for violence, but violence is aimed more broadly, targeting collaborators' families and villages in an effort to deter collaboration among the wider population.

Cleansing

Strategies of cleansing are similar to strategies of control in that they seek to sever connections between the opponent and its civilian base of support; the difference is that rather than using violence to coerce changes in civilian behavior, strategies of cleansing use violence to remove civilians from contested territory entirely.[60] This distinction between violence aimed at coercing civilians and violence aimed at removing or eliminating civilians is often blurry. In some cases, violence aimed at eliminating civilians may involve coercion; for example, civilians may witness violence against neighboring families or villages and decide to flee before being forced to do so. In the longer term, however, violence aimed at removing civilians from contested territory has no audience; once a belligerent has succeeded in relocating or killing civilians from the contested territory, the belligerent does not have any expectation that a wider audience will alter its behavior. Cleansing may serve a second purpose as well; in addition to removing an opponent's base of civilian support, cleansing a territory of a particular ethnic or religious group serves to homogenize the territory, allowing the government or rebel group to make a more forceful claim that the territory rightfully belongs to their own ethnic or religious constituency.

Low-casualty cleansing involves the physical removal of civilians from territory without imposing direct, intentional civilian casualties; often, this type of violence is referred to as forced relocation or forced displacement.[61] Governments or rebel groups, for example, may physically relocate civilian populations into guarded villages or concentration camps; although the conditions in relocation camps may be poor, leading to deaths resulting from disease and malnutrition, such strategies do not involve the direct killing of large numbers of civilians. In most cases, relocation is intended to be temporary.

[60] Valentino 2000; Valentino 2004; Downes 2006; Downes 2008.
[61] On the strategic use of forced displacement, see Steele 2009; Greenhill 2010; Steele 2011.

High-casualty cleansing involves more severe violence, aimed at the permanent removal of civilians from a particular territory. Strategies of high-casualty cleansing place few limits on violence, attacking any civilians belonging to a particular ethnic or religious group. Entire villages may be forced violently from their homes, with crops and houses burned to prevent their return; forced migration and scorched earth campaigns are often accompanied by mass killings, both to eliminate members of the target group and to induce other members of the group to flee. Moving even further along the spectrum of violence, genocide aims to eliminate a particular ethnic or religious population entirely. The goal is not relocation, but eradication. The line between high-casualty cleansing and genocide is difficult to draw, with experts often disagreeing about whether a case qualifies as genocide; it has been widely debated, for example, whether Sudan's violence against African ethnic groups in Darfur ought to be considered genocide.[62] For the purposes of this book, I put aside debates about defining genocide and group genocide together with high-casualty cleansing.

Existing research has examined the causes of genocide and mass killing;[63] documented ethnic cleansing and genocide in Bosnia, Rwanda, and Darfur;[64] and criticized the international community for failing to respond effectively to genocide.[65] Yet cleansing is one among several possible strategies of violence against civilians; often cleansing is used in conjunction with other forms of violence, as part of a larger strategy for waging civil war. In this book, therefore, I analyze high-casualty cleansing and genocide alongside other forms of violence in an effort to understand why some governments and rebel groups take violence against civilians to this extreme, while other governments and rebel groups do not. Because my focus is on wartime violence against civilians, I do not address cases of cleansing and genocide that occur outside the context of civil war.[66]

Terrorism

While governments and rebel groups often use violence as a means of coercing civilians into providing supplies, sharing intelligence, or abandoning territory, civilians are not always the intended audience for violence. Governments and rebel groups may also use violence against civilians as a means

---

[62] On the debate over whether Darfur constitutes genocide, see Prunier 2005; Straus 2005.

[63] Harff 2003; Valentino 2004; Straus 2012.

[64] On the genocide in Rwanda, see, for example, Prunier 1995; Des Forges 1999; Mamdani 2001; Straus 2006; Fujii 2009. On Darfur, see, for example, Prunier 2005. On Bosnia, see, for example, Woodward 1995.

[65] Power 2002; Barnett 2003.

[66] On forms of cleansing and genocide, including cleansing and genocide occurring outside of the context of civil war, see Valentino 2000; Valentino 2004.

of coercing a third party actor – <u>in particular, as a means of coercing their opponent into making political concessions</u>. Perhaps the most obvious way to compel one's opponent to negotiate or to reduce their war aims is through direct military pressure – military denial – by attacking the opponent's military bases, equipment, and troops; seizing and maintaining control over disputed territory; or targeting sources of military supply in an effort to demonstrate that military victory is unlikely. Governments and rebel groups may also pressure the opponent indirectly, attacking civilian targets rather than military targets, in the hope that by increasing the costs of the conflict for the opponent's civilian constituents, the opponent will be forced to make political concessions or negotiate an end to the conflict. Civilians may be a particularly attractive target because they are unarmed, unlikely to mount as formidable a resistance to attack as armed and trained soldiers; similarly, civilian infrastructure and residential areas are not as well guarded or fortified against attack as are military installations and bases.[67]

The use of violence as a means of inflicting enough suffering that the opponent is forced to make concessions is often referred to as a strategy of punishment,[68] but this type of violence would also qualify as terrorism according to many definitions of the term.[69] The definition of terrorism has been the subject of extensive debate,[70] but many scholarly definitions emphasize the idea that terrorism aims to convey a message to an audience other than those targeted with violence, an emphasis that is similar to the distinction made in Figure 1.1 between the different target audiences for violence.[71] In Hoffman's words, "terrorism is specifically designed to have far-reaching psychological effects beyond the immediate victim(s) or object of the terrorist attack. It is meant to instill fear within, and thereby intimidate, a wider 'target audience' that might include a rival ethnic or religious group, an entire country, a national government or political party, or public opinion in general."[72] While some definitions of terrorism include violence against government and military personnel not actively engaged in military operations,[73] in order to maintain this book's focus on violence against civilians, I restrict my definition of terrorism to

---

[67] Downes 2006; Downes 2008. [68] Pape 1996.

[69] Stanton 2013. Referring to this strategy of violence as terrorism as opposed to punishment also helps to avoid confusion with strategies of control. Strategies of control aim to punish civilians for aiding the opponent, while strategies of terrorism aim to punish the opponent.

[70] On the challenges of defining terrorism, see, for example, Crenshaw 1995; Hoffman 2006.

[71] Weinberg, Pedahzur, and Hirsch-Hoefler 2004.   [72] Hoffman 2006, 40–41.

[73] In its annual Country Reports on Terrorism, for example, the U.S. State Department defines terrorism as "premeditated, politically motivated violence perpetrated against noncombatant targets by subnational groups or clandestine agents." According to chapter 7 of the Country Reports on Terrorism 2009, the State Department interprets the term "noncombatant targets" to include "in addition to civilians, military personnel (whether or not armed or on duty) who are not deployed in a war zone or a war-like setting."

violence against civilian targets.[74] And although it is more common to apply the term "terrorism" to violence perpetrated by nonstate actors than to violence perpetrated by state actors, to maintain consistency across the analyses of government and rebel group violence, I use the term "terrorism" to refer to government and rebel group violence that shares a common characteristic: violence that targets the opponent's civilian constituents, with the aim of achieving a political objective through the intimidation or coercion of the opponent.

While violence aimed at terrorizing the opponent may seem similar to violence aimed at controlling or cleansing territory, in that civilians are the primary target of attack, the distinction is important. When violence is used as a means of terrorism, civilians are still the target of violence, but are not the target audience for violence; attacks are intended not to coerce civilians themselves, but to coerce *the opponent* into making concessions. Most governments and rebel groups are willing to accept some civilian losses during war. Attacks, therefore, are likely to focus on targets that are of high value to the opponent – for example, residential areas of towns or villages where members of the opponent's civilian constituency reside or, if the opponent is the government, targets essential to the functioning of civilian infrastructure and the national economy, such as oil pipelines and power stations.

All terrorism strategies inflict damage on civilian targets in an effort to impose costs on the opponent, but terrorism strategies differ from one another in the types of targets attacked. Some governments and rebel groups attack civilian targets with the aim of imposing high costs, but few casualties. Examples of low-casualty terrorism include attacks on civilian homes or businesses after civilians have already evacuated the area; attacks on civilian infrastructure targets such as bridges, roadways, or power stations; and attacks on economic targets such as oil pipelines. At the far end of the spectrum, high-casualty terrorism involves more extreme forms of violence. Rebel groups may explode bombs in populated public areas such as bus stations or restaurants, while governments may use aerial bombardment or artillery shelling of residential areas of neighborhoods believed to be rebel strongholds.

THE BENEFITS OF VIOLENCE

In addition to considering the costs of violence, governments and rebel groups also assess the extent to which a particular form of violence will aid in the pursuit of their political objectives. When the costs of violence are extremely low, even a minimal benefit to violence may be enough to entice a belligerent to attack civilians, whereas when the costs of violence are extremely high, even

---

[74] Much of the research on transnational terrorism uses a similar definition of terrorism (Stanton 2013).

significant benefits to violence will not outweigh these costs. I posit that how a government or rebel group weighs the benefits of each of the three different strategies of violence – control, cleansing, and terrorism – depends in large part on an assessment of *the opponent's* relationship with its civilian constituents. The greater the civilian support for the opponent in the disputed territory, the greater the threat these civilians pose for the belligerent and, therefore, the greater the benefit a belligerent is likely to obtain from using violence to control or eliminate these individuals.[75] The smaller and more geographically concentrated the opponent's civilian constituency, the more feasible it is for a belligerent to eliminate this constituency entirely, as part of a strategy of cleansing. Finally, governments and rebel groups consider the extent to which the opponent's political institutions constrain decision making, creating incentives for leaders to respond to the demands of their domestic civilian constituents. The greater an opponent's sensitivity to losses among its civilian constituents, the more likely it is that the opponent will respond to violence by making political concessions, thus making a strategy of terrorism more appealing. I now turn to a more detailed discussion of how belligerents calculate the benefits of each of these three strategies of violence: control, cleansing, and terrorism.

Strategies of Control

Limited violence aimed at forcing civilians to cooperate – a strategy of control – is likely to be useful in almost any civil war. Nearly all governments and rebel groups will, at some point, need to elicit information or resources from uncooperative civilians.[76] Although belligerents may establish bases in their home regions, where civilian support is high, fighting a war often requires conducting military operations in regions where civilian loyalties lie with the opponent. In addition, even within the belligerent's home region, support might not be unanimous and civilian cooperation might not be forthcoming.

In his study of civil war violence, Stathis Kalyvas contends that it is not useful to think of civilians as having a particular loyalty to one side or the other in a civil war and that during times of intense conflict, civilians support whichever side is able to provide effective security.[77] Others, however, argue that civilian loyalties may not shift so easily.[78] Jason Lyall, Graeme Blair, and Kosuke Imai, for example, in their study of the conflict in Afghanistan,

---

[75] In her research on violence against civilians in conventional civil wars, Balcells 2011 similarly emphasizes the extent of support for the opponent in disputed territory. She argues that belligerents use indirect violence – bombardment of civilians – against territories under their opponents' control, and are more likely to do so when civilian support for the opponent in these territories is high. In such cases, belligerents see civilians as a threat to their ability to gain control over these territories in the future.

[76] Kalyvas 2006.   [77] Ibid.   [78] Downes 2007; Steele 2011; Lyall, Blair, and Imai 2013.

demonstrate that not only are preexisting loyalties persistent, but that these loyalties shape civilian perceptions of government and insurgent violence.[79] Like these scholars, I argue that civilians do often possess preexisting loyalties, and these loyalties shape belligerent incentives to adopt strategies of control. When popular support for the opponent is low, strategies of low-casualty control are likely to be sufficient to deter collaboration with the opponent; belligerents can identify suspected collaborators and target these individuals for punishment. As long as casualties remain low, domestic or international backlash is likely to remain low; governments and rebel groups can point to a specific transgression on the part of the targeted individual, claiming this as evidence that the individual posed a significant enough threat to warrant arrest, torture, or even death. The low domestic and international costs of a strategy of low-casualty control, combined with its high value in eliciting cooperation from civilians, make it highly likely that belligerents will adopt such a strategy.

High-casualty strategies of control are likely to draw greater domestic and international criticism and, therefore, come with higher domestic and international costs. Thus, governments and rebel groups are only likely to pursue a strategy of high-casualty control when the benefits are significant enough to outweigh the high costs: when popular support for the opponent is high. In such cases, belligerents may increase violence in an attempt to deter civilians from aiding the opponent; rather than detaining or killing individual collaborators, however, belligerents are likely to target larger groups of civilians – perhaps entire families or villages.

Kalyvas argues that violence aimed at controlling civilians is likely to be highest when control over a particular territory is contested.[80] Although periods of high contestation are also likely to be periods of high suspicion regarding civilian loyalties, this is not always the case. In some conflicts, despite high military contestation over a particular territory, a group may be certain that it has strong civilian support, limiting the need to use violence as a means of controlling civilians. In Darfur, for example, territorial contestation was intense in the early years of the conflict, but the rebel groups – which had strong backing from civilians – did not use high levels of violence against civilians. Conversely, even if a group possesses monopoly control over an area, the group may not be assured of civilian loyalties.

Some might argue that at the highest levels of support for the opponent, violence aimed at controlling civilians is unlikely, as belligerents know that controlling these territories is exceedingly difficult and would require violence on an extreme scale.[81] This might help to explain why violence aimed at controlling civilians varies across space within a given conflict; however, this argument is less useful for understanding variation in violence *across* civil wars.

---

[79] Lyall, Blair, and Imai 2013.   [80] Kalyvas 1999; Kalyvas 2006.
[81] Balcells 2010; Balcells 2011.

Once conflicts reach a high enough level of violence to qualify as a civil war, contestation over civilian loyalties is likely to be significant at the national level, meaning that belligerents are unlikely to reach the point at which popular support for the opponent is so high that violence against these supporters becomes futile.

H5: *The greater the civilian support for the opponent within the contested territory, the more likely it is that a belligerent will adopt a strategy of high-casualty control.*

Strategies of Cleansing

Many belligerents might prefer if they could eliminate the opponent's base of civilian support entirely, but engineering the complete removal of a population from disputed territory is beyond the capacity of most belligerents. The physical challenge of carrying out a strategy of cleansing is extraordinary; forcing massive population movements, as part of a strategy of low-casualty cleansing, or exterminating entire communities, as part of a strategy of high-casualty cleansing, demands not only extensive military resources, but also complex logistical coordination. The benefits of a strategy of cleansing, therefore, depend on the extent to which it is feasible to relocate or exterminate the opponent's civilian constituents; this, in turn, depends on the size of the opponent's civilian constituency in the territory under dispute as well as the degree to which the opponent's civilian constituency is geographically concentrated within that territory.[82] Larger, more geographically dispersed groups are more challenging to cleanse; under such circumstances, the benefits of cleansing are minimal.

For governments, whether the territory in dispute is the entire country or a separatist region, the calculation regarding the benefits of cleansing is likely to be the same. If the rebel group draws its civilian support from a small, geographically concentrated group – for example, a concentrated ethnic or religious minority – the government may see eliminating this group as both desirable, to cut the rebel group off from its civilian base, and attainable, because the group aiding the rebels is small enough that killing or forcibly relocating most group members is within the government's means. Furthermore, when the group of civilians supporting the rebellion constitutes only a small percentage of the country's total population, the government may be able to use propaganda to marginalize this small minority, minimizing domestic criticism of government violence.

---

[82] Downes 2007 similarly argues that indiscriminate violence can be an effective counterinsurgency strategy if the population supporting the insurgency is small and if the territory being contested is also small.

For rebel groups, however, the calculation regarding the benefits of cleansing is slightly different. While governments can call on existing bureaucratic structures – using police forces and local government officials in addition to the military – to implement a strategy of cleansing,[83] rebel groups have more limited institutional resources. Thus, even if the government draws support from a geographically concentrated ethnic or religious minority, rebel groups may have difficulty carrying out a strategy of cleansing if the minority group inhabits a region far removed from the rebel group's base of operations.

Separatist rebel groups, however, may see cleansing as both strategically beneficial and logistically feasible. Separatist rebel groups often perceive "outsider" civilians living in the separatist region – civilians from a minority ethnic or religious group – as a threat to the rebel group; apart from their potential disloyalty, the presence of a large population of "outsider" civilians may also call into question the rebel group's claim to the disputed territory. By homogenizing the population within the separatist region, the rebel group may believe that it will be able to make a stronger demand for autonomy, based on claims that the separatist region has an ethnic or religious population that is distinct from the rest of the country. For example, Susan Woodward argues that in Bosnia, leaders were aware that obtaining international recognition for a separatist region would likely require a referendum; ethnic cleansing thus served as a means of both militarily securing territory for the separatist group and ensuring a political majority in favor of autonomy.[84] However, even when cleansing may benefit the rebel group, if the "outsider" civilian population is large or geographically dispersed throughout the separatist region, cleansing may not be militarily feasible.

Most governments and rebel groups that perceive a benefit to cleansing are likely to opt for strategies of low-casualty cleansing, using threats of violence to intimidate civilians into departing "voluntarily" from disputed territory or forcibly evacuating villages without killing their inhabitants. Because strategies of high-casualty cleansing use extreme violence to remove civilians from disputed territory, only those governments and rebel groups who perceive high benefits to violence, as well as low domestic and international costs to violence, will adopt such a strategy.

H6:   *Governments are more likely to adopt strategies of high-casualty cleansing when the rebel group draws support from a small, geographically concentrated civilian constituency.*

H7:   *Rebel groups are more likely to adopt strategies of high-casualty cleansing when they have separatist aims and the government draws support from a small, geographically concentrated civilian constituency within the separatist region.*

---

[83] During the 1994 genocide in Rwanda, for example, local government officials were often instrumental in helping to carry out violence (Straus 2006).

[84] Woodward 1995.

Strategies of Terrorism

While we often think of wars as ending in a victory for one side or the other, in fact, since the end of the Cold War, outright military victories in civil war have been rare.[85] With the large majority of civil wars ending through negotiated settlements rather than military victories, belligerents often aim to elicit the greatest political concessions possible from their opponents. Strategies of terrorism, which involve attacking the opponent's civilian constituents as a means of increasing the costs of the conflict, are one way in which governments and rebel groups may attempt to secure greater concessions. A strategy of terrorism will only work, however, if the opponent is sensitive to losses among its civilian constituents and responds to losses by making concessions. When weighing the benefits of terrorism, therefore, governments and rebel groups make calculations about their opponent's sensitivity to civilian losses; they make such calculations based largely on the nature of their opponent's political institutions. In the section on the domestic costs of violence, I posited that governments and rebel groups whose political institutions encourage leaders to respond to the demands of the domestic public face high domestic costs to using violence against the *opponent's civilian constituents*. For the same reasons, these governments and rebel groups are likely to be sensitive to violence directed at their *own civilian constituents*. As civilian losses rise, these governments and rebel groups are likely to face rising public discontent and pressure to put an end to violence, even if doing so means making political concessions. When facing an opponent whose political institutions encourage responsiveness to the public, therefore, belligerents are likely to perceive the opponent as sensitive to civilian losses and, therefore, as a potential target for terrorism.

For governments, assessing whether a rebel group is likely to be sensitive to violent attacks on its constituency is difficult. Although some rebel groups appear to behave as representative and responsive governing bodies, the political institutions that rebel groups create in the territories under their control are often not fully formed, making it difficult to assess whether these institutions can hold rebel group leaders accountable to their civilian constituencies and, therefore, whether the group will respond to civilian suffering by giving in to government demands. Still, as I argued in the section on the domestic costs of violence, rebel group political institutions vary, with some rebel groups developing complex political institutions that perform a variety of tasks of governance and other rebel groups lacking any political structure. The more developed a rebel group's political institutions, the more likely it is that the government will perceive the rebel group as responsive to the demands of its civilian constituents and the more likely it is that the government will view a strategy of terrorism as potentially valuable.

---

[85] DeRouen and Sobek 2004; Toft 2009.

Rebel groups also evaluate their opponent's sensitivity to civilian losses, making use of available information about government political institutions.[86] Because political institutions and norms in democratic countries create incentives for leaders to be responsive to the domestic public, rebel groups are likely to perceive democratic governments as vulnerable to domestic public pressure. Rebel groups facing democratic governments seek to exploit this vulnerability in their opponents by using violence deliberately in an attempt to manipulate public opinion.[87] Generating enough public pressure to force government concessions is challenging, but the broader institutional setting within democratic countries – in particular, the tendency for democratic countries to protect the freedom of the press – makes it easier for rebel groups to capture public attention.[88] Because democratic governments have greater difficulty controlling the dissemination of information, it is more likely that details on terrorist attacks will be available to the domestic public, increasing the potential for such attacks to generate public demands for government concessions.

Rebel groups are likely to perceive autocratic governments as less susceptible to domestic public pressure. As discussed in the section on the domestic costs of violence, in comparison to democratic governments, autocratic governments have fewer institutional incentives to respond to the demands of the domestic public. Efforts to use terrorist attacks as a means of mobilizing public pressure on the government to make concessions are unlikely to be effective against an autocratic opponent. Thus, the more democratic the government opponent, the more likely it is that the rebel group will adopt terrorist tactics. Rebel groups use terrorist tactics as a means of increasing the costs of the conflict, with the hope that this will increase domestic pressure on the government to resolve the conflict, forcing the government to make concessions that it previously was unwilling to make.

Some might challenge the argument that the public in a democracy is likely to respond to terrorist attacks by pressuring the government to make concessions, and instead claim that the public is just as likely to respond to terrorist attacks by rallying in support of the government. Studies of the rally 'round the flag effect, however, show that although an initial surge in public support for the government may follow dramatic events that occur during a war, this rally effect is likely to decline as the costs of a conflict mount.[89] Once the public gains access to negative information – for example, about casualties incurred during a terrorist attack – it is difficult for a democratic government to counteract this information, thus making an increase in opposition to government policies more likely.[90] As studies of terrorism in Israel have argued, although public support for parties or candidates advocating hardline policies may increase in the short term, terrorist violence may encourage the public to support more

---

[86] Stanton 2013.   [87] Merom 2003.   [88] Li 2005.
[89] Mueller 1973; Gartner and Segura 1998; Mueller 2005.   [90] Merom 2003.

moderate, conciliatory policies over the long term.[91] Rebel groups are aware of the risk of backlash associated with a strategy of terrorism, but choose this strategy both because their time horizons are long – they are willing to wait for public pressure on the government to build over time – and because other available alternatives for coercing the government are limited.

H8: *Governments and rebel groups are more likely to adopt strategies of terrorism when fighting against opponents whose political institutions encourage accountability to civilian constituents.*

Although all belligerents have incentives to use terrorist attacks when fighting against opponents with political institutions that encourage responsiveness to civilian constituents, the form that terrorism takes will vary depending on how the belligerent weighs the domestic costs of violence. Governments and rebel groups that seek to maintain broad civilian constituencies – governments and rebel groups with inclusive political systems – cannot afford to use violence in ways that might lead to popular backlash. These governments and rebel groups use terrorism selectively, seeking to pressure the opponent by imposing high civilian costs, but not necessarily high civilian casualties – for example, by attacking infrastructure targets or destroying evacuated homes – in the hopes that avoiding civilian casualties will minimize backlash. Governments and rebel groups with narrower constituencies have greater flexibility in their use of violence; these governments and rebel groups are more likely to attack high-casualty targets.

H9: *Among governments and rebel groups using terrorism, governments and rebel groups with exclusionary political systems are more likely than governments and rebel groups with inclusive political systems to adopt high-casualty strategies of terrorism.*

Table 1.1 summarizes these hypotheses on government and rebel group strategies of restraint, control, cleansing, and terrorism.

ALTERNATIVE EXPLANATIONS FOR VIOLENCE AND RESTRAINT

Three broad strands of argument dominate the literature on civilian targeting, emphasizing (1) the organizational structure of armed groups, (2) the military context, and (3) the influence of international factors. These arguments fall short, however, in that they emphasize particular costs or particular benefits to the use of violence against civilians. In contrast, the argument of this book addresses a wider range of costs and benefits within a single theoretical framework, in an effort to explain how governments and

[91] Berrebi and Klor 2006; Berrebi and Klor 2008.

TABLE 1.1 *Summary of Hypotheses*

Strategy	Hypotheses
Restraint	H1: political institutions encourage leader responsiveness to public demands → government and rebel group restraint H2: inclusive political system → government and rebel group restraint H3: government need for domestic and international support (unstable regime) → government restraint H4: rebel group need for international support (autocratic opponent) → rebel group restraint
High-Casualty Control	H5: high civilian support for the opponent in contested territory → government and rebel group high-casualty control
High-Casualty Cleansing	H6: rebel group constituency is small and concentrated → government high-casualty cleansing H7: government constituency in separatist region is small and concentrated → rebel group high-casualty cleansing
Terrorism and High-Casualty Terrorism	H8: opponent's political institutions encourage accountability to constituents → government and rebel group terrorism H9: exclusionary political system → government and rebel group high-casualty terrorism

rebel groups weigh these different incentives in making decisions about whether and how to target civilians.

Organizational Structure

The first strand of argument focuses on the organizational structure of armed groups as a key determinant of behavior. Some scholars within this strand of argument see restraint as the preferred strategy of belligerents; to succeed in civil war, belligerents need civilian support and, therefore, have incentives to treat civilians well. When violence does occur, it often takes place in the context of looting and is the work of individual soldiers, rather than a deliberate strategy on the part of the group. According to this view, restraint is most likely when groups have the organizational capacity to control soldiers' use of violence.[92] Jeremy Weinstein offers an explanation for why some rebel groups

---

[92] Weinstein 2005; Humphreys and Weinstein 2006; Weinstein 2007. See also Azam 2002; Azam 2006.

lack the capacity to control their members, positing that rebel groups who have access to external funding – obtained from a foreign government or through the trafficking of natural resources – are dominated by recruits interested primarily in short-term rewards, creating organizational structures plagued with discipline problems that lead to abuses of civilians.[93] Rebel groups without access to external funding, in contrast, attract recruits with the promise of long-term political gains and support their operations by developing strong ties with local communities. Because these groups depend heavily on civilians for support, they face particularly high domestic costs to violence, creating incentives for restraint. And comprised of members highly committed to the cause, these groups are better able to enforce discipline within their organizations, leading to lower levels of violence against civilians.

Although it is certainly true that some portion of the violence against civilians that takes place during civil war is individually motivated, these arguments about organizational control fail to acknowledge that governments and rebel groups may perceive benefits to the use of violence against civilians. Governments and rebel groups often incorporate civilian targeting into their strategies for waging war, using attacks on civilians as a means of undermining their opponent's base of support or increasing the costs of the conflict for the opponent; in these cases, effective discipline and control are likely to lead to increased, rather than decreased, violence against civilians.[94] In addition, while these arguments acknowledge that groups may face different domestic costs to the use of violence, these arguments do not consider the international costs of violence.

More recent work on the organizational dynamics of armed groups acknowledges that violence against civilians is often strategically motivated, but emphasizes that nonstrategically motivated violence, or opportunistic violence, is also common in civil war and can plague even those armed groups that seek to restrain violence.[95] These approaches are best conceived as arguments that can coexist with the strategic arguments advanced in this book, rather than as alternatives. Amelia Hoover Green, for example, contends that in order for armed groups to control the use of violence, leaders must use discipline to reward desired behavior and punish transgressions, as well as implement political education to align the preferences of armed group members with those of the group leadership.[96] Similarly, Devorah Manekin finds that limiting opportunistic violence requires a strong military hierarchy and an effective command structure, able to enforce discipline, while Elisabeth Wood makes

---

[93] Weinstein 2005; Weinstein 2007. See also Hovil and Werker 2005; Salehyan, Siroky, and Wood 2014. Hovil and Werker point to another mechanism through which external financing may increase incentives for violence, arguing that rebel groups may attack civilians to convince an external sponsor that they are active.

[94] For a discussion of this point, see Wood 2009.

[95] Wood 2006; Wood 2009; Hoover Green 2011; Manekin 2013.   [96] Hoover Green 2011.

similar arguments regarding the organizational structures that help groups to prevent their members from perpetrating sexual violence in war.[97]

Also within this organizational strand of argument, Dara Cohen argues that much of the sexual violence occurring during civil war is driven not by a lack of organizational control, leading to opportunistic violence, but by other organizational imperatives – in particular, the need for armed groups to build group cohesion.[98] She argues that armed groups lacking social cohesion, such as governments or rebel groups that rely on forced conscription or abduction to fill their ranks, may use group-perpetrated sexual violence as a means of strengthening group bonds. Again, such organizational motivations for violence might be present alongside strategic motivations for violence against civilians.

Military Context

The second strand of argument focuses on the way in which the military context affects belligerent behavior. Two of the most common arguments regarding the military context view civilian targeting as a strategy belligerents adopt when they have few other options for confronting their opponent militarily. In his analysis of civilian targeting in interstate war, Alexander Downes argues that it is only when conflicts become too costly to bear that governments are willing to carry out large-scale attacks on an opponent's civilian constituency.[99] While governments often refrain from targeting civilians at the outset of a war, when conflicts develop into wars of attrition, governments become desperate to reduce costs to their own troops and society and use attacks on the opponent's civilian population as a substitute for fighting costly military engagements.[100] It is possible that a similar logic drives civilian targeting in civil wars, with governments and rebel groups attacking civilians out of desperation to minimize their own losses. In an interstate war, however, targeting the opponent's civilian constituents involves attacking *foreign* civilians, whereas in a civil war, targeting the opponent's civilian constituents involves attacking *citizens of one's own country*. A government facing a domestic rebellion may be able to limit its military losses by attacking the rebel group's civilian base of support instead of engaging the rebel group militarily, but in doing so, the government would still be incurring costs in the form of damage to its own citizens, infrastructure, and territory as well as potential domestic backlash. Thus, the domestic costs of civilian targeting may be higher in civil wars than in interstate wars.

A second military context argument makes a similar claim, arguing that belligerents target civilians when they have few other available military options. Rather than emphasizing the costs of the conflict, however, this argument posits

---

[97] Wood 2006; Wood 2009; Manekin 2013.   [98] Cohen 2013.
[99] Downes 2006; Downes 2008.   [100] Downes 2006; Downes 2008.

that the relative strength of the belligerents drives strategy. A government or rebel group that is weak in comparison to its opponent or that has suffered significant military losses may use attacks on the opponent's constituents as a substitute for fighting direct military engagements.[101] Strong belligerents are likely to refrain from attacks on civilians; such groups are able to confront their opponents militarily and do not need to use extreme tactics to attain victory. Others have suggested an alternate mechanism, positing that weak rebel groups and rebel groups depleted by military losses have difficulty eliciting voluntary civilian cooperation and thus have incentives to obtain resources through looting or coercion, leading to increased violence against civilians.[102]

A third military context argument argues that violence against civilians is linked to contestation over territory. Stathis Kalyvas posits that when contestation over territory is high, governments and rebel groups have incentives to use selective violence against individuals suspected of aiding the opponent as a means of coercing civilian cooperation and thereby extending control over territory.[103] When territorial control is complete, belligerents do not need to use violence to elicit cooperation; the pervasive presence of the armed group and its threat of violence is enough to prompt "voluntary" collaboration. In areas of partial control, however, some individuals may choose to provide information to the opponent, increasing belligerent incentives to use violence as a means of deterring collaboration with the enemy. In addition, the availability of information about suspected collaborators makes it possible to identify and target these individuals. Thus, as contestation increases – when one side's monopoly control over territory is challenged – violence against civilians may escalate as governments and rebel groups attempt to convince civilians that aiding the other side will be costly.[104] As a belligerent's control over territory declines, the belligerent's access to reliable sources of information also declines, making it more difficult to identify suspected enemy collaborators and, thus, increasing the likelihood that the belligerent will use indiscriminate violence rather than selective violence.

Scholars have pointed to at least two other aspects of the military context that may influence behavior: guerrilla warfare and the number of warring factions. Arguments about guerrilla warfare hypothesize that because rebel groups using guerrilla warfare rely heavily on civilians for support, governments have stronger incentives to attack civilians in conflicts involving guerrilla warfare than in conflicts involving conventional warfare.[105] As Laia Balcells has shown, however, even in conventional civil wars, belligerents may have incentives to target civilians. When prewar political mobilization is high, civilians often develop strong ties to one side or the other; when civilians loyal to the

---

[101] Valentino, Huth, and Balch-Lindsay 2004; Hultman 2007. See also research on terrorism, such as Crenshaw 1981; Pape 2003.
[102] Wood 2010; Wood, Kathman, and Gent 2012; Wood 2014a; Wood 2014b.
[103] Kalyvas 2006.   [104] Kalyvas 1999.   [105] Valentino, Huth, and Balch-Lindsay 2004.

opponent are present behind the frontlines, belligerents may seek to eliminate this civilian threat.[106]

Within the literature on terrorism, some have argued that the number of insurgent factions influences patterns of violence. According to this view, groups use terrorist violence as a means of outbidding rival factions for support from civilian constituencies, meaning that conflicts involving multiple rebel groups are associated with a greater likelihood of rebel group terrorism.[107] It is also possible that the presence of multiple rebel groups affects government incentives for violence, increasing the strain on the government's military resources and, thus, increasing the likelihood that the government will target civilians as a substitute for fighting costly military engagements.

All of these arguments regarding the military context rightly point out that belligerent incentives for violence vary across cases of civil war. And it is reasonable to argue that characteristics of the military context influence incentives for violence. Yet the military context is only one set of factors that belligerents weigh in assessing the value of violence against civilians. The strategic context is also defined by the opponent's relationship to its civilian constituents – the strength of the opponent's civilian support and its sensitivity to civilian losses. A more complete analysis of violence against civilians requires an understanding of how belligerents weigh these incentives for violence against the potential domestic and international costs of violence.

International Factors

A final set of alternative arguments looks at the influence of international factors on belligerent behavior. Although these arguments acknowledge that violence against civilians may be costly internationally, many of these arguments miscalculate how governments and rebel groups respond to the international costs of violence. Some international legal scholars, for example, argue that by ratifying an international agreement, a government signals that the agreement is in its interest; for this reason, governments generally comply with the agreements they ratify.[108] Scholars focusing on international human rights law have challenged this view, however, demonstrating that governments do not always intend to comply with the human rights treaties they ratify – for example, some governments may view ratification as a means of distracting attention from their poor human rights record. Thus, treaty ratification does not necessarily predict compliance.[109] Even if a government believes compliance with international humanitarian law is in its interest at the time of ratification, however, interests may change, particularly when a government is faced with a

---

[106] Balcells 2010; Balcells 2011.   [107] Bloom 2005; Kydd and Walter 2006; Chenoweth 2010.
[108] See, for example, Chayes and Chayes 1993.
[109] Hathaway 2002; Neumayer 2005; Hafner-Burton and Tsutsui 2007; Hafner-Burton, Tsutsui, and Meyer 2008; Vreeland 2008.

challenge to its domestic authority. Incentives to target civilians are strong during civil war and, for some governments, may outweigh the international costs associated with violating an international agreement.

Other scholars have argued that in interstate wars, reciprocity can motivate compliance with international humanitarian law: governments may be more likely to abide by their international legal commitments when they believe that their opponent will do so as well.[110] As James Morrow points out, however, although reciprocity may motivate belligerents to abide by some types of international humanitarian legal commitments, such as commitments requiring respect for prisoners of war, reciprocity may be weaker with regard to violence against civilians because even if the other side retaliates by attacking civilians, soldiers are not directly harmed.[111] In addition, in civil wars, governments might not trust their rebel opponents to abide by international law, particularly since rebel groups cannot commit themselves formally by ratifying international agreements.

Another argument, also emphasizing international factors, posits that economic and political interdependence can encourage government restraint. In a country whose economy is heavily reliant on international trade, for example, the government may be concerned that civilian targeting will offend key trading partners, while a government that participates extensively in international organizations may face pressure to maintain a favorable reputation.[112] This strand of argument is right to claim that some governments are more sensitive than others to the international consequences of their actions. Economically and politically interdependent states, however, are not the states most likely to weigh heavily the international costs of their behavior during civil war; most states, even highly interdependent states, can withstand the loss of trade or decline in reputation that might result from abusing civilians during civil war. Instead, it is the states that need domestic and international support to secure their domestic rule that are most sensitive to the international consequences of their actions.

Similarly, some claim that rebel groups receiving backing from democracies are less likely to target civilians, as democracies are likely to withhold aid from abusive groups and to pressure groups they support to comply with international human rights standards.[113] It is true that rebel groups seeking support from Western international constituencies face higher international costs to violence. However, a rebel group's need for support from Western constituencies depends on the domestic context – in particular, on the rebel group's ability to generate domestic pressure on the government to negotiate. Rebel groups unable to generate domestic pressure on the government need diplomatic backing from international actors as a means of mobilizing additional

[110] Morrow and Jo 2006; Morrow 2007; Morrow 2014.   [111] Morrow 2014.
[112] Harff 2003.   [113] Salehyan, Siroky, and Wood 2014.

pressure on the government. These rebel groups exercise restraint *in the hope* of winning international support, but are not always successful, meaning that rebel group restraint is not necessarily correlated with backing from Western or democratic governments or intergovernmental organizations.

CONCLUSION

In this chapter, I have argued that much of the violence that governments and rebel groups direct against civilians during civil war is strategic. Governments and rebel groups use violence against civilians in an attempt to control civilians or territory, to cleanse territories with heterogeneous populations, or as a form of terrorism, to force the opponent into making concessions. Exercising restraint with respect to civilian populations is also often a strategic decision, taken in an effort to obtain advantages in the conflict. Which of these strategies of violence a government or rebel group chooses to adopt with respect to civilian populations depends on how the government or rebel group weighs the costs and benefits of violence and, in particular, on how they expect domestic and international constituencies to respond to violence. Governments and rebel groups weigh the costs of violence based on an assessment of *their own relationship* with domestic and international constituencies, while governments and rebel groups weigh the benefits of violence based on an assessment of *their opponent's relationship* with its constituents. To assess these hypotheses, I constructed an original data set on government and rebel group violence against civilians, which I describe in detail in Chapter 2. This new data set, which includes all civil wars from 1989 to 2010, measures not only the level of government and rebel group violence against civilians, but also the many forms that abuse of civilians may take.

2

A New Data Set on Violence against Civilians
in Civil War

This chapter presents an original data set on government and rebel group violence against civilians. The data set, which includes all civil wars from 1989 to 2010, measures a number of different forms of government and rebel group violence against civilians, all of which are violations of international humanitarian law as codified in major international legal treaties. To date, no existing work has collected cross-conflict data on *forms* of government and rebel group violence against civilians or on types of international humanitarian law violation during civil war.[1] Although several scholars studying wartime violence against civilians have identified cases of civilian targeting across conflicts, these scholars use measures of the number of civilians killed – either the number of civilians killed during military combat with the opponent or the number of civilians killed in one-sided violence, when no military engagement with the opponent was ongoing.[2] Obtaining reliable data on civilian deaths that occur in the context of civil war, however, is difficult; the quality and depth of reporting may vary widely across countries and across time, raising questions about the feasibility of using count data as a basis for cross-country comparison.[3] In addition, count data do not provide information on the context within which civilians were killed or what forms of violence governments and rebel groups used in attacking civilians.

After describing the universe of cases, I discuss how the data set measures the strategies of government and rebel group violence outlined in Chapter 1 – control, cleansing, and terrorism – as well as government and rebel group

---

[1] For data on government violations of international humanitarian law during interstate war, see Morrow and Jo 2006; Morrow 2014.

[2] Valentino, Huth, and Balch-Lindsay 2004; Eck and Hultman 2007; Hultman 2007; Weinstein 2007; Hultman 2012.

[3] Kalyvas 2006.

restraint. An overview of the data shows that governments and rebel groups vary widely in the forms of violence used against civilians during civil war. In additon, more than 40 percent of governments and rebel groups do not target civilians and exercise restraint in their fighting.

A NEW DATA SET ON FORMS OF GOVERNMENT AND REBEL GROUP VIOLENCE AGAINST CIVILIANS

To analyze patterns of civil war violence, I created an original data set, measuring different *forms* of government and rebel group violence against civilians in all civil wars from 1989 to 2010. The cases are drawn from the Uppsala Conflict Data Program (UCDP)/Peace Research Institute, Oslo (PRIO) Armed Conflict Dataset, which defines internal armed conflict as "a contested incompatibility that concerns government or territory or both where the use of armed force between two parties results in at least 25 battle-related deaths" and "occurs between the government of a state and internal opposition groups."[4] Following standard definitions of civil war, I focus on conflicts with at least 1,000 battle-related deaths.[5]

I limit my universe of cases to post–Cold War civil wars – civil wars that either began or were ongoing after 1989. Multiple, detailed sources of information are available for post–Cold War conflicts, reducing the likelihood of biased coding. Theoretically, it makes sense to focus on this time period, as the strategic context confronting belligerents changed dramatically at the end of the Cold War when groups could no longer rely on ideology to attract superpower backing.[6]

In cases where a government is fighting multiple rebel groups simultaneously, I consider each conflict to be a separate civil war, as long as each rebel group maintained separate leadership; in some cases, the same government behaves differently toward different insurgent groups. In total, the data set includes 115 cases of civil war (115 conflict dyads); Table 2.3 at the end of the chapter lists the cases.[7]

Issues in Measuring Civilian Targeting

All of the forms of violence against civilians included in this data set are prohibited under international humanitarian law.[8] Three international treaties form the core of international humanitarian law as it applies to civil wars: the

---

[4] Gleditsch et al. 2002, 618–619.   [5] Fearon and Laitin 2003; Doyle and Sambanis 2006.

[6] For a broader discussion of how the end of the Cold War impacted civil wars, see Kalyvas and Balcells 2010.

[7] In Somalia, after the overthrow of Siad Barre in 1991, the central government collapsed, leaving multiple rebel groups fighting for control; I do not record government behavior for this case.

[8] On the development of the distinction between combatants and noncombatants, see Best 1994. See also Robertson 1999 on the history of international humanitarian law.

1949 Geneva Convention Relative to the Protection of Civilian Persons in Time of War; the 1977 Protocol Additional to the Geneva Conventions of 12 August 1949, and Relating to the Protection of Victims of Non-International Armed Conflicts (Protocol II); and the Rome Statute of the International Criminal Court.[9] The basic protections outlined in these three treaties are also considered customary international law,[10] defined by the Statute of the International Court of Justice as rules that have become "a general practice accepted as law."[11] As such, all actors engaged in conflict – governments and rebel groups – are obligated to abide by these rules, regardless of whether they have ratified the relevant treaties. This body of international humanitarian law explicitly prohibits a wide range of violence against civilians, including murder, rape, torture, mutilation, and abduction, as well as indiscriminate bombing of civilian areas, forced relocation of civilian populations, and the use of civilians as hostages or human shields.

In measuring violence against civilians, I focus on violence that is intentional, in which sources indicate that government or rebel group attacks on civilian populations or civilian targets were deliberate. I do not include incidents of collateral damage, in which civilians are harmed or civilian targets are destroyed during a military engagement with the opponent. To do so would require making judgments about the necessity and proportionality of a military action, as well as whether the actor responsible made adequate attempts to avoid civilian casualties.[12] I am interested in capturing patterns of behavior – forms of violence that are repeated throughout the conflict. Parties to a conflict, and even international lawyers, often disagree about the extent to which a particular action violates international humanitarian law.[13] Focusing on patterns of conduct limits the need to make judgments about the legality of particular incidents of violence, and reduces the likelihood of attributing individual criminal acts to the armed group as a whole.

To minimize problems of measurement, I use multiple sources in my coding. Since the late 1970s the U.S. Department of State has published annual *Country Reports on Human Rights Practices* for each country in the world, providing

---

[9] See Geneva Convention Relative to the Protection of Civilian Persons in Time of War, 75 UNTS 287, Entered Into Force 21 October 1950; Protocol Additional to the Geneva Conventions of 12 August 1949, and Relating to the Protection of Victims of Non-International Armed Conflicts (Protocol II), 1125 UNTS 609, Entered Into Force 7 December 1978; Rome Statute of the International Criminal Court, 2187 UNTS 90, Entered Into Force 1 July 2002.

[10] Henckaerts and Doswald-Beck 2005.

[11] Statute of the International Court of Justice, Article 38(1)(b), 26 June 1945.

[12] Under customary international law, military attacks should be proportional "in relation to the concrete and direct military advantage anticipated" (Henckaerts and Doswald-Beck 2005, 25).

[13] A number of scholars have made attempts to measure compliance with specific obligations under international law, including Simmons 2000; Hathaway 2002; Hafner-Burton 2005; Neumayer 2005; Morrow and Jo 2006; Valentino, Huth, and Croco 2006; Hafner-Burton and Tsutsui 2007; Morrow 2014.

detailed information on each country's respect for "internationally recognized individual, civil, political and worker rights, as set forth in the Universal Declaration of Human Rights,"[14] including a section discussing violations of international humanitarian law. To supplement the U.S. State Department *Country Reports on Human Rights Practices*, for each conflict, I consulted all of the relevant annual reports and in-depth reports published by Amnesty International, Human Rights Watch, International Crisis Group, and the United Nations, as well as secondary historical sources and newspaper reports. Although these sources provide extensive information on civil war violence, the level of detail available varies from year to year, raising concerns about the accuracy of annual data on violence against civilians. For this reason, I measure violence and restraint for each conflict as a whole, prioritizing the reliability of the data over obtaining finer-grained annual measures. Although doing so precludes quantitative analysis of variation over time in government and rebel group violence, I look at variation over time in the case study chapters.

Comparisons to Existing Data on Civilian Targeting

Existing work on wartime violence against civilians has used measures of the number of civilians killed to identify cases of civilian targeting.[15] Benjamin Valentino, Paul Huth, and Dylan Balch-Lindsay, for example, use a threshold level of violence – 50,000 intentional civilian deaths over a period of five years or less – to identify cases of government mass killing during interstate and civil wars from 1945 to 2000; while Kristine Eck and Lisa Hultman's data on one-sided violence counts the number of civilians killed in incidents involving "the intentional and direct use of violence" by governments and rebel groups in conflicts from 1989 to 2011.[16] Like the data introduced in this book, these two data sources examine intentional violence against civilians, excluding accidental violence or collateral damage. Valentino et al., however, restrict their analysis to the far end of the spectrum of government violence, excluding cases in which governments targeted civilians intentionally, but did not inflict sufficiently high casualties to qualify as having engaged in "mass killing." Eck and Hultman examine a wider range of violence, including government and rebel group violence against civilians that exceeds 25 civilian deaths per year. Still, their data set excludes violence that leads to significant destruction of civilian targets, but does not kill large numbers of civilians – for example, scorched earth campaigns, which destroy civilian homes and crops, but do not always

---

[14] U.S. Department of State, 2006 Country Reports on Human Rights Practices, "Overview and Acknowledgements." Available online at www.state.gov.
[15] Valentino, Huth, and Balch-Lindsay 2004; Eck and Hultman 2007; Hultman 2007; Weinstein 2007; Wood 2010; Hultman 2012; Wood, Kathman, and Gent 2012; Salehyan, Siroky, and Wood 2014; Wood 2014a; Wood 2014b.
[16] Eck and Hultman 2007, 235.

lead immediately to civilian deaths. In addition, the Eck and Hultman data set uses count data on the number of civilians killed by each actor during incidents of one-sided violence. While count data offer the advantage of permitting an assessment of the scale of violence, even the most carefully collected data on civilian deaths may be problematic. Civilian deaths are often not well documented and the availability of information may vary significantly across countries and across time, making it difficult to rely on count data as a basis for cross-country comparison.[17]

The data set in this book thus differs in several key ways from existing data on wartime violence against civilians. First, it addresses concerns regarding the reliability of count data by focusing on *forms* of violence, such as massacres, the burning of civilian homes or crops, and the bombing of civilian targets. For most civil wars, sources report on general patterns of violence, even if they do not provide estimates of the numbers of civilians killed. For this reason, the data set presented in this book is less likely to overlook incidents in which civilian casualties were poorly documented. In addition, the data set presented here includes a wider range of cases of violence against civilians, including forms of violence such as scorched earth campaigns or small-scale bombings that intend to cause significant harm to civilians through the destruction of civilian targets, but do not always lead to immediate civilian deaths. Finally, the data set presented in this book focuses on the most severe forms of violence against civilians – high-casualty civilian targeting, in which belligerents collectively target groups of civilians rather than singling out particular individuals for attack. Although belligerents frequently target individual civilians during civil war – using torture, rape, and targeted killing – these forms of violence are present in nearly all civil wars. More than 95 percent of the governments and rebel groups fighting in civil wars from 1989 to 2010 killed individual civilians suspected of aiding the opponent – what is often referred to as selective violence. In some cases, the targeting of individual civilians takes place on a large scale and thus, ought to be considered a form of high-casualty civilian targeting. In nearly all of these cases, however, the belligerent also used other forms of high-casualty violence against civilians.

Measuring Restraint

Strategies of restraint are characterized by deliberate efforts to avoid attacking civilian populations, civilian residential areas, and civilian infrastructure such as schools and hospitals. It is important to note that the concept of restraint used in this book does not indicate a complete absence of violence against civilians; rather, it represents an absence of the most severe forms of violence against civilians. Governments or rebel groups exercising restraint may engage

[17] Kalyvas 2006.

in limited, small-scale violence against civilians, such as the targeted killing of individuals suspected of aiding the opponent, but governments and rebel groups exercising restraint do not commit large-scale abuses against civilians, such as massacres or the burning of villages. While violence is restrained with respect to civilian targets, violence is not necessarily restrained with respect to military targets.

I create dichotomous variables for *Government Restraint* and *Rebel Group Restraint*, measuring whether each government and each rebel group refrained from the most severe forms of civilian abuse. A government or rebel group is coded as having exercised restraint if it did *not* use any of the following four forms of violence against civilians: massacres; scorched earth campaigns; forced expulsion of a particular ethnic or religious group from territory; or deliberate bombing and shelling of populated civilian targets. Massacres are defined as the deliberate killing of a group of five or more civilians at close range in a single incident.[18] Civilians killed by bombs or killed in the crossfire during a battle are not included. Only those groups that were responsible for more than five massacres during the course of the conflict are coded as having used this form of violence.[19] Scorched earth strategies involve the intentional burning or destruction of villages and/or agricultural land, while forced expulsion is the forced, permanent removal of a particular civilian population from a particular region.[20] Coding the deliberate bombing and shelling of civilian areas is slightly more complicated, as governments and rebel groups often claim that aerial bombardment or artillery shelling is aimed at military targets, only mistakenly hitting nearby civilian targets. For this reason, I only include sustained bombing or shelling that was reported to be intentionally directed at populated civilian targets such as residential areas of towns or cities. For rebel groups, this includes the use of small-scale bombs to attack populated civilian targets such as buses, restaurants, or public markets, but does not include the use of small-scale bombs only to attack infrastructure

---

[18] International legal sources do not specify the number of deaths required for an incident to be considered a massacre or collective punishment. For measurement purposes, however, it was necessary to establish a threshold number of deaths for identifying a massacre.

[19] It is possible that in longer conflicts, governments and rebel groups are more likely to reach this five-massacre threshold. The measure of government massacres is positively correlated with conflict duration, but the coefficient is substantively small (0.2087; p=0.0353), while the measure of rebel group massacres is not significantly correlated with conflict duration (0.0178, p=0.8585). Controlling for conflict duration does not alter the findings for the main variables of interest. These analyses (shown in the online Appendix), however, do indicate that governments and rebel groups are less likely to exercise restraint in conflicts of longer duration.

[20] Forced expulsion is distinct from other forms of forced displacement. Governments, for example, often forcibly relocate civilians into government-protected villages during counterinsurgency operations. This form of displacement is intended to be temporary, distinguishing it from the permanent displacement intended with forced expulsion.

targets such as power lines or oil pipelines. These four forms of violence – massacres, scorched earth tactics, forced expulsion, and the deliberate bombing and shelling of civilian targets – are common during civil war; still, 49 percent of governments and 41.8 percent of rebel groups refrained from *all four* of these forms of violence against civilians, exercising restraint in their fighting.

In confronting Maoist insurgents, the government of Nepal, for example, used mass arrest and interrogation to undermine popular support for the rebellion, but did not engage in more severe forms of violence against civilians. Similar cases of government restraint include the British government in its fight against the rebellion in Northern Ireland, the Algerian government in its counterinsurgency operations against the Islamic Salvation Army (AIS) and later the Armed Islamic Group (GIA), and the Philippine government in its confrontations with the Moro National Liberation Front (MNLF) and the Moro Islamic Liberation Front (MILF). Cases of rebel group restraint include the National United Front for an Independent, Neutral, Peaceful, and Cooperative Cambodia (Front Uni National pour un Cambodge Indépendent, Neutre, Pacifique, Et Coopératif, FUNCINPEC) and the Khmer People's National Liberation Front (KPNLF) in their efforts to overthrow the Vietnamese-backed Cambodian government, the Free Aceh Movement (Gerakan Aceh Merdeka, GAM) and the Revolutionary Front for an Independent East Timor (Frente Revolucionária do Timor Leste Independente, Fretilin) during their struggles against the Indonesian government to gain independence for Aceh and East Timor, and both separatist and revolutionary insurgent groups fighting against Mengistu Haile Mariam's regime in Ethiopia.

The dichotomous measures of *Government Restraint* and *Rebel Group Restraint* have the advantage of clearly delineating between belligerents that refrain from *all* of the most severe forms of violence against civilians and belligerents that abuse civilians. Among belligerents that abuse civilians, however, some are responsible for more extreme violence than others. To capture this variation, I create an alternate measure of restraint, which distinguishes between levels of government and rebel group violence against civilians. For this measure, the highest category of restraint is the same as in the dichotomous measure – indicating a government or rebel group that did *not* use any of the following four forms of violence against civilians: massacres; scorched earth campaigns; forced expulsion of a particular ethnic or religious group from territory; or deliberate bombing and shelling of populated civilian targets. At the other end of the spectrum, the category of highest violence includes governments or rebel groups that used either of the highest casualty forms of violence against civilians: massacres or indiscriminate bombing or shelling of populated civilian targets. The intermediate category captures governments and rebel groups that used lower-casualty forms of violence against civilians – scorched earth campaigns, bombing of economic or infrastructure targets, or forced expulsion of civilians from territory – but did not use either of the highest casualty forms of violence (massacres or bombing of populated civilian targets). For example, in its fight against the Kurdistan Workers' Party (Partiya Karkerên Kurdistanê, PKK), the Turkish government carried out a scorched earth campaign – burning and destroying thousands of Kurdish villages – but it did so without inflicting high civilian casualties. Using the dichotomous measure of restraint, the Turkish government is coded as not having exercised restraint; however, using the categorical measure of restraint, the Turkish government falls into the intermediate category – as a government that used scorched earth strategies, but did not use higher-casualty forms of violence.

To simplify the presentation of the statistical findings, in Chapter 3, I discuss only the results of the analyses using the dichotomous measures of *Government Restraint* and *Rebel Group Restraint*. The results for all of the main variables of interest remain consistent, however, when using the alternate, categorical measures of government and rebel group restraint. This consistency – while reassuring – is not particularly surprising, as the dichotomous measures should present more difficult tests for the hypotheses on government and rebel group restraint. In the dichotomous measures, cases such as Turkey – in which the government or the rebel group exercised partial, but not full, restraint – are coded as cases of nonrestraint. Thus, if the statistical tests find support for the hypotheses using this narrower definition of government and rebel group restraint, this should be interpreted as particularly persuasive evidence in support of the arguments advanced in this book.

A final challenge to measuring restraint is variation in the availability of information across cases. I address this issue in two ways. First, I examine the relationship between restraint and freedom of the press.[21] If information on civilian targeting is more limited in countries with greater restrictions on press freedom – most commonly, autocratic countries – then civil wars in these countries might appear to involve less violence than they actually do. Press freedom is not correlated strongly with either *Government Restraint* or *Rebel Group Restraint*, indicating that the measure of restraint is not simply capturing a lack of information on violence.[22] Second, I do not code *Government Restraint* and *Rebel Group Restraint* for 12 cases in which information on the conduct of fighting is extremely limited, or in which differentiating between the behavior of various warring parties is difficult; these cases do not enter into the data analysis.[23] If I were to keep these cases in the data set, they might skew the results; the lack of information would make it appear as if there were no civilian targeting to report.

[21] Data on press freedom are from Freedom House, available at www.freedomhouse.org.

[22] The correlation between press freedom and *Rebel Group Restraint* is negative, but the coefficient is substantively small (-0.2695, $p=0.0059$). Press freedom is not significantly correlated with *Government Restraint* (0.0936, $p=0.3494$).

[23] See Table 2.3 at the end of this chapter.

Measuring Control

Because the hypotheses examine the conditions under which governments or rebel groups are likely to use different forms of high-casualty violence, the data set focuses on measuring high-casualty forms of control, cleansing, and terrorism. Strategies of control use violence as a means of coercing civilian cooperation and deterring civilians from providing aid to the opponent. Achieving this deterrent effect requires a close association between collaboration and the violence intended to punish this collaboration.[24] Low-casualty forms of control are highly discriminate, involving the identification of specific individuals believed to be providing assistance to the opponent; these individuals are then detained, tortured, or killed. Rather than targeting only the individual collaborating with the opponent, high-casualty forms of control target other individuals associated with the collaborator, such as the collaborator's family members, neighbors, or fellow villagers. Although high-casualty forms of control are more expansive in their use of violence, they still require some level of discrimination to identify the family, neighborhood, or village associated with suspected collaborators. Without some degree of discrimination, the link between violence and the behavior being punished would be lost. For this reason, belligerents using strategies of high-casualty control most often carry out violence through direct, face-to-face encounters between armed forces and civilians. Soldiers identify particular groups for attack, often issuing explicit threats to make clear that violence is punishment for the group's collaboration with the opposing side.

I measure high-casualty control using two dichotomous variables, *Government High-Casualty Control* and *Rebel Group High-Casualty Control*, capturing whether a government or rebel group carried out more than five massacres of civilians during the civil war. Massacres are consistent with the definition of high-casualty control in that they represent a form of violence against civilians that is discriminate in regard to the group – violence is directed at a particular group of individuals – but indiscriminate in its targeting of individuals within that group. If a government or rebel group used massacres in combination with forced expulsion of a particular ethnic or religious group, the case is coded as a case of high-casualty cleansing, rather than a case of high-casualty control, as discussed in the following section. Using this measure, 17 of the 102 governments (16.7 percent) fighting civil wars from 1989 to 2010 adopted strategies of high-casualty control, while 26 of the 103 rebel groups (25.2 percent) used strategies of high-casualty control. Examples of belligerents who used high-casualty control include the Ethiopian government, which carried out at least 18 massacres of civilians in regions of Eritrean separatist activity and seven massacres of civilians in regions where the Tigray People's Liberation Front

---

[24] Kalyvas 2006.

(TPLF) was active from 1987 to 1991, and the Revolutionary United Front (RUF) in Sierra Leone, which was responsible for more than 15 massacres of civilians believed to be sympathetic to the government.

Measuring Cleansing

In strategies of cleansing, as in strategies of control, civilians are the target of coercion; but whereas strategies of control aim to coerce civilians into providing intelligence or material support, strategies of cleansing seek to coerce the civilian population into abandoning a particular territory. Low-casualty strategies of cleansing relocate civilians by force, but do so without inflicting high casualties; for example, governments may relocate civilians into designated camps or villages, while rebel groups may threaten civilians, urging them to leave a particular territory. In many cases, this form of cleansing is intended to be temporary. High-casualty strategies of cleansing, in contrast, use more extreme violence to permanently remove civilians of a particular ethnic or religious group from the contested territory; in the most extreme cases, violence is intended not to expel civilians, but to exterminate them. Governments and rebel groups who use high-casualty cleansing often combine forced expulsion with massacres and scorched earth campaigns to eliminate members of the targeted population and to deter survivors from returning to the region. Because the attempt to expel civilians from territory may involve massacres, it can be challenging to distinguish between strategies of high-casualty control and strategies of high-casualty cleansing. I focus, therefore, on forced expulsion as the defining characteristic of high-casualty cleansing.

I code as *Government High-Casualty Cleansing* and *Rebel Group High-Casualty Cleansing* cases in which a government or rebel group forcibly expelled civilians from a particular ethnic or religious group from contested territory *and* also used scorched earth tactics and/or massacres. Only 12.8 percent of governments and 9.7 percent of rebel groups used strategies of high-casualty cleansing. The Sudanese government, for example, used high-casualty cleansing in Darfur, targeting civilians from three ethnic groups – the Fur, the Masalit, and the Zaghawa – believed to be supportive of the insurgency. During attacks on villages, the Sudanese government burned civilian homes and crops, killed livestock, massacred civilians, and issued threats against the remaining civilians urging them to flee. During the Bosnian war, both Croatian and Serbian insurgent groups used high-casualty cleansing to rid territories under their control of civilians from other ethnic groups.

Measuring Terrorism

Terrorism differs from other forms of violence against civilians in that it seeks to influence an audience beyond those directly targeted with violence. Civilians are the target of violence but not the target audience for violence; attacks are intended not to coerce civilians but to coerce the opponent into making concessions. Two key characteristics distinguish terrorism from other forms of violence against civilians: the first related to the target of violence and the second related to the nature of violence. First, because terrorism aims to coerce a wider audience beyond those immediately targeted for attack, terrorism does not require the identification of specific individuals for attack or the ability to convey a direct coercive threat to civilians. The target of violence, therefore, is not as narrow as in other strategies of violence against civilians. For this reason, terrorism does not need to involve face-to-face encounters; violence may be more removed. Second, because the aim of terrorism is to generate public pressure on the opponent to make concessions, violence is likely to be visible and public, aimed at imposing material and psychological damage on a broad section of the opponent's constituency. While some attacks on civilians using small arms may achieve public visibility and inflict widespread damage, in most cases, violence aimed at terrorism requires more substantial firepower. The use of explosives to attack civilian targets is the form of violence that most closely matches these characteristics; it is highly destructive, public violence with a broad target.

Rebel Group Terrorism is a dichotomous variable, measuring whether or not a rebel group used small-scale bombs, such as car bombs, suicide bombs, or improvised explosive devices (IEDs), to attack civilian targets; the measure does not include artillery shelling or bombing of towns or cities. I further differentiate between *Rebel Group Low-Casualty Terrorism* and *Rebel Group High-Casualty Terrorism* by focusing on the target of attack. Low-casualty terrorism includes cases in which the rebel group bombed infrastructure targets, such as power stations, oil pipelines, or bridges; although attacking these types of targets imposes high costs on civilians by disrupting electric and sanitation services or impeding transportation, casualties are rare. High-casualty terrorism includes cases in which the rebel group bombed populated civilian targets, such as buses, restaurants, and markets. Thirty-eight of the 103 rebel groups in the data set, or 36.9 percent, used strategies of terrorism. Of these, 30 groups engaged primarily in high-casualty terrorism, while eight groups engaged primarily in low-casualty terrorism. The Farabundo Martí National Liberation Front (Frente Farabundo Martí para la Liberación Nacional, FMLN) in El Salvador, for example, used a strategy of low-casualty terrorism: the group employed small-scale bombs to attack infrastructure targets such as power and telephone lines more than 1,000 times during the civil war, but rarely attacked populated civilian targets. The PKK in Turkey, in contrast, used high-casualty terrorism, regularly bombing populated civilian targets such as buses, hotels, and shopping centers.

For governments, the measure of terrorism is slightly different, reflecting differences in the tactics that governments use to inflict violence on civilians. Because governments have access to more advanced military equipment than rebel groups, when governments deliberately bomb or shell civilian targets, they tend to use artillery or aerial bombardment rather than small-scale bombs and IEDs. *Government High-Casualty Terrorism* captures cases in which the government engaged in intentional bombing and shelling of populated civilian targets – for example, the bombing of a village at a time when no rebel military forces or military bases were present and when no military engagement with the rebel group was ongoing. Bombing or shelling directed at the rebel group's troops, weapons, or military bases is excluded, even if civilians were killed in the crossfire. Using this measure, 21.6 percent of governments adopted strategies of high-casualty terrorism. Examples include the Russian government's bombardment of Grozny and other towns during the conflicts in Chechnya and the Burmese government's repeated shelling of villages and refugee camps during its conflicts with the Karen, Karenni, and Shan insurgencies. Identifying cases of government low-casualty terrorism is more difficult. In these cases, although sources may report that government bombing and shelling was indiscriminate and failed to distinguish between military and civilian targets, governments often dispute this, claiming that rebels were active in the area. For this reason, I only examine quantitatively the arguments about government high-casualty terrorism.

Table 2.1 provides a summary of the measures used for each strategy of violence. Table 2.3, at the end of the chapter, lists all of the civil wars in the data set, as well as the coding of government and rebel group strategies of restraint, control, cleansing, and terrorism for each conflict.

TABLE 2.1 *Measures of Government and Rebel Group Strategies of Violence*

Strategy	Government Measure	Rebel Group Measure
Restraint	No massacres; no scorched earth; no forced expulsion; no deliberate bombing or shelling of populated civilian targets	No massacres; no scorched earth; no forced expulsion; no deliberate bombing or shelling of populated civilian targets
High-Casualty Control	Massacres, without forced expulsion	Massacres, without forced expulsion
High-Casualty Cleansing	Forced expulsion of a particular ethnic or religious group from territory; in combination with massacres or scorched earth tactics	Forced expulsion of a particular ethnic or religious group from territory; in combination with massacres or scorched earth tactics
High-Casualty Terrorism	Deliberate bombing or shelling of populated civilian targets	Deliberate use of small-scale bombs against populated civilian targets

Measuring the Domestic Costs of Violence

The first set of hypotheses I presented in Chapter 1 argues that the characteristics of a government or rebel group's political system influence the domestic costs of violence and, therefore, the likelihood of restraint. I focus on three characteristics: (1) the degree to which institutions encourage leaders to be responsive to their constituents, (2) the inclusiveness of the political system, and (3) the consolidation of political power. To capture the extent to which a government's political institutions create incentives for leaders to be responsive to their constituents, I measure *Government Level of Democracy* in the year the conflict began, using the country's polity score from the Polity IV Project; polity scores range from −10 (most autocratic) to +10 (most democratic).[25] The majority of conflicts, 78.4 percent, took place in states with nondemocratic regimes, split fairly evenly between autocratic regimes (polity scores less than or equal to −6) and anocratic regimes (polity scores from −5 to +5). Twenty-two of the 102 governments in the data set, or 21.6 percent, are democratic (polity scores greater than or equal to +6).[26]

For rebel groups, an ideal measure of institutional incentives for responsiveness would gauge the extent to which rebel group political structures allow civilian supporters to participate in rebel group governance and to influence leaders' decisions, holding leaders accountable to the preferences of their constituents. Detailed data on characteristics of rebel group governance structures are not available across conflicts, but it is possible to observe whether a rebel group established any form of governance at all. *Rebel Group Governance* measures whether a rebel group created political structures to govern territory or populations under its control – structures aimed at providing public services such as adjudication of disputes, provision of humanitarian relief, maintenance of sanitation or transportation infrastructure, or certification of marriage or other contracts.[27] The provision of governance is not synonymous with controlling territory. Some groups that control territory do not establish political institutions or administrative structures; rebel groups in Cambodia provide an example.[28] And even groups that operate within contested territory may establish political structures that serve their constituents, as GAM did in Aceh. Nearly all rebel groups use some form of civilian taxation to finance their

---

[25] Marshall and Jaggers 2009. Polity scores measure six aspects of government regime type, all of which are relevant in capturing the degree to which institutions encourage leaders to be responsive to constituents. Results are robust to alternate measures of government regime type; see the online Appendix.

[26] Several democratic governments (Colombia, India, Israel, and the Philippines) have fought multiple civil wars. Although 22 of the conflicts in the data set involve democratic governments, only 9 democracies have fought civil wars.

[27] I code this variable using information from secondary historical sources. For further discussion, including the list of sources used, see the online Appendix.

[28] Asia Watch 1992.

operations;[29] thus, in order to qualify as having governance structures, a rebel group's administrative apparatus must extend beyond structures aimed at extracting taxes or exploiting local resources. Fifty of the 103 rebel groups (48.5 percent) in the data set established governance structures.

The inclusiveness of a government or rebel group's political system refers to the extent to which the political system permits individuals from diverse groups to gain access to political power. *Inclusive Government Regime* relies on data from the Ethnic Power Relations (EPR) data set; governments in which one or more ethnic groups have "dominant" or "monopoly" control are coded as having exclusionary regimes, while those in which no ethnic group has "dominant" or "monopoly" control are coded as having inclusive regimes.[30] The concept of an inclusive regime is distinct from regime type. A government may have democratic institutions that encourage accountability to the public and constrain executive decision making, and yet the government may be dominated by individuals from a single ethnic group. In democratic Turkey, for example, the Turkish majority controls the political system, excluding both the Kurds and the Roma. Similarly, a government may have autocratic institutions, but the political system may allow for the involvement of multiple ethnic groups. In autocratic Uganda, for example, Southwestern ethnic groups are powerful politically, but they share power with the Baganda and Basoga ethnic groups. Nearly 55 percent of governments have inclusive regimes.

Similar data capturing the degree to which a rebel group's political system excludes particular ethnic or national groups from access to political power are not available, but the EPR data set provides information on whether rebel groups are pursuing ethnically inclusive political objectives. *Inclusive Rebel Group* distinguishes between inclusive groups, whose political objectives "would pertain to the country's entire population," and exclusionary groups, whose "stated objective is to provide selective benefits" for particular ethnic groups.[31] Rebel groups pursuing sectarian religious objectives are also coded as exclusionary. Exclusionary rebel groups are more prevalent in the data set, at 70.9 percent of cases, than inclusive rebel groups.

For governments, *Unstable Government Regime* measures whether the government experienced a change in regime or an attempted coup within the five years prior to the start of the conflict.[32] In some cases, regime change represents a move toward a more democratic or more autocratic form of government; in other cases, regime change takes place following the end of a civil war or following the creation of a new state. About two-thirds of governments experienced a change in regime or an attempted coup within five years of the start of the conflict.

---

[29] Kalyvas 2001.   [30] Wimmer, Cederman, and Min 1999.

[31] Wucherpfennig et al. 2012, 95.

[32] I use Polity IV's data and definition of regime change: A three or more point shift in polity score within a three-year period (Marshall and Jaggers 2009). Data on coups are from Powell and Thyne 2011; Marshall and Marshall 2014.

Measuring the International Costs of Violence

According to the second set of hypotheses, the international costs of violence depend on belligerents' relationships with international constituencies – in particular, Western international constituencies. Governments whose regimes are unstable need support from international constituencies to bolster their legitimacy, while rebel groups facing autocratic opponents need international support to force government concessions. These belligerents face high international costs to violence, increasing the likelihood of restraint. The measure of regime stability described earlier – *Unstable Government Regime* – reflects not only a government's need to build domestic support, but also its need to build international support. To capture the regime type of the rebel group's opponent I use *Government Level of Democracy*.

The end of the Cold War and the concomitant decline of ideologically based appeals for international support created greater space for belligerents to use international human rights and humanitarian norms as a basis for seeking international support. Thus, if the argument of this book is correct and belligerents do, in fact, use restraint strategically to appeal for international support, the likelihood of restraint should be highest in conflicts beginning after the end of the Cold War. *Post-1989 Conflict* is a dichotomous variable measuring whether the conflict began after 1989.

Measuring the Benefits of Violence

The final set of hypotheses presented in Chapter 1 turns to variation in forms of violence. These hypotheses posit that governments and rebel groups decide which form of violence to use – control, cleansing, or terrorism – based on calculations regarding the benefits of each form of violence. How a belligerent weighs these benefits depends, in turn, on an assessment of the opponent's civilian constituency: the strength and location of civilian support for the opponent and the degree to which the opponent is responsive to its civilian constituents.

The first of these hypotheses, positing that the strength of civilian support for the opponent is linked to strategies of high-casualty control, is difficult to examine using statistical analyses. Measuring civilian support for a political group can be challenging even in liberal democratic countries with strong media institutions capable of carrying out public opinion polling. During a civil war, obtaining accurate estimates of the strength of support for a particular belligerent is even more difficult, given the incentives respondents may have to misrepresent their loyalties.[33] For this reason, I do not test this hypothesis statistically; instead, I examine arguments regarding strategies of control in the case studies.

[33] Blair, Imai, and Lyall 2014.

The hypothesis on government cleansing focuses on the degree of geographic concentration of the rebel group's civilian constituency. To capture this, I begin by identifying conflicts in which the rebel group draws its primary civilian support from individuals of a particular ethnic group. Although it is possible for rebel groups without an ethnic base of support to have geographically concentrated civilian constituencies, data on the location and size of nonethnic rebel constituencies are not available. *Concentrated Rebel Group Constituency* is a dichotomous variable constructed using data from the Minorities at Risk (MAR) Project, capturing whether a rebel group's ethnic base of support is located in one region of the country; in addition, 25 percent or more of the group's population must live in the region and the group must constitute "the predominant portion of the population" in the region.[34] Slightly more than half (58.3 percent) of the rebel groups in the data set derive support from a regionally concentrated ethnic group.

The hypothesis on rebel group cleansing posits that separatist rebel groups are likely to use cleansing when the government has a small, geographically concentrated constituency of supporters within the separatist region. *Concentrated Government Constituency* captures whether the government has a base of support that constitutes between 5 and 50 percent of the population in the separatist region;[35] of the 43 governments fighting separatist insurgencies, 26 have such a civilian constituency.

Finally, the first hypothesis on terrorism posits that governments and rebel groups are more likely to adopt strategies of terrorism when they believe that their opponent's political institutions create incentives for the opponent to be responsive to its constituents. To measure the degree to which a government or rebel group is responsive to its civilian constituents, I use the same measures – *Government Level of Democracy* and *Rebel Group Governance* – discussed in the section on restraint. The second hypothesis on terrorism predicts that among belligerents using terrorism, governments and rebel groups with inclusive political systems will be wary of inflicting high civilian casualties, instead adopting strategies of low-casualty terrorism. I measure inclusiveness using the variables discussed in the section on the domestic costs of violence.

Control Variables

I include a number of additional variables, both to test alternative arguments and to control for other factors that might influence civil war violence. Arguments regarding organizational control posit that armed groups possessing greater control over their members are less likely to target civilians and, further, that rebel groups with access to external sources of financing are least likely to

---

[34] Minorities at Risk Project 2007, 8. This variable is from the Minorities at Risk variable GC2.

[35] These data were compiled using primary sources, such as census data, as well as secondary sources. For further discussion, including the list of sources used, see the online Appendix.

control the use of violence among their members. Measures of organizational control are not available for governments, but several options exist for testing this argument with respect to rebel groups. *Contraband* is a dichotomous variable indicating whether there is "evidence of major reliance by the rebels on income from production or trafficking in contraband" such as cocaine, diamonds, or opium.[36] I also use the Non-State Actor Data , a data set measuring rebel group characteristics, to construct a four-point index, *Rebel Group Organizational Control*, ranging from no central command structure to a central command structure exercising a high degree of control over its forces.[37]

To assess the second set of alternative arguments, claiming that the military context influences belligerent behavior, I include *Relative Strength*, a ratio of average government troop strength to average rebel group troop strength, constructed using annual data from *The Military Balance* and the *SIPRI Yearbooks*.[38] *Conflict Intensity*, which captures the costs of the conflict, measures average annual battle-related deaths, logged.[39] *Guerrilla Conflict* measures whether a conflict was fought primarily using tactics of guerrilla or irregular warfare.[40] *Multiparty Conflict* is a dichotomous variable capturing whether a conflict involved multiple rebel groups fighting for similar political objectives.[41] While most of the military context arguments lend themselves to cross-national quantitative analysis, an exception is the argument that Stathis Kalyvas makes regarding contestation over territory; this argument makes predictions about the relationship between *subnational* variation in territorial contestation and the likelihood of violence. For this reason, I do not test this argument quantitatively, instead addressing this argument in the case study chapters.

[36] This measure is from Fearon 2004, 284. Weinstein 2007 uses this measure, as well as a measure of rebel group aid from foreign governments. I do not use the measure of aid from foreign governments because, according to my argument, rebel group behavior may influence whether the group receives foreign assistance in the first place.

[37] Cunningham, Gleditsch, and Salehyan 2009. To simplify the presentation of the statistical results, the regression tables in the text only show the results of the analyses controlling for *Contraband*. The results of the analyses using the measure of *Rebel Group Organizational Control* from the Non-State Actor Data are shown in the online Appendix.

[38] The International Institute for Strategic Studies 1989–2010; Stockholm International Peace Research Institute (SIPRI) 1989–2010. For conflicts that began before 1989, I use data from 1989 onwards. Government troop estimates are for active armed forces, excluding paramilitary forces such as police. In robustness checks, I substituted an alternate measure of relative strength from Cunningham, Gleditsch, and Salehyan 2009. This does not alter significantly the statistical results.

[39] Data are from the PRIO Battle Deaths Dataset, 1946–2005, and Duration Data v1-2006. See Gleditsch et al. 2002; Lacina and Gleditsch 2005; Gates and Strand 2006. In robustness checks, I used several alternate measures of conflict costs, including total battle-related deaths, battle-related deaths logged, and conflict duration; substituting these measures does not alter significantly the statistical results.

[40] Coding is from Kalyvas and Balcells 2010; robustness checks use data from Valentino, Huth, and Balch-Lindsay 2004.

[41] Coding of multiparty conflicts is from the UCDP/PRIO Armed Conflict Dataset.

The third set of alternative arguments posits that international factors, such as political and economic interdependence or the ratification of relevant instruments of international humanitarian law, influence government behavior. To examine economic interdependence, I look at the extent of a country's involvement in *International Trade*, measured as the sum of total exports and imports of goods and services as a percentage of GDP.[42] I also consider political interdependence, using data on *IGO Membership*, which measure the ratio of the number of intergovernmental organizations (IGOs) of which the country was a member to the number of IGOs of which the country *could* have been a member, in the year the conflict began.[43] *Ratified Additional Protocol II* captures whether a government ratified the Second Additional Protocol to the Geneva Conventions, which provides protections for civilians in civil wars, prior to the start of the civil war.[44] Ratification of the Second Additional Protocol binds all parties to an internal conflict – the government as well as the rebel group; I thus include this variable in the analyses of both government and rebel group restraint. In all of the analyses I control for the *Per Capita GDP* of the country in which the civil war is taking place; this variable is logged.[45] Table 2.2 summarizes the hypotheses and the independent variable measures used to evaluate each hypothesis.

A FIRST LOOK AT THE VARIATION IN VIOLENCE

Figure 2.1 shows the percentage of governments and rebel groups that engaged in each of the strategies of violence: high-casualty control, high-casualty cleansing, high-casualty terrorism, and restraint. As these data show, it is not the case that all governments engage in severe abuses of civilian populations during civil war, nor is it the case that governments rarely target civilians during civil war. Similarly, rebel group strategies with respect to civilians vary substantially, with some rebel groups engaging in very little civilian targeting during civil war, exercising restraint in their fighting, and others responsible for high levels of civilian abuse. Governments and rebel groups do often comply

---

[42] Data are from the World Bank, *World Development Indicators*, available online at: data .worldbank.org. I use data for the year before the conflict began because the onset of hostilities often interferes with trade.

[43] Mansfield and Pevehouse 2006. Data are available through 2000; for conflicts beginning after 2000, I use IGO memberships from 2000.

[44] The Second Additional Protocol was signed in 1977, meaning that all governments in the data set had the opportunity to ratify this treaty prior to the period of study. The Rome Statute of the International Criminal Court was adopted in July 1998. Twenty-two civil wars in the data set began after the Rome Statute's adoption, but only one government (Democratic Republic of Congo in its conflict with the National Congress for the Defence of the People, CNDP) ratified the Rome Statute prior to the start of the conflict. The Congolese government did exercise restraint in this conflict.

[45] Data are from Gleditsch 2002. Because civil war onset often leads to a decline in GDP, I measure per capita GDP in the year prior to conflict onset. For conflicts that began prior to 1989, I use data from 1988.

TABLE 2.2 *Summary of Independent Variable Measures*

Hypotheses	Independent Variable Measures
Hypotheses on Restraint	
H1: political institutions encourage leader responsiveness to public demands → government and rebel group restraint	government level of democracy; rebel group governance
H2: inclusive political system → government and rebel group restraint	inclusive government regime; inclusive rebel political system
H3: government need for domestic and international support → government restraint	unstable government regime
H4: rebel group need for international support → rebel group restraint	autocratic government opponent
Hypothesis on High-Casualty Control	
H5: high civilian support for the opponent in contested territory → government and rebel group high-casualty control	none; hypothesis not tested quantitatively
Hypotheses on High-Casualty Cleansing	
H6: rebel group constituency is small and concentrated → government high-casualty cleansing	concentrated rebel group constituency
H7: government constituency in separatist region is small and concentrated → rebel group high-casualty cleansing	concentrated government constituency in separatist region
Hypotheses on Terrorism and High-Casualty Terrorism	
H8: opponent's political institutions encourage accountability to constituents → government and rebel group terrorism	rebel group governance; government level of democracy
H9: exclusionary political system → government and rebel group high-casualty terrorism	inclusive government regime; inclusive rebel political system

with international humanitarian law during civil war; more than 40 percent of governments and rebel groups adopted strategies of restraint.

The nature of violence also varies considerably. About 25.2 percent of rebel groups and 16.7 percent of governments adopted strategies of high-casualty control, while 29.1 percent of rebel groups and 21.6 percent of governments used strategies of high-casualty terrorism. High-casualty cleansing, perhaps the most extreme of these three forms of violence, is the least common strategy,

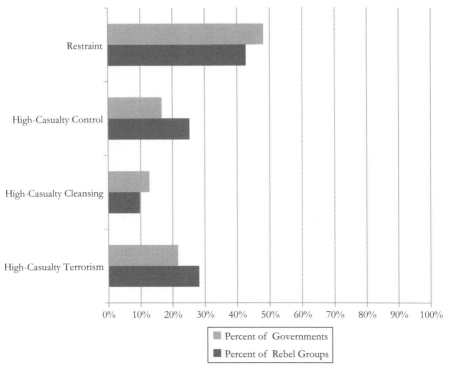

FIGURE 2.1 Distribution of Government and Rebel Group Strategies of Violence.

with less than 13 percent of governments and less than 10 percent of rebel groups adopting this strategy of violence. The next chapter uses quantitative analyses to examine in greater detail this variation in strategies of violence and restraint.

CONCLUSION

Existing work on wartime violence against civilians uses counts of the number of civilians killed as the primary measure of civilian targeting. During war, however, civilians are killed in multiple ways – by direct contact with armed forces, as civilians are shot at close range; by aerial bombardment; by small-scale bombs exploded in public places. And much wartime violence against civilians – torture, forced expulsion, scorched earth tactics – inflicts severe suffering without killing large numbers of civilians. An improved understanding of the causes of wartime violence against civilians requires a better understanding of the dynamics of conflict and of the multiple forms that violence against civilians may take. In this chapter, I presented an original data set, measuring forms of government and rebel group violence against civilians in all civil wars from 1989 to 2010. An overview of the data shows that although many governments and rebel groups do engage in severe forms of violence against civilians, restraint is not an uncommon strategy for either governments or rebel groups. More than 40 percent of governments and rebel groups refrained from using the most severe forms of violence against civilians during civil war. Chapter 3 uses this new data set to evaluate the hypotheses on government and rebel group violence and restraint.

TABLE 2.3 *Strategies of Violence and Restraint in Civil War, 1989–2010*

| | Conflict | | | | Government Strategies | | | | Rebel Group Strategies | | | |
Government	Rebel Group	Start	End	Restraint	High-Casualty Control	High-Casualty Cleansing	High-Casualty Terrorism	Restraint	High-Casualty Control	High-Casualty Cleansing	High- or Low-Casualty Terrorism
Afghanistan (Najibullah gov't)	Mujahideen	1978	1992	X				X			
Afghanistan (Rabbani gov't)	Taliban	1994	1996	X				X			
Afghanistan (Taliban gov't)	Northern Alliance	1996	2001		X			X			
Afghanistan (Karzai gov't)	Taliban	2003	—	X							High
Algeria	AIS/FIS	1992	1997	X				X			Low
Algeria	GIA	1992	2006	X					X		High
Algeria	GSPC, AQIM	1998	—	X					X		High
Angola	UNITA	1975	2002				X		X		
Azerbaijan	Nagorno-Karabakh	1992	1994	X						X	
Bangladesh	Chittagong Hills/Shanti Bahini	1975	1997			X				X	
Bosnia	Croat Republic/HVO	1992	1994							X	
Bosnia	Serbian Republic/BSA	1992	1995			X				X	
Burma	Karens/KNU	1948	—				X	X			
Burma	Shan/SSA	1959	—		X		X	X			
Burma	Kachins/KIO	1961	1992	insufficient information; coded as missing				insufficient information; coded as missing			
Burma	Karenni/KNPP	1992	2005				X	X			
Burundi	CNDD, CNDD-FDD	1994	2003		X				X		
Burundi	Palipehutu	1997	—		X				X		

Country	Group						
Cambodia (Hun Sen gov't)	FUNCINPEC	1978	1991	X		X	
Cambodia (Hun Sen gov't)	KPNLF	1978	1991	X		X	
Cambodia (Hun Sen gov't)	Khmer Rouge	1978	1993	X			
Cambodia (coalition gov't)	Khmer Rouge	1993	1998	X		X	
Chad	MPS	1982	1990	insufficient information; coded as missing			
Chad	MDD	1991	1997	X		X	
Chad	MDJT	1999	2005	insufficient information; coded as missing			
Chad	FUCD	2005	2006	X		X	
Colombia	EPL	1965	1989	insufficient information; coded as missing			
Colombia	ELN	1965	—	X	X		Low
Colombia	FARC	1965	—	X	X	X	High
Congo-Brazzaville	Cobras	1997	1997	X		X	
Congo-Brazzaville	Cocoyes	1997	1999	insufficient information; coded as missing			
Congo-Kinshasa	AFDL	1996	1997	X	X		
Congo-Kinshasa	RCD, RCD-ML	1998	2001	X		X	
Congo-Kinshasa	MLC	1998	2001	X		X	
Congo-Kinshasa	CNDP	2006	2008	X		X	
Cote D'Ivoire	MPCI, MPIGO, MJP, FN	2002	2004	X		X	
Croatia	Serbian Republic of Krajina	1992	1995	X	X	X	
Djibouti	FRUD	1991	1994	X		X	
Egypt	Al-Gamaa al-Islamiyya	1993	1998	X	X		High
El Salvador	FMLN	1979	1991	X	X		Low
Ethiopia	Eritrea	1972	1991	X	X	X	
Ethiopia	TPLF	1976	1991	X	X	X	
Ethiopia	Oromo/OLF	1992	—	X	X		Low
Ethiopia	Ogaden/ONLF	1994	—	X			
Georgia	Abkhazia	1992	1994	X		X	

(continued)

TABLE 2.3 (continued)

Conflict				Government Strategies				Rebel Group Strategies			
Government	Rebel Group	Start	End	Restraint	High-Casualty Control	High-Casualty Cleansing	High-Casualty Terrorism	Restraint	High-Casualty Control	High-Casualty Cleansing	High- or Low-Casualty Terrorism
Georgia	Ossetia	1992	1994	insufficient information; coded as missing				insufficient information; coded as missing			
Guatemala	URNG	1966	1995	X							Low
Guinea	RFDG	2000	2001	insufficient information; coded as missing				insufficient information; coded as missing			
Guinea Bissau	Military faction	1998	1999	X				X			
India	Manipur/PLA	1982	2007	insufficient information; coded as missing				insufficient information; coded as missing			
India	Sikhs	1983	1993	X					X		High
India	Kashmir	1989	—		X				X		High
India	Assam/ULFA	1990	—	X							High
India	Naxalites	1990	—	X							Low
India	Tripura/ATTF	1992	1999	insufficient information; coded as missing				insufficient information; coded as missing			
India	Nagaland/NSCN	1992	2000	X					X		
India	Manipur/UNLF	1993	2009	insufficient information; coded as missing				insufficient information; coded as missing			
India	Bodoland/NDFB	1993	2010	X					X		High
India	Tripura/NLFT	1995	2006	X					X		
Indonesia	East Timor/Fretilin	1975	1999		X			X			
Indonesia	Aceh/GAM	1989	2005		X			X			
Iran	KDPI	1979	1996	insufficient information; coded as missing				insufficient information; coded as missing			
Iraq	Kurds/KDP	1961	1991			X	X	X			
Iraq	Kurds/PUK	1976	1996			X	X	X			
Iraq	Shiites/SCIRI	1991	1996			X	X	X			
Iraq	Al-Mahdi Army	2004	2008	X							
Iraq	Ansar al-Islam	2004	—	X							High
Iraq	ISI	2004	—	X							High
Israel	Fatah	1965	—								High
Israel	Hamas	1993	—				X				High
Israel	PIJ	1995	—								High
Israel	Hezbollah	1990	2006				X				High

Country	Multiple factions			insufficient information; coded as missing	insufficient information; coded as missing	insufficient information; coded as missing	
Lebanon	Multiple factions					X	
Liberia	NPFL	1989	1995			X	
Liberia	INPFL	1990	1992		X		
Liberia	LURD	2000	2003		X		
Moldova	Dniester Republic	1992	1992	X	X		
Morocco	Western Sahara/Polisario	1975	1989	X		X	
Mozambique	RENAMO	1976	1992			X	
Nepal	CPN-M, UPF	1996	2006	X			High
Nicaragua	Contras	1981	1990	X	X		
Pakistan	Baluchistan/BLA	2004	—	X	X		Low
Pakistan	TTP	2007	—	X	X		High
Peru	Sendero Luminoso	1981	2000	X		X	High
Philippines	MNLF	1972	1993	X			High
Philippines	CPP/NPA	1972	—				High
Philippines	MILF	1990	—	X		X	High
Philippines	ASG	1993	—	X		X	High
Russia	Chechnya	1994	1996	X	X		
Russia	Chechnya	1999	2007	X			High
Russia	Caucasus Emirate	2007	—	X			High
Rwanda	RPF	1990	1994	X			
Rwanda	Former FAR, interahamwe	1997	2004	X		X	
Senegal	Casamance/MFDC	1990	2003			X	
Sierra Leone	RUF	1991	2000	X		X	
Somalia	SNM	1981	1991	X	X		
Somalia	USC faction led by Aideed	1991	2002	no government actor coded		X	
Somalia	ARS/UIC	2006	—	X		X	

(continued)

TABLE 2.3 (continued)

Conflict				Government Strategies				Rebel Group Strategies			
Government	Rebel Group	Start	End	Restraint	High-Casualty Control	High-Casualty Cleansing	High-Casualty Terrorism	Restraint	High-Casualty Control	High-Casualty Cleansing	High- or Low-Casualty Terrorism
Somalia	Al-Shabaab	2008	—	X							High
South Africa	ANC	1976	1994					X			Low
Sri Lanka	LTTE	1983	2009		X		X			X	High
Sri Lanka	JVP	1987	1990	X				X			
Sudan	SPLA	1983	2004		X		X	X			
Sudan	Darfur/JEM	2003	—			X	X	X			
Sudan	Darfur/SLA	2003	—			X	X	X			
Tajikistan	UTO	1992	1998	X				X			
Thailand	Patani insurgents	2003	—	X							High
Turkey	Kurds/PKK	1984	—								High
Uganda	UPA	1987	1991		X				X		
Uganda	LRA	1987	—	X					X		
Uganda	ADF	1996	1999	X							High
United Kingdom	PIRA	1970	1999	X							High
Yemen	South Yemen	1994	1994	X				X			
Yugoslavia	Croatia	1991	1991			X	X	X			
Yugoslavia	Kosovo/KLA	1998	1999			X	X			X	

Notes: for cases beginning before 1989, coding reflects behavior from 1989 onward. All four strategies are blank for cases in which the government or rebel group used either scorched earth tactics or forced expulsion, but did not use these tactics in combination. These cases involve significant violence against civilians and, therefore, are not cases of restraint; but these cases do not meet the definition for high-casualty cleansing (which requires the use of forced expulsion in combination with scorched earth tactics or massacres).

3

Quantitative Analysis of Government and Rebel Group Violence and Restraint

Using the original data set on government and rebel group violence against civilians introduced in Chapter 2, this chapter presents the results of a series of quantitative analyses. The quantitative evidence lends support to this book's central argument: that governments and rebel groups use violence and restraint strategically, weighing the costs of violence based on an assessment of *their own* relationship with domestic and international constituents and weighing the benefits of violence based on an assessment of *their opponent's* relationship with its constituents. The first part of the chapter presents the findings on government and rebel group strategies of restraint; these findings show that governments and rebel groups facing high *domestic* costs to the use of violence – governments and rebel groups with broad domestic civilian constituencies and with institutional incentives to be responsive to these constituencies – are more likely to exercise restraint toward civilians. In addition, governments and rebel groups facing high *international* costs to violence – governments with unstable regimes and rebel groups confronting autocratic opponents – are more likely to adopt strategies of restraint.

The second part of the chapter presents the findings on government and rebel group strategies of cleansing and terrorism. The results of these analyses show that strategies of high-casualty cleansing are more likely when the opponent's civilian constituency is small and geographically concentrated, making it possible for a government or rebel group to eliminate entirely its opponent's civilian support base. The evidence demonstrates that governments and rebel groups also consider their opponent's likely response to violence. Governments and rebel groups are more likely to adopt strategies of terrorism when they perceive their opponent as sensitive to the civilian costs of conflict, and thus likely to make concessions in response to violent attacks on civilians. But the findings also show that the form that terrorism takes depends on how governments and rebel groups weigh the costs of violence; the lower the domestic costs of violence – the smaller the government or rebel group's own civilian constituency – the greater the likelihood that terrorism will take the form of high-casualty attacks on populated civilian targets. In the final section of the chapter, I analyze the findings in light of alternative explanations for wartime violence against civilians; the quantitative evidence raises questions about the ability of many of the most common hypotheses on civilian targeting to account for patterns of violence across cases of civil war.

QUANTITATIVE ANALYSES

Because all of the dependent variables are dichotomous, I use binary logit models for the statistical analyses. A number of countries in the data set have experienced multiple civil wars; I report robust standard errors, clustering cases by country. Table 3.1 again summarizes the hypotheses, as well as the measures used to evaluate each hypothesis. Table 3.2 reports the results of the statistical analyses for government strategies of violence and restraint, while Table 3.3 reports the results for rebel group strategies of violence and restraint. I also conduct a variety of robustness checks, including analyses using alternate measures of the main variables of interest and incorporating additional control variables; the results of these robustness checks are shown in the online Appendix to the book. In the sections that follow, I discuss the findings on strategies of restraint, strategies of cleansing, and, finally, strategies of terrorism.

GOVERNMENT AND REBEL GROUP RESTRAINT

H1:   *The stronger the institutional incentives for government and rebel group leaders to be responsive to public demands, the greater the likelihood of restraint.*

H2:   *The more inclusive a government or rebel group's political system, the greater the likelihood of restraint.*

H3:   *Governments in need of building domestic and international support – in particular, governments with unstable regimes – are more likely to adopt strategies of restraint.*

H4:   *Rebel groups in need of building international support – in particular, rebel groups facing more autocratic opponents – are more likely to adopt strategies of restraint.*

Government Restraint

Figure 3.1 shows the percent of governments adopting strategies of restraint, broken down by the three regime characteristics I argue drive government behavior: regime type, regime inclusiveness, and regime stability. The data lend support to the first hypothesis, positing that restraint is most common among governments with strong institutional incentives to be responsive to the public. More than half (54.6 percent) of the governments with democratic regimes

TABLE 3.1 *Summary of Hypotheses and Independent Variable Measures*

Hypotheses	Independent Variable Measures
Hypotheses on Restraint	
H1: political institutions encourage leader responsiveness to public demands → government and rebel group restraint	government level of democracy; rebel group governance
H2: inclusive political system → government and rebel group restraint	inclusive government regime; inclusive rebel political system
H3: government need for domestic and international support → government restraint	unstable government regime
H4: rebel group need for international support → rebel group restraint	autocratic government opponent
Hypothesis on High-Casualty Control	
H5: high civilian support for the opponent in contested territory → government and rebel group high-casualty control	none; hypothesis not tested quantitatively
Hypotheses on High-Casualty Cleansing	
H6: rebel group constituency is small and concentrated → government high-casualty cleansing	concentrated rebel group constituency
H7: government constituency in separatist region is small and concentrated → rebel group high-casualty cleansing	concentrated government constituency in separatist region
Hypotheses on Terrorism and High-Casualty Terrorism	
H8: opponent's political institutions encourage accountability to constituents → government and rebel group terrorism	rebel group governance; government level of democracy
H9: exclusionary political system → government and rebel group high-casualty terrorism	inclusive government regime; inclusive rebel political system

exercised restraint in their counterinsurgency operations, whereas less than 30 percent of governments with autocratic regimes exercised restraint. The patterns evident in Figure 3.1 are also consistent with the expectations of the second hypothesis; restraint is more common among governments with inclusive regimes than among governments with exclusionary regimes. Nearly two-thirds of governments with inclusive regimes exercised restraint, as compared with less than one-third of governments with exclusionary regimes. In addition,

TABLE 3.2 *Binary Logit Results: Government Strategies of Violence and Restraint*

	Model 1 Restraint (Basic Model)	Model 2 Restraint (International Variables)	Model 3 Restraint (Military Context Variables)	Model 4 High-Casualty Cleansing	Model 5 High-Casualty Terrorism
Government Level of Democracy	0.133** (0.060)	0.145** (0.061)	0.124** (0.062)	-0.357*** (0.122)	-0.119 (0.083)
Inclusive Government Regime	1.539** (0.671)	1.687** (0.677)	1.824** (0.714)	0.158 (0.836)	-1.495* (0.835)
Unstable Government Regime	2.033*** (0.730)	2.486*** (0.879)	2.392*** (0.834)	-1.479 (0.949)	-1.527 (1.037)
Concentrated Rebel Group Constituency	-0.282 (0.635)	-0.243 (0.622)	-0.240 (0.677)	1.722** (0.832)	0.119 (0.927)
Rebel Group Governance	-1.598*** (0.527)	-1.686*** (0.636)	-1.637*** (0.519)	0.215 (1.047)	2.785*** (1.073)
Relative Strength – Ratio of Gov't to Rebel Troops, Logged	-0.001 (0.146)	-0.032 (0.184)	-0.045 (0.149)	-0.365* (0.214)	0.216 (0.313)
Conflict Intensity – Average Annual Battle Deaths, Logged	-0.010 (0.219)	0.223 (0.278)	-0.020 (0.221)	-0.225 (0.396)	0.249 (0.266)
Per Capita GDP, Logged	0.409 (0.472)	0.390 (0.464)	0.488 (0.496)	1.041* (0.602)	0.608 (0.384)
Rebel Group Restraint	0.373 (0.560)	0.350 (0.619)	0.396 (0.541)	-0.010 (1.045)	0.373 (0.660)

	(1)	(2)	(3)	(4)	(5)
Post-1989 Conflict	—	1.375**	—	—	—
		(0.665)			
International Trade	—	0.003	—	—	—
		(0.009)			
IGO Membership	—	3.287	—	—	—
		(3.140)			
Ratified Additional Protocol II	—	-0.009	—	—	—
		(0.731)			
Guerrilla Conflict	—	—	0.635	—	—
			(0.604)		
Multiparty Conflict	—	—	-0.768	—	—
			(0.550)		
Constant	-4.550	-8.655**	-5.357	-9.225*	-9.157**
	(3.366)	(4.101)	(3.691)	(5.259)	(3.993)
Wald Chi²	27.54***	23.61**	29.00***	24.43***	21.46**
Pseudo R²	0.2648	0.3150	0.2892	0.3917	0.4428
N	102	102	102	102	102

Note: Robust standard errors in parentheses; *** p < 0.01, ** p < 0.05, * p < 0.10.

TABLE 3.3 *Binary Logit Results: Rebel Group Strategies of Violence and Restraint*

	Model 1 Restraint (Basic Model)	Model 2 Restraint (International Variables)	Model 3 Restraint (Military Context Variables)	Model 4 High-Casualty Cleansing	Model 5 Terrorism	Model 6 High-Casualty Terrorism
Government Level of Democracy	-0.152***	-0.161***	-0.153***	-0.025	0.244***	0.236***
	(0.046)	(0.047)	(0.049)	(0.107)	(0.091)	(0.071)
Rebel Group Governance	1.188**	1.337**	1.284**	0.150	0.357	-0.711
	(0.581)	(0.574)	(0.543)	(1.339)	(0.647)	(0.528)
Inclusive Rebel Group	1.585***	1.888***	1.708**	—	-0.641	-1.858***
	(0.590)	(0.617)	(0.699)		(0.767)	(0.671)
Concentrated Government Constituency	—	—	—	4.109***	—	—
				(1.142)		
Relative Strength – Ratio of Gov't to Rebel Troops, Logged	0.201	0.254*	0.302	-1.072***	0.498**	0.253
	(0.136)	(0.148)	(0.185)	(0.267)	(0.222)	(0.193)
Conflict Intensity – Average Annual Battle Deaths, Logged	0.215	0.267	0.181	-0.093	-0.073	-0.036
	(0.176)	(0.196)	(0.163)	(0.415)	(0.209)	(0.186)
Per Capita GDP, Logged	-0.328	-0.398	-0.364	0.518	0.242	0.576*
	(0.308)	(0.329)	(0.331)	(0.675)	(0.353)	(0.347)
Government Restraint	0.382	0.207	0.455	-2.060**	1.043	0.307
	(0.502)	(0.546)	(0.468)	(1.020)	(0.781)	(0.703)
Contraband	0.176	0.299	0.224	-0.919	-0.243	0.421
	(0.513)	(0.554)	(0.537)	(1.126)	(0.714)	(0.753)

Post-1989 Conflict	—	0.882	—	—	—	—
		(0.697)				
Ratified Additional Protocol II	—	-0.403	—	—	—	—
		(0.561)				
Guerrilla Conflict	—	—	-0.881	—	—	—
			(0.772)			
Multiparty Conflict	—	—	-0.182	—	0.993	0.576
			(0.560)		(0.635)	(0.592)
Constant	-1.383	-1.987	-0.681	-5.319	-4.417	-5.928*
	(2.515)	(2.476)	(2.576)	(5.610)	(2.885)	(3.144)
Wald Chi²	20.57***	22.20**	24.23***	52.10***	26.90***	63.94***
Pseudo R²	0.2240	0.2384	0.2410	0.5557	0.4611	0.4407
N	102	102	102	102	102	102

Note: Robust standard errors in parentheses; *** $p < 0.01$, ** $p < 0.05$, * $p < 0.10$.

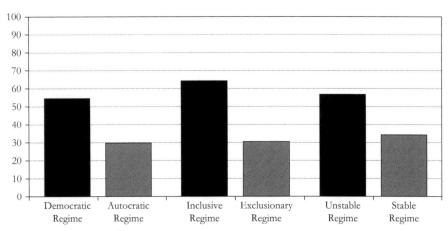

FIGURE 3.1 Percent of Governments Exercising Restraint.

the empirical evidence supports the claim that governments with unstable regimes are more likely to adopt strategies of restraint. Of the 67 governments that experienced regime change or an attempted coup in the five years prior to the start of the conflict, 38 (56.7 percent) refrained from targeting civilians. In contrast, among governments with stable regimes, only 34.3 percent exercised restraint.

Turning to the results of the regression analyses, shown in Models 1, 2, and 3 of Table 3.2, the findings provide support for all three of the hypotheses regarding government restraint. Consistent with the first hypothesis (H1), regime type, as measured by a government's polity score, is both substantively and statistically significant at the 0.05 level in all three models; the coefficients for *Government Level of Democracy* are positive, indicating that more democratic governments are more likely to adopt strategies of restraint. The results shown in Table 3.2 also support the second hypothesis (H2); the variable measuring *Inclusive Government Regime* is positive and statistically significant at the 0.05 level, meaning that governments with inclusive regimes are more likely than governments with exclusionary regimes to adopt strategies of restraint. Finally, providing evidence in support of the third hypothesis (H3), the relationship between *Unstable Government Regime* and *Government Restraint* is positive and statistically significant at the 0.01 level in all three specifications of the model. Governments with unstable regimes are more likely than governments with stable regimes to exercise restraint.

The results for these three main variables of interest – *Government Level of Democracy, Inclusive Government Regime,* and *Unstable Government Regime* – hold even after controlling for the strength of the government relative to the rebel group, the intensity of the conflict, per capita GDP, and the behavior of the rebel group. Model 2 incorporates controls for international

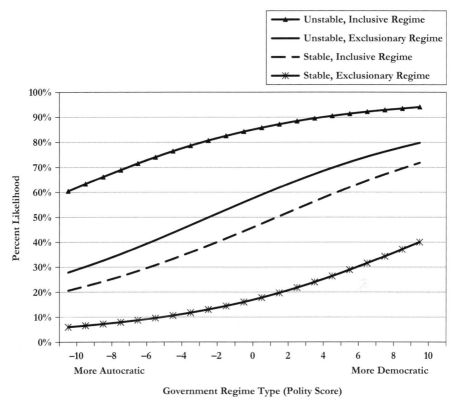

FIGURE 3.2 Likelihood of Government Restraint.
Note: To improve readability, 95 percent confidence intervals are omitted from this graph, but are included in the online Appendix.

factors, including ratification of the Second Additional Protocol to the Geneva Conventions and the degree to which the government is economically and politically interdependent; Model 3 adds controls for characteristics of the military context, including rebel group use of guerrilla tactics and the presence of multiple combatants. The findings for the three main variables of interest remain remarkably consistent in these alternate model specifications.

If the argument of this book is correct – if governments use restraint, in part, to appeal to international constituencies – then the likelihood of restraint should be highest in conflicts beginning after the end of the Cold War. The end of the Cold War brought a decline in ideologically based appeals for international support, creating space for belligerents to use the framework of international human rights and humanitarian law as a means of seeking international support. Consistent with this expectation, governments fighting in conflicts that began after the end of the Cold War are more likely to exercise restraint; the coefficient for *Post-1989 Conflict* is positive and statistically significant at the 0.05 level in Table 3.2, Model 2.

To illustrate the substantive impact of the independent variables on the likelihood of government restraint, Figure 3.2 shows the calculated probability of restraint for governments with regime types ranging from autocratic to democratic; this figure also allows for comparisons between governments with inclusive and exclusionary regimes, as well as between governments with stable and unstable regimes.[1]

As Figure 3.2 shows, the relationship between government regime type and restraint is substantively large. The likelihood that a democratic government will exercise restraint is between 1.5 and 6.1 times greater than the likelihood that an autocratic government will exercise restraint.[2] In addition, governments with inclusive regimes are more likely than governments with exclusionary regimes to exercise restraint. The likelihood of restraint is between 1.2 and 3.4 times greater for governments with inclusive regimes than for governments with exclusionary regimes. Finally, governments with unstable regimes have a likelihood of restraint that is between 1.3 and 4.6 times greater than the likelihood of restraint among governments with stable regimes.

Rebel Group Restraint

Turning to the evidence on rebel group restraint, Figure 3.3 shows the percentage of rebel groups exercising restraint, broken down by the regime type of the government opponent and characteristics of the rebel group's political system. The first two hypotheses on rebel group restraint emphasize the domestic costs of violence, positing that rebel groups with institutional incentives to be responsive to public demands (H1) and rebel groups with inclusive political systems (H2) face high domestic costs to violence, and, thus, are more likely to exercise restraint. As the first hypothesis predicts, among rebel groups that possess

---

[1] I used *Clarify* to generate all of the probabilities in this chapter. See King, Tomz, and Wittenberg 2000. For Figure 3.2, I used Model 1 in Table 3.2, holding relative strength, conflict intensity, and per capita GDP at their mean values. I calculated the probabilities for the modal government: a government facing a rebel group with a regional base of civilian support, but lacking governance institutions, which targets civilians. Throughout this chapter, when calculating probabilities for an autocratic government or for a rebel group fighting against an autocratic government, I use a polity score of −9. While it is possible for a government to have a polity score of −10, among governments in this data set, the lowest polity score is −9. When calculating probabilities for anocratic governments, I use a polity score of 0; for democratic governments, I use a polity score of 10.

[2] Some might claim that a selection effect is influencing these results – because democratic political institutions allow minority groups to express their demands nonviolently, the insurgencies that challenge democratic governments tend to be extreme groups, with little popular support. What appears to be restraint on the part of democratic governments, therefore, may simply be a lack of need to use high levels of violence against a group's civilian supporters. The majority of rebel groups fighting democratic governments, however, are well above the mean for the data set in terms of their strength relative to the government, suggesting that these groups are not extremist groups lacking popular support.

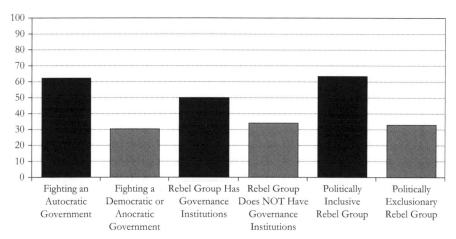

FIGURE 3.3 Percent of Rebel Groups Exercising Restraint.

governance institutions – a measure of whether rebel groups have incentives to be responsive to civilian demands – 50 percent adopted a strategy of restraint; in comparison, only 34 percent of rebel groups without governance institutions refrained from violence against civilians. The second hypothesis also finds strong support in the data. Nearly two-thirds of rebel groups with inclusive political systems exercised restraint; restraint is much less common among rebel groups with exclusionary political systems, with less than one-third of these rebel groups exercising restraint. The final hypothesis on rebel group restraint focuses on the international costs of violence, predicting that the more autocratic a rebel group's government opponent, the more likely it is that the rebel group will use restraint (H4). This first look at the data provides support for this hypothesis as well. Twenty-three of the 37 rebel groups challenging autocratic governments, or 62.2 percent, exercised restraint, while only 30.3 percent of the rebel groups fighting democratic or anocratic governments exercised restraint. The next section analyzes these hypotheses using regression analysis.

The results of statistical analyses, shown in Table 3.3, provide strong support for the first hypothesis. The coefficient for *Rebel Group Governance* is positive and statistically significant at the 0.05 level in all of the models analyzing the likelihood of rebel group restraint (Models 1–3); rebel groups that create political structures to govern their constituents are more likely to exercise restraint than rebel groups without such governance institutions. The findings also provide strong support for the second hypothesis. The coefficient for *Inclusive Rebel Group* is positive and statistically significant at the 0.01 or 0.05 level in all of the analyses of rebel group restraint, indicating that rebel groups with inclusive political objectives are more likely than rebel groups with exclusionary political objectives to exercise restraint. In addition, the results support the final hypothesis on rebel group restraint, predicting that restraint should be more likely among rebel groups facing autocratic governments. The coefficient for *Government Level of Democracy* is negative and statistically significant at the 0.01 level in all three models, indicating that the more democratic a rebel group's government opponent, the less likely the rebel group is to exercise restraint.

For all three of these main variables of interest – *Rebel Group Governance, Inclusive Rebel Group*, and *Government Level of Democracy* – the results are robust to the inclusion of a variety of control variables, including the strength of the rebel group relative to the government, the intensity of the conflict, per capita GDP, the government's behavior, the availability of financing from contraband, the use of guerrilla tactics, and the presence of multiple insurgent groups.

As in the analysis of government restraint, the findings regarding post–Cold War conflicts lend additional support to the claim that rebel groups use restraint strategically to appeal for international support; however, the relationship between the timing of the conflict and the likelihood of restraint is slightly weaker for rebel groups than for governments. The coefficient for *Post-1989 Conflict* just misses standard levels of statistical significance in the analyses of rebel group restraint (Model 3), but the coefficient is positive, suggesting that rebel groups fighting in post–Cold War conflicts may be more likely than rebel groups fighting during the Cold War to exercise restraint.

Figure 3.4 illustrates the substantive impact of the three main variables of interest, showing the probability of restraint for four types of rebel groups, when fighting against governments of different regime types: an inclusive group with and without governance institutions, as well as an exclusionary group with and without governance institutions.[3] The relationship between rebel group governance and rebel group restraint is large in substantive terms. Rebel groups that establish governance institutions are between 1.2 and 2.5 times more likely to exercise restraint than rebel groups lacking governance structures. In addition, Figure 3.4 shows that the behavior of inclusive rebel groups differs markedly from the behavior of exclusionary rebel groups. For a rebel group with an inclusive political system, the likelihood of restraint is between 1.3 and 3.8 times higher than the likelihood of restraint for a rebel group with an exclusionary political system. Finally, rebel groups fighting against autocratic governments are much more likely to abide by international humanitarian law and to refrain from using violence against civilians than are rebel groups fighting against anocratic or democratic governments. The likelihood of restraint for rebel groups confronting autocratic governments is between 2.4 and 8.3 times higher than the likelihood of restraint for rebel groups facing democratic governments.

---

[3] I used Model 1 in Table 3.3, holding relative strength, conflict intensity, and per capita GDP at their mean values. I calculated the predicted probability of restraint for the modal rebel group: one that does not finance its operations through the trafficking of contraband and is fighting against a government that targets civilians.

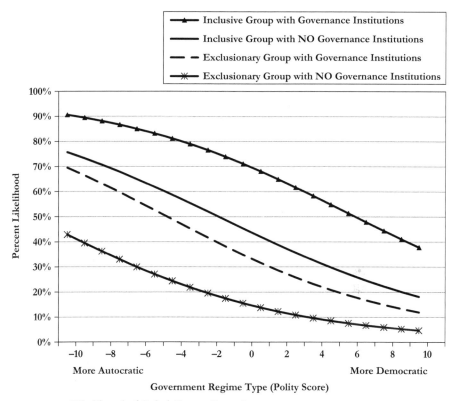

FIGURE 3.4 Likelihood of Rebel Group Restraint.
Note: To improve readability, 95 percent confidence intervals are omitted from this graph, but are included in the online appendix.

Rebel Group Restraint and the Search for International Support

The analysis performed here demonstrates that rebel groups facing autocratic governments are, indeed, more likely to exercise restraint. I posit that the causal mechanism linking government regime type to rebel group restraint is the rebel group's need to appeal to Western international constituencies for diplomatic support. Rebel groups facing autocratic opponents have difficulty using domestic pressure to elicit government concessions; instead, these groups seek to build international support, and use restraint to do so. One key observable implication of this argument is that rebel groups that decide to exercise restraint should then use this good behavior to appeal to Western actors for diplomatic support, assuming they have the capacity to do so. To examine this, I analyze rebel group international lobbying efforts.

It would be ideal to have data on rebel group activity at the UN, but the UN does not keep records of active groups that are not registered nongovernmental organizations (NGOs). Two other sources of information on rebel

group lobbying, however, are available. First, the U.S. government requires
that any representative of a foreign individual or group engaging in political
activities in the United States register with the Department of Justice.[4] Several
other countries regulate lobbyists, but most do not have mandatory registration systems for foreign groups.[5] Although the United States is only one
among many Western governments from which a rebel group might seek
diplomatic support, during the post–Cold War period, the United States has
been the most powerful state in the international system and has become
involved in many ongoing conflicts. If rebel groups that exercise restraint
are more likely to make international appeals, this pattern should be evident
in rebel group lobbying efforts in the United States.

During its 1973 to 1996 war against the Iraqi government, for example, the
Patriotic Union of Kurdistan (PUK) hired Commonwealth Consulting Corpor-
ation as its representative in the United States, stating in its Foreign Agents
Registration Act (FARA) registration documents that:

Commonwealth Consulting Corporation proposes to assist the client in developing and
fostering a policy of continued United States government support for the Kurdish people
of Iraq. Activities will include media relations as well as advocacy of this policy before
U.S. government officials. An additional area of concern is the humanitarian plight of the
Kurdish people of Iraq and the Commonwealth Consulting Corporation will seek to
develop a greater understanding of the desperate condition of the Kurdish people in
northern Iraq and the need for greater humanitarian assistance from the United States
and other western nations.[6]

The second available source of data on rebel group international lobbying
efforts is historical membership data from the Unrepresented Nations and
Peoples Organization (UNPO), an international NGO providing training and
other resources to aid unrepresented nations and minority groups in their
efforts to lobby international actors; most UNPO members are seeking greater
autonomy or independence for their group.[7] The UNPO is nonviolent, but
many of its members are affiliated with armed rebel groups.

Rebel Group Lobbying is a dichotomous variable, measuring whether the
rebel group lobbied the U.S. government or joined the UNPO while the conflict
was ongoing. Using this measure, slightly more than one-third of rebel groups

---

[4] The database is available through the U.S. Department of Justice, Foreign Agents Registration Act
(FARA) website at www.fara.gov.
[5] Malone 2004; OECD 2009; OECD 2012. Canada established a mandatory registration system in
1989, but the Canadian system is directed at lobbyists from corporate and nonprofit enterprises,
rather than foreign political actors.
[6] "Patriotic Union of Kurdistan," Exhibit B To Registration Statement Pursuant to Foreign Agents
Registration Act of 1938, Registration # 4647, Date Stamped: 1 March 1992. Available online at
www.fara.gov.
[7] Unrepresented Nations and Peoples Organization (UNPO) website, available at http://unpo.org.

TABLE 3.4 *Binary Logit Results: Rebel Group Lobbying*

	Model 1
Rebel Group Restraint	0.994**
	(0.479)
Government Restraint	-0.957*
	(0.513)
Distance to United States	0.0001
	(0.00009)
Government is U.S. Ally	-0.388
	(0.491)
Conflict Intensity – Average Annual Battle-Related Deaths, Logged	0.342*
	(0.182)
Conflict Duration, Logged	0.400
	(0.252)
Per Capita GDP, Logged	0.459*
	(0.268)
Constant	-9.322***
	(2.940)
Wald Chi^2	20.53***
Pseudo R^2	0.1621
N	102

Note: Robust standard errors in parentheses; *** $p < 0.01$, ** $p < 0.05$, * $p < 0.10$.

engaged in international lobbying efforts. Among the 43 rebel groups that exercised restraint, however, nearly half (48.8 percent) either had registered representatives in the United States or were members of the UNPO during the conflict, whereas only 28.3 percent of rebel groups that targeted civilians maintained representatives in the United States or were members of the UNPO.

Statistical analysis confirms this positive relationship between rebel group restraint and the likelihood of rebel group lobbying. Table 3.4 shows the results of a binary logit analysis, in which *Rebel Group Lobbying* is the dependent variable, with robust standard errors, clustered by country, shown in parentheses. The analysis controls for a number of other variables that may account for patterns of rebel group lobbying. Rebel groups fighting in particularly intense or lengthy conflicts may be more likely to seek international support; I thus control for *Conflict Intensity* and *Conflict Duration*. *Government Restraint* accounts for the possibility that rebel groups may have difficulty making international appeals when the government refrains from violence against civilians. Rebel groups in wealthier countries, as measured by *Per Capita GDP*, may have access to greater resources – for example, a more educated population from which to recruit members or a wealthier base from which to raise funds – which may make overseas lobbying more feasible. *Distance to the United States*, measuring the distance in kilometers between Washington, D.C., and the capital

TABLE 3.5 *Likelihood of Rebel Group Lobbying*

	Government Restraint	
	Government exercises restraint toward civilians	Government targets civilians
Rebel Group Restraint		
Rebel group exercises restraint toward civilians	39.7%	61.2%
Rebel group targets civilians	19.8%	37.4%
Difference	19.9% (1.9, 41.3)	23.8% (2.9, 43.0)

Note: 95% confidence interval shown in parentheses for the first differences.

city in the rebel group's country of origin, also accounts for variation in the logistical obstacles to lobbying.[8] Finally, rebel groups may be less likely to seek American support if their government opponent has close ties with the United States; *Government is U.S. Ally* measures whether the government had an alliance with the United States that was in force during the civil war.[9]

The analysis shows that rebel groups that exercise restraint are more likely than rebel groups that target civilians to engage in international lobbying; the coefficient for *Rebel Group Restraint* is positive and statistically significant at the 0.05 level. Not surprisingly, the relationship between government restraint and rebel group lobbying is negative and statistically significant at the 0.10 level, indicating that rebel groups are *less* likely to make appeals for international support when the government exercises restraint with respect to civilians and *more* likely to do so when the government targets civilians. Notably, these relationships between rebel group lobbying, rebel group restraint, and government restraint hold even when controlling for conflict intensity, as measured by average annual battle-related deaths.

To provide a sense of the magnitude of the relationship between rebel group lobbying and rebel group restraint, Table 3.5 calculates the predicted probability of international lobbying for a rebel group that exercises restraint and a rebel group that does not.[10] As this table shows, the likelihood that a rebel group will lobby international actors is between 19.9 and 23.8 percentage points higher for a rebel group that exercises restraint than for a rebel group that targets civilians.

---

[8] Gleditsch and Ward 2001.

[9] Data are from the Alliance Treaty Obligations and Provisions (ATOP) data set (Leeds et al. 2002).

[10] I calculated these probabilities for a rebel group fighting against a government that is not a U.S. ally (the modal category for this variable), holding all other variables at their mean.

GOVERNMENT AND REBEL GROUP CLEANSING

H6: *Governments are more likely to adopt strategies of high-casualty cleansing when the rebel group draws support from a small, geographically concentrated civilian constituency.*

H7: *Rebel groups are more likely to adopt strategies of high-casualty cleansing when they have separatist aims and the government draws support from a small, geographically concentrated civilian constituency within the separatist region.*

Government Cleansing

The hypothesis on government cleansing (H6) predicts that governments should be more likely to use cleansing when facing a rebel group whose civilian constituency is geographically concentrated. High-casualty cleansing is not a common strategy – only 12.8 percent of all governments used this strategy – but the data do suggest that characteristics of the rebel group's constituency influence government incentives to use cleansing. Among governments fighting rebel groups with a regional base of support, 18.3 percent adopted strategies of high-casualty cleansing, while less than 5 percent of governments used high-casualty cleansing when facing a rebel group without a regional base of support. Of the 13 cases in which governments used strategies of high-casualty cleansing, all but two were cases in which the rebel group had a base of support that was concentrated in a single region of the country.

The results of the regression analyses for government high-casualty cleansing, shown in Table 3.2, Model 4, provide additional confirmation of this relationship. The coefficient for *Concentrated Rebel Group Constituency* is positive and statistically significant at the 0.05 level, indicating that the likelihood of government high-casualty cleansing is higher in conflicts in which the rebel group's constituents are concentrated in a particular region. This model controls for a variety of other factors that might influence government strategy, including the strength of the government relative to the rebel group, the intensity of the conflict, per capita GDP, rebel group behavior, and variables capturing the nature of government and rebel group institutions. The results also indicate that more democratic governments are less likely to use strategies of high-casualty cleansing; the coefficient for government regime type is negative and statistically significant at the 0.01 level. This finding is consistent with the arguments I make in this book about the institutional constraints within democracies; if a democratic government were to engage in an extreme form of violence, such as ethnic cleansing, the government would likely face backlash from its constituents, even if cleansing was directed against a marginalized group.

To gain a better sense of the magnitude of the relationship between the geographic concentration of the rebel group's civilian constituency and

TABLE 3.6 *Likelihood of Government High-Casualty Cleansing*

	Government Regime Type		
	Autocratic	Anocratic	Democratic
Rebel Group Constituency			
Rebel group supporters are regionally concentrated	45.9%	4.9%	0.7%
Rebel group supporters are *not* regionally concentrated	17.1%	1.0%	0.1%
Difference	28.8%	3.9%	0.6%
	(1.7, 59.8)	(0.08, 17.2)	(0.000002, 4.1)

Note: 95% confidence interval shown in parentheses for the first differences.

government cleansing, Table 3.6 shows the predicted probability that governments of different regime types will adopt a strategy of high-casualty cleansing.[11]

As Table 3.6 illustrates, the degree to which rebel group constituents are concentrated geographically has a large, substantive impact on the predicted probability that a government will adopt a strategy of high-casualty cleansing. For democratic and anocratic governments, the likelihood of high-casualty cleansing remains low even when rebel group supporters are concentrated geographically. But for autocratic governments, the likelihood of high-casualty cleansing is substantially greater when a rebel group's civilian constituents are concentrated in a single region of the country. Among autocratic governments, the probability of high-casualty cleansing is 17.1 percent when the rebel group's civilian constituents are dispersed geographically, but increases nearly 29 percentage points – to 45.9 percent – when the government is fighting against a rebel group whose constituents are concentrated in a particular region. For all types of governments, the difference the predicted probability of high-casualty cleansing when fighting a rebel group with highly concentrated supporters and when fighting a rebel group without geographically concentrated supporters is statistically significant at the 0.05 level; the 95 percent confidence intervals all remain above zero.

Rebel Group Cleansing

According to the argument developed in Chapter 1, rebel groups are most likely to adopt strategies of high-casualty cleansing when they have separatist aims

[11] To calculate the predicted probabilities of government high-casualty cleansing, I used Model 4 in Table 3.2, holding relative strength, conflict intensity, and per capita GDP at their mean values. I calculated the predicted probability of high-casualty cleansing for the modal government: one with an inclusive, unstable regime fighting against a rebel group without governance institutions that targets civilians.

and when a small group of the government's civilian supporters live in a geographically concentrated area of the separatist region. Fewer than 10 percent of rebel groups used high-casualty cleansing. Even so, the difference in rebel group behavior, based on the size and geographic location of government supporters, is noticeable. Twenty-six rebel groups confronted a government possessing a small, geographically concentrated group of constituents living within the separatist region; of these 26 rebel groups, 30.8 percent used high-casualty cleansing. In contrast, 76 rebel groups faced governments whose supporters were not geographically concentrated within a separatist region; only one of these rebel groups used high-casualty cleansing.

The statistical analysis of rebel group high-casualty cleansing, shown in Table 3.3, Model 4, supports the claim that rebel groups assess the government's civilian constituency when choosing whether to adopt a strategy of high-casualty cleansing. The coefficient for *Concentrated Government Constituency* is positive and statistically significant at the 0.01 level, indicating that rebel groups are more likely to adopt strategies of high-casualty cleansing when facing a government with a small group of constituents living in the separatist region.

Rebel group use of high-casualty cleansing is not correlated with either the regime type of the government opponent or the presence of rebel group governance structures. These results set high-casualty cleansing apart from rebel group violence more generally, indicating that when a small, concentrated group of government constituents is located within a separatist region, the incentives for the rebel group to adopt a strategy of cleansing are so great as to overpower the factors that would otherwise encourage restraint, such as the presence of rebel group governance institutions or the challenge of confronting an autocratic opponent.

To examine the magnitude of the relationship between concentrated government constituencies and the likelihood of high-casualty cleansing, Table 3.7

TABLE 3.7 *Likelihood of Rebel Group High-Casualty Cleansing*

	Rebel Group Governance	
	Governance Institutions	No Governance Institutions
Government Constituency		
Government has small, concentrated constituency within separatist region	36.5%	32.7%
Government does *not* have small, concentrated constituency within separatist region	1.5%	1.5%
Difference	35.0% (4.7, 78.5)	31.2% (4.0, 75.1)

Note: 95% confidence interval shown in parentheses for the first differences.

shows the predicted probability that a rebel group will adopt a strategy of high-casualty cleansing for conflicts in which the government has a small, concentrated constituency living inside the separatist region and conflicts in which the government does not possess such a constituency.[12] The likelihood of rebel group high-casualty cleansing is high when the government has a small, concentrated constituency of supporters living in the separatist region, ranging from 32.7 percent for rebel groups without governance institutions to 36.5 percent for rebel groups with governance institutions. In contrast, the probability that a rebel group will adopt a strategy of high-casualty cleansing drops to less than 2 percent when the government does not possess a small, concentrated constituency living within the separatist region.

GOVERNMENT AND REBEL GROUP TERRORISM

H8:   *Governments and rebel groups are more likely to adopt strategies of terrorism when fighting against opponents whose political institutions encourage accountability to civilian constituents.*

H9:   *Among governments and rebel groups using terrorism, governments and rebel groups with exclusionary political systems are more likely than governments and rebel groups with inclusive political systems to adopt high-casualty strategies of terrorism.*

Government Terrorism

In Chapter 1, I argued that governments are more likely to adopt strategies of terrorism when facing a rebel group whose political institutions create incentives for rebel group leaders to be responsive to their constituents; governments perceive these groups as more likely to make concessions in response to rising civilian losses. Further, inclusive governments tend to be concerned about maintaining a broad base of civilian support and, therefore, are unlikely to use strategies of high-casualty terrorism. Because it is difficult to develop reliable cross-country measures of government low-casualty terrorism, I look only at government high-casualty terrorism in this section. Figure 3.5 permits an examination of whether governments behave differently when facing an opponent whose institutions demand accountability to civilians. Of the 50 governments facing rebel groups that have established governance structures, 40 percent adopted a strategy of high-casualty terrorism. In striking contrast, in the 52 conflicts in which rebel groups lacked political institutions governing

---

[12] I calculated these probabilities using Model 4 in Table 3.3; the probabilities reflect a rebel group that does not finance its operations through the trafficking of contraband and that is fighting against a government that targets civilians (the modal categories in the data set), holding government regime type, relative strength, conflict intensity, and per capita GDP at their means.

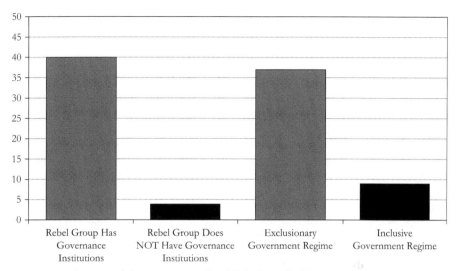

FIGURE 3.5 Percent of Governments using High-Casualty Terrorism.

civilians under their control, only two governments used a strategy of high-casualty terrorism. This initial examination of the data also lends support to the hypothesis claiming that governments needing to build a broad base of support will be wary of using high-casualty terrorism. Governments with inclusive political systems rarely engage in high-casualty terrorism; only five of the 56 governments (8.9 percent) with inclusive regimes used high-casualty terrorism, whereas 37.0 percent of governments with exclusionary regimes chose this strategy of violence.

The results of the statistical analyses, shown in Table 3.2, Model 5, provide additional support for the arguments on government high-casualty terrorism. The coefficient for *Rebel Group Governance* is substantively large, positive, and statistically significant at the 0.01 level, indicating that governments fighting against rebel groups with governance institutions are more likely than governments fighting against rebel groups without governance institutions to adopt strategies of high-casualty terrorism. Also predicted by the hypotheses, the relationship between government inclusiveness and high-casualty terrorism is negative and statistically significant at the 0.10 level, indicating that governments with inclusive regimes are less likely than governments with exclusionary regimes to engage in high-casualty terrorism. These relationships hold even after controlling for government regime type and regime stability, the geographic concentration of rebel group supporters, rebel group behavior, the strength of the government relative to the rebel group, the intensity of the conflict, and per capita GDP.

Also of note are the findings regarding other government regime characteristics. The coefficients for *Government Level of Democracy* and *Unstable Government Regime* are negative, but fall short of standard levels of statistical

TABLE 3.8 *Likelihood of Government High-Casualty Terrorism, Unstable Regime*

	Government Regime		Difference
	Exclusionary	Inclusive	
Rebel Group Governance			
Governance institutions	34.3%	11.8%	22.5%
			(−3.6, 48.8)
No governance institutions	4.5%	1.2%	3.3%
			(−0.3, 14.1)
Difference	29.8%	10.6%	
	(7.1, 57.1)	(1.9, 29.7)	

Note: 95% confidence interval shown in parentheses for the first differences.

TABLE 3.9 *Likelihood of Government High-Casualty Terrorism, Stable Regime*

	Government Regime		Difference
	Exclusionary	Inclusive	
Rebel Group Governance			
Governance institutions	66.2%	37.3%	28.9%
			(−4.4, 58.1)
No governance institutions	19.3%	5.8%	13.5%
			(−0.6, 49.9)
Difference	46.9%	31.5%	
	(9.3, 78.1)	(4.8, 67.2)	

Note: 95% confidence interval shown in parentheses for the first differences.

significance, suggesting that more democratic governments and governments with unstable regimes may be less likely to use strategies of high-casualty terrorism. These findings are consistent with the hypotheses on government restraint; governments with more democratic, inclusive, and unstable regimes have greater incentives to exercise restraint in their fighting and to avoid the most extreme forms of violence – in this case, deliberate artillery or aerial bombardment of rebel supporters, as part of a strategy of high-casualty terrorism.

To illustrate the substantive effects, Tables 3.8 and 3.9 show the predicted probability that a government will use high-casualty terrorism, with Table 3.8 showing the results for a government with an unstable regime and Table 3.9 showing the results for a government with a stable regime.[13] As these tables

---

[13] I used Model 5 in Table 3.2, holding government regime type, relative strength, conflict intensity, and per capita GDP at their mean values. I calculated the probabilities for a rebel group that targets civilians and whose supporters are concentrated in a regional base (the modal categories for these variables).

show, the presence of rebel group governance institutions has a large, substantive effect on the likelihood that a government will use high-casualty terrorism. Among governments with exclusionary regimes, the likelihood of government high-casualty terrorism is between 29.8 and 46.9 percentage points greater when the rebel group has governance institutions than when it does not. And although the probability of high-casualty terrorism is lower for governments with inclusive regimes, even among these governments the likelihood of high-casualty terrorism increases by between 10.6 and 31.5 percentage points when the rebel group has governance institutions, as compared with cases in which the rebel group does not have governance institutions.

Comparing the exclusionary government columns with the inclusive government columns shows that governments with exclusionary regimes are much more likely than governments with inclusive regimes to adopt strategies of high-casualty terrorism. The likelihood of high-casualty terrorism is between 1.8 and 3.8 times greater for a government with an exclusionary regime than for a government with an inclusive regime.

Rebel Group Terrorism

The hypotheses on rebel group terrorism make two claims: first, that rebel groups are more likely to adopt strategies of terrorism when facing a democratic opponent, and second, that the target of terrorist attacks should vary, depending on whether the rebel group has inclusive political objectives. The descriptive statistics provide preliminary support for these arguments. Table 3.10 displays the number of groups that used a strategy of terrorism, when fighting against democratic, anocratic, and autocratic opponents. Among the 22 rebel groups fighting democratic opponents, terrorism is the dominant tactic, with 90.9 percent (20 rebel groups) carrying out bomb attacks against civilian targets. Among rebel groups fighting against nondemocratic governments, the use of terrorism is much less common. Of the 44 rebel groups fighting against anocratic governments – governments possessing both democratic and autocratic characteristics – only 15 groups (34.1 percent) bombed civilian targets. The percentage of groups using terrorism drops even further for

TABLE 3.10 *Rebel Group Use of Terrorism*

	Rebel Groups Using Terrorism	Rebel Groups *Not* Using Terrorism	Total
Democratic Government	20 (90.9%)	2 (9.1%)	22 (100%)
Anocratic Government	15 (34.1%)	29 (65.9%)	44 (100%)
Autocratic Government	3 (8.1%)	34 (91.9%)	37 (100%)

TABLE 3.11 *Rebel Group Use of High- and Low-Casualty Terrorism*

	Bombings of High-Casualty Civilian Targets	Bombings of Low-Casualty Civilian Targets	Total High- and Low- Casualty Terrorism
Inclusive Rebel Groups	3 (42.9%)	4 (57.1%)	7 (100%)
Exclusionary Rebel Groups	27 (87.1%)	4 (12.9%)	31 (100%)

rebel groups fighting against autocratic governments; only 3 of 37 rebel groups (8.1 percent) used terrorism when faced with an autocratic opponent.

Among rebel groups using terrorism, inclusive and exclusionary groups focus their attacks on different types of targets, as Table 3.11 shows. Inclusive rebel groups whose political objectives demand a broad base of civilian support tend to direct attacks against low-casualty targets, while exclusionary groups with narrower civilian constituencies tend to attack high-casualty targets. Of the seven inclusive rebel groups that used terrorism, 57.1 percent focused their attacks on low-casualty targets, whereas among the 31 exclusionary rebel groups that used terrorism, only 12.9 percent attacked primarily low-casualty targets. High-casualty terrorism, in contrast, is much more common among rebel groups with exclusionary political objectives. More than 87 percent of the exclusionary rebel groups using terrorism attacked high-casualty targets, while only 42.9 percent of the inclusive insurgencies using terrorism attacked high-casualty targets.

To further explore the relationship between rebel group terrorism, government regime type, and rebel group political goals, I run two sets of statistical analyses, the results of which are shown in Table 3.3, Models 5 and 6. Model 5 is an analysis of rebel group terrorism in general, including the bombing of low- and high-casualty targets, while Model 6 is an analysis of high-casualty terrorism. Looking first at the results for terrorism in general, the coefficient for *Government Level of Democracy* is substantively large and statistically significant at the 0.01 level; the coefficient is positive, indicating that, as predicted, the more democratic a rebel group's opponent, the more likely it is that the rebel group will use terrorism. This relationship between government regime type and rebel group terrorism holds even after controlling for the rebel group's political institutions, the military strength of the rebel group, the intensity of the conflict, per capita GDP, rebel group financing, and the presence of multiple rebel groups.[14]

---

[14] In robustness checks, I controlled for the region where the conflict took place, which does not alter the results for government regime type or the inclusiveness of the rebel group's political system. These analyses indicate that rebel groups in Eastern Europe, Latin America, and North

Turning to the analyses of high-casualty terrorism, the results in Model 6 are similar to the results for terrorism in general (Model 5), but the one notable difference is that the coefficient for *Inclusive Rebel Group*, although negative in both of the analyses, reaches statistical significance only in Model 6. This finding indicates that while rebel groups with inclusive political objectives are not any less likely than exclusionary rebel groups to use terrorism in general, they are less likely to use high-casualty forms of terrorism, as the hypothesis on rebel group political objectives predicts.

To facilitate interpretation of these statistical results, Figure 3.6 shows the probability that a rebel group will adopt a strategy of terrorism when fighting against governments of different regime types; I calculate these probabilities for the modal rebel group: an exclusionary rebel group without governance institutions.[15]

As Figure 3.6 illustrates, the likelihood that a rebel group will use terrorism increases dramatically as government regime type moves from autocratic to democratic; when confronting a fully autocratic government, the likelihood that a rebel group will use terrorism is only 7.4 percent, lending support to the argument that rebel groups think a strategy of terrorism will be ineffective when directed against an autocratic government unresponsive to public demands. The probability that a rebel group will pursue a strategy of terrorism is nearly five times greater, increasing to 35.4 percent, when the rebel group is fighting against an anocratic government. Perhaps most striking, however, is the result for democracy; when facing a fully democratic government, the likelihood that a rebel group will use a strategy of terrorism increases by about 45 percentage points to 80.5 percent. These results provide strong support for the hypothesis put forth in this book, positing that rebel groups make calculations about whether to engage in terrorism based on an assessment of the government's sensitivity to the demands of its domestic constituents.

To examine the second hypothesis on rebel group terrorism, regarding the relationship between rebel group political objectives and high-casualty terrorism, Table 3.12 shows the probability of attacking high-casualty targets for inclusive rebel groups as compared with exclusionary rebel groups.[16] Since the

Africa and the Middle East are more likely to use terrorism, while rebel groups in North Africa and the Middle East are more likely to use high-casualty terrorism.

[15] To calculate the probabilities in Figure 3.6 I used Model 5 shown in Table 3.3, holding relative strength, conflict intensity, and per capita GDP at their mean values. The reported probabilities are for a rebel group without governance institutions that does not finance its operations through the trafficking of contraband and that is fighting in a multiparty conflict, against a government that targets civilians (the modal categories for these variables).

[16] To calculate these probabilities I used Table 3.3, Model 6, holding relative strength, conflict intensity, and per capita GDP at their mean values. The reported probabilities are for a rebel group without governance institutions that does not finance its operations through the trafficking of contraband and that is fighting in a multiparty conflict, against a government that targets civilians (the modal categories for these variables).

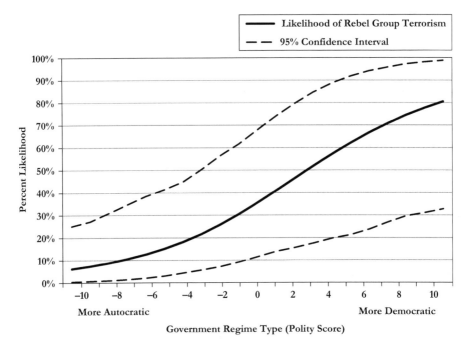

FIGURE 3.6 Likelihood of Rebel Group Terrorism, Exclusionary Rebel Group.

TABLE 3.12 *Likelihood of Rebel Group High-Casualty Terrorism*

	Government Regime Type		
	Autocratic	Anocratic	Democratic
Rebel Group Political Objectives			
Exclusionary	9.1%	39.7%	84.0%
Inclusive	2.3%	12.1%	51.1%
Difference	6.8%	27.6%	32.9%
	(0.9, 20.3)	(8.7, 49.0)	(3.6, 61.5)

Note: 95% confidence interval shown in parentheses for the first differences.

findings on terrorism indicate that rebel groups, indeed, are more likely to engage in terrorism the more democratic their opponent, the probabilities for rebel groups fighting against democracies are most relevant. For an exclusionary rebel group with a narrow base of civilian support, the likelihood of engaging in high-casualty terrorism is high, at 84.0 percent. The probability of attacking high-casualty targets drops nearly 33 percentage points, to 51.1

percent, for an inclusive rebel group – one whose political objectives demand support from a broad constituency.

ASSESSING ALTERNATIVE EXPLANATIONS

Alternative Explanations for Government Violence and Restraint

The quantitative evidence provides little support for alternative arguments claiming that the military context influences patterns of government behavior across conflicts. Research has shown that in interstate conflicts high conflict costs are associated with a greater likelihood of civilian targeting, but the results of the analyses shown in Table 3.2 indicate that the same does not hold true for civil wars. The coefficient for *Conflict Intensity* is not statistically significant in the analyses of government high-casualty cleansing or government high-casualty terrorism. In civil wars, governments fighting in intense, costly conflicts are no more likely to target civilians with violence than governments fighting in less intense, less costly conflicts. Nor is conflict intensity associated with the likelihood of government restraint; governments fighting in low-intensity conflicts are no more likely to respect the immunity of civilians than governments fighting in high-intensity conflicts.

The findings regarding *Relative Strength* are mixed. This variable is measured as the ratio of government to rebel group troops; higher values represent governments that are stronger, relative to their rebel opponents. Thus, the negative relationship between relative strength and government high-casualty cleansing indicates that militarily strong governments are less likely than militarily weak governments to adopt a strategy of high-casualty cleansing. But the relative strength of the belligerents does not show any clear association with the likelihood of either government restraint or government high-casualty terrorism; in these models, the coefficients for *Relative Strength* are far from standard levels of statistical significance.

Arguments positing that governments are more likely to target civilians and less likely to exercise restraint in conflicts involving guerrilla warfare find little support in the data. In fact, the results suggest that the opposite may be true: in the analysis of government restraint (Model 3), the coefficient for *Guerrilla Conflict* is positive, but does not reach statistical significance; these results suggest that, if anything, governments may be more likely to exercise restraint and less likely to use violence in conflicts fought using guerrilla tactics. And, finally, the evidence provides some weak support for the claim that the belligerents behave differently in conflicts involving multiple insurgent groups, with the evidence suggesting that governments may be more likely to target civilians and less likely to exercise restraint when facing multiple insurgent groups. The *Multiparty Conflict* coefficient is negative, as this argument would predict, but falls just short of standard levels of statistical significance.

Turning to international factors, the findings do not provide strong support for arguments claiming that restraint is more likely among economically and politically interdependent governments or among governments that have ratified relevant instruments of international humanitarian law (Table 3.2, Model 2). The variable measuring the extent of a country's involvement in *International Trade* is positively associated with government restraint, as is the variable measuring *IGO Membership*, but the coefficients for these variables are far from standard levels of statistical significance. Governments that rely heavily on international trade and that participate in IGOs are no more likely to exercise restraint than governments that are not highly involved in the activities of the international community. In addition, contrary to the expectations of international legal scholars, governments that ratified relevant international humanitarian law treaties are no more likely to refrain from attacking civilians than governments that had not ratified these treaties prior to the conflict; the coefficient for the variable capturing whether a government *Ratified Additional Protocol II* is far from statistical significance.

A final alternative explanation argues that a dynamic of reciprocity may lead to mutual restraint in civil war. If the reciprocity hypothesis is correct, the relationship between government behavior and rebel group behavior should be positive; restraint among governments should be matched with restraint among rebel groups. The results do not support this hypothesis. Although the relationship between government and rebel group restraint is positive, the coefficient does not achieve statistical significance.

The findings also suggest that governments with high levels of GDP per capita may be more likely to adopt strategies of high-casualty cleansing. This may reflect the fact that high-casualty cleansing is an intensely violent strategy, which requires the devotion of substantial military resources to eliminating entirely the insurgent's base of support, something that may be more feasible for wealthier governments.

Alternative Explanations for Rebel Group Violence and Restraint

While the arguments put forth in this book emphasize the strategic calculation that rebel groups make regarding their need to build support from domestic and international constituencies, some have posited that rebel group behavior is closely linked to the organizational structure of the armed group. These arguments claim that restraint is most likely, and violence least likely, among armed groups that have a high degree of control over the use of violence among their members. Jeremy Weinstein argues that rebel groups without access to external sources of financing are the groups most likely to develop effective means of controlling their members and, therefore, most likely to refrain from violence against civilians, while rebel groups with access to external sources of financing are more likely to abuse civilians. The quantitative evidence does not, however, provide support for these arguments. The *Contraband* coefficient is far from achieving statistical significance in the analyses of rebel group restraint, high-casualty cleansing, and terrorism. This result contrasts sharply with the common wisdom; although rebel groups such as the Revolutionary United Front (RUF) in Sierra Leone have made headlines with their horrific atrocities against civilians and their exploitation of diamond resources, the evidence indicates that these two conflict characteristics – natural resource exploitation and violence against civilians – are not, in fact, correlated with one another across cases of civil war.

Another means of assessing whether an armed group's organizational structure might be tied to violence against civilians is to look at more direct measures of *Rebel Group Organizational Control*, capturing the extent to which leaders exert control over their forces (results shown in the online Appendix).[17] The coefficient for *Rebel Group Organizational Control* is not statistically significant in any of the analyses of rebel group restraint, rebel group high-casualty cleansing, rebel group terrorism, or rebel group high-casualty terrorism, but this is not particularly surprising in light of the argument of this book. For groups with strategic incentives to use violence against civilians, mechanisms of organizational control are likely to lead to more effective perpetration of violence, while for groups with incentives to exercise restraint, mechanisms of organizational control are likely to lead to more effective limits on the use of violence.[18] Measures of organizational control should not, therefore, be associated with any particular strategy of violence or with restraint.

Turning to arguments regarding the military context, the findings do not show evidence of a relationship between the intensity of the conflict and the likelihood of rebel group violence or restraint. The coefficients for *Conflict Intensity* do not reach statistical significance in any of the models; in civil wars, rebel groups do not appear to use violence against civilians as a means of coping with rising conflict costs, nor are rebel groups fighting in low-intensity conflicts any more likely to exercise restraint.

Contrary to the common claim that violence against civilians is a weapon of the weak and that strong rebel groups have little need to engage in violence, the quantitative evidence indicates that the strength of the rebel group has little bearing on the likelihood of restraint across cases of civil war. If anything, the results of the statistical analyses indicate that the relationship between rebel group strength and rebel group behavior may be the opposite. The *Relative Strength* variable measures the ratio of government to rebel group troops; higher values of this measure represent stronger governments and weaker rebel groups. Although the coefficient for *Relative Strength* is not statistically significant, it is positive, suggesting that weak rebel groups may be more likely – not less likely – than strong rebel groups to use restraint.

The results do, however, indicate that the relative strength of the belligerents may be relevant to understanding rebel group strategies of high-casualty

---

[17] Cunningham, Gleditsch, and Salehyan 2009.   [18] Wood 2009.

cleansing. The negative and statistically significant coefficient for *Relative Strength* in Table 3.3, Model 4 indicates that weak rebel groups are less likely to adopt strategies of high-casualty cleansing. This finding – that strong rebel groups are more likely to adopt strategies of high-casualty cleansing – is broadly consistent with the strategic hypothesis put forth in this book. I argue that separatist rebel groups use cleansing when a small, geographically concentrated group of the government's supporters lives inside the separatist region. Such rebel groups expel government constituents from the separatist region as a means of solidifying their own ethnonational group's claim to the territory. Such a strategy – of creating a de facto autonomous region – requires some degree of strength. Only those rebel groups that already possess the means to rule the separatist region are likely to attempt such a strategy.

The coefficient measuring *Relative Strength* is positive and statistically significant in the analysis of rebel group terrorism, indicating that weaker rebel groups are more likely to engage in terrorism. This finding is consistent with the common claim that terrorism is a weapon of the weak. Interestingly, this does not extend to rebel group high-casualty terrorism; in this analysis (Model 6), the coefficient for *Relative Strength*, though positive, is not statistically significant, suggesting that rebel group decisions to engage in high-casualty attacks on public civilian targets are not driven by a need to compensate for military weakness.

Government Restraint has little influence on the likelihood of rebel group restraint or rebel group terrorism, but is negatively correlated with rebel group high-casualty cleansing; conflicts in which the rebel group engages in high-casualty cleansing appear to involve high levels of atrocities on both sides. Finally, although the coefficient for *Guerrilla Conflict* does not reach standard levels of statistical significance in the analysis of rebel group restraint, the coefficient is negative, suggesting that rebel groups may be less likely to use restraint when fighting in conflicts that involve guerrilla warfare. This is consistent with arguments claiming that incentives to target civilians are greater in conflicts involving guerrilla warfare, in which civilians are deeply enmeshed in conflict. However, arguments regarding guerrilla warfare have typically focused on governments, arguing that governments are more likely to target civilians and less likely to exercise restraint when confronting a guerrilla insurgency. Interestingly, the findings here suggest that rebel groups, not governments, may be less restrained during guerrilla war.

Several other findings are worth noting. First, the coefficient for *Per Capita GDP* is positive and statistically significant at the 0.10 level in the analysis of high-casualty terrorism. Studies of transnational terrorism have found that transnational groups are more likely to target wealthier countries;[19] the findings here suggest a similar pattern among domestic insurgencies. If the argument of this book is correct and rebel groups use terrorism as a means of

---

[19] Krueger and Laitin 2008.

increasing the costs of the conflict for the government, it is not particularly surprising that rebel groups are more likely to use terrorism against wealthy opponents; accustomed to a high standard of living, citizens in wealthy countries may be particularly likely to lobby for a change in government policy as a means of halting further terrorist violence. Second, the coefficient for *Multiparty Conflict* is not statistically significant in any of the models. This finding is difficult to reconcile with the theoretical logic of the outbidding hypothesis, which claims that rival groups compete with one another for popular support by carrying out dramatic attacks on the opponent's civilian constituency. If this theoretical logic were correct, one would expect that multiparty conflicts should be associated with terrorism in general as well as with the most sensational forms of terrorism – high-casualty attacks on populated civilian targets. In addition, one would expect restraint to be less common in multiparty conflicts.

CONCLUSION

Using original data on government and rebel group violence against civilians, the quantitative analyses in this chapter lend support to the claim that government and rebel group behavior is driven by strategic calculations. In making these calculations, governments and rebel groups weigh the costs of violence based on an assessment of their own relationship with domestic and international constituencies. For governments and rebel groups that seek support from broad domestic and international constituencies, the costs of engaging in violence are high; as the quantitative analyses of restraint show, it is these governments and rebel groups that are most likely to exercise restraint. Governments and rebel groups weigh the benefits of violence based on their opponent's relationship with its civilian constituents. The more geographically concentrated the opponent's civilian constituents, the more feasible a strategy of cleansing becomes. This bears out in the statistical analyses, where the findings indicate that governments facing rebel groups with highly concentrated constituents are more likely to adopt strategies of high-casualty cleansing, while rebel groups are more likely to use high-casualty cleansing when fighting against governments with small, concentrated groups of constituents living within the separatist region. Finally, the evidence provides support for the contention that governments and rebel groups make calculations about the opponent's likely response to civilian losses; governments and rebel groups are more likely to adopt strategies of terrorism when facing an opponent likely to be sensitive to civilian losses.

In addition, the quantitative analyses in this chapter suggest the need to refine much of the common wisdom regarding civilian targeting. Measures of organizational control cannot account for patterns of either government or rebel group violence or restraint across conflicts, likely because organizational capacity can be used either to propagate violence, or to enforce restraint. The evidence does not support the claim that either governments or rebel groups target civilians out of desperation when conflict costs are high; this is an important way in which the determinants of civilian targeting in civil war differ from the determinants of civilian targeting in interstate war. In addition, the evidence shows that the impact of belligerent strength on the likelihood of violence against civilians varies, depending on the strategy of violence or restraint one examines. Although weak rebel groups are more likely to use terrorism, they are not any more likely to use the highest casualty forms of terrorism and are *less* likely to use high-casualty cleansing. In addition, strong rebel groups are not any more likely to exercise restraint. The analyses of government behavior indicate that weak governments are more likely to use high-casualty cleansing, but government strength is not associated with either government high-casualty terrorism or government restraint. The remaining five empirical chapters of the book are organized by strategy of violence and use case studies to examine more carefully the theoretical arguments put forth in this book.

4

Government Restraint in Indonesia

As the evidence presented in Chapters 2 and 3 shows, governments vary widely in the extent to which they direct violence against civilians during civil war. Although it is true that many civil wars involve brutal attacks on civilians, it is also true that more than 40 percent of governments waging civil war do not commit extreme abuses against civilians, largely complying with international legal standards requiring respect for the immunity of noncombatants. The governments most likely to exercise restraint in their fighting are governments facing high domestic and international costs to violence. How governments weigh the costs of violence depends on the government's relationship with its own domestic and international constituencies. Governments that need support from broad domestic and international constituencies face the greatest constraints on their use of violence; these governments are likely to exercise restraint rather than risk domestic and international backlash by targeting civilians. The statistical results provide support for this claim, showing that of the 102 governments engaged in civil wars from 1989 to 2010, governments with democratic regimes, inclusive regimes, and unstable regimes, indeed, were more likely than other types of governments to refrain from violence against civilians.

While the statistical analyses provide strong evidence that these patterns of government behavior hold true across cases of civil war, case studies can help to shed light on the causal mechanisms driving the statistical correlations. Cases in which key variables of interest, such as government regime type, changed during the conflict are particularly useful in exploring these causal mechanisms. In the post–Cold War period, only two governments transitioned from autocracy to democracy during an ongoing civil war: Indonesia and Nepal. In Nepal, the regime transition took place, in large part, because of political pressure resulting from the ongoing conflict with

Maoists.[1] In Indonesia, however, the regime transition was caused by factors unrelated to ongoing conflicts, making this a particularly useful case for examining arguments regarding the impact of regime type and transition on government and rebel group behavior.

For more than thirty of its first fifty years of independence, Indonesia was ruled by the autocratic regime of President Suharto. During his rule, which lasted from 1965 until 1998, three separatist movements developed in Indonesia – in East Timor, Aceh, and Irian Jaya (Papua). I focus in this chapter on the conflicts in Aceh and East Timor, as more detailed information is available about these conflicts. The insurgencies in Aceh and East Timor were both ongoing in the late 1990s, when Indonesia's transition to democracy began. Although Suharto's regime had faced growing domestic political opposition in the 1990s, and increasing pressures for liberalization of the political system, it retained its authoritarian hold on power and avoided major political reform until the Asian financial crisis hit the region.[2] The financial crisis contributed to the collapse of the Indonesian economy, precipitating widespread popular protests that ultimately brought down Suharto's regime in 1998 and ushered in a transition to democracy.

This chapter examines the Indonesia case in depth, tracing government counterinsurgency operations in Aceh and East Timor before, during, and after democratic transition, while the next chapter examines rebel group strategies in Aceh and East Timor. Both chapters incorporate evidence from interviews I conducted in Indonesia's capital city of Jakarta and in the Acehnese provincial capital of Banda Aceh in July and August 2006. I interviewed a diverse set of individuals with expertise on the conflicts in Aceh and East Timor, including government officials, rebel group members, human rights activists, scholars, journalists, and officials from Indonesian and international nongovernmental organizations (NGOs).[3] As the argument of this book would predict, during its democratic transition, the Indonesian government made significant changes in its strategies for confronting the insurgencies in Aceh and East Timor – acknowledging past human rights abuses, initiating military and police reforms to improve respect for human rights, altering counterinsurgency strategies to reduce attacks on civilians, and pursuing peace talks with both rebel groups. The case study also highlights the challenges new leaders face as they struggle to reform government institutions and policies, often in the face of opposition from members of the old regime. In Indonesia, new civilian leaders confronted resistance to their policy changes from members of the still-powerful military.

---

[1] Shah 2008.   [2] Liddle 1996; Aspinall 2005.
[3] I identify these sources by their affiliation rather than by name. Although some of those I interviewed did not object to the use of their name, others preferred anonymity.

COUNTERINSURGENCY UNDER SUHARTO: STRATEGIES OF
HIGH-CASUALTY CONTROL AND CLEANSING

Background to the Conflicts in Aceh and East Timor

Aceh and East Timor are located at the northern and southern tips of the
Indonesian archipelago, respectively. Both regions have populations that are
ethnically distinct from other regions of Indonesia. Indonesia's largest and most
politically dominant ethnic group is the Javanese, constituting more than
40 percent of the population, but in Aceh, the Acehnese are the largest ethnic
group and in East Timor, the Timorese are the ethnic majority. East Timor,
however, is smaller in size than Aceh, and more ethnically homogenous. Population figures for Aceh are available for 1980, several years after the insurgency
began, estimating the total population at more than 2.6 million living in a
territory of more than 55,000 square kilometers.[4] According to the 1980
census, 67.5 percent of the population spoke Acehnese at home, with a number
of other ethnic groups accounting for the remainder of the population.[5] At the
start of its insurgency in 1975, East Timor was about one-quarter the size of
Aceh in terms of both its population and its territory, with a population of
about 650,000 and a territory of about 15,000 square kilometers.[6] In addition,
East Timor's population was more ethnically homogenous; in the last census
prior to the insurgency more than 98 percent of the population identified as
Timorese.[7]

Unlike the regions of Aceh and Papua, which were incorporated into Indo-
nesia after the country gained independence from Dutch colonial rule in 1949,
East Timor was a Portuguese colony until 1975. During the process of decol-
onization from Portugal, two major political parties emerged – the Timorese
Democratic Union (União Democrática Timorense, UDT), which advocated a
gradual progression toward independence, and the Revolutionary Front for an
Independent East Timor (Frente Revolucionária do Timor Leste Independente,
Fretilin), which called for more immediate independence. As Fretilin's popularity grew and transition to an independent government seemed imminent, the
UDT, with the support of the Indonesian government, launched a coup attempt
in September 1975, forcing the departure of Portuguese officials and prompting
a brief armed conflict with Fretilin. Fretilin had retaken control of the region by
October 1975, but the Indonesian government invaded East Timor on December 7, 1975, and forcibly annexed the territory.[8] Following the invasion,

---

[4] From Indonesian census data, available online from Statistics Indonesia at www.bps.go.id.
[5] Aspinall 2009, 4–5.　　[6] Kiernan 2003, 591; Staveteig 2007, 14.
[7] Hajek 2000, 217; Kiernan 2003, 590; Silva and Ball 2006, 13.
[8] On the events leading up to Indonesia's annexation, see Taylor 1999b. See also "Indonesia Tidies
the Map: The Spectre of a Mini-Angola in East Timor Means that Indonesia Will Probably Get
Away with Grabbing It," *Economist*, 13 December 1975.

Fretilin withdrew to the mountainous interior of East Timor and organized armed opposition to Indonesia, with the group's forces estimated at 2,500 regular troops, 7,000 militia members, and 20,000 reserves.[9] Although Indonesian forces occupied several major towns, they were unable to gain control over much of the territory of East Timor.

The separatist rebellion in Aceh began on December 4, 1976, when the Free Aceh Movement (Gerakan Aceh Merdeka, GAM) issued a declaration of independence from Indonesia. The insurgency had its roots in a history of grievance against the Indonesian government related, in large part, to frustration with the Indonesian government's repeated failure to follow through with plans for regional autonomy – what one GAM member referred to as "empty promises."[10] Shortly after Indonesia gained independence in 1949, the government revoked Aceh's status as a province and incorporated the region into the neighboring province of Northern Sumatra, precipitating an Acehnese insurgency, called the Darul Islam rebellion.[11] To end the rebellion, the Indonesian government granted special status to Aceh, which purportedly gave Acehnese leaders control over religion, education, and customary law in the province; in practice, however, special status had little impact.[12] Many of GAM's early members participated in the Darul Islam rebellion and as Edward Aspinall, an expert on the Acehnese conflict, argues, the experience of the Darul Islam rebellion likely contributed to the development of a sense of unique Acehnese national identity.[13] GAM's founder and leader, Hasan di Tiro, in mobilizing popular support for renewed rebellion in the 1970s, argued that Aceh constituted a unique nation, deserving of independence from what he portrayed as Indonesian colonial rule.[14]

During the early years of its rebellion, GAM remained small, focusing primarily on mobilizing popular support for the insurgency and, as one GAM member phrased it, working "to remind people of their separate identity as Acehnese."[15] GAM carried out its first violent attacks in late 1977, targeting industrial sites near Lhokseumawe, which was the region's industrial center and the base for foreign corporations involved in oil and natural gas extraction.[16] The Indonesian government's refusal to share natural resource revenues with the Acehnese was among GAM's central grievances.[17] The Indonesian government responded by sending a military Special Forces (Kopassus) unit to combat the insurgency; by the early 1980s most of GAM's leadership had been killed or

---

[9] Taylor 1999b, 70.

[10] Interview with GAM member and delegate to peace negotiations, Banda Aceh, 8 August 2006.

[11] Aspinall 2006; Miller 2006.   [12] Miller 2006; Sulaiman 2006.

[13] Aspinall 2006; Aspinall 2007a; Aspinall 2007b.   [14] Aspinall 2002; Aspinall 2007a.

[15] Interview with GAM political leader, Banda Aceh, 7 August 2006. See also di Tiro 1984; Schulze 2003.

[16] Robinson 1998; Schulze 2003; Schulze 2004.

[17] Di Tiro 1984; Schulze 2003. On the role that natural resources have played in the Acehnese conflict, see Aspinall 2007a.

arrested, or had fled into exile.[18] Still led by di Tiro, who had gone into exile in Sweden, GAM spent the 1980s regrouping. It recruited members from within the Acehnese diaspora in Malaysia and, in the late 1980s, sent several hundred GAM members to Libya for training.[19] The newly trained GAM forces returned to Aceh in May 1988 and, with weapons smuggled through Thailand, began launching small-scale guerrilla attacks on government and military targets.[20]

Indonesian Counterinsurgency Operations under Suharto

During the rebellions in East Timor and Aceh, Indonesia was led by President Suharto, a general in the Indonesian armed forces who had taken power following a 1965 military coup. Suharto's government drew support from a narrow domestic civilian constituency, and thus faced low domestic costs to violence – particularly violence directed at ethnic minorities in the distant regions of Aceh and East Timor. The military played an important role in government under Suharto and although opposition parties were permitted, their activities were severely restricted and elections were routinely manipulated to retain power for Suharto's Golkar party.[21] On its 21-point scale, ranging from most democratic (+10) to most autocratic (–10), the Polity IV Project rated Suharto's government as a –7 (an autocracy) for nearly all of the years it was in power. In addition, Suharto's regime was both exclusionary and stable; the Javanese were the dominant political group and the government had been in power for about a decade by the time the Acehnese and Timorese insurgencies began. Furthermore, Suharto came to power in the midst of the Cold War and positioned himself as an anti-Communist leader, helping him to avoid any serious international criticism of his counterinsurgency operations and obviating the need for his government to use restraint as a means of appealing for support from a broader international constituency.

Sustained in power by narrow domestic and international constituencies, Suharto's government had few incentives to exercise restraint in its confrontations with insurgents in Aceh and East Timor. As the argument of this book would predict, Suharto's government, when faced with insurgencies receiving significant support from Acehnese and Timorese civilians, adopted high-casualty counterinsurgency strategies. Suharto refused to negotiate with either

---

[18] "Rebel 'Commander' Captured in Aceh," BBC Summary of World Broadcasts, 14 July 1982; "Rebel Commander Captured," BBC Summary of World Broadcasts, 23 December 1982.

[19] Schulze 2003. Interviews with former GAM senior military commander, Jakarta, 5 August 2006; GAM political leader, Banda Aceh, 7 August 2006.

[20] "5 Killed in Raid on Military Outpost in Aceh," *Straits Times*, 29 May 1990; "Two Suspected Aceh Rebels Killed by Indonesian Troops," *Straits Times*, 7 June 1990. Interviews with former GAM senior military commander, Jakarta, 5 August 2006; GAM political leader, Banda Aceh, 7 August 2006; Indonesian journalist, Jakarta, 3 August 2006; former commander in charge of Indonesian military operations in Aceh, Jakarta, 3 August 2006.

[21] On Suharto's rule and the collapse of his government, see Aspinall 2005.

Fretilin or GAM; sent military combat units to both regions; and restricted access by journalists, NGOs, and foreigners.[22] However, the form of government violence differed slightly in East Timor as compared with Aceh. In the smaller, more ethnically homogenous East Timor, the government adopted a strategy of high-casualty cleansing, seeking to physically separate the Fretilin insurgents from their base of support. In the larger, more ethnically heterogeneous Aceh, a strategy of cleansing would have been difficult to implement; instead, the government used high-casualty control, targeting suspected insurgent collaborators as a means of deterring others from aiding the insurgency.

In East Timor, as part of its strategy of high-casualty cleansing, the Indonesian government forcibly relocated hundreds of thousands of Timorese into government-run villages located in peripheral areas, away from the center of Fretilin operations in the interior of the country.[23] To force civilians out of the interior and to pave the way for ground offensives against Fretilin, Indonesia used aerial and naval bombardment to destroy vegetation, crops, and villages and used ground forces to surround the civilian population and forcibly transport them to resettlement areas.[24] The most severe government abuses occurred in the first years of the conflict, with one scholar estimating that during the five years following Indonesia's invasion, approximately 150,000 East Timorese were killed.[25] A 1985 Amnesty International report placed the number of East Timorese killed in the ten years since Indonesia's invasion at 200,000 – amounting to one-third of East Timor's population.[26]

During ground operations, the destruction of villages and killing of civilians was common. In August 1976, for example, it was reported that Indonesian forces burned six villages near Zumalai in the western region of East Timor, killing all of the civilians living in these villages.[27] Another village in the western region, Arsabai, was targeted by Indonesian forces in early 1978; all of the civilians in Arsabai were killed.[28] In an attempt to flush Fretilin out of East Timor's mountainous terrain, the government forced civilians to participate in massive search operations, referred to as "fence of legs" operations, in which civilians were made to walk in front of Indonesian troops as they scoured East Timor's interior for Fretilin units and bases. During these search operations in the early 1980s thousands of civilians believed to be supporters of Fretilin were arrested and in 1983, the Indonesian government admitted that it was holding 4,000 individuals in a detention center on Atauro Island off the northern coast of East

---

[22] Taylor 1999b, 71. See also "East Timor: Remember Us?" *Economist*, 26 May 1979; Human Rights Watch World Report 1992; Amnesty International 1993a; Amnesty International 1994.
[23] Taylor 1999b.
[24] *New York Times* Abstracts, 4 January 1976. Amnesty International 1985.
[25] Kiernan 2003, 593–594.   [26] Amnesty International 1985, 6.   [27] Taylor 1999b, 71.
[28] Taylor 1999b, 85.

Timor.[29] Many other civilians believed to be sympathetic to Fretilin were killed. In one of the most extreme incidents reported, Indonesian troops killed approximately 400 civilians in September 1981 at Mount Aitana near the town of Lacluta in the central region of East Timor.[30] Indonesian forces carried out similar massacres in 1983, killing several hundred civilians and burning homes in a series of massacres in the village of Kraras and surrounding areas.[31]

In addition to the civilians killed directly by Indonesian forces during these early years of counterinsurgency, many thousands of Timorese civilians died of hunger and disease, as destruction of crops and displacement of entire villages took their toll on food production. Reports in 1979 estimated that in some villages, death rates from hunger and disease were as high as 12 people per day and that approximately 300,000 people – more than half of the population – were in need of food aid.[32]

With the Timorese civilian population decimated, counterinsurgency operations decreased in intensity during the late 1980s and early 1990s. Still, Indonesian forces continued to detain, interrogate, and kill civilians believed to be Fretilin sympathizers.[33] Many of these killings were incidents in which one or several unarmed civilians were killed, but in several cases Indonesian forces killed large groups of unarmed civilians at once.[34] The most publicized of these incidents was the November 12, 1991 massacre, which took place in the Santa Cruz Cemetery in the capital city of Dili following a memorial service for a proindependence activist killed by Indonesian forces.[35] Indonesian forces fired deliberately into a crowd of 3,000–4,000 unarmed civilians who were participating in a procession after the memorial service. Estimates place the total number of civilians killed somewhere between 75 and 200, with some estimates as high as 270.[36] Reports suggest that the government's attack was planned in advance and that Indonesian forces tried to cover up the massacre in the days following the attack by killing an additional 60 to 80 civilians who had witnessed the events or had been active in lobbying for independence, and arresting more than 300 others.[37]

---

[29] William J. Holstein, "Indonesia Admits Wholesale Detentions on East Timor," *United Press International*, 3 February 1983.

[30] Amnesty International 1985.

[31] Commission for Reception, Truth and Reconciliation in East Timor (CAVR) 2005, 168–173; U.S. Embassy in Jakarta 2008a; U.S. Embassy in Jakarta 2008b; Jolliffe 2009.

[32] "East Timor: The Next Cambodia," *Economist*, 10 November 1979; Jill Jolliffe, "East Timor Guerrillas Defy Starvation and Jakarta's Bombs," *Globe and Mail*, 4 September 1979.

[33] Amnesty International 1991b; UN Commission on Human Rights 1992.

[34] Human Rights Watch/Asia 1994.   [35] UN Commission on Human Rights 1994b.

[36] Human Rights Watch 1991a; Amnesty International 1991a; Amnesty International 1991c; UN Commission on Human Rights 1994b.

[37] Amnesty International 1991a; UN Commission on Human Rights 1994b.

Although Indonesian counterinsurgency operations in East Timor slowed in the late 1980s and early 1990s, operations in Aceh intensified as Indonesia challenged the resurgence of GAM. In 1989, the government launched Operasi Jaring Merah (Operation Red Net) and by July 1990 it was reported that about 12,000 Indonesian troops – combined military and Kopassus forces – were stationed in Aceh.[38] This period of government military operations, which lasted from 1989 to 1998, is often referred to as the Daerah Operasi Militer (Military Operations Zone) period, or DOM, indicating that formal military operations were ongoing in the province.[39]

In addition to direct attacks on GAM units and bases, the Indonesian government used a strategy of high-casualty control in an attempt to deter civilians from providing intelligence and other forms of support to GAM – what interviewees referred to as attempts "to scare the population," to teach civilians a lesson, or to show civilians the consequences of backing demands for independence.[40] As in East Timor, the military forced civilians to participate in "fence of legs" operations, positioning civilians in front of government troops as they searched Aceh's mountains and jungles for GAM units.[41] In addition to search operations and direct attacks on GAM units, government counterinsurgency operations frequently targeted civilians believed to be sympathetic to the insurgency. Government forces targeted the families of GAM members, torturing, raping, and, in some cases, holding individuals hostage in an attempt to force the surrender of GAM members.[42] Government forces also targeted other individuals believed to be aiding GAM, burning collaborators' homes and torturing, raping, and frequently killing these individuals – sometimes in front of their families – their dead bodies deliberately left in public places, near places of worship, or along roadways as a warning to others who might be aiding the insurgency.[43] One GAM member I interviewed alleged that villagers, in some cases, were not permitted to remove the bodies for several days, so that civilians would be forced to pass by the bodies repeatedly.[44] Many of these individuals

---

[38] Sukma 2001, 382; Sukma 2004.
[39] Some dispute whether Aceh was ever formally labeled as an area of military operations. See Widjajanto and Kammen 1999.
[40] Interviews with GAM senior political leader, Banda Aceh, 7 August 2006; GAM member and delegate to peace negotiations, Banda Aceh, 8 August 2006; Acehnese NGO leader, Banda Aceh, 9 August 2006.
[41] Human Rights Watch 1991b; Human Rights Watch 1992; Amnesty International 1993a; Robinson 1998; Sukma 2004; Schulze 2006.
[42] Human Rights Watch 1990; Amnesty International 1993a; Schulze 2006.
[43] Human Rights Watch 1990; Human Rights Watch 1991b; Amnesty International 1993a; Robinson 1998; Schulze 2006. Interviews with Acehnese human rights activist, Jakarta, 1 August 2006; former GAM senior military commander, Jakarta, 5 August 2006; senior international NGO official and expert on Indonesia, Jakarta, 5 August 2006; Acehnese human rights activist, Banda Aceh, 7 August 2006; GAM member and delegate to peace negotiations, Banda Aceh, 8 August 2006; representative in Indonesian legislature, Banda Aceh, 9 August 2006.
[44] Interview with senior GAM political leader, Banda Aceh, 7 August 2006.

appear to have been killed under similar circumstances – shot at close range, with the bullets often removed from the corpse; their hands or feet bound, indicating that they had been captured before being killed; and their bodies bearing signs of beating or torture.[45] In a memoir published in 1989, President Suharto admitted that during the mid-1980s the Indonesian government had used similar tactics for dealing with unrest in other regions of the country, saying, "Some of the corpses were left [in public places] just like that. This was for the purpose of shock therapy.... This was done so that the general public would understand that there was still someone capable of taking action to tackle the problem of criminality."[46] Many interviewees adopted this term – "shock therapy" – to explain the government's counterinsurgency strategies in Aceh.[47]

Attacks on civilians were not isolated incidents; rather, government targeting of civilians was frequent and pervasive, what one observer has termed the "institutionalization of terror."[48] One interviewee recollected several examples of attacks that took place during this time period, arguing that while some attacks targeted specific individuals, such as the shooting of an Acehnese academic in his car, other incidents involved attacks on larger groups of civilians and seemed intended to instill fear in the population.[49] Other interviewees attested that the military attacked whole villages; if an incident occurred in one village – for example, the discovery of a GAM collaborator – Indonesian security forces would also target neighboring villages with violence, engaging in what one interviewee referred to as "collective punishment" of villages.[50] Rapes of Acehnese women were not uncommon and, according to several individuals I interviewed, were intended to humiliate, shame, and frighten the civilian population.[51]

Reporting on human rights abuses was limited because many individuals feared punishment for publicizing abuses, but in late 1990, local Acehnese leaders confirmed that Indonesian forces were regularly executing individuals believed to be sympathetic to the insurgency. When questioned by Reuters regarding these claims of frequent killings, an Indonesian soldier admitted that the military was using these methods as a means of terrorizing civilians, saying "Okay, that does happen. But they use terrorist strategies so we are forced to

---

[45] Amnesty International 1993a; "Discovery of Corpses in Aceh Reported," BBC Monitoring Service: Asia-Pacific, 19 August 1998.

[46] Quoted in Amnesty International 1993a, 20.

[47] Interviews with Acehnese human rights activist, Jakarta, 1 August 2006; senior GAM political leader, Banda Aceh, 7 August 2006; Acehnese NGO leader, Banda Aceh, 9 August 2006.

[48] Robinson 1998, 140.

[49] Interview with Acehnese human rights activist, Jakarta, 1 August 2006.

[50] Interviews with Acehnese human rights activist, Banda Aceh, 7 August 2006; senior international NGO official and expert on Indonesia, Jakarta, 5 August 2006.

[51] Interviews with Acehnese human rights activist, Jakarta, 1 August 2006; senior GAM political leader, Banda Aceh, 7 August 2006; GAM member and delegate to peace negotiations, Banda Aceh, 8 August 2006.

use anti-terrorist strategies."[52] Even most of the military officials I interviewed were willing to admit that the security forces under Suharto had engaged in misconduct or "misbehavior" and had been insensitive to the need to win the hearts and minds of civilians in Aceh, contributing to increased support for the insurgency.[53]

Amnesty International estimated that from 1989 to 1993 approximately 2,000 civilians were killed by Indonesian armed forces in Aceh;[54] attacks declined in the late 1990s, with one interviewee attributing this to the fact that the military had successfully extended its control over the territory and thus no longer needed to use violence to force civilians to submit to the government's control.[55] After Suharto's fall from power in 1998, fact-finding missions sent to Aceh to investigate allegations of government abuse reported that evidence indicated widespread government abuses of the civilian population; the missions confirmed the existence of a number of mass graves, believed to have been used by the military to dispose of groups of individuals killed during the DOM period.[56] A member of the National Commission on Human Rights (Komnas HAM) fact-finding mission announced that "The discovery (of the skeletal remains) has convinced us beyond doubt that reports on widespread military atrocities over the past nine years in Aceh are an undisputed fact."[57]

When asked why the Suharto government used such brutality in its counter-insurgency operations in Aceh and East Timor, interviewees pointed to three key factors.[58] First, they emphasized the character of Indonesian political institutions and the ways in which military dictatorship contributed to particular strategies for confronting the insurgencies – in effect, pointing out that Suharto drew support from a narrow constituency of military backers and had few institutional incentives to appeal to a broader domestic audience. Under Suharto's rule, the military held enormous sway; military leaders were given powerful positions in the national bureaucracy and legislature, as well as in regional and local levels of government. In this atmosphere of military

---

[52] Elizabeth Pisani, "Corpses Litter Indonesia's Aceh Province, Residents Say," *Reuters News*, 23 November 1990.

[53] Interviews with former commander in charge of Indonesian military operations in Aceh, Jakarta, 3 August 2006; retired senior Indonesian military official, Jakarta, 1 August 2006.

[54] Amnesty International 1993a, 16.

[55] Interview with Acehnese human rights activist, Jakarta, 1 August 2006.

[56] International Crisis Group 2001b. Ali Kotarumalos, "Rights Activist Says 11 Mass Graves Found in Indonesian Province," *Associated Press*, 5 August 1998; "The Aceh Killing Fields," *Jakarta Post*, 6 August 1998; "Rights Group Says 781 People Killed, 163 Missing in Indonesian Province," *Agence France-Presse*, 25 August 1998; "Wiranto Criticizes Rights Commission Over Aceh Probe," *Jakarta Post*, 27 August 1998.

[57] Pandaya, "Team Finds Skeletons in 'Killing Field,'" *Jakarta Post*, 22 August 1998; Patrisia Prakarsa, "Indonesian Rights Team Ends Fact Finding Mission in Troubled Aceh," *Agence France-Presse*, 23 August 1998; Pandaya, "Skeletons Excavated from North Aceh Grave," *Jakarta Post*, 23 August 1998.

[58] This section draws on multiple interviews in Jakarta and Banda Aceh, July and August 2006.

dominance, a military response to the conflict was, in the words of one interviewee, "the only tool available" to the government. They argued that Suharto was "a military man" committed to "a military solution" to the conflicts in Aceh and East Timor; Suharto would have viewed any political negotiation with the rebel groups as admitting the government's weakness. Although domestic opposition to government attacks on civilians in Aceh and East Timor did develop, particularly in the late 1990s as reporting on military abuses became more frequent, Suharto refused to alter his strategy because his "personalistic" rule did not require him to be responsive to public criticism, and after more than thirty years as president, Suharto had become "overconfident" in his ability to remain in power despite public opposition. One interviewee likened Suharto's rule to that of a king, saying that Suharto possessed control over all aspects of Indonesian life including politics, economics, and even culture.

Second, interviewees emphasized that Suharto legitimated his rule by claiming that a military government was best able to uphold the ideals of Pancasila, a set of ideological principles laid out at Indonesia's independence as a guide for governing the country. Central to the Pancasila ideology was the idea of Indonesia as a unitary state. This professed commitment to upholding the ideals of Pancasila, including the country's unity, added to the government's stubborn unwillingness to negotiate with separatist groups.[59]

The third explanation interviewees offered for government violence against civilians in Aceh and East Timor pointed to the importance of the international context and the fact that Suharto's government did not need to behave well in order to garner support from a broad international constituency. Not only did Suharto's personalistic autocratic rule insulate him from domestic criticism, but his staunch anticommunist stance protected him from international condemnation. During the Cold War, international actors, eager to maintain Indonesia as a Western ally in the fight against communism, did not pressure Suharto to alter his policies in Aceh or East Timor. It was not until the 1990s – particularly following the 1991 Dili massacre – that foreign governments began to raise more serious questions about Indonesia's human rights practices.[60]

Throughout Suharto's tenure, the Indonesian government refused to negotiate with either Fretilin or GAM and although in 1997 the United Nations mediated discussions between Indonesia and Portugal over the status of East Timor, the Indonesian government was unwilling to make concessions.[61] When Suharto's 1998 fall from power ushered in a transitional regime, however, the government began to consider alternatives to military repression in Aceh and East Timor.

---

[59] This commitment to the Pancasila ideology may also have been tied to Indonesia's ethnic makeup. As Walter (2009) demonstrates, in countries with many minority groups demanding greater autonomy, governments are particularly resistant to negotiations, out of a fear of setting a precedent for other groups.

[60] Smith 2003; Murphy 2010.

[61] "UN Vows to Accelerate E.Timor Settlement," *Jakarta Post*, 17 December 1997.

COUNTERINSURGENCY IN TRANSITION: STRATEGIES OF
RESTRAINT IN INDONESIA'S NEW DEMOCRACY

The Fall of Suharto and Indonesia's Transition to Democracy

In the months leading up to the collapse of Suharto's government, domestic pressure for democratic reform was intense. Student groups organized mass protests throughout the country calling for political reform, an end to government corruption, and the removal of Suharto from power; it is estimated that some of the largest demonstrations, held in Yogyakarta and Bandung in mid-May 1998, drew half a million people each.[62] Many prominent opposition leaders, including Megawati Sukarnoputri, leader of the opposition PDI party, and Amien Rais, head of a major Islamic organization called Muhammadiyah, echoed protestors' calls for reform and insisted that significant political change required first ousting Suharto. When the government responded harshly to demonstrations in the spring of 1998, domestic criticism mounted. Indonesian NGOs, such as the Indonesian Legal Aid Institute (LBH), issued statements accusing the military of attacks on demonstrators and formed a new organization, called the Commission for "the Disappeared" and Victims of Violence (Kontras), to investigate reports that Indonesian security forces were involved in the disappearance of members of the political opposition.[63]

Calls for political and military reform did not end with Suharto's May 21 resignation and the transfer of power to Vice President B. J. Habibie; many were skeptical of Habibie's willingness to undertake serious reform, viewing his government as an extension of Suharto's autocratic rule. Protests continued, demanding that Habibie make moves toward democratization.[64] The new government under Habibie faced heavy pressure from both domestic and international constituencies to prove its commitment to democratic transition and to the redress of human rights abuses committed under Suharto. It was no longer possible for the government to remain in power with only the backing of a narrow domestic constituency. The economically weak and politically unstable new regime under Habibie needed support from a wider domestic and international constituency – and in the post–Cold War era, the government could no longer use anticommunist appeals to secure international backing.

---

[62] Aspinall 2005.
[63] See, for example, "RI May Face Trouble in UN Rights Meeting," *Jakarta Post*, 17 April 1998; Kafil Yamin, "After IMF, Jakarta Runs into Students' Growing Ire," *Inter Press Service*, 22 April 1998; Human Rights Watch World Report 1998; Aspinall 2005.
[64] See, for example, Bhimanto Suwastoyo, "Habibie Announces Cabinet as Army Intervenes Between Rival Demonstrators," *Agence France-Presse*, 22 May 1998; Bhimanto Suwastoyo, "Military Sweeps Away Student Protest as New Government Consolidates," *Agence France-Presse*, 23 May 1998; "Students Continue with Demonstrations for Reform," *Jakarta Post*, 23 May 1998; Christopher Torchia, "Indonesia's New President Faces Growing Calls for Early Elections," *Associated Press*, 24 May 1998.

Domestic opinion polls shed additional light on the nature of the domestic pressure urging Habibie's government to implement policy changes. Because independent public opinion polling was not permitted under Suharto, Indonesia's polling infrastructure was not well developed at the time of the political transition, but a few organizations did conduct polls during this period.[65] One of the earliest polls was conducted by the International Foundation for Election Systems (IFES) in December 1998 through February 1999, in advance of the parliamentary elections scheduled for June 1999.[66] Although the survey did not ask respondents questions related directly to the conflicts in Aceh or East Timor, it did ask more general questions regarding democratic transition and political rights. The poll confirmed that public pressure for a full transition to democracy was widespread, as the mass public protests suggested; 70 percent of respondents said that Indonesia "should strive to be a democracy."[67] Respondents also indicated significant dissatisfaction regarding the government's respect for individual rights. Only 9 percent of respondents indicated that they were "very satisfied" with government respect for the rights of citizens; an additional 41 percent reported they were "somewhat satisfied" with government respect for the rights of citizens. Most respondents linked respect for individual rights to the process of democratization, with 84 percent of respondents agreeing that "when government officials must be elected by the people in order to keep their position in government, they will have more respect for the rights of the people."[68] And although the survey did not make specific reference to the Acehnese or Timorese people in asking respondents about political rights, it did ask whether "members of all ethnic groups in Indonesia should have the same rights as citizens"; 87 percent responded affirmatively,[69] suggesting that public support for a more conciliatory policy toward minority groups was strong.

In the days following Suharto's resignation, international actors also urged Habibie to pursue democratization. U.S. President Clinton released a statement saying, "We welcome President Suharto's decision, which provides an opportunity to begin a process leading to a real democratic transition for Indonesia – an opportunity for the Indonesian people to come together and build a stable democracy for the future.... We urge Indonesia's leaders to move forward promptly with a peaceful process that enjoys broad public support."[70] The EU response was similar, calling on Habibie "to put in place democratic structures and institutions that create a government that is accountable to the people of Indonesia,"[71] while the UN spokesperson announced that UN

---

[65] Mietzner 2009b. [66] Wagner 1999. [67] Ibid., 47. [68] Ibid., 49. [69] Ibid., 56.
[70] Andrea Shalal-Esa, "U.S. Urges Indonesia Leaders to Move toward Democracy," *Reuters*, 21 May 1998.
[71] "Clinton, Asian Nations Hail Suharto Resignation," *Agence France-Presse*, 21 May 1998.

Secretary-General Kofi Annan "hopes that Indonesia will now be able to rebuild social peace based on democratic principles and values and revive its economy."[72]

In addition to calling for a transition to democracy, international actors also pushed specifically for improvement in the military's human rights record and change in the government's policies toward Aceh and East Timor. In early August 1998, U.S. Secretary of Defense William Cohen met with Indonesian government and military leaders in Jakarta. In a press conference after the meetings, Cohen stated, "I do know that the Indonesian Government has a number of investigations under way in terms of any abuses of human rights. It's important that such investigations be carried out openly, honestly, with integrity. And if that is done, it will enjoy the support of the Indonesian people and the commendation of the world community."[73] While East Timor had long been on the international agenda, foreign governments and the United Nations pressured Habibie to take immediate action. EU members issued a statement pushing Indonesia to hold democratic elections, to release political prisoners, and to work with the United Nations on resolving the East Timor issue.[74] Even Australia, which was one of the few countries to officially recognize Indonesia's 1975 annexation of East Timor, urged Habibie to address the issue.[75] Although the United Nations avoided mentioning East Timor in its public statements following Suharto's resignation, reports suggest that UN officials were pressuring the Habibie government privately to change its position.[76]

Policy Change under Presidents Habibie and Wahid

In response to pressure from domestic and international constituencies, Habibie's government made a number of public attempts to distance itself from the repressive policies of Suharto. As one government official I interviewed observed, Habibie initiated changes in government policy because both "international support and the government's survival depended on it"; another interviewee commented on the sense of urgency post-transition – that there was a "rush" to pass government reforms.[77] Following the new government's first cabinet

---

[72] "UN's Annan Expresses Relief over Indonesia Power Transfer," *Dow Jones International News*, 21 May 1998.

[73] Philip Shenon, "U.S. Officials, in Indonesia, Warn Rulers to Respect Rights," *New York Times*, 2 August 1998; Cindy Shiner, "Cohen 'Encouraged' by Indonesia but Presses Human Rights Issue," *Washington Post*, 2 August 1998.

[74] "EU Urges Indonesia to Step Up Reforms," *Agence France-Presse*, 25 May 1998; "EU Urges Glasnost for Indonesia, Welcomes Poll," *Reuters News*, 25 May 1998.

[75] "Ramos Horta and Australian Government Urge Action on East Timor," *Agence France-Presse*, 24 May 1998.

[76] Robert H. Reid, "UN Hopes Power Shift in Indonesia May Lead to Progress on East Timor," *Associated Press*, 21 May 1998.

[77] Interviews with senior official in Indonesian government under Suharto, Jakarta, 29 July 2006; former UN official and participant in peace negotiations with GAM, Jakarta, 3 August 2006.

meeting on May 25, the Justice Minister announced that "the government is studying the question of East Timorese who are in prison" and acknowledged that "we should change our position" on East Timor.[78] Several weeks later, Indonesia announced the release of 16 East Timorese political prisoners, though it still refused to release Fretilin leader Xanana Gusmão, who had been in Indonesian custody since 1992.[79] Habibie also expressed his willingness to grant limited autonomy to East Timor, though he insisted that the region must remain a part of Indonesia.[80] In July and August, Indonesia began to withdraw some of its military troops from East Timor, as a signal of its commitment to pursuing a new policy.[81]

Habibie's government demonstrated its intention to reform policies in Aceh as well. It allowed both the National Human Rights Commission (Komnas-HAM) and the legislature to send missions to Aceh to investigate allegations of military abuse.[82] In response to the findings of these missions and extensive public criticism of the military's operations in Aceh, Indonesia's Minister of Defense and Commander of the Armed Forces, General Wiranto, announced that Aceh would no longer be considered an area of military operations and promised to withdraw some military troops from the province.[83] Wiranto even expressed publicly his regret for the military's past abuses, saying, "I sincerely apologise to all Aceh people for the acts of some soldiers"[84] and "on behalf of Indonesia's armed forces, I apologise to the people of Aceh if during military operations the armed forces have made you suffer."[85] In a speech given to commemorate Indonesia's independence, Habibie apologized as well, stating, "I, on behalf of the Government, would like to express my deepest regret for the human rights violations in several regions committed by individuals from the state apparatus. I apologise to the Indonesian people, in particular to the families of the victims."[86] On August 20, 1998, the government began withdrawing troops from Aceh.[87] Habibie released

[78] "Indonesia Takes Softer Approach to East Timor Question," *Reuters News*, 25 May 1998.

[79] "Presidential Decree Frees 16 East Timor Political Prisoners," BBC Summary of World Broadcasts, 11 June 1998; "Indonesia: Zingabust," *Economist*, 13 June 1998.

[80] "Indonesia Prepared to Grant Special Status to East Timor," *Associated Press*, 9 June 1998.

[81] "More Indonesian Troops Pull Out from East Timor," *Agence France-Presse*, 8 August 1998.

[82] Sukma 2001.

[83] Sukma 2001; Schulze 2006; Jemadu 2006; Patrisia Prakarsa, "Indonesia to Withdraw Troops from Aceh as Mass Graves to Be Dug Up," *Agence France-Presse*, 7 August 1998; Irwan Firdaus, "Indonesian Official Says Troops Will Withdraw from Northern Province," *Associated Press*, 7 August 1998; Maskur Abdullah, "Indonesia to End Military Operations in Aceh," *Reuters News*, 7 August 1998.

[84] Irwan Firdaus, "Indonesian Official Says Troops Will Withdraw from Northern Province," *Associated Press*, 7 August 1998.

[85] Maskur Abdullah, "Indonesia to End Military Operations in Aceh," *Reuters*, 7 August 1998.

[86] Louise Williams, "Sorry for Abuses, Habibie Tells the Nation," *Sydney Morning Herald*, 17 August 1998.

[87] "Indonesian Military Pulls Out First Troops from Troubled Aceh," *Agence France-Presse*, 20 August 1998.

39 Acehnese political prisoners in March 1999 and later that month traveled to Aceh, where he again apologized for abuses of the Suharto era.[88]

After spending his first few months as president seeking to distance the new government from Suharto, Habibie then began to make more substantial changes in the government's policies toward Aceh and East Timor. The government decided at a cabinet meeting in late January 1999 that it would consider independence for East Timor if no agreement could be reached on autonomy; at a news conference after the meeting, Information Minister Yunus Yosfiah announced the decision: "A regional autonomy 'plus' will be accorded to East Timor. If this is not accepted by the mass in East Timor, we will suggest to the new membership of the People's Consultative Assembly formed as the result of the next elections, to release East Timor from Indonesia."[89] Several weeks later, the government moved Gusmão from a Jakarta prison to a local house, where he remained in detention, but was freer to participate in negotiations over the status of East Timor.[90] While the government still pressed for East Timor to remain an autonomous province within Indonesia, it agreed in March 1999 to allow East Timor to vote on the proposed autonomy agreement.[91] The UN Assistance Mission in East Timor (UNAMET) was deployed in June of that year to facilitate voting. In the August 30 referendum, 78.5 percent voted against becoming an autonomous republic within Indonesia, thus demonstrating their desire for full independence.

Habibie made efforts to reform the government's policy toward Aceh as well. In September 1999, the government passed a new law on the "Special Status of the Province of Aceh Special Region" (Law No. 44/1999), which gave Aceh greater control over religion, education, and cultural issues.[92] Although GAM opposed the law, saying that the new autonomy provisions were not sufficient to resolve the conflict, the law did signal the government's willingness to pursue a political resolution to the conflict. Efforts to negotiate a political settlement in Aceh continued under Habibie's successor, Abdurrahman Wahid, who agreed to the government's first ever negotiations with GAM. According to a representative in the Indonesian legislature I interviewed, the new civilian government realized that even if they could destroy the insurgency in Aceh, the human costs of doing so would be high; in his view, high civilian costs were no longer acceptable to the Indonesian government after

---

[88] Sukma 2001; Jemadu 2006.

[89] "Indonesia Mulls Letting Go of East Timor," *Agence France-Presse*, 27 January 1999; "Indonesia May Release Grip on East Timor," *Jakarta Post*, 28 January 1999.

[90] "Jailed Timorese Rebel Leader Accepts House Detention," *Agence France-Presse*, 29 January 1999; "Jailed East Timorese Rebel Moved from Prison to House Arrest," *Associated Press*, 9 February 1999; "Jailed Rebel Leader Gusmão Pledges to Work for Free East Timor," *Agence France-Presse*, 10 February 1999.

[91] "Portugal, Indonesia Agree on E.Timor UN-Sponsored Direct Vote," *Agence France-Presse*, 11 March 1999.

[92] Miller 2006.

the fall of Suharto.[93] Mediated by the Henri Dunant Centre, an international NGO based in Geneva, negotiations between government and GAM representatives began in January 2000 and led to the May 12 signing of a "Joint Understanding on a Humanitarian Pause for Aceh."[94] Although the humanitarian pause agreement did not address the political issues at the root of the conflict, it was the first time that the two sides had agreed on a formal ceasefire, intended to facilitate the provision of humanitarian assistance to civilians in Aceh.

Obstacles to Reform

Despite these efforts at political resolution of the conflicts in East Timor and Aceh, security forces continued to abuse civilians in both regions, even after Suharto's resignation. In the months leading up to the referendum in East Timor, Indonesian security forces organized, financed, and armed local militias, which supported East Timor's integration with Indonesia. Prointegration militias regularly attacked and harassed representatives of UNAMET and individuals who favored Timorese independence.[95] Violence escalated after the September 4 announcement of the referendum results. With the support of Indonesian security forces, prointegration militias engaged in widespread violence, burning homes and public buildings, attacking civilians seen as supportive of independence, and forcibly displacing an estimated 400,000 Timorese, who fled to the interior of the country and across the border into West Timor.[96] The United Nations estimated that more than 1,000 people were killed in postreferendum violence, stating that while much of the violence was "selective and targeted against specific individuals or families, some atrocities were of a more indiscriminate nature and were apparently aimed at terrorizing and intimidating entire villages or communities perceived as hostile to the prointegration cause."[97] An Indonesian commission created to investigate reports of human rights abuses surrounding the referendum concluded in their January 2000 report that "the facts and evidence also indicate that the civil and military apparatus, including the police, cooperated with the militia, creating a situation and conditions that supported the occurrence of crimes against humanity, which were carried out by the civil, military, police, and militia group apparatuses."[98] Habibie's inability to control security forces following the referendum forced him to withdraw his bid for the presidency in 1999 and to permit the deployment of a UN intervention force to restore order in East Timor.[99]

In Aceh, security operations against GAM continued under Habibie's presidency. The government transferred formal control over security operations

---

[93] Interview with representative in the Indonesian legislature, Banda Aceh, 9 August 2006.
[94] Sukma 2001; Jemadu 2006.   [95] KPP HAM 2000.
[96] This estimate of the total number of displaced is from UN General Assembly 1999, 8.
[97] UN General Assembly 1999, 7.   [98] KPP HAM 2000, 57.   [99] Huxley 2002.

from the military to the police, in an effort "to create an impression that the new government was now taking a more civil approach to the problem in the province."[100] A journalist I interviewed confirmed this, saying that democratization and the push for reform forced the government to appear to be taking action on the issue of military abuses.[101] However, this transfer of command did little to change operations on the ground, with the military still playing a prominent role in counterinsurgency operations.[102] A number of abuses of civilians were reported during Indonesia's first post-Suharto operation, Operasi Wibawa. On January 3, 1999, Indonesian troops fired into a crowd of civilians who were protesting police raids, killing 11, injuring 32, and arresting 170. Many of those arrested were later tortured; four died and 23 were injured while in government custody.[103] Similar incidents were reported in February, May, and July of that year, when Indonesian troops fired into crowds of civilians, killing nine civilians in February at Idi Cut village, 40 in Krueng Guekueh near Lhokseumawe in May, and 58 at a boarding school in Beuteng Ateuh in July.[104] Like Habibie, President Wahid lacked control over the military and reports of military abuse in Aceh continued even after the signing of the "humanitarian pause" in May 2000. In December 2000, for example, the military reportedly killed three members of an Acehnese NGO who were working to support torture victims.[105] During a visit to Aceh that same month, Wahid apologized for his inability to control the military.[106]

The Indonesian government, however, did attempt to reign in military abuse. With the creation of a national human rights commission, Komnas-HAM, and a commission to investigate reports of military abuse in Aceh, the government signaled that it would no longer overlook human rights abuses by the military or police. The government initiated programs to professionalize the military, including counterinsurgency training as well as human rights training, provided by the International Committee of the Red Cross and the UN High Commission for Refugees.[107] Although the military mounted intense counterinsurgency operations against GAM from 2001 to 2003, these counterinsurgency operations also prioritized programs intended to win over the Acehnese population – such as programs aimed at reeducating surrendered GAM members and encouraging civilians to declare loyalty to Indonesia. More than 6,000 villages were forced to pronounce their loyalty to Indonesia in 2001 and 2002.[108] Rather than killing civilians or destroying villages suspected of aiding GAM, as was common under Suharto, the military issued identity cards to aid in distinguishing civilians from insurgents and forcibly relocated civilians from a number of villages in order to separate GAM from their civilian base of

---

[100] Sukma 2004, 14.   [101] Interview with Indonesian journalist, Jakarta, 3 August 2006.
[102] International Crisis Group 2000a; Sukma 2004.   [103] Sukma 2001, 388; Sukma 2004.
[104] International Crisis Group 2001b; Sukma 2001, 388–389; Sukma 2004.
[105] Schulze 2006, 254.   [106] Reid 2004.   [107] Schulze 2006.   [108] Schulze 2006, 257.

support.[109] These tactics were not without problems – for example, conditions in camps for displaced populations were often dismal – but they did represent a shift away from more direct forms of violence against civilians. The military also committed increased resources to improving rule of law, promoting economic development, and providing humanitarian aid.[110] Independent journalists and NGO officials I spoke with, who reported on Aceh in the post-transition period, acknowledged these changes in government behavior, saying that the improvement in the government's treatment of civilians was noticeable; torture and detention of individuals without due process declined.[111] One interviewee noted that military personnel often complained during the post-transition period that human rights awareness was impeding their effectiveness in Aceh and tying their hands.[112]

Political and Military Responses under President Megawati

Pressure from domestic and international constituencies for policy change remained strong throughout the early years of democratic transition in Indonesia. Two national, representative surveys – one conducted in June 2001 and another in April 2002 – included direct questions regarding the ongoing conflict in Aceh. In the June 2001 survey, 69 percent of respondents said that the best way to resolve the situation in Aceh was through "dialogue with the people of Aceh," while only 12 percent said that "military force" was the best means of addressing the issue.[113] When the same question was asked in a second survey conducted in April 2002, the breakdown of responses was nearly identical, with 69.4 percent advocating dialogue with the people of Aceh and 11.8 percent supporting the use of military force.[114] International actors also continued to urge the Indonesian government to find a peaceful resolution to the conflict in Aceh. During an April 2001 visit to Aceh, the U.S. ambassador to Indonesia called on the government to use a "humanitarian approach" in resolving the conflict, rather than a military approach.[115] When a new U.S. ambassador to Indonesia was appointed, he, too, traveled to Aceh and urged a peaceful resolution to the conflict, saying, "The United States strongly supports the territorial integrity of Indonesia. However we also sincerely believe that the problem of Aceh can only be solved through dialogue, justice and accountability and a government policy that embraces the people of Aceh."[116]

---

[109] International Crisis Group 2003a; Schulze 2006.   [110] Sukma 2004; Schulze 2006.
[111] Interviews with Indonesian journalist, Jakarta 3 August 2006; senior international NGO official and expert on Indonesia, Jakarta, 5 August 2006.
[112] Interview with senior international NGO official and expert on Indonesia, Jakarta, 5 August 2006.
[113] International Foundation for Election Systems (IFES) 2002, 13–14.   [114] Ibid., 13–14, 39.
[115] "U.S. Ambassador Offers Training for Aceh Police," *Jakarta Post*, 6 April 2001.
[116] "U.S. Envoy Calls for Dialogue in Indonesia's Aceh as Nine More Killed," *Agence France-Presse*, 12 February 2002.

Megawati Sukarnoputri, who replaced Abdurrahman Wahid as president in July 2001, continued to pursue political negotiations with GAM. In August 2001, the government passed a second law on autonomy for Aceh (Law No. 18/2001), which promised Aceh a greater share of revenues from natural resource exploitation in the province; created an Islamic court system in Aceh, based in shari'a law; and allowed for a figurehead leader to represent the region. The law was not, however, well received in Aceh; many felt that the Acehnese population had not been given adequate opportunity to participate in its creation and were skeptical that it would lead to real change, particularly since the law failed to address past human rights abuses.[117] As negotiations with GAM slowed in late 2002, international pressure to find a peaceful resolution mounted, with the EU, Japan, the United States, and the World Bank organizing a conference in Tokyo in early December to coordinate international financial backing for a peace agreement.[118] Several days later, on December 9, representatives of the Indonesian government and GAM signed a Cessation of Hostilities Agreement (COHA).[119] Individuals close to the negotiations admitted that international pressure was instrumental in getting the two sides to reach a final accord.[120]

Implementation of the COHA stalled, however, as GAM resisted disarmament and reiterated its demands for Acehnese independence at the same time as the Indonesian government insisted that GAM abandon its calls for independence. As tensions rose, the government withdrew from the COHA on May 19 and announced the implementation of martial law in Aceh.[121] At first glance, the move toward more aggressive military operations in Aceh seems at odds with Indonesian public opinion and with international pressure to find a diplomatic resolution to the conflict. A national, representative survey carried out by IFES in June–July 2003, however, suggests that Indonesian public opinion shifted following the breakdown of the COHA. In the 2003 survey, only 27 percent said they preferred that the Indonesian government use dialogue to resolve the conflict in Aceh, as compared with 69 percent who preferred dialogue in the 2001 and 2002 surveys. While only 12 percent preferred the use of military force in 2001 and 2002, by 2003 50 percent of respondents preferred some form of military operation.[122]

Almost immediately following the announcement of martial law in Aceh, reports emerged that government forces were engaging in more frequent abuses

---

[117] Miller 2006.   [118] Aspinall and Crouch 2003.

[119] For an overview of the negotiations see Centre for Humanitarian Dialogue Annual Report 2002, Geneva, September 2003, available online at www.hdcentre.org.

[120] Interviews with former GAM senior military commander, Jakarta, 5 August 2006; GAM member and delegate to peace negotiations, Banda Aceh, 8 August 2006; former senior cabinet minister under Wahid, Jakarta, 3 August 2006.

[121] Aspinall and Crouch 2003; Huber 2004; Jemadu 2006.

[122] International Foundation for Election Systems (IFES) 2003, 21–22.

of civilians. In October 2004, Amnesty International estimated that at least 24 individuals working for local human rights and humanitarian aid organizations had been arrested since May 2003.[123] Following investigations in Aceh in early June 2003, the National Commission on Human Rights reported that they had found evidence of arrest, torture, and killing of civilians, including an incident on May 21 in which military forces are believed to have shot seven unarmed civilians in the northern district of Bireuen.[124] The investigation of reported abuses became more difficult as the period of martial law wore on – in particular, following Megawati's announcement on June 16 of a presidential decree imposing restrictions on access to Aceh by journalists and humanitarian aid organizations.[125] Although security force abuses of civilians increased under martial law, the government did make some efforts to prevent abuse. The military continued issuing identity cards to civilians and relocating villages near areas of GAM operations.[126] The military also demonstrated a new willingness to hold soldiers accountable for attacks on civilians.[127]

The Military and Resistance to Reform

The transition to democracy in Indonesia brought significant change in the government's policies toward Aceh and East Timor, with all three of the post-Suharto governments seeking to improve respect for human rights during military operations and advocating political solutions to Indonesia's separatist conflicts, but the shift away from the harsh military repression of the Suharto era was not a smooth process. As the first post-Suharto president, Habibie made a number of public attempts to separate his government from the country's authoritarian past – forming a National Human Rights Commission to investigate reports of military abuse, withdrawing troops from East Timor and Aceh, passing a law to expand Aceh's regional autonomy, and agreeing to a referendum on East Timor's independence. These efforts to moderate the government's policies toward Aceh and East Timor were plagued, however, by reports of continuing military abuse, including violence surrounding the East Timor referendum. Wahid agreed to the first ever government negotiations with GAM, which led to the signing of a "humanitarian pause" agreement, but found himself unable to reign in the military, and in December 2000 apologized publicly for his inability to prevent military abuses in Aceh. Much like the two

---

[123] Amnesty International 2004, 14. See also Muninggar Sri Saraswati, "Aceh Police Targeting Rights Activists, Offices," *Jakarta Post*, 10 June 2003.

[124] Muninggar Sri Saraswati, "Rights Body Confirms Murder of Unarmed Civilians in Bireuen," *Jakarta Post*, 14 June 2003.

[125] Matthew Moore, "Indonesia Limits, But Does Not Ban, Outside Access to Province," *Sydney Morning Herald*, 19 June 2003; "Indonesia Bans Foreign Tourists from Aceh," *Reuters News*, 17 June 2003; Human Rights Watch 2003; Davies 2006.

[126] International Crisis Group 2003a. [127] Human Rights Watch 2003, 44–45.

presidents that preceded her, Megawati pursued a policy toward Aceh that combined political and military elements – passing new autonomy legislation for Aceh, engaging in negotiations with GAM, and signing the COHA, and yet launching a major military offensive against GAM with the declaration of martial law in May 2003.

The fact that the military continued to play a central role in government, even after the fall of Suharto, helps to account for the halting changes in government policy during Indonesia's transition to democracy. In interviews, former government and military officials emphasized the challenges of transitioning the military from its role under Suharto's authoritarian government to its role under the civilian control of Indonesia's new democratic leaders, acknowledging that abuses continued because the transition was still in progress.[128] Under Habibie's government, the process of extricating the military from political affairs began with a reduction in the number of seats allocated to the military in national and local legislatures, a separation of military and police forces, and an agreement that active military officers would no longer be permitted to occupy cabinet positions.[129] Still, the military remained a powerful political force and when heavily contested elections were held in July and October 1999, each of the major candidates turned to the military for support. As Wahid stated, "You still can't become President in Indonesia without the military. They're out of the bureaucracy, and all of that, but that's nonsense. Nonsense! They're still strong and [General] Wiranto will support me to become President."[130]

After taking over the presidency in October 1999, Wahid initiated an ambitious program of military reform, which included the removal of conservative military leaders from active command by offering them cabinet positions, the appointment of a new head of the armed forces, and the installation of a civilian academic as Minister of Defense.[131] Although the military reforms carried out under Habibie and Wahid reduced the military's role in politics, civilian oversight of military operations remained limited until the passage of laws in 2002 and 2004, which gave the Defense Ministry greater control over the military.[132] In addition, the military's territorial command structure, which consisted of a dense network of military units spread throughout every region of the country, remained untouched in the period following Suharto's departure.[133] By failing to dismantle the territorial command structure, the post-Suharto governments allowed the military to retain a strong influence over local and regional affairs and to continue to engage in business operations throughout the country, which have long provided the military with an

---

[128] Interviews with senior official in Indonesian government under Suharto, Jakarta, 29 July 2006; retired senior Indonesian military official, Jakarta, 1 August 2006.
[129] International Crisis Group 2000b; Mietzner 2006; Mietzner 2009a.
[130] Quoted in Mietzner 2006, 17.   [131] Mietzner 2009a.   [132] Mietzner 2006.
[133] International Crisis Group 2000b; Kingsbury 2003.

independent source of funding.[134] The military's financial independence has impeded efforts to implement effective civilian control over the military, helping to explain why, despite efforts by civilian presidents to pursue more conciliatory policies toward separatist regions and to prove the government's commitment to human rights, incidents of military abuse continued even after the transition to democracy.

ASSESSING THE ALTERNATIVE ARGUMENTS

I have argued in this chapter that the transition to democracy forced Indonesian leaders to seek support from broader domestic and international constituencies. This increased the domestic and international costs of violence, increasing incentives to exercise restraint in counterinsurgency operations in Aceh and East Timor. In this section I examine several alternative explanations for the Indonesian government's behavior in these two cases.

Among scholars who focus on the organizational structure of armed groups, some posit that much of the violence against civilians occurring during civil war is opportunistic violence, carried out by individual members of an armed group and made possible by ineffective structures of organizational control. The violence of the Suharto era, however, is not consistent with this view. Evidence from East Timor and Aceh shows that the government's counterinsurgent violence against civilians was deliberate. In East Timor, the government forcibly relocated hundreds of thousands of Timorese, used its superior naval and aerial power to bombard East Timor in the early years of the civil war, and carried out systematic attacks against civilians in the interior. In Aceh, even Suharto admitted that violence was intentional, aimed at terrorizing the population into submission.

Other scholars who point to the role of organizational control accept that violence against civilians is often strategic, but point out that when armed groups seek to exercise restraint toward civilians, their ability to do so depends on organizational characteristics, such as the group's ability to enforce discipline. Organizational control arguments most often emphasize the organizational challenges facing militaries – the problems of enforcing discipline within military organizations and preventing individual soldiers from abusing civilians. In Indonesia, the military did face some of these kinds of organizational control issues; a former commander in charge of Indonesian military operations in Aceh during the post-Suharto period, for example, noted the challenges of enforcing discipline within the military during this period.[135] But for Indonesia, the major challenge of organizational control was a broader one – a challenge at the level of the national government, with

---

[134] Interview with scholar and expert on Indonesia, 27 July 2006. On military involvement in business activities see International Crisis Group 2000b; Kingsbury 2003; Mietzner 2009a.
[135] Interview with retired senior Indonesian military official, Jakarta, 1 August 2006.

the civilian leadership unable to exert effective control over the military in order to implement its strategy of restraint.

Turning to arguments focusing on the military context, some scholars claim that a government's capabilities are the primary determinant of its counter-insurgency strategy. Governments that have powerful militaries and extensive resources are capable of carrying out complex counterinsurgency operations; these governments are able to combine intensive policing of towns and cities with military strikes against rebel bases and units, and have little need to resort to brutal attacks on civilian sympathizers. This argument finds little support in the evidence from Indonesia. As the discussion earlier in this chapter shows, the behavior of the Indonesian government shifted as the transition to democracy began in May 1998. The strength of the Indonesian military, however, did not change significantly during this transition period; the military remained intact when Habibie took over the government in 1998, with General Wiranto remaining commander in chief of the Indonesian armed forces and with the size of the military remaining relatively constant throughout the period of transition. And although the political transition did involve efforts to exert greater civilian control over the military and to decrease the military's influence over politics in Indonesia – Wahid, for example, appointed a civilian minister for defense and secured Wiranto's resignation – it did not significantly alter the military's strength.[136]

In addition, the new government that took over began the move toward a strategy of restraint at a moment of economic weakness, not economic strength. Economically, the months surrounding the May 1998 transition to democracy were a low point for Indonesia; as the Asian financial crisis progressed, Indonesia's GDP plummeted, registering a negative 13 percent growth rate for 1998, leading to a drop in GDP per capita from US$906 in 1997 to US$777 in 1998, declining again in 1999 to US$773, the lowest level in six years.[137] Inflation exploded to 58 percent in 1998 and remained at 20 percent in 1999, and the value of the Indonesian currency tanked; with a collapsing economy, Suharto was forced to accept a loan package from the IMF and, ultimately, to relinquish power. Although the size of the military remained consistent during the transition, economic crisis meant that the new government had fewer resources to allocate to the military. Total government military expenditure had increased steadily in the years preceding transition, but by 1999 government spending on the military had stagnated. Government military expenditure declined from an average of 14.4 percent of central government expenditure in the five years preceding transition to only 6 percent of central government expenditure in 1999.

---

[136] Chandra and Kammen 2002.

[137] All economic data are from the World Bank, *World Development Indicators*, multiple years, available online at data.worldbank.org. Per capita GDP is measured in constant 2000 U.S. dollars.

Although Indonesia experienced a particularly rapid and steep economic decline before and during its transition to democracy, it is not unusual for a transitional government to be faced with economic hardship. In fact, many regime transitions take place in the context of economic and institutional weakness. It is difficult, therefore, for the capabilities hypothesis, which suggests that restraint is linked to government economic and military strength, to account for restraint among these transitional governments.

A second military context hypothesis suggests that governments exercise restraint when the costs of the conflict are low; civilian targeting is a strategy of last resort and it is only when conflicts become too costly to bear that governments are willing to carry out large-scale attacks on a rebel group's civilian constituency. Low conflict costs, however, do not appear to have driven government restraint in either of these cases. In East Timor, the most intense period of fighting and the period of highest government, rebel, and civilian casualties took place during the first few years of conflict, immediately following Indonesia's annexation of the region. By the 1990s, the conflict had settled into a low-intensity guerrilla struggle, with occasional Fretilin ambushes of military units and sporadic clashes between government and rebel forces. This low level of conflict intensity persisted during and after the 1998 transition to democracy; the hypothesis on costs of conflict, therefore, cannot explain why the government's counterinsurgency strategy shifted toward restraint in 1998, despite the fact that the costs of the conflict had been at a low level for more than a decade prior to the government's change in strategy. In Aceh, the conflict intensified during the transition to democracy, as GAM expanded its recruiting efforts, extended its geographic reach beyond its strongholds in northern and eastern Aceh, and began taking control of local administrative structures throughout the region; GAM's territorial control increased, as did the group's access to financial resources and weapons.[138] As GAM's operations expanded, the Indonesian government faced rising costs in Aceh. Here, too, the evidence does not match the predictions of the hypothesis regarding the costs of conflict, for it was as the costs of conflict were rising in Aceh, not declining, that the government began shifting toward a strategy of restraint.

Arguments emphasizing contestation over territory may help to explain changes in levels of civilian targeting under Suharto, but these explanations are unable to account for the shift to restraint following Suharto's demise. In both Aceh and East Timor, contestation over territory was high in the first few years of the insurgencies and, consistent with the expectations of contestation arguments, government violence against civilians was also high. When the government gained greater control over these territories – by the mid-1980s in East Timor and by the late 1990s in Aceh – violence did decline, again as a contestation argument would predict. And in fact, as mentioned earlier, one interviewee attributed the decline in violence in Aceh to the government's

---

[138] Schulze 2003; Schulze 2004.

achievement of effective control over the territory, which meant the government no longer needed to use violence to elicit civilian cooperation.[139] Contestation arguments, however, cannot explain the government's shift to restraint in 1998. In East Timor, contestation over territory was low in the 1990s and throughout the transition to democracy; although the level of contestation over territory did not change with democratization, government behavior did. Meanwhile, contestation over territory in Aceh increased as GAM expanded its geographic reach following the collapse of Suharto's regime, but the Indonesian government improved its human rights record during this period of increased fighting, contrary to the predictions of the contestation hypothesis.

Among alternative arguments emphasizing international factors, one of the primary arguments posits that states that have signed relevant international human rights and humanitarian law treaties are more likely to exercise restraint. The evidence from Indonesia does not support this claim. Every single state in the international system is a party to the 1949 Geneva Conventions; more than 70 states ratified the Geneva Conventions shortly after they were negotiated in the 1950s and newly independent states, in most cases, joined the Geneva Conventions after gaining independence. Indonesia follows this pattern, having acceded to the conventions in 1958. The timing of ratification of the Geneva Conventions, therefore, cannot explain variation in government behavior; like the conflicts in Indonesia, most contemporary civil wars began well after the governments involved had joined the Geneva Conventions.

The 1977 Second Additional Protocol to the Geneva Conventions and the 1998 Rome Statute, which outline in greater detail the protections accorded to civilians during internal conflicts, have been less widely adopted and, therefore, may provide more leverage for understanding whether treaty ratification is associated with changes in state behavior. As of 2015, however, the Indonesian government had not ratified either the Second Additional Protocol or the Rome Statute; ratification of international humanitarian law treaties, therefore, cannot provide any insight into the government's dramatic shift toward restraint that began in 1998.

The two final alternatives to the arguments presented in this chapter are challenges directed specifically at the hypothesis on governments with unstable regimes. The first of these arguments suggests that transitional governments may adopt strategies of restraint not because they are eager to gain support from domestic and international constituencies, but because the new leaders who take power after a regime transition tend to be more moderate in their policy preferences. In Indonesia, the first transitional president was B. J. Habibie, who had been vice president under General Suharto; Habibie was not a political moderate and would likely have continued the policies of the Suharto era, were it not for heavy pressure on the government to democratize. In fact, many Indonesians were opposed to the idea of a Habibie presidency precisely

---

[139] Interview with Acehnese human rights activist, Jakarta, 1 August 2006.

because they believed that his leadership would not be much different from Suharto's; large public protests erupted in Jakarta following the announcement that Habibie would assume the presidency, with Indonesians demanding a more definitive break from Suharto's authoritarian rule.[140] As one former UN official I interviewed explained, although many reforms were passed under Habibie, this was not because Habibie himself sought reform, but because of the "agitation surrounding reformasi [reform]" and the pressure to prove the government was committed to change.[141] In the face of widespread domestic unrest, Habibie had little choice but to move forward with democratization and to implement more moderate policies with respect to the insurgencies in Aceh and East Timor.

Indonesia's second post-Suharto president, Abdurrahman Wahid, was more moderate in his political leanings, having been a vocal member of the opposition during Suharto's rule. The third post-Suharto president, Megawati Sukarnoputri, was not as moderate as Wahid, but she had also been a prominent opposition figure prior to democratic transition. Although Wahid and Megawati may have had more moderate political preferences than Suharto and Habibie, and although these preferences were likely important factors in their decisions to initiate political and military reforms, what is striking is that senior members of the Indonesian military and bureaucracy – individuals who were not political moderates – consented to these far-reaching reforms. According to interviews, it was the pressure of transition – the strength of domestic and international demands for political change – that forced conservative leaders to accept a significant reduction in the military's role in politics and changes in government policies toward Aceh and East Timor.

The second alternative argument is relevant to cases in which a regime transition takes place during the civil war, as it did in Indonesia. In these cases, this alternative argument suggests, peace negotiations with the rebel group often accompany the regime transition; government restraint may simply be related to the process of peace negotiations and may have little to do with the instability of government institutions and the desire to build support from domestic and international constituencies. Certainly, in any conflict, some of the variation over time in government and rebel group behavior will be driven by the dynamics of that particular conflict – by the initiation or breakdown of peace talks; by seasonal changes that increase or decrease force mobility; or by particular events such as elections or assassinations or even natural disasters, like the 2004 tsunami that hit Aceh. In Indonesia, democratic transition was accompanied by attempts to resolve the conflicts in Aceh and East Timor through peace negotiations; in both cases, the Indonesian government began to exercise restraint around the same time that the process of political dialogue began. In Aceh, however, peace negotiations repeatedly broke down; several

---

[140] Aspinall 2005.
[141] Interview with former UN official and participant in negotiations with GAM, Jakarta, 3 August 2006.

times the government returned to full scale military operations, and in 2003, even instituted martial law in the province. And although Indonesian forces did commit abuses of Acehnese civilians during these military operations, these abuses were far less severe than those committed under Suharto's rule. Government efforts to reform the military and to improve its human rights performance continued, even as peace talks collapsed and conflict escalated.

CONCLUSION

The case study of Indonesia in this chapter lends additional support to the hypotheses on government restraint by answering a question that the statistical analyses could not address: if a government experiences a change in regime – and thus a change in its relationship with domestic and international constituencies – during an ongoing civil war, does this impact the government's counterinsurgency strategy? If government relationships with domestic and international constituencies influence calculations regarding the costs of violence and the value of restraint, then changes in regime type during a conflict should correspond with changes in government behavior. The Indonesian government is the only government since 1989 to have undergone a democratic transition while fighting an ongoing civil war, in which the conflict itself did not directly cause the political transition. Rather, the political transition in Indonesia was largely the result of an exogenous economic shock – the 1997 Asian financial crisis, which led to a sharp decline in the Indonesian economy, sparking widespread popular protests demanding political and economic reforms. The Indonesian case thus provides a unique opportunity to trace how this sudden and dramatic change in the government's regime type influenced the government's counterinsurgency strategies in Aceh and East Timor.

The transitional government that took power in Indonesia in 1998 following the collapse of Suharto's autocratic government was under heavy domestic and international pressure to distance itself from the repressive policies of the Suharto era and to demonstrate a commitment to democratic transition. Domestic protests demanding policy change continued after Suharto's departure, while international donors signaled that their continued support was contingent on moves toward democratization. The new government did make dramatic changes to its strategies in East Timor and Aceh, apologizing for human rights abuses committed under Suharto, establishing a national human rights commission, releasing Timorese prisoners, withdrawing some of its troops from Aceh, granting increased regional autonomy to Aceh, and ultimately engaging in peace negotiations with both rebel groups. As the Indonesia case studies make clear, however, transitional governments may have a difficult time changing their counterinsurgency strategies. Although the civilian leadership in Indonesia appeared to be committed to restraint as a means of building legitimacy and support from domestic and international constituencies, effective implementation of such a strategy required military support as well, which at times was difficult for the government to secure.

5

Rebel Group Restraint in Aceh and East Timor

Rebel groups, like governments, often restrict their use of violence in civil war; of the 103 rebel groups that have waged insurgencies since 1989, 41.8 percent exercised restraint in their fighting, largely avoiding attacks on civilian targets. And like governments, rebel groups are more likely to exercise restraint when they calculate that the domestic and international costs of violence are high. Rebel groups make this calculation based on their relationship with their own domestic and international constituents. The broader the constituencies to which a rebel group must appeal, the higher the costs of violence and the greater the incentives for restraint. The statistical analyses in Chapter 3 provide support for these arguments, confirming that rebel groups with broad constituencies – those with governance institutions, inclusive political systems, and facing autocratic governments – indeed are more likely to exercise restraint; however, these analyses are limited in what they can tell us about *why* these particular types of rebel groups are more likely to use restraint. This chapter examines these theoretical arguments about rebel group restraint in greater depth, through a continuation of the case study of Indonesia, focusing on the behavior of the two insurgent groups: the Revolutionary Front for an Independent East Timor (Frente Revolucionária do Timor Leste Independente, Fretilin) in East Timor and the Free Aceh Movement (Gerakan Aceh Merdeka, GAM) in Aceh.

Indonesia's two major separatist insurgencies are useful cases for comparison in several respects. First, both groups faced conflicting incentives with regard to the use of violence against civilians. Although both groups established political institutions, creating incentives for group leaders to be responsive to their civilian constituents, neither group was inclusive;

both were separatist groups with narrow civilian constituencies made up of individuals from the dominant ethnic group in the separatist region. These narrow civilian constituencies should have given GAM and Fretilin the flexibility to use violence against minority ethnic groups within the separatist region – in particular, against the Javanese, who were the Indonesian government's traditional base of support – or against government constituents living in neighboring regions. And yet, neither GAM nor Fretilin engaged in deliberate attacks on civilians. At the time that the Acehnese and Timorese insurgencies began, Suharto ruled Indonesia as an autocracy; within this domestic political context, the insurgencies had little hope of generating domestic pressure on the government to make concessions and instead appealed to the international community for support. Restraint was a response to the high international costs of using violence.

The second advantage of studying the insurgencies in Aceh and East Timor is the same as the advantage in studying the Indonesian government: because Indonesia transitioned to democracy while the conflicts were ongoing, these cases provide an opportunity to examine how insurgent groups respond to a changing domestic context. The argument of this book might expect a shift in the behavior of GAM and Fretilin, away from strategies of restraint and toward strategies of terrorism, as the Indonesian government transitioned to democracy and leaders became more vulnerable to pressure from the domestic public. Interestingly, neither rebel group shifted from its strategy of restraint. For Fretilin, the explanation is fairly straightforward. One of the government's earliest policy changes was related to East Timor, thus eliminating the need for Fretilin to use violence as a means of pressuring the government. For GAM, however, the persistence of restraint is more puzzling. GAM's continued commitment to a strategy of restraint was linked strongly to the group's observation of events in East Timor. When East Timor won a referendum, GAM thought this would be possible for Aceh too, failing to appreciate the difference in the way the international community viewed these two regions of Indonesia. Because East Timor had been a Portuguese colony, and was annexed forcibly by Indonesia in 1975, the international community was more sympathetic to Fretilin's demand for self-determination. Aceh, in contrast, having been a Dutch colony like the rest of Indonesia and having joined the Indonesian state voluntarily when the country gained its independence, had a more difficult time garnering international support. A key aspect of GAM's strategy that did change, however, was the group's efforts to mobilize domestic public pressure on the Indonesian government to negotiate. GAM took advantage of the political opening during the transition to build ties with civil society groups in Indonesia and to push for greater concessions – an indication that GAM was taking into consideration the government's changing relationship with its political constituents and altering its strategies in response, as the argument of this book would predict.

FRETILIN AND THE STRUGGLE FOR EAST TIMORESE INDEPENDENCE

Fretilin's Political Constituency

Fretilin originated as a political party established during the process of Portuguese decolonization; in the years leading up to Indonesia's annexation of East Timor, Fretilin built a significant base of support from a broad Timorese constituency. Fretilin possessed a well-developed political structure at both the national level and the local level, with a national political leadership as well as local political representatives who consulted with civilians and developed close ties to local communities. This governance structure likely created incentives for Fretilin leaders to be responsive to their civilian constituents, increasing the domestic costs of engaging in violence against fellow Timorese and increasing incentives for restraint. Fretilin's political objectives, however, were not inclusive. Fretilin was a separatist group fighting for independence on behalf of a particular ethnic group: the Timorese. Thus, although Fretilin had incentives to exercise restraint toward Timorese civilians, Fretlin likely faced fewer constraints on its ability to use violence against non-Timorese civilians.

Several other parties emerged during the period of decolonization, each advocating a different vision for the future status of the territory. Fretilin argued for a quick transition to independence and emphasized in its political manifesto the right of the Timorese people to self-determination, saying, "Fretilin struggles against colonialism and any form of domination of our people."[1] The Timorese Democratic Union (União Democrática Timorense, UDT) also advocated independence, but its plan was more conservative and initially proposed federation with Portugal, while the Timorese Popular Democratic Association (Associação Popular Democrática Timorense, Apodeti) supported integration with Indonesia. Although Fretilin and the UDT formed a coalition in early 1975, intended to facilitate the transition to independence, observers report that Fretilin remained the more popular of the two parties, with support from about 60 percent of the Timorese population.[2] Fretilin's administrative structure consisted of a 50-person central committee as well as a system of regional subcommittees, which were responsible for developing ties to local communities and implementing programs for economic development, literacy, and health.[3] These efforts to support social and economic development in 1974 and 1975 helped Fretilin to develop a strong network of support throughout East Timor particularly in rural areas.[4] After a failed UDT coup attempt in August 1975, Fretilin took control of East Timor, with Xavier do Amaral serving as president and Nicolau Lobato as prime minister.[5] Sources report

---

[1] Nicol 2002, 95.   [2] Jolliffe 2009, 67.   [3] Taylor 1999b; Niner 2001.
[4] Jolliffe 1978; Taylor 1999b, 32–43.   [5] Jolliffe 1978; Niner 2001.

that the party enjoyed significant popular support in the months prior to Indonesia's invasion.[6]

Following Indonesia's annexation of East Timor in December 1975, Fretilin retreated to the interior of the country and created a separate armed wing, called Falintil, which maintained a force of approximately 2,500 regular troops, with an additional 7,000 militia and 20,000 reserves.[7] Fretilin remained the group's political wing and created a local administrative structure, carrying out political functions and coordinating education, healthcare, and food production in zones of insurgent control.[8] According to one expert on the region, Fretilin's political structure during this period, "although a shadow of the pre-invasion period, still retained its essential participatory democratic features,"[9] with the group holding political meetings and appointing political commissioners in order to consult with the civilian population regarding resistance to the Indonesian occupation. In addition to this political structure on the ground in East Timor, Fretilin had a number of political representatives abroad, the most prominent of whom was José Ramos-Horta, whose responsibilities included advocating on behalf of the group with foreign governments and international organizations.[10]

As Indonesian military operations intensified in the late 1970s, Fretilin was no longer able to maintain zones of control in the interior of the country. In place of local administrative structures, Fretilin established unarmed units responsible for gathering intelligence and maintaining the group's ties to villages and civilians, while Falintil adopted a traditional guerrilla strategy, using highly mobile armed units to mount small-scale guerrilla attacks on Indonesian military targets – for example, ambushes of army patrols and attacks on weapons caches.[11] During this period, Xanana Gusmão took over the group's leadership; he later resigned from Fretilin to become head of the National Council of Maubere Resistance (Conselho Nacional da Resistência Maubere, CNRM), a nonpartisan umbrella group that included Fretilin as well as other political parties active in the Timorese resistance. Falintil remained the armed wing of the insurgency, while Ramos-Horta continued to represent the insurgency abroad, under the title of Special Representative of the CNRM.[12]

---

[6] Taylor 1999b; Jolliffe 2009.   [7] Taylor 1999b, 70.   [8] Taylor 1999b; Niner 2001.
[9] Taylor 1999b, 82.   [10] Ramos-Horta 1987.
[11] Taylor 1999b; Niner 2001. See, for example, Jill Jolliffe, "East Timor Guerrillas Defy Starvation and Jakarta's Bombs," *Globe and Mail*, 4 September 1979; James M. Markham, "Refugees Say Rebels in East Timor Are Still Fighting the Indonesians," *New York Times*, 29 July 1980; Colin Campbell, "Indonesia Squeezing Guerrillas in East Timor," *New York Times*, 21 November 1982; Madeleine Prowse, "Indonesia Mounts 'No Mercy' Assault on Guerrillas in Timor," *Globe and Mail*, 10 September 1983; Barbara Crossette, "War Goes in in Indonesia Isle," *New York Times*, 19 July 1985; Graham Williams, "The Forgotten War: Fretilin Fights On," *Sydney Morning Herald*, 15 April 1987; "Four Killed in East Timor Ambush," *Agence France-Presse*, 19 March 1993; Colin Nickerson, "Once Mighty East Timor Separatists Dying Breed," *Boston Globe*, 29 June 1993.
[12] Pinto and Jardine 1997.

On the ground in East Timor, Indonesia's strategy of forced relocation made it difficult for Fretilin to maintain its local networks. Precise estimates of the numbers of resettled civilians are difficult to obtain, but reports suggest that nearly half of the population may have been forcibly resettled into government-run camps. The last Portuguese census of East Timor prior to Indonesia's invasion had estimated the Timorese population at 609, 477 in 1970, with more than 98 percent of the population identifying as ethnically Timorese.[13] Although no census was taken in 1975, demographers estimate that the population had grown to approximately 650,000 by the time of the invasion.[14] In December 1978, the Indonesian government estimated that between 268,644 and 318,921 people had been resettled into relocation centers.[15] Even so, Fretilin continued to cultivate a complex network of civilian support, which extended throughout the interior of the country among villages that had not been forcibly displaced and even reached into government-run resettlement camps.[16]

Javanese Migrants in East Timor

The argument of this book posits that governments and rebel groups weigh not only the costs of violence, but also its benefits – and do so mainly by evaluating the opponent's relationship with its constituents. The greater the civilian support for the opponent, the greater the incentives to use a strategy of high-casualty control, in order to force civilian cooperation and establish control over territory. In separatist conflicts, the presence of government constituents within the separatist region can create incentives for cleansing – particularly if this constituency is small in size and geographically concentrated. Fretilin had significant support from Timorese civilians, meaning that incentives to use violence as a means of controlling Timorese civilians were low. Fretilin did, however, have incentives to use violence against non-Timorese – in particular, against the Javanese, who were seen as the traditional base of support for the Indonesian government. In the years following the invasion, Indonesia encouraged Javanese and Balinese migration into East Timor as part of its transmigration program. Because Indonesian censuses during this period conducted only limited surveys of East Timor and did not provide information on the ethnic makeup of the population, it is challenging to develop estimates of the number of transmigrants in East Timor. The first transmigrants arrived in 1980 and by 1987 sources estimate that tens of thousands of transmigrants were living in East Timor.[17] At the same time, the Timorese population was in decline, as a result of violent deaths that occurred during the invasion and subsequent

---

[13] Hajek 2000, 217; Kiernan 2003, 590; Silva and Ball 2006, 13.
[14] Kiernan 2003, 591; Staveteig 2007, 14.
[15] Taylor 1999a; Taylor 1999b; Silva and Ball 2006, 6.   [16] Taylor 1999b.
[17] Kiernan 2003, 592.

conflict, as well as deaths related to disease and starvation. Thus, the transmigrant population may have made up as much as 10–15 percent of the total population in East Timor. The transmigrant population continued to grow throughout the 1980s and early 1990s, reaching 150,000–200,000 by 1999.[18] Many of these individuals lived in transmigrant villages, making them easy targets for attack. Tensions between Timorese and transmigrant populations ran high throughout Indonesia's occupation, with occasional clashes and riots breaking out between the two groups.[19]

Fretilin repeatedly expressed its opposition to transmigration into East Timor, viewing it as an attempt to dilute and marginalize the Timorese population in the region. Ramos-Horta voiced this opposition in an interview with the *New York Times*, saying, "They [non-Timorese migrants] have taken over the best land, the best jobs, even the small shops in the streets. In public service jobs only 3 out of 10 is Timorese. In the streets, selling in the markets, the average we estimate is one Timorese for nine Indonesians ... if the trend continues for the next 10 years, the Timorese will be completely outnumbered."[20] Ending transmigration into East Timor was a key component of the group's agenda; in an interview with the *Australian* in 1996, Ramos-Horta called for action to address key issues, saying, "We have to move forward for the pressing matters on the ground. Namely the excessive presence of the military, the excessive presence of Indonesian transmigrants in the country, the arbitrary arrests, summary executions and torture."[21] At times, Fretilin even suggested that it might be willing to take more aggressive action toward the transmigrant population. In a column published in the *Sydney Morning Herald* in 1995, Ramos-Horta wrote, "The CNRM will continue to pursue armed resistance and escalate it if and when feasible; it will continue to make Indonesian presence in the cities, towns and villages unsafe, and the future of Indonesian transmigrants uncertain. Indonesian cultural imperialism will be rejected. On the diplomatic front it will pursue even more aggressively every possible idea to increase the costs for Indonesia."[22] In the lead-up to the referendum in East Timor in 1998, Ramos-Horta warned of possible violence between Timorese and transmigrants.[23]

---

[18] Taylor 1999a, 32.
[19] See, for example, Paul Jacob, "Dili under Police Control after Five Days of Rioting," *Straits Times*, 10 September 1995; Sue Neales, "Two Decades of Death, Despair and Torture in Indonesia's Achilles Heel," *Sydney Morning Herald*, 21 October 1995.
[20] Barbara Crossette, "Wave of Migration is Altering East Timor," *New York Times*, 30 October 1994. See also "Resistance Leader Horta Interviewed by Portuguese TV," *BBC Monitoring Service*, 1 November 1996.
[21] Sarah Stock and Patrick Walters, "Nobel Winner Hopes for Clinton Role in E.Timor," *Australian*, 15 November 1996.
[22] José Ramos-Horta, "East Timorese Resistance Resolves to Fight On," *Sydney Morning Herald*, 20 January 1995.
[23] "Timorese Leader Demands Right of Referendum to Find Solution," *BBC Monitoring Service: Asia-Pacific*, 4 June 1998.

Given these tensions between Timorese and non-Timorese, some portion of Fretilin's Timorese constituency might have supported, or at least acquiesced to, the targeting of the transmigrant population. Despite the incentives to engage in violence against non-Timorese, however, Fretilin did not use violence against this population. Throughout the insurgency – both in the early years when Fretilin still controlled significant portions of East Timor and in the later years when the group had evolved into a more traditional guerrilla force – Fretilin avoided attacks on civilian targets. In the next section, I argue that Fretilin's restraint with respect to civilians was a response to the high international costs to using violence against civilians.

Domestic Constraints and Fretilin's Search for International Support

Although Fretilin launched a guerrilla campaign against Indonesian military targets and worked to build a broad base of civilian support within East Timor, these domestic efforts were unlikely to force concessions from Indonesia's strong, entrenched autocratic government. In fact, Ramos-Horta has indicated that this assessment of the Indonesian government was part of the group's thinking, saying in an interview, "The problem was I was dealing with a dictatorship that does not understand that dialogue, concessions, and flexibility allow all sides to win. The military only understands the 'we win' concept."[24]

Unable to mount sufficient domestic pressure on the Indonesian government to force concessions, Fretilin sought to internationalize the conflict. In his 1987 autobiography, Ramos-Horta explicitly outlined this logic:

Most wars of national liberation end in negotiations. There is almost no precedent of a guerrilla movement defeating an established government by military means alone.... East Timor is in fact one case in which the West could play an effective and constructive role.... A combined effort by the U.S. and Great Britain, with which Australia could be associated, would certainly persuade the Indonesian generals to seriously negotiate an end to the war.... A combination of the Secretary-General's moral weight and diplomatic ability, with the constant prodding of the Indonesians by Washington and other industrialized countries, would be certain to bring about a breakthrough.[25]

Fretilin reached out to foreign governments, foreign nongovernmental organizations (NGOs), and the United Nations, in the hopes of drawing international attention to the conflict and increasing diplomatic support for the insurgency's cause. Most of Fretilin's diplomatic outreach was organized by an external delegation, made up of Fretilin leaders who had left East Timor just prior to Indonesia's 1975 invasion and others who had been representing Fretilin abroad during its years as a new political party in 1974 and 1975. The group's primary representative was Ramos-Horta, who served as Fretilin's foreign minister and spent much of his time lobbying foreign governments and the

---

[24] Kennedy 2000, 164.   [25] Ramos-Horta 1987, 206.

United Nations, to build diplomatic opposition to Indonesia's annexation of East Timor and to strengthen support for Timorese independence.[26]

Ramos-Horta succeeded in encouraging the UN General Assembly to pass annual resolutions from 1975 through 1982, rejecting Indonesia's annexation of East Timor and insisting on the region's right to self-determination.[27] The UN Security Council passed similar resolutions in 1975 and 1976.[28] In addition, Fretilin sought to win the support of individual foreign governments; for example, in Portugal in May 1979, Fretilin representatives held a seminar with prominent supporters from Portugal, Mozambique, the United States, and Europe to raise international awareness about East Timor.[29] Ramos-Horta described the seminar as follows:

> The objectives which we want to achieve through this seminar are to alert the Portuguese public, denounce the policy of passiveness and silence followed to date by all Portuguese governments since the April 1974 revolution, and to bring pressure to bear on the Portuguese Government to adopt a more active stand on the East Timor issue, at the level of the United Nations. Contrary to what the people in Portugal and other parts of the world are led to believe by the Western press, armed resistance continues throughout the territory, where Indonesia has stationed several thousand troops. It is very tragic that whereas the armed struggle against Indonesian troops still continues in a large part of East Timor, the people abroad believe that there is no war, that Indonesia is in full control and that the East Timor people are happy about the situation. This is absolutely untrue. This is the real tragedy of the situation. This is what needs to be pointed out.[30]

In response to the seminar, the Portuguese legislature passed resolutions condemning Indonesia's annexation of East Timor and expressing support for Timorese resistance to Indonesian rule.[31]

Fretilin's external delegation achieved a number of other minor diplomatic successes in the 1980s, including a July 1984 public statement by the Pope and a letter sent the same month from members of the U.S. Congress to the Indonesian government, both of which called on Indonesia to end human rights abuses in East Timor.[32] Several years later, in 1987, Ramos-Horta published a

---

[26] Bernard D. Nossiter, "A 'Depressing' Cause at U.N.: Independence for East Timor," *New York Times*, 9 February 1983; Claude Robinson, "East Timor: New Diplomatic Pressure on Indonesia Expected," *Inter Press Service*, 27 July 1984; Michael Simmons, "Ten Years of Terror: Interview with Ramos Horta, East Timor's Representative at the UN," *Guardian*, 20 December 1985; Henry Kamm, "Post-Colonial Oppressors," *New York Times*, 11 January 1987.

[27] UN General Assembly Resolutions 3485 (XXX) 12 December 1975, 31/53 (1976) 1 December 1976, 32/34 (1977) 28 November 1977, 33/39 (1978) 13 December 1978, 34/40 (1979) 21 November 1979, 35/27 (1980) 11 November 1980, 36/50 (1981) 24 November 1981, 37/30 (1982) 23 November 1982.

[28] UN Security Council Resolutions 384 (1975) 22 December 1975 and 389 (1976) 22 April 1976.

[29] "East Timor: Remember Us?" *Economist*, 26 May 1979.

[30] "International Seminar Held in Portugal," BBC Summary of World Broadcasts, 28 May 1979.

[31] Ibid.

[32] Henry Kamm, "Pope Condemns South African Racial Policies," *New York Times*, 8 July 1984; Patrick Slavin, "United States: Congressmen Urge Action on East Timor," *Inter Press Service*,

book detailing Fretilin's struggle to gain independence for East Timor, which was reviewed in the *New York Times*, but by this time East Timor had largely faded from the international spotlight.[33]

It was not until the November 1991 Dili massacre, when Indonesian forces fired into a crowd of Timorese demonstrators in East Timor's capital, killing an estimated 75 to 200 civilians, that international attention again turned to the Timorese struggle for independence. Ramos-Horta made clear that Fretilin's goal in the aftermath of Dili was to generate as much international pressure on Indonesia as possible in the hope of forcing a negotiated settlement to the conflict, saying, "In due course we will step up our offensive in every area and that will include (the) diplomatic and I am confident that international pressure will increase on Indonesia."[34] Ramos-Horta immediately called on the UN Security Council to convene to discuss the events in Dili and urged foreign governments to institute an arms embargo on Indonesia.[35] The European Parliament responded by passing a resolution recommending that the European Community and the United Nations ban arms sales to Indonesia.[36] Within several weeks of the Dili massacre, the Netherlands became the first country to halt official aid to Indonesia; Canada followed in early December by cutting some of its official development assistance to Indonesia.[37] A number of members of the U.S. Congress called for reductions in U.S. aid to Indonesia and in October 1992 the United States ended its military training assistance to Indonesia in response to persistent human rights abuses in East Timor.[38]

Perhaps Fretilin's most significant diplomatic breakthrough in the months following the Dili massacre was a December 1991 meeting between Fretilin representatives and Australia's Prime Minister and Minister of Foreign Affairs. Australia was one of the few countries that had formally recognized Indonesia's annexation of East Timor, maintaining its support for Indonesia despite domestic and international opposition; the fact that one of Indonesia's strongest allies conceded to a high-level meeting with Timorese representatives suggested that

12 July 1984; Bernard Gwertzman, "Shultz Expresses Concern on Rights," *New York Times*, 12 July 1984.

[33] Henry Kamm, "Post-Colonial Oppressors," *New York Times*, 11 January 1987.

[34] "Indonesian Leaders 'Will Pay for Their Crimes' Separatists Say," *Agence France-Presse*, 14 November 1991.

[35] "Fretilin Asks for UN Security Council Meeting," *Agence France-Presse*, 12 November 1991; "Indonesian Leaders 'Will Pay for Their Crimes' Separatists Say," *Agence France-Presse*, 14 November 1991; "East Timor Rebels Seek Ban on Arms to Indonesia," *Agence France-Presse*, 14 November 1991.

[36] "European Parliament Wants Arms Ban on Indonesia after Shooting," *Reuters News*, 21 November 1991.

[37] "Shame and Blame over East Timor Massacre," *Economist*, 30 November 1991; "U.S. Says Timor Inquiry Must Be Credible, Canada Cuts Some Aid," *Reuters News*, 9 December 1991.

[38] "U.S. Congress Passes Bill Aiding Russia, Israel," *Reuters News*, 6 October 1992; "House of Representatives Adopts Foreign Aid Package," *Agence France-Presse*, 5 October 1992.

refusing to negotiate over East Timor was no longer a viable option for Indonesia.[39] In December 1992 Indonesia agreed to take part in UN-mediated talks with Portugal over the status of East Timor.[40] According to Ramos-Horta, Fretilin's strategy of international diplomatic pressure had been successful in forcing Indonesia to the negotiating table. He reasoned that Indonesia's willingness to negotiate

is due to the fact that Indonesia knows that it lost the battle inside Timor, despite its total military occupation, and to pressure from the United States and the European Community.... The U.S. Congress cut military aid to Indonesia in September of this year, as a result of the massacre of over 200 Timorese in November last and because of the continuous denunciations of human rights violations ... [another thing that] had a big impact is that, for the first time, the so-called "major media" in the United States, both the written press and television, began to speak about Timor, after a news blackout lasting more than 15 years.[41]

In building international support for East Timor, Fretilin framed the conflict both in terms of international law and human rights.[42] When Fretilin leader Xanana Gusmão was sentenced to life in prison for engaging in rebellion against the Indonesian state, he read a statement in court arguing that Indonesia did not have legal jurisdiction over his case because Indonesia had taken control of East Timor by force and, therefore, did not exercise legitimate rule over the territory and its citizens, which remained by law part of Portugal. He also requested that the United Nations intervene to resolve the conflict in East Timor in accordance with principles of international law.[43] Throughout the conflict, Fretilin maintained this position, arguing that East Timor had a legal right to self-determination following Portuguese decolonization; this claimed right to self-determination was the basis for demanding a referendum that would allow Timorese to choose between integration with Indonesia and independence.

Fretilin also portrayed East Timor as a human rights issue, tapping into growing international concern for human rights in the post–Cold War period. Fretilin leaders accused the Indonesian government of grave human rights abuses in East Timor, drawing attention to the scale of the abuses by citing estimates of 60,000 to 100,000 killed during the early years of Indonesia's occupation and, at times, referring to Indonesian actions in East Timor as genocide and citing the 1951 Convention on the Prevention and Punishment

---

[39] Mark Metherell, "Hawke to Meet Timor Guerrillas," *Age*, 3 December 1991; Mike Seccombe, "PM Attacked over Line on Dili Horror," *Sydney Morning Herald*, 4 December 1991.

[40] Phillip McCarthy, "East Timor Impasse Remains," *Sydney Morning Herald*, 19 December 1992.

[41] "East Timor: Resistance Demands Inclusion in Negotiations," *Inter Press Service*, 15 October 1992.

[42] See Bob 2005 for a discussion of how local movements frame their struggles to win increased international attention.

[43] "East Timor: Exiled Leader Protests Gusmão's Life Sentence," *Inter Press Service*, 21 May 1993.

of the Crime of Genocide.[44] Fretilin raised these concerns repeatedly with the UN Human Rights Commission, calling on foreign governments to cut aid to Indonesia.[45] In 1992, when the Commission passed a resolution criticizing Indonesia, Ramos-Horta applauded the decision, saying, "It is the first time that an absolute majority supported a condemnation of Indonesia for the violation of human rights in Timor."[46]

Fretilin also worked closely with international human rights NGOs to raise awareness of the situation in East Timor. In May 1994, Fretilin helped to organize an Asia-Pacific Conference on East Timor in the Philippines, which according to Ramos-Horta sought to "enhance the international profile of the plight of East Timor under Indonesian occupation. It also intended to foster dialogue between East Timorese nationalists and the Indonesian pro-democracy movement, and South-east Asian human-rights defenders with the aim of encouraging co-operation in the search for self-determination in East Timor and democracy in Indonesia."[47] A similar conference of the Southeast Asian Human Rights Network was held in Bangkok in July 1994 to coincide with a meeting of the Association of Southeast Asian Nations (ASEAN).[48] Under pressure from Indonesia to prevent the conferences from taking place, the Philippine and Thai governments banned foreign participants from entering their respective countries, but the conferences took place anyway and harshly criticized Indonesia for human rights abuses in East Timor.

Throughout the mid- to late 1990s, Fretilin continued its efforts to increase international pressure on the Indonesian government. As a result of the ongoing UN-mediated talks between Indonesia and Portugal, the Indonesian Foreign Minister agreed to meet with Ramos-Horta in October 1994.[49] Although the meeting was informal and Indonesia continued to refuse direct negotiations with Fretilin, the meeting did represent significant progress in Fretilin's efforts to use international attention as a means of bringing Indonesia to the negotiating table. In 1996 Bishop Carlos Ximenes Belo and José Ramos-Horta were awarded the Nobel Peace Prize "for their work towards a just and peaceful solution to the conflict in East Timor." The Nobel Committee said that it hoped awarding the prize to Bishop Belo and Ramos-Horta would "spur efforts to

[44] Ramos-Horta 1987, 175. See, also, "East Timor Rebels Seek Ban on Arms to Indonesia," *Agence France-Presse*, 14 November 1991.

[45] Victor Ego Ducrot, "Human Rights: East Timor Rebel Leader Pleads for U.N. Support," *Inter Press Service*, 25 February 1993.

[46] "East Timor: Optimism over U.N. Condemnation of Indonesia," *Inter Press Service*, 28 August 1992.

[47] Nirmal Ghosh, "Ramos Defuses Crisis, Bans Non-Filipinos from Meeting," *Straits Times*, 21 May 1994.

[48] Robert Birsel, "Thais Fear Indonesia, East Timor Activist Says," *Reuters News*, 20 July 1994.

[49] "Alatas to Meet Separatist Leader of East Timor," *Jakarta Post*, 4 October 1994; Farhan Haq, "East Timor: Resistance Holds Direct Talks with Indonesian Envoy," *Inter Press Service*, 7 October 1994.

find a diplomatic solution to the conflict in East Timor based on the peoples' right to self-determination."[50] In interviews following the prize announcement as well as in his Nobel Lecture, Ramos-Horta urged Australia, the European Union, and the United States to pressure Indonesia to settle the conflict in East Timor, calling for "serious dialogue under United Nations auspices to resolve the problem."[51] Although international pressure mounted in the late 1990s, it was not until after the collapse of Suharto's government in May 1998 that the Indonesian government finally conceded to a referendum on East Timor's independence.

GAM AND THE STRUGGLE FOR ACEHNESE INDEPENDENCE

GAM's Political Constituency

Like Fretilin, GAM received support from Acehnese civilians and possessed a complex governance structure, increasing incentives for GAM leaders to be responsive to their civilian constituents. GAM's top political leader was the group's founder, Hasan di Tiro, who fled Aceh in 1978 and eventually took up residence in Sweden, which became the base for the group's exiled political leadership. Other key political leaders living in exile in Sweden included Malik Mahmud, who served as the group's minister of state and later its prime minister, and Zaini Abdullah, who was minister of education and later foreign minister.[52] The group's military wing, called the Forces of the Free Aceh Movement (Angkatan Gerakan Aceh Merdeka, AGAM) and later the Army of the State of Aceh (Tentara Negara Aceh, TNA), was led by Abdullah Syafi'i; when Syafi'i died in 2002, Muzakkir Manaf seceded him as GAM's top military commander.[53] Despite their physical distance, GAM's political and military leadership maintained regular communications, with the political leadership outlining general policies and representing the group abroad, and the military leadership responsible for translating these policy directives into military operations.[54]

In addition to designating a set of political leaders responsible for communicating the group's political agenda, GAM also created its own local government structure, to serve as an alternative to Indonesian local institutions and to develop links with the local population throughout Aceh.[55] As di Tiro wrote

[50] Norwegian Nobel Committee, Press Release, 11 October 1996.
[51] Philippe Naughton, "Nobel Laureate Says East Timor's Ordeal Must End," *Reuters News*, 11 October 1996. See, also, Ramos-Horta's Nobel Lecture, available online at www.nobel prize.org.
[52] Schulze 2004; Aspinall 2009.   [53] Schulze 2004; Aspinall 2009.
[54] Schulze 2004; Aspinall 2009.
[55] Interviews with former senior GAM military commander, Jakarta, 5 August 2006; GAM member and delegate to peace negotiations, Banda Aceh, 8 August 2006; Acehnese NGO leader, Banda Aceh, 9 August 2006; Indonesian journalist, Jakarta, 3 August 2006.

in his 1984 memoir, winning support from Acehnese civilians was essential to the success of the insurgency. He argued that GAM's "first task, therefore, should be to restore the national consciousness, to revive the national memory, then to organize and to mobilize ourselves. Now, all these are not military activities but political, cultural, and educational. They are absolutely necessary to prepare before we can engage in armed struggle."[56]

GAM's shadow government carried out tax collection, issued birth and marriage certificates, and included a court system to adjudicate local disputes.[57] GAM taxed individuals, local businesses, village development funds received from the central government, aid organizations, and large corporations such as Exxon Mobil.[58] The development of an alternative local administrative structure, combined with GAM's intimidation of Indonesian local government officials, severely undermined the ability of the Indonesian government to function at the local level in Aceh; reports in May 2003 indicated that Indonesian local government structures were no longer functioning in 4,750 of 5,947 villages in Aceh.[59]

Brutal repression under Suharto's government made it difficult to gauge the extent of popular support for GAM during the early 1990s, but one journalist who spent considerable time embedded with GAM claims that local support for the insurgency was high from the outset, arguing that it was because so many Acehnese civilians were aiding GAM that the military engaged in such severe abuses against civilians during the 1990s.[60] Even if many civilians were supportive of GAM from the start of the insurgency, almost everyone I interviewed, including military officials, GAM members, and independent observers, pointed out that local support increased dramatically during the 1990s as the government's attacks on civilian populations backfired, generating greater antipathy and resistance to the Indonesian government.[61]

With significant support from the Acehnese population, particularly in the later years of the insurgency, and a political institutional structure that tied GAM to these constituents, the costs of violence against Acehnese civilians were high, increasing incentives for restraint.[62] But, like Fretilin, GAM possessed a narrow political constituency. GAM sought autonomy for the Acehnese and in

---

[56] Di Tiro 1984, 73.
[57] Interviews with former senior GAM military commander, Jakarta, 5 August 2006; Acehnese NGO leader, Banda Aceh, 9 August 2006; Indonesian journalist, Jakarta, 3 August 2006. See also International Crisis Group 2000a; Schulze 2003; Schulze 2004; Schulze 2006.
[58] Reid 2004; Schulze 2004.   [59] International Crisis Group 2001a; Schulze 2006, 231.
[60] Nessen 2006.
[61] Interviews with Indonesian scholar and expert on Aceh, Jakarta, 31 July 2006; human rights activist, Jakarta, 31 July 2006; Acehnese human rights activist, Jakarta, 1 August 2006; former commander in charge of Indonesian military operations in Aceh, Jakarta, 3 August 2006; senior cabinet minister under Wahid, Jakarta, 3 August 2006; GAM senior political leader, Banda Aceh, 7 August 2006; Acehnese human rights activist, Banda Aceh, 7 August 2006; GAM member and delegate to peace negotiations, Banda Aceh, 8 August 2006.
[62] Interview with GAM member and delegate to peace negotiations, Banda Aceh, 8 August 2006.

laying out its case for independence from Indonesia emphasized the distinctness of Acehnese identity; according to GAM, the Acehnese people had their own history, language, culture, and characteristics that made them a nation worthy of their own government. In making this case for Acehnese independence, GAM frequently expressed its opposition to the presence of non-Acehnese in the region. Thus, although GAM's civilian constituency may not have tolerated high levels of violence against fellow Acehnese, it is unlikely that opposition to violence against non-Acehnese living in the region would have been as strong. As one expert on the region notes, "anti-Javanese animus was by this time [post-1998] a widely shared attitude in Aceh."[63]

Javanese Migrants in Aceh

Like East Timor, Aceh had a significant Javanese population, creating incentives for violence aimed at controlling or cleansing these government constituents. The Indonesian government began encouraging transmigration to Aceh in 1975. Over the next several decades, the government helped to establish 126 transmigrant villages, totaling about 160,000 non-Acehnese migrants, most of whom were Javanese.[64] According to Indonesia's 1990 census, 65 percent of the population in Aceh reported speaking Acehnese at home, while six percent reported speaking Javanese; actual numbers of Acehnese and Javanese were likely higher than these percentages suggest, however, as some number of individuals in each of these two groups likely reported speaking Indonesian at home.[65] One expert on Aceh estimates that the Javanese constituted approximately 10 percent of Aceh's population of 3.9 million in 2000; although the Indonesian census for that year reports a higher percentage of Javanese, census officials did not have access to areas of Aceh with higher concentrations of Acehnese individuals.[66] Another scholar cites a roughly similar estimate given by a Javanese elder, placing the Javanese population at about 500,000 in 2003.[67] In a survey taken in between censuses in 2003, 82.7 percent of the population identified as ethnically Acehnese.[68]

From the earliest days of the insurgency, GAM expressed strong opposition to the presence of the transmigrant population in Aceh. Javanese migrant populations in the region were viewed as evidence of government attempts to extend its colonization of the region.[69] In a book chronicling the insurgency's origins and early years, GAM's leader, di Tiro, wrote:

---

[63] Aspinall 2009, 173. Several interviewees also noted the tensions in Aceh as a result of Javanese migration to the region (interview with senior international NGO official and expert on Indonesia, Jakarta, 5 August 2006; interview with GAM member and delegate to peace negotiations, Banda Aceh, 8 August 2006).

[64] Aspinall 2008, 134; Badan Pusat Statistik - Statistics Indonesia 2011.

[65] Aspinall 2008, 134.   [66] Ibid.   [67] Davies 2006, 187.   [68] Aspinall 2009, 4.

[69] Aspinall 2008; Aspinall 2009.

Our political objective is to discourage, and eventually to stop the Javanese settlers/ colonizers/"transmigrants" from coming illegally (without our permission) to our country to devour our resources, to ruin our economy, to take away our jobs, to rob us of our land, and finally to constitute themselves as Javanese fifth columns in our midst, until our country can no longer be defended against Javanese aggression, and against Javanese takeover.[70]

In addition to stating publicly its opposition to the presence of transmigrants in the region, GAM took more aggressive action against transmigrant communities, urging transmigrants to leave Aceh and threatening them with violence. In 2001, for example, a senior GAM military commander, Sofyan Daud, issued a statement announcing the deployment of GAM troops and urging non-Acehnese to leave:

To non-Acehnese residents, we ask you to leave the country of our forebears as soon as possible.... With all respect, we ask our brothers from the Javanese ethnic groups to temporarily move out, because we do not want you, who have been thrown out of your own region, to become the unnecessary victims should war break out between GAM guerrillas and Indonesian security troops.[71]

While GAM does not admit to targeting Javanese migrants, violent attacks on migrant communities were reported throughout the insurgency.[72] In most of the reported cases Javanese were harassed, threatened, and told to leave Aceh; in some cases, Javanese homes were burned and Javanese civilians attacked physically.[73] As a result, many transmigrants left Aceh; in 2005 the government estimated that 130,000 transmigrants had left since the 1998 resurgence of violence in the region.[74]

The level of violence against transmigrants was higher in Aceh than it was in East Timor. Still, GAM's leadership maintained its distance, publicly encouraging transmigrants to leave, but without condoning violence against these non-Acehnese civilians. As in East Timor, the high international costs of violence outweighed the potential benefits of a strategy of control or cleansing, encouraging GAM to limit violence against Javanese transmigrants. As Edward Aspinall explains, "in the post-1998 period, GAM was reconfiguring its agenda in terms of human rights discourse, and the movement's more sophisticated leaders were aware that ethnic hostility could undermine its attempts to garner international support."[75]

---

[70] Di Tiro 1984, 330. Cited in Aspinall 2008, 135.
[71] "Aceh Rebels Prepare for All-Out Resistance against Indonesian Forces," *Agence-France Presse*, 22 April 2001.
[72] Sheila Tefft, "Homesteaders Face Violence," *Christian Science Monitor*, 14 August 1990; "The Free Aceh Movement: A Thorn in Indonesia's Flank for Decades," *Agence France-Presse*, 27 March 1998. See also International Crisis Group 2001a; Schulze 2004; Aspinall 2009.
[73] Agus Maryono, "Terrorized Transmigrants Leave Aceh," *Jakarta Post*, 9 September 1999.
[74] Aspinall 2009, 173. [75] Ibid.

GAM's Military Strategy

GAM's strategy for confronting the Indonesian government was similar to Fretilin's strategy in East Timor, possessing three key components: guerrilla attacks on Indonesian government and military targets, attempts to build local support for the insurgency, and efforts to generate international pressure on the Indonesian government to negotiate. The military component of GAM's strategy involved armed attacks on Indonesian government, police, and military targets in Aceh. Although GAM was heavily outnumbered by the Indonesian military, it relied on its superior knowledge of Acehnese territory, its access to intelligence through links with local communities, and its ability to retreat within Aceh's mountainous interior to carry out small-scale guerrilla attacks.[76] GAM carried out frequent ambushes of military and police vehicles,[77] attacks on military and police posts, and surprise assaults on police or military units as they patrolled communities.[78] In the later years of the insurgency, GAM also targeted government buildings such as courthouses or local government offices,[79] as well as intimidated, harassed, and sometimes killed judges and local government officials.[80]

Like most insurgencies that employ guerrilla warfare, the aim of the military component of GAM's strategy was to wear down the Indonesian government and military, with the expectation that the financial and political costs of the conflict would ultimately force concessions. As a GAM representative explained, "From a military perspective there is no way for us to defeat them and for them to defeat us. We want to tie down as many of their troops as possible in Aceh. We want them to spend more money on this operation. We want to exhaust them financially."[81] Another GAM member made a similar

---

[76] Sukma 2001; Davies 2006; Schulze 2006.

[77] "Free Aceh Movement Says It Was Responsible for Shootings," BBC Monitoring Service: Asia-Pacific, 2 June 1999; "Army Patrol Ambushed in Aceh, One Soldier Killed," BBC Monitoring Service: Asia-Pacific, 15 July 1999; "Violence in Indonesia's Troubled Aceh Claims 11 Lives," *Agence France-Presse*, 21 August 1999.

[78] "National Liberation Front of Aceh Continues Fight for Independence," *Economist*, 8 September 1990; "Aceh Rebels Blamed for Death and Injuries in Indonesia Ambush," *Agence France-Presse*, 16 April 1998; "Guerrillas, Anti-Riot Troops Clash in Aceh," BBC Monitoring Service: Asia-Pacific, 20 August 1999; "Rebels Injure Four Policemen in New Violence in Troubled Aceh," *Agence France-Presse*, 13 December 1999; "Three Policemen Killed in Aceh," *Jakarta Post*, 20 December 1999; "Rebel Blast Injures Policemen in Aceh," *Agence France-Presse*, 23 December 1999.

[79] "Five Killed in Aceh Province Violence," *Agence France-Presse*, 18 September 2000; "Violence Claims More Victims in Restive Aceh," *Agence France-Presse*, 21 September 2000; "Humanitarian Pause Brought More Casualties, Says Graito," *Jakarta Post*, 22 September 2000; "Two More Govt Offices Attacked in Banda Aceh," *Jakarta Post*, 1 October 2000; "Six Killed in New Violence in Indonesia's Aceh Province," *Agence France-Presse*, 3 November 2000.

[80] Schulze 2004; Schulze 2006. "Grenade Attack on Aceh's Indonesian Governor," *Agence France-Presse*, 10 December 2000.

[81] Quoted in Schulze 2006, 228.

observation, saying, "We know that we cannot win militarily," but pointing out that Indonesia also is unable to defeat GAM; the aim, he said, was to prevent Indonesia from winning the war, while simultaneously encouraging support for independence among the Acehnese.[82]

For the most part, GAM refrained from using violence against civilians.[83] GAM did, however, argue that some civilian targets were closely tied to the Indonesian government and, therefore, constituted legitimate targets for attack; this included individual civilians believed to be aiding the Indonesian government, major foreign corporations operating in Aceh, and Javanese migrant communities in Aceh. A senior GAM military commander, whom I interviewed, explained in detail how the group identified legitimate targets for attack.[84] For GAM, he explained, there were three types of hostile individuals: an individual carrying a weapon and using the weapon against GAM; an individual carrying a weapon, but not using it at that particular moment; and an individual not carrying a weapon, but engaging in "hostile" conduct against GAM, such as providing information to the Indonesian government. In the first case, when an individual is armed and attacking, the commander argued that GAM was justified in responding with force. In the second and third cases – when an individual is armed, but not attacking or is an unarmed government collaborator – GAM troops were instructed to detain and interrogate the individual; often suspects were tried through a GAM court system. If the individual was found guilty of aiding the government, the punishment would depend on the extent of collaboration with the government and whether this collaboration was intentional, with the most serious punishment being death. Certainly GAM courts were not impartial – they were run by members of the rebel group – and it is unlikely that all suspected collaborators did, in fact, receive a trial before punishment as the GAM commander claimed, but it is clear that GAM did try to identify and punish specific individuals believed to be aiding the government, rather than using violence indiscriminately to attack whole families or entire villages.[85]

GAM also viewed foreign corporations as closely tied to the Indonesian government, and therefore, as legitimate targets for attack. As GAM's military commander for North Aceh explained, foreign corporations involved in oil and natural gas extraction and logging are "exploiting Aceh's land for the benefit of the colonialist government in Jakarta while our people are starving and killed by Indonesian security forces."[86] Most of these attacks targeted Indonesian

---

[82] Interview with GAM senior political leader, Banda Aceh, 7 August 2006.

[83] Interviews with Indonesian journalist, Jakarta, 3 August 2006; senior international NGO official and expert on Indonesia, Jakarta, 5 August 2006; Acehnese human rights activist, Banda Aceh, 7 August 2006; GAM member and delegate to peace negotiations, 8 August 2006.

[84] Interview with former GAM senior military commander, Jakarta, 5 August 2006.

[85] On reports of GAM attacks on government collaborators, see International Crisis Group 2001a.

[86] "Rebels Urge Mobil Oil to Leave Aceh Province for Safety Reasons," *Agence France-Presse*, 3 January 2001.

security forces guarding oil and natural gas sites, and avoided attacks on civilian employees.[87] Exxon Mobil was a frequent target, and GAM specifically called on Exxon Mobil to remove its employees from Aceh, announcing that "we cannot be held responsible for any damage suffered by Mobil Oil in the event that we attack Indonesian soldiers in the company's complex."[88]

Domestic Constraints and GAM's Search for International Support

Under Suharto, the political institutional structure left little space for domestic political opposition. Interviewees noted that during this period, citizens were afraid to express opposition to Suharto's policies; restrictions on freedom of speech and association, as well as government control over the media, made it difficult for citizens to mobilize politically or to establish civil society organizations. Generating domestic pressure on the government to alter its policies in Aceh was simply not a viable option.[89] Within this constrained domestic political context, GAM turned to the international community, seeking to generate international pressure on the Indonesian government to negotiate by raising international awareness of Acehnese grievances, drawing attention to Indonesian human rights abuses in Aceh, and actively lobbying governments, NGOs, and the United Nations for support. In his 1984 memoir, di Tiro argued that the Acehnese "as a people have been put under externally imposed isolation for so long that we have been effectively isolated internationally. To solve all our problems as a nation, we have to get back into international political currents, out of our isolation."[90]

GAM began making appeals to the international community in the 1980s, after the government's harsh response to the insurgency forced many GAM leaders to take refuge overseas. GAM opened offices in Malaysia, Singapore, Australia, the United States, and Europe.[91] While in exile in Sweden, di Tiro wrote a number of articles developing GAM's ideology and defending Aceh's right to self-determination. He also regularly attended international conferences and seminars, in an effort to increase awareness of the situation in Aceh.[92] In November 1991, for example, di Tiro gave a talk at the Hoover

---

[87] "Fourteen Killed as Violence Escalates in Indonesia's Restive Aceh," *Agence France-Presse*, 13 September 2000; "Eight Injured as Aceh Rebels Attack Indonesian Security Forces," *Agence France-Presse*, 12 December 2000; "At Least Six Killed, Eight Injured in Aceh Violence," *Agence France-Presse*, 12 January 2001.

[88] "Rebels Urge Mobil Oil to Leave Aceh Province for Safety Reasons," *Agence France-Presse*, 3 January 2001. See also Wayne Arnold, "Exxon Mobil, in Fear, Exits Indonesian Gas Fields," *New York Times*, 24 March 2001; "Aceh Rebels Attack Airplane," *Jakarta Post*, 1 April 2000; Jay Solomon, "Fueling Fears: Mobil Sees Gas Plant Becoming Rallying Point for Indonesian Rebels," *Wall Street Journal*, 7 September 2000.

[89] Interviews with senior international NGO official and expert on Indonesia, Jakarta, 5 August 2006; Acehnese NGO leader, Banda Aceh, 9 August 2006.

[90] Di Tiro 1984, 72.   [91] Schulze 2003.   [92] Sukma 2001.

Institution at Stanford University, titled "Acheh: Freedom at Issue," in which he made the following argument for international intervention in Aceh:

Today, all Human Rights organizations in the world, notably Amnesty International, Asia Watch, International Committee of the Red Cross, British and other Parliamentary Human Rights Groups, United Nations Human Rights Commission, which I addressed last August, all had expressed concerned about Human Rights violations in *Acheh* by the military regime of Indonesia. Especially the European Parliament had adopted a Resolution in February, 1991, condemning the regime of Javanese Indonesia for violating the Human Rights of the Achehnese people.... The obvious avenue for solution in Acheh would seem to be this: the UN or preferably the U.S., should intervene on legitimate humanitarian ground to put an end to the crime of genocide being perpetrated by the Indonesian regime in Acheh. A plebiscite under the UN or the U.S. auspices should be carried out to let the people of Acheh exercise their right of self determination.[93]

Hasan di Tiro and other GAM leaders also appealed to the United Nations, seeking to increase international attention to Acehnese grievances by testifying before the UN Commission on Human Rights and its Sub-Commission on Prevention of Discrimination and Protection of Minorities.[94] GAM leaders abroad also participated in the activities of the Unrepresented Nations and Peoples Organization (UNPO), which was created in 1991 to aid indigenous populations and minority groups in bringing their concerns to the attention of the international community and, in particular, to the attention of the United Nations.[95] In addition, GAM sought to develop relationships with international NGOs, in the hope that NGOs might help to raise awareness of Acehnese grievances against Indonesia.[96]

Early GAM statements emphasized Aceh's right to self-determination based on the claim that Aceh had never consented to incorporation into Indonesia,[97] but in the post–Cold War period, as human rights issues gained greater prominence internationally, GAM played up the human rights dimension of the

---

[93] Hasan di Tiro, "Acheh: Freedom at Issue," speech at Hoover Seminar, Hoover Institution, Stanford University, 13 November 1991.

[94] Hasan di Tiro submitted testimony to the UN Commission on Human Rights, Sub-Commission on Prevention of Discrimination and Protection of Minorities on 19 August 1992 (UN Commission on Human Rights, Sub-Commission on Prevention of Discrimination and Protection of Minorities 1992). Schulze 2004 also cites Hasan di Tiro as having appealed to the Sub-Commission on 23 August 1991 and to the UN Human Rights Commission on 29 January 1992. Yusuf Daud submitted testimony to the UN Commission on Human Rights, Sub-Commission on Prevention of Discrimination and Protection of Minorities on 11 August 1994 (UN Commission on Human Rights, Sub-Commission on Prevention of Discrimination and Protection of Minorities 1994). Syahbuddin Rauf submitted testimony to the UN Commission on Human Rights on 3 March 1993 and to the UN Commission on Human Rights, Sub-Commission on Prevention of Discrimination and Protection of Minorities on 11 August 1993 (UN Commission on Human Rights 1993b; UN Commission on Human Rights, Sub-Commission on Prevention of Discrimination and Protection of Minorities 1993).

[95] Unrepresented Nations and Peoples Organization 1997.   [96] Aspinall 2002.

[97] Di Tiro 1980.

conflict, arguing that Indonesian security forces were responsible for severe abuses of civilians in Aceh and that these human rights violations warranted international intervention on Aceh's behalf.[98] GAM's references to Indonesian human rights violations began in the early 1990s, as di Tiro and other GAM leaders made appeals to the UN Commission on Human Rights. At a meeting of the UN Commission on Human Rights, Sub-Commission on Prevention of Discrimination and Protection of Minorities in August 1993, GAM representative Syahbuddin Rauf "expressed the hope that a special rapporteur should be sent to Aceh to investigate the atrocities committed by the Indonesian forces."[99] GAM argued that the Acehnese constituted a distinct ethnic group and accused the Indonesian government of engaging in ethnic cleansing and even genocide against the Acehnese.[100] In his March 1993 statement before the UN Commission on Human Rights, Rauf suggested that Indonesia's "reign of terror imposed on the Achehnese was akin to the ethnic cleansing practised in Bosnia and Herzegovina."[101]

GAM's Post-Suharto Strategy

After the fall of Suharto in 1998 and the move toward democratic government in Indonesia, GAM intensified both its military operations on the ground in Aceh and its efforts to win diplomatic support internationally. The argument put forth in this book posits that rebel groups fighting against democratic governments are likely to adopt strategies of terrorism, targeting civilians in an effort to increase the costs of the conflict and to generate domestic public pressure that will force the government to make concessions. As Indonesia democratized, however, GAM did not shift from a strategy of restraint to a strategy of terrorism. Instead, GAM continued to exercise restraint in its dealings with civilians, even as it increased its attacks on government and military targets.

I posit that there are two key reasons that GAM did not alter its strategy of restraint. First, the new Indonesian government installed after the collapse of Suharto's authoritarian regime was a transitional government and had not yet established itself as a democracy. Although the Indonesian public and the international community welcomed the departure of Suharto, they remained unsure of the new government's commitment to democratic reform. In addition, as discussed in Chapter 4, the military retained a powerful role in

---

[98] Aspinall 2002; Schulze 2004; Aspinall 2006; interview with Indonesian scholar and expert on Aceh, Jakarta, 31 July 2006.

[99] UN Commission on Human Rights, Sub-Commission on Prevention of Discrimination and Protection of Minorities 1993, 5.

[100] Aspinall 2002. In his 1992 testimony to the UN Commission on Human Rights, Sub-Commission on Protection of Minorities and Prevention of Discrimination, di Tiro suggested that Indonesia was carrying out genocide in Aceh (UN Commission on Human Rights, Sub-Commission on Prevention of Discrimination and Protection of Minorities 1992).

[101] UN Commission on Human Rights 1993b.

government, even after Indonesia began to democratize. Rebel groups challenging full democracies often have difficulty making international appeals because the governments they are fighting against are already perceived as legitimate by most domestic and international actors. Rebel groups challenging governments that have not yet established their democratic credentials, however, do not face this same barrier to building international support. In fact, during the transition to democracy, governments are often particularly sensitive to domestic and international criticism, as they attempt to legitimize their rule. Several interviewees noted the government's weakness during this period of transition, emphasizing that GAM sought to take advantage of the new government's vulnerability by increasing its efforts to generate domestic and international pressure on the Indonesian government to negotiate.[102]

The second reason GAM did not alter its strategy of restraint was that GAM was influenced heavily by the events in East Timor. Indonesia's decision to allow East Timor to hold a referendum on independence demonstrated the effectiveness of international pressure in forcing the government to make concessions to separatist movements. GAM members and independent observers I interviewed emphasized that events in East Timor had a strong impact on GAM, saying that GAM believed that they might be able to generate enough international pressure to compel the Indonesian government to agree to a similar settlement for Aceh.[103]

One aspect of GAM's strategy that did change as the government democratized was an increase in GAM's efforts to bring domestic pressure to bear on the Indonesian government. Under Suharto's autocratic rule, the ability of domestic groups to criticize the government was severely restricted by harsh government repression of opposition. Furthermore, because the government was autocratic, government institutions did not create incentives for Indonesian leaders to be responsive to what little public criticism did emerge. With democratization, however, public criticism became both more possible and more likely to influence the behavior of the government. As the power of Indonesian civil society increased, GAM sought to build relationships with Indonesian NGOs and student activist groups, in an effort to generate domestic pressure on the government to resolve the conflict in Aceh. Indonesian NGOs – groups such as the Commission for "the Disappeared" and Victims of Violence (Kontras) and the Indonesian Legal Aid Institute (LBH) – served an important role in investigating and reporting on abuses committed by the Indonesian military in Aceh.[104] In addition to mobilizing domestic pressure on the Indonesian

---

[102] Interviews with former senior GAM military commander, Jakarta, 5 August 2006; Acehnese human rights activist, Banda Aceh, 7 August 2006; Acehnese NGO leader, Banda Aceh, 9 August 2006.

[103] Interviews with Indonesian journalist, Jakarta, 3 August 2006; senior GAM political leader, Banda Aceh, 7 August 2006; GAM member and delegate to peace negotiations, Banda Aceh, 8 August 2006. See also Schulze 2004; Schulze 2006.

[104] International Crisis Group 2001a; Aspinall 2002; Schulze 2006.

government, these Indonesian NGOs also networked with international NGOs, helping to raise awareness about human rights abuses and repression in Indonesia.[105] Even within Aceh itself, civil society groups grew more active during the transition period. The Aceh Referendum Information Centre (Sentral Informasi Referendum Aceh, SIRA), one of the largest student activist organizations that emerged after the fall of Suharto, was established in Aceh in February 1999. Although the Indonesian government accused SIRA of being part of GAM and often arrested and interrogated SIRA leaders, SIRA maintained its own leadership and organizational structure.[106] SIRA did, however, cooperate with GAM.[107] As a new organization, SIRA had not yet developed the ties to local communities necessary to build a mass movement in favor of an Aceh referendum. GAM, in contrast, had a strong local network extending into villages throughout Aceh; in cooperation with SIRA, GAM used this existing civilian network to build support for Acehnese independence.[108]

SIRA and other Acehnese civil society groups organized frequent rallies calling for Indonesia to hold a referendum for Aceh. Small rallies were reported in early October 1999,[109] but momentum surged after October 20, when Abdurrahman Wahid was elected as the new Indonesian president; several months earlier Wahid had indicated his support for a referendum in Aceh.[110] Thousands were estimated to have attended referendum rallies in East and South Aceh in mid-October 1999,[111] while tens of thousands gathered for rallies in Banda Aceh, Lhokseumawe, and Pidie at the end of October and beginning of November.[112] The largest of the rallies, held on November 8 in Banda Aceh, attracted somewhere between 500,000 and one million people.[113]

---

[105] Interviews with GAM senior political leader, Banda Aceh, 7 August 2006; Acehnese human rights activist, Banda Aceh, 7 August 2006; GAM member and delegate to peace negotiations, Banda Aceh, 8 August 2006.

[106] Aspinall 2006.

[107] Interviews with GAM member and delegate to peace negotiations, Banda Aceh, 8 August 2006; Acehnese NGO leader, Banda Aceh, 9 August 2006. See also Schulze 2004.

[108] Interviews with Indonesian journalist, Jakarta, 3 August 2006; GAM member and delegate to peace negotiations, Banda Aceh, 8 August 2006.

[109] "Aceh Students Demand Referendum on Self-Determination," *Agence France-Presse*, 4 October 1999; "Thousands Protest: Student Dies as Indonesia Armed Forces Day Celebrated," *Agence France-Presse*, 5 October 1999.

[110] "Muslim Leader Supports Referendum Calls in Indonesia Province," *Associated Press*, 19 May 1999.

[111] "'Tens of Thousands' March in Aceh to Demand Referendum," BBC Monitoring Service: Asia-Pacific, 16 October 1999; "Protest Calls for Referendum in Indonesia's Aceh," *Reuters News*, 23 October 1999.

[112] "More Separatist Protests Shake Indonesia," *Reuters News*, 28 October 1999; "Thousands Rally to Demand Referendum in Indonesia's Aceh Province," *Agence France-Presse*, 29 October 1999; "Tens of Thousands Gather in East Aceh Town to Demand Referendum," *Agence France-Presse*, 4 November 1999.

[113] "Hundreds of Thousands Call for Referendum in Indonesia's Volatile Aceh," *Agence France-Presse*, 8 November 1999.

Mass demonstrations were intended to draw the attention of the Indonesian government as well as the attention of the international community. SIRA demonstrations in Jakarta in 2000 explicitly encouraged the United Nations and the United States to intervene.[114] Some national organizations in Indonesia even expressed their support for a referendum; the Islamic Students Association, for example, announced that if the government did not begin investigating reports of human rights abuses in Aceh, the group would support a referendum for Aceh.[115] Graffiti with the word "referendum" appeared throughout Aceh;[116] as one journalist I interviewed observed, many Acehnese did not know exactly what a referendum would entail, but knew that East Timor had gotten one and, therefore, wanted one for Aceh.[117]

Not only did the process of democratization create greater space for civil society organizations to operate in Aceh and throughout Indonesia, but it also led to fewer restrictions on travel to Aceh. This loosening of travel restrictions gave GAM leaders on the ground in Aceh greater access to foreign journalists; they used this increased media access to reach out to international actors for support. Abdullah Syafi'i, who was GAM's senior military commander in Aceh until his death in January 2002, met with numerous Indonesian and foreign journalists in 1999. During these meetings, Syafi'i, like GAM's leaders in exile, emphasized that Indonesian forces were responsible for serious human rights abuses against civilians.[118] In an August 1999 interview with the *Jakarta Post*, Syafi'i accused Indonesian troops of attacking civilians, saying that "Many civilians have been massacred.... They rape, they kill ... they plunder the belongings of the Acehnese. They have been running from the realities and refused to take responsibility."[119] Syafi'i appealed to the international community for support and called for international intervention to end the Indonesian government's harsh treatment of Acehnese. In the *Jakarta Post* interview, Syafi'i was quoted as saying, "Why is the international world still so silent? Do they see Acehnese as subhuman? Please do not abandon us.... We do not have any ties whatsoever with war criminals. We just hope that the international world, especially the Netherlands which surrendered Aceh to the colonial powers of Indonesia, will solve the situation and be responsible for the suffering of the Acehnese."[120] In an interview with the London-based *Guardian* Syafi'i acknowledged that GAM sought to increase international awareness of the conflict in Aceh; he again urged the international community to intervene,

---

[114] Aspinall 2002; Aspinall 2006.   [115] Aspinall 2006.

[116] Interview with Indonesian journalist, Jakarta, 3 August 2006. See also Sukma 2001.

[117] Interview with Indonesian journalist, Jakarta, 3 August 2006.

[118] For a discussion of GAM's emphasis on Indonesian human rights abuses during this period, see Aspinall 2006.

[119] "AGAM Chief Calls for World Attention on Aceh," *Jakarta Post*, 4 August 1999.

[120] Ibid.

comparing Aceh to Kosovo and asking, "Why doesn't the world open its eyes to the atrocities here. Why does it let this happen to us? If it can intervene in Kosovo, why can't it do the same here? . . . Without outside help there will never be peace in Aceh."[121]

Syafi'i often made reference to international law in his calls for international support, insisting that Indonesia's human rights abuses in Aceh justified international intervention on Aceh's behalf. He compared Aceh to Kosovo, Kuwait, and Yugoslavia, arguing that just as foreign governments had intervened to stop atrocities and to protect threatened minority groups in these countries, so should they intervene to end atrocities against the Acehnese in Indonesia. In an interview with an Australian journalist, Syafi'i insisted that the international community take action against Indonesia:

Aceh has always been its own nation. We ask for the help of the international community to acknowledge this. Our nation has been attacked, oppressed, and raped by the Dutch and the Indonesians. We ask: is justice in this world only in the textbooks? . . . Those who are wrong have to be punished. International law has to be enforced for us. Is our blood different from Yugoslav blood? From Kuwaiti blood? The international community must listen to us. That is why we are pleased to meet foreign journalists, to meet foreign friends.[122]

As GAM military commanders on the ground in Aceh became more vocal in lobbying for international support after the fall of Suharto, GAM's civilian leadership abroad also stepped up its efforts to generate international pressure on the governments of Presidents Habibie, Wahid, and Megawati. GAM leaders used three key strategies for building international support during this period: first, emphasizing that despite the Indonesian government's stated commitment to democratic reform, government security forces continued to engage in human rights abuses in Aceh; second, portraying GAM as a national separatist insurgency and downplaying the religious elements of the group's ideology; and third, using peace negotiations with the Indonesian government as an opportunity to increase the group's international profile.

First, GAM pointed out that even after democratization, the Indonesian military continued to engage in abuses against civilians in Aceh. GAM sought to draw sharp contrasts between the Indonesian government's repressive, abusive behavior toward civilians in Aceh and the insurgency's respect for human rights. In a July 4, 2002, press release, Zaini Abdullah, a senior GAM leader and one of its primary negotiators, stated, "We believe in and uphold the Geneva Conventions and follow the dictates of International Humanitarian Law. Under no circumstances does GAM purposely target civilians or their property. However, under such circumstances, GAM will, when necessary, question people but will never harm or unnecessarily detain

---

[121] John Aglionby, "'Our Freedom Must Be Complete,'" *Guardian*, 10 August 1999.
[122] Johanson 1999, 10.

non-combatants."[123] A GAM military commander I interviewed insisted that the group was knowledgeable about international humanitarian law and trained its troops to abide by these international standards; he claimed that GAM wanted to sign the First Additional Protocol to the Geneva Conventions applicable to international armed conflicts – to signal the group's commitment to international humanitarian law and to emphasize that GAM viewed Aceh as an independent nation and, therefore, viewed the conflict as an international armed conflict rather than an internal conflict.[124]

Some scholars have argued that GAM sought intentionally to provoke the Indonesian security forces, in the hope that Indonesia's harsh counterinsurgency tactics would prompt international actors to intervene.[125] Little evidence is available, however, to support this claim. Although GAM likely expected the government's counterinsurgency operations to be harsh, GAM does appear to have tried to protect civilians from government abuses when possible. For example, in December 1999, to commemorate the twenty-third anniversary of GAM's founding, GAM planned a massive flag-raising ceremony, but when the military threatened to crack down on flag raisings, GAM leaders canceled the planned ceremony and made public appeals to civilians not to fly the GAM flag. A GAM spokesman explained the cancellation, saying, "What is the point of hoisting the flag if the people are shot by the Indonesian military and police," while GAM's military commander, Abdullah Syafi'i, was quoted as saying, "Our main concern is the safety of all people. Anyone – Acehnese, Chinese, or Javanese – who lives in Aceh is not allowed to fly the flag."[126]

Second, GAM downplayed the role of Islam in the conflict. From the start of its rebellion, GAM argued that Aceh had a unique ethnic and national identity, distinct from the Indonesian national identity. Although GAM saw Islam as an important component of Acehnese identity, the group insisted that the conflict was not simply about gaining greater control over religion in Aceh, but about the right to self-determination.[127] In the early years of its rebellion, GAM received training from the Libyan government and made more frequent reference to the Islamic component of Acehnese identity, but GAM later realized that the group's links to Islam might create obstacles to winning support among Western governments and the United Nations.[128] When the Indonesian government tried to

---

[123] Text of press release reprinted in "Aceh Rebel Negotiator Says 18 Civilians 'Detained' in Indonesia to Be Released," *BBC Monitoring: Asia-Pacific*, 4 July 2002.

[124] Interview with former senior GAM military commander, Jakarta, 5 July 2006.

[125] See, for example, Schulze 2004. This is similar to the moral hazard argument made by Kuperman (2006), who suggests that groups often launch rebellions with the hope that the government will overreact and commit large-scale abuses of human rights that will force international intervention.

[126] Victor Tjahjadi, "Aceh Rebels Urge Residents Not to Fly Separatist Flag on Anniversary," *Agence France-Presse*, 2 December 1999.

[127] Aspinall 2007a; Aspinall 2007b.

[128] Interviews with former senior GAM military commander, Jakarta, 5 August 2006; senior GAM political leader, Banda Aceh, 7 August 2006. Schulze (2004) points out that while GAM

address the conflict in Aceh by passing legislation that would allow for the implementation of Islamic shari'a law, GAM opposed the legislation and argued that religion was not, as the government claimed, the cause of the conflict.[129] In interviews, GAM leaders suggested that the Indonesian government was using the implementation of shari'a law in Aceh to portray GAM as an Islamist group, thereby marginalizing GAM internationally.[130] GAM's attempts to downplay the influence of Islam increased after September 11, 2001, as the international community became even warier of groups linked to Islam. GAM made public statements condemning the September 11 attacks on the United States and expressed opposition to al-Qaeda and other Islamic extremist organizations.[131] GAM also repudiated any links with Indonesian Islamic extremist organizations.[132]

The third, and perhaps most important, strategy that GAM used in seeking to build international support was to use peace negotiations with the Indonesian government as a means of increasing international awareness of the Achenese conflict and building international pressure on the Indonesian government to concede to independence for Aceh.[133] The first negotiations began in January 2000, with a series of meetings in Geneva between the Indonesian ambassador to the United Nations in Geneva, Hassan Wirajuda, and GAM's leader, Hasan di Tiro. The Henry Dunant Centre (later renamed the HD Centre or the Centre for Humanitarian Dialogue) helped to facilitate and mediate the talks, leading to the signing of a "Joint Understanding of Humanitarian Pause for Aceh" on May 12, which was intended to serve as a temporary ceasefire to allow for the provision of humanitarian assistance and to pave the way for continued negotiations.[134] For GAM, the fact that these first talks with the Indonesian government took place in Europe and were mediated by an international NGO was important for several reasons: it drew international attention to the conflict in Aceh and it signaled that GAM was a legitimate actor, deserving of serious negotiations with the Indonesian government.[135] One of GAM's senior representatives at the peace negotiations acknowledged that GAM sought to use the

representatives abroad emphasized Achenese nationalism and ethnicity, GAM leaders in Aceh relied more heavily on religion as a means of recruiting members. On the realization that Islam might impede the group's ability to win international support, see Aspinall 2007b.

[129] Aspinall 2007b.

[130] Interviews with senior GAM political leader, Banda Aceh, 7 August 2006; human rights activist, Jakarta, 1 August 2006. Aspinall 2007b suggests that the Indonesian government may also have sought to marginalize GAM domestically. By portraying Islam as GAM's central grievance, the government could claim that there was no need for separation from Indonesia since the newly democratic government was more accepting of a role for Islam than the Suharto government had been.

[131] Aspinall 2007b. See also Bertil Lintner, "Indonesia – Birthday Bash: Aceh Separatists Mark Their 25th Anniversary Facing Major New Challenges," *Far Eastern Economic Review*, 13 December 2001.

[132] Amy Chew, "Aceh Links to al Qaeda Dismissed," CNN.com, 12 July 2002.

[133] Aspinall and Crouch 2003; Schulze 2004.

[134] For an analysis of the HD Centre's mediation efforts in Aceh, see Huber 2004.

[135] Aspinall and Crouch 2003; Schulze 2004.

negotiations as a means of building international support, in the hope that this would force the government to concede:

It [GAM's strategy] is based on three pillars: first the Acehnese people, second the Indonesians, and third the international community. If the Indonesians want to give us our freedom, the conflict is over. But at the moment we have only the first pillar and the third. . . . Regarding the third – we give information to the international community about the situation here. The dialogue is part of this, too. Everything needs to be conducted outside of Aceh and Indonesia! If all three elements work, then the struggle for an independent Aceh will be a success. The second pillar is the most difficult. We need to get the Acehnese people to influence the Indonesians and the international community to pressure Jakarta.[136]

Negotiations broke down after Megawati took over the presidency in July 2001, as the government stepped up its military operations in Aceh. When the prospect of renewed negotiations was raised toward the end of 2001, senior members of the Indonesian government demanded that negotiations take place without foreign mediators, claiming that the conflict in Aceh was a domestic issue that should be resolved within Indonesia.[137] GAM, still intent on making the conflict in Aceh an international issue, insisted that negotiations take place outside Indonesia with representatives of the national government.[138] The two sides eventually agreed to negotiations in Geneva, again facilitated by the HD Centre and attended by five retired foreign diplomats from Sweden, Thailand, the United Kingdom, the United States, and Yugoslavia, who were intended to provide support for the peace process.

GAM's strategy of increasing international pressure on the Indonesian government through negotiations appeared to be working, as foreign governments increasingly urged the Indonesian government to find a peaceful resolution to the conflict. The U.S. ambassador to Indonesia, for example, called for a negotiated settlement during visits to Aceh in 2001 and 2002, while the EU, Japan, the United States, and the World Bank organized a conference in late 2002 to coordinate financial support to back a peace agreement.[139] Within days, representatives of the Indonesian government and GAM signed the Cessation of Hostilities Agreement (COHA); individuals close to negotiations agree that international pressure was key to securing the final agreement.[140]

---

[136] As quoted in Schulze 2004, 53.
[137] "Indonesia Rules Out Foreign Mediator in Talks with Aceh Rebels," *Agence France-Presse*, 4 January 2002.
[138] "Indonesian Military Kills Top Aceh Rebel Commander," *Agence France-Presse*, 23 January 2002. Interviews with former senior GAM military commander, Jakarta, 5 August 2006; former UN official and participant in peace negotiations, 3 August 2006; Indonesian journalist, Jakarta, 3 August 2006.
[139] Aspinall and Crouch 2003.
[140] Interviews with former GAM senior military commander, Jakarta, 5 August 2006; GAM member and delegate to peace negotiations, Banda Aceh, 8 August 2006; former senior cabinet minister under Wahid, Jakarta, 3 August 2006.

The COHA established terms for a ceasefire and provided for a monitoring team, including a number of international representatives to aid in the implementation of the ceasefire. GAM agreed to turn in its weapons and begin demobilizing its military forces, while the Indonesian government agreed to halt offensive operations against GAM and relocate its military and police units.[141] Although the COHA did not resolve the political issues at stake in the conflict, both sides agreed to take part in further negotiations once the ceasefire was in place. The first few months following the signing of the COHA saw a decline in violence in Aceh, but the agreement began to break down in early 2003. GAM was hesitant to demobilize, fearing that the Indonesian government would return to military operations once GAM had surrendered its weapons. The Indonesian government, too, resisted making any significant changes in its security force structure in Aceh. The peace process collapsed entirely following negotiations held in April and May 2003, in which the Indonesian government took a harsher stance than it had in previous peace talks. Although GAM expressed its willingness to continue negotiations, it refused to accept the Indonesian government's terms for peace. The government withdrew immediately from negotiations, imposed martial law in Aceh, and launched a renewed military offensive against GAM.

Through the process of peace negotiations, mediated by an international NGO and held at international venues, GAM had succeeded in drawing increased international attention to the conflict in Aceh – Japan, the EU, the United States, and the World Bank initiated the December 2002 conference to coordinate financial support for the peace process and sponsored the May 2003 peace talks in Tokyo, while the Philippines and Thailand sent observers to aid in the implementation of the COHA agreement. But despite this increased international attention, foreign governments proved unwilling to pressure the Indonesian government to concede Acehnese independence. The U.S. ambassador to Indonesia and the Japanese prime minister, for example, both urged the Indonesian government to negotiate, but at the same time confirmed their commitment to uphold Indonesian territorial integrity.[142] GAM likely overestimated its ability to win international support for Acehnese independence, perhaps not realizing that international actors would view Aceh and East Timor so differently – that the international justification for East Timor's independence rested heavily on the idea that Indonesia's 1975 invasion and annexation of the former Portuguese colony was illegal.[143]

In the end, GAM was unable to translate increased international attention into pressure for Acehnese independence. Following the government's

---

[141] Aspinall and Crouch 2003; Huber 2004.

[142] "U.S. Envoy Calls for Dialogue in Indonesia's Aceh as Nine More Killed," *Agence France-Presse*, 12 February 2002; "Koizumi Urges Peace in Aceh, Offers Help," *Jakarta Post*, 9 October 2003.

[143] Interview with Indonesian scholar and expert on Aceh, Jakarta, 31 July 2006.

declaration of martial law in May 2003, government military operations against GAM intensified. It was not until late 2004 that the government again offered to negotiate with GAM, this time through secret negotiations arranged by newly elected Indonesian vice president Yusuf Kalla. When a tsunami hit Aceh on December 26, 2004, killing more than 200,000 people, GAM declared an immediate ceasefire to allow for the provision of humanitarian assistance and although the government did not formally reciprocate the ceasefire, it did make efforts to facilitate the distribution of aid. Formal peace negotiations, mediated by former Finnish President Martii Ahtisaari, began the following month in Helsinki and led to the signing of a Memorandum of Understanding (MOU) on August 15, 2005. Unlike previous agreements, the MOU resolved many of the major political issues at stake in the conflict, establishing provisions for the creation of local political parties in Aceh, the holding of local elections, the distribution of revenues from natural resource exploitation in the province, the granting of amnesty to GAM members, and the creation of a truth and reconciliation commission for Aceh, among other provisions.[144] An Aceh Monitoring Mission, run by the EU and ASEAN, was organized to monitor the implementation of the agreement.

Reflecting on the outcome of the conflict in Aceh as compared with East Timor, several GAM members and other interviewees attributed the difference to patterns of international support, noting that diplomatic support from a third-party government – Portugal – as well as from the UN was crucial to East Timor's ability to pressure the Indonesian government into granting independence, while the lack of such support from foreign governments or from the UN meant that Aceh had to settle for regional autonomy.[145]

ASSESSING THE ALTERNATIVE ARGUMENTS

An organizational control perspective would emphasize the characteristics of Fretilin and GAM's organizational structures that made it possible for the two groups to implement strategies of restraint toward civilians – perhaps pointing to efforts on the part of both groups to enforce discipline and to maintain control over the use of violence within their organizations. This articulation of the organizational control perspective is not in direct conflict with the argument of this chapter. I focus on how the insurgencies' relationships with their domestic and international constituencies generated incentives for restraint, whereas organizational control arguments are interested in understanding why some groups are better able to implement such strategic choices. Fretilin and GAM both possessed organizational characteristics – such as well-trained

---

[144] Memorandum of Understanding Between the Government of the Republic of Indonesia and the Free Aceh Movement, signed in Helsinki, Finland, 15 August 2005.

[145] Interviews with Acehnese human rights activist, Jakarta, 1 August 2006; GAM senior political leader, Banda Aceh, 7 August 2006.

forces and a clear command structure with military forces subordinate to the political leadership – that likely contributed to their ability to carry out strategies of restraint. Fretilin's Central Committee, comprised of 15 members, including a president and vice president, was the primary body responsible for decision making; the group's military wing, Falintil, was subordinate to the Committee political leadership.[146] In the early years of the rebellion, Falintil was led by Rogério Lobato, who had previous military experience in the Portuguese army. In fact, many of Falintil's members had formal military experience, with one source estimating that of Falintil's 20,000 troops, 2,500 were professional soldiers and an additional 7,000 had received formal military training as part of the Portuguese armed forces; the remaining troops received shorter military training sessions.[147] GAM's military wing, AGAM, was also subordinate to the group's political leadership based in Sweden; while this geographic separation necessitated giving AGAM commanders some autonomy to make military decisions on the ground, political leaders in Sweden were in regular contact with the group's military leaders in Aceh.[148] Although AGAM soldiers lacked the professional military experience of Falintil soldiers, many did receive training in guerrilla warfare tactics in Libya in the late 1980s.[149]

The main challenge to the argument put forth in this chapter comes from arguments emphasizing the military context and, in particular, arguments emphasizing the relative strength of the belligerents; the claim is that rebel groups fighting against autocratic governments are so weak and so constrained by harsh government repression that they are simply unable to engage in violence against civilian populations. Thus, although it may be true empirically that rebel groups fighting against autocratic governments are less likely to engage in violence against civilians, this lack of violence against civilians is not the result of deliberate rebel group strategies of restraint. Rather, what looks like rebel group restraint is, in fact, simply an inability of the rebel group to engage in any violent activity, as a result of the effectiveness of repression under autocratic governments. The evidence from the Aceh and East Timor cases does not, however, support this claim. In both cases, the rebel groups faced a highly repressive autocratic government under Suharto, were heavily outmatched in terms of military troops and equipment by the powerful Indonesian military, and yet were able to carry out regular ambushes on Indonesian police and military units and to continue to do so over a period of many years. Both rebel groups had the capacity to attack families or villages suspected of sympathizing with the government – in particular, Javanese transmigrants – if they had chosen to do so. In addition, Fretilin and GAM both maintained networks of representatives in foreign cities, and GAM also had the resources to send several hundred members for military training in Libya; with a strong Islamic history and identity, GAM

---

[146] Hill 2002.   [147] Dunn 1996, 258.   [148] Schulze 2004.

[149] Ibid. Interviews with former senior GAM military commander, Jakarta, 5 August 2006; senior GAM political leader, 7 August 2006.

might also have developed connections with Jemaah Islamiyya or other jihadist groups active in Southeast Asia, much like the Moro Islamic Liberation Front (MILF) did in the Philippines. It is likely that both Fretilin and GAM could have used their international resources to carry out attacks on civilian targets within Indonesia, but neither group even attempted to direct violence against Javanese civilians within the separatist regions or beyond.

A second military context argument suggests that governments and rebel groups only resort to civilian targeting when the costs of continued fighting rise to unacceptable levels, when attacks on the opponent's military forces have proven ineffective; rebel groups are most likely to exercise restraint, therefore, when the costs of the conflict are low, making civilian targeting unnecessary. This explanation holds little weight in the Aceh and East Timor cases. In East Timor, Fretilin was nearly wiped out in the early years of the insurgency, as the Indonesian military depleted the rebel group's civilian base by forcibly relocating hundreds of thousands of civilians into resettlement camps; used heavy aerial and naval bombardment to attack the interior of the country; and launched massive search operations to hunt down Fretilin units and bases. Even as the costs of the conflict threatened to destroy the insurgency entirely, Fretilin continued to direct violence primarily at police and military targets.

At several points during the Acehnese conflict, the costs of the conflict for GAM and its Acehnese civilian base were also extremely high. When GAM emerged in the late 1970s, the Indonesian government responded with a harsh crackdown on the organization; most of GAM's leaders and members were killed, imprisoned, or forced to flee to Malaysia. GAM regrouped, sending several hundred members for military training in Libya and launching renewed operations against the Indonesian government from 1989 to 1991. Throughout the 1990s, Aceh was declared a region of active military operations; the Indonesian government intensified its attacks on GAM and suspected GAM sympathizers. Although the fall of Suharto in 1998 brought several attempts at peace negotiations, negotiations broke down in 2001 and again in 2003, leading to renewed military operations in the region and increased GAM casualties. Despite suffering high costs during each of these periods of intense government counterinsurgency operations, GAM continued to focus its attacks on government and military targets, never resorting to attacks on civilians.

A third military context argument posits that when contestation over territory is high, governments and rebel groups use violence as a means of forcing civilians to cooperate and deterring them from aiding the opponent. According to this view, governments and rebel groups are most likely to refrain from targeting civilians during periods when contestation over territory is low. This explanation, too, fails to account for rebel group behavior in Aceh and East Timor. As discussed in Chapter 4, contestation over territory in East Timor was high during the first few years of the insurgency, as the Indonesian government struggled to wrest control of the region's interior from Fretilin. By the late 1980s, this had largely been achieved, with Fretilin no longer possessing control over territory in the interior of the country; throughout the 1990s the conflict persisted at a low level of intensity, with Fretilin maintaining small, highly mobile units able to launch hit-and-run attacks on Indonesian police and military targets. Even during the period of highest contestation over territory in the late 1970s and early 1980s, however, Fretilin did not target civilians; although the level of contestation declined dramatically in the 1990s, Fretilin's treatment of civilians remained unchanged. The conflict in Aceh saw three periods of high contestation over territory – when GAM first emerged in the 1970s, after the return of the Libyan-trained GAM members in 1989–1991, and after the breakdown of peace negotiations in 2001 and 2003 – but GAM, like Fretilin, did not alter its strategy and refrained from attacking civilians throughout the insurgency.

CONCLUSION

The argument of this book predicts that relationships with domestic and international constituencies shape government and rebel group behavior. Fretilin and GAM both had governing structures tying them to their Timorese and Acehnese constituents, and generating strong incentives for restraint toward these groups of civilians. The presence of Javanese transmigrants in both regions, however, also created incentives for violence, to purge these government constituents from the separatist region. As groups with exclusionary political objectives, Fretilin and GAM likely could have used violence against Javanese civilians without risking backlash from their Timorese and Acehnese supporters. Pressure to build support from international constituencies, however, urged both rebel groups to exercise restraint toward transmigrants. In fact, leaders of both rebel groups explicitly stated that Suharto's autocratic rule made it seem impossible to use domestic pressure to force government concessions, encouraging the turn to international actors for support.

The contrast between the outcomes of the Aceh case, in which GAM was forced to accept regional autonomy within the Indonesian state, and the East Timor case, in which international support helped Fretilin to obtain independence, illustrates the difficulties that rebel groups face in trying to bring their cases to the international community. The argument of this book posits that rebel groups in need of support from Western international constituencies – rebel groups facing autocratic governments – will exercise restraint in their fighting in an effort to garner international diplomatic backing, but it does not suggest that all rebel groups will be equally *successful* in their bids to win the support of international actors. Although both the GAM insurgency in Aceh and the Fretilin insurgency in East Timor did exercise restraint in their fighting and did appeal to international actors by contrasting their own good behavior with the repressive and abusive policies of the Suharto government, Fretilin was more successful than GAM in publicizing and framing its case internationally.

6

Variation in Government Violence against Civilians: Turkey and Sudan

As illustrated in the statistical analyses in Chapter 3, for governments with narrow domestic and international constituencies, the costs of violence are low, increasing the likelihood of civilian targeting. However, the character of government violence varies significantly across cases. This chapter explores this variation in government violence through case studies of conflicts in Turkey and Sudan. The argument of this book posits that governments evaluate the benefits of different strategies of violence based on an assessment of their rebel opponent and, in particular, the rebel group's relationship with its civilian constituents. The greater the civilian support for the rebel group in the disputed territory, the greater the threat these civilians pose and, therefore, the greater the benefit a government is likely to obtain from using violence as part of a strategy aimed at controlling or eliminating these individuals. The form of violence a government uses, however, depends on the size and geographic concentration of the rebel group's civilian constituency. The smaller and more geographically concentrated the rebel group's civilian constituency, the more feasible it is to eliminate this constituency entirely, as part of a strategy of cleansing. Finally, the greater the rebel group's sensitivity to losses among its civilian constituents, the more likely it is that the rebel group will respond to violence by making political concessions, thus increasing government incentives to use a strategy of terrorism.

The statistical analyses provide support for these arguments. An autocratic government facing a rebel group whose civilian constituents are geographically concentrated is 2.7 times more likely to adopt a strategy of high-casualty cleansing than an autocratic government facing a rebel group whose constituents are not geographically concentrated. And a government facing a rebel group likely to be sensitive to losses among its constituents is between 3.4 and 9.8 times more likely to adopt a strategy of high-casualty terrorism than a government facing a rebel group lacking incentives to be responsive to its constituents. This chapter analyzes these patterns in greater depth, through two case studies: the first focusing on the Sudanese government's response to the rebellion in Darfur and the second examining Turkey's counterinsurgency strategies against the Kurdistan Workers' Party (Partiya Karkerên Kurdistanê, PKK). These two case studies allow for analysis of aspects of government behavior that are difficult to capture in the statistical analysis – in particular, how governments weigh the benefits of violence against its costs, and the extent to which an assessment of domestic and international constituencies influences strategic decisions regarding the use of violence.

The Darfur case study explores how a government behaves in the absence of constraints on the use of violence; this case study focuses on the first few years of the conflict, when the fighting was most intense. This is not a case of conflicting incentives. Rather, this is a case in which incentives to engage in violence against civilians were high and almost entirely unregulated by any concern for losing domestic or international support. As a long-standing autocratic government already unpopular with international actors, the Sudanese government had narrow domestic and international constituencies and little sensitivity to domestic and international criticism. In addition, it faced an insurgency whose civilian supporters were predominately from ethnic groups concentrated in the western region of Darfur. Under these conditions – facing a rebellion with strong civilian support, concentrated in a particular geographic region – the Sudanese government had strong incentives to use extreme violence against civilians and calculated that the costs of this violence would be low, given the government's stable autocratic institutions and lack of engagement with the international community. As the argument of this book would predict, the Sudanese government adopted a strategy of high-casualty cleansing.

The second case study in this chapter turns to Turkey's use of low-casualty cleansing and terrorism in its fight against the PKK. This is a case in which the government faced conflicting incentives regarding its use of violence in counterinsurgency operations. The potential benefits of violence were high. The PKK possessed significant support among Kurds in the disputed territory, increasing government incentives to use violence as a means of extending its territorial control. The PKK also had governance institutions, indicating that group leaders likely would be responsive to losses among their Kurdish constituents and generating incentives for the government to adopt a strategy of terrorism. In addition, the government had an exclusionary political system, meaning that it relied on a narrow domestic constituency to remain in power and thus could engage in violence against civilians outside that constituency – against Kurdish civilians – without risking significant public backlash. The domestic costs of violence were to some extent limited.

The Turkish government, however, was also constrained in its use of violence by pressure from domestic and international constituencies. Turkey was a full democracy throughout the PKK insurgency; thus, although the government was exclusionary, the open political system permitted public criticism from members of the political opposition, increasing domestic pressure on the government to exercise restraint in its counterinsurgency operations. Turkey also faced heavy pressure from international constituencies – in particular, European actors, who insisted that Turkey improve its human rights performance prior to continuing along the path toward membership in the EU. Thus, the Turkish government, a stable democracy facing pressure from domestic and international actors to demonstrate respect for human rights, did attack the rebel group's base of civilian support, but sought to limit civilian casualties.

THE SUDANESE GOVERNMENT AND CLEANSING IN DARFUR

Darfur Rebel Groups and Their Political Constituents

The two main rebel groups that launched the conflict in Darfur in 2003 – the Sudan Liberation Army (SLA) and the Justice and Equality Movement (JEM) – were revolutionary groups, calling for the overthrow of the government, the establishment of democratic institutions at the national level, and a more equitable distribution of political power and economic resources among Sudan's regions.[1] Sudan had been an autocracy since June 1989, when a group of military officers, led by Omar Hassan al-Bashir, overthrew the democratically elected civilian government in a military coup; suspended the constitution; and installed the Revolutionary Command Council, made up of 15 military officers, as the primary governing body of the state. The Sudanese government maintained heavy restrictions on the media and political participation and, until 2002, did not permit opposition parties to operate in the country.[2] The Polity IV Project gave Bashir's regime a score of −7 (autocracy) beginning with the coup in 1989 and continuing through 2002; Sudan's polity score increased slightly to −6 (still an autocracy) in 2003 and remained at this level during the early years of the conflict in Darfur. In addition, Bashir's government was exclusionary throughout this period. The Ethnic Power Relations data set lists three Arab groups, the Shaygiyya, Ja'aliyyin, and Danagla, representing approximately 15 percent of Sudan's total population, as exercising dominant power over Sudan's political institutions since the mid-1980s; Bashir is a member of the Ja'aliyyin ethnic group.[3]

---

[1] The outbreak of war in 2003 was preceded by a long history of tension and small-scale conflict in Darfur between nomadic (often identified as "Arab") and sedentary agriculturalist (often identified as "African") groups over access to land and water, exacerbated by government policies that marginalized peripheral regions of Sudan and African ethnic groups living in those regions. To reinforce their policies, the Sudanese government backed local Arab militias; other ethnic groups in the region responded with the creation of their own militia forces. For background to the conflict in Darfur see International Crisis Group 2004a; Prunier 2005; Daly 2007; de Waal 2007; Tubiana 2007.

[2] Daly 2007; Collins 2008; Gallab 2008.   [3] Natsios 2012, 81.

In justifying their rebellion, the Darfur rebel groups pointed to the government's autocratic political institutions as well as its policies of political exclusion, citing systematic political and economic marginalization of regions such as Darfur. The JEM demanded a redress of regional inequality and, in its manifesto, advocated the creation of a federal, democratic government "based on political pluralism, the rule of law, independence of the judiciary and the principle of separation of powers."[4] The SLA issued a similar manifesto in March 2003 protesting against the "marginalisation, racial discrimination and exploitation that had disrupted the peaceful coexistence between the region's African and Arab communities";[5] calling for the establishment of a secular, decentralized government with increased autonomy for Darfur and other regions; and promoting the "restructuring of power and an equal and equitable distribution of both power and wealth in all their dimensions."[6] The two rebel groups maintained separate leadership, but often collaborated in their military operations. In early 2003, the SLA and the JEM launched their first armed assaults against government targets. The rebel groups attacked a military base in the town of Golu on February 26, killing a number of Sudanese soldiers, and on April 25 attacked military targets in the capital of Northern Darfur, el-Fashir, destroying four military helicopters and two military planes at the town's airport, capturing significant amounts of ammunition, and killing between 75 and 89 government soldiers.[7]

Details on the organizational structures of the rebel groups are sparse. It appears that both groups made efforts to establish distinct political institutions, but were not particularly successful in doing so. The JEM was led by Khalil Ibrahim, who served as the group's main political representative, while Abubakar Hamid Nur is said to have served as JEM's general coordinator, responsible for military operations.[8] Several years into the conflict, the JEM established a more defined political structure, which included representatives from across Sudan on an executive board, a legislative committee, and a General Congress, but these bodies had little power, with Ibrahim retaining tight control over the group.[9] The SLA established a three-part leadership structure, with each of the three major positions occupied by a member of one of the group's three main ethnic constituencies. A Fur representative, Abdel Wahid Mohamed al Nur, was selected as chairman and a Zaghawa

---

[4] JEM manifesto quoted in Flint 2007, 162.   [5] International Crisis Group 2003b.
[6] SLA manifesto quoted in Flint 2007, 160. Many have noted that SPLA officials likely assisted the SLA in developing its political manifesto, which is evident in the similarity between SLA and SPLA stated political goals.
[7] "New Rebel Group Seizes West Sudan Town," *Agence France-Presse*, 26 February 2003; "Rebels Claim Capture of Sudan State Capital, Khartoum Denies," *Agence France-Presse*, 25 April 2003; International Crisis Group 2003b.
[8] Flint and de Waal 2008, 102, 243.   [9] Ibid., 111.

representative, Abdalla Abakir, as military commander; the deputy chairman position was reserved for a Masalit representative, but this position was not filled until several years after the group's creation.[10] Following Abdalla Abakir's death in early 2004, Minni Arkoi Minawi took over as the secretary general in charge of military operations.[11] The group's organizational structures, however, remained weak and by October 2005, growing tensions between the Fur and Zaghawa factions led to a split in the SLA, with Abdel Wahid leading one faction and Minni Minawi the other.[12]

Despite advocating broad political reforms at the national level, both groups derived support primarily from three main ethnic groups – the Fur, Masalit, and Zaghawa – concentrated in the western region of Sudan, in the states of North Darfur, South Darfur, and West Darfur. Experts on the conflict agree that support for the rebel groups was high among civilians in Darfur, increasing as the insurgency gained strength.[13] In Sudan's last reliable national census, conducted in 1956, "Western" (or "African") ethnic groups were estimated at approximately 57 percent of the total population of the Darfur region, with the Fur and Masalit being the largest of these groups.[14] The UN estimated the total prewar (2003) population of Darfur at 6.3 million.[15] Assuming that "African" ethnic groups were still about 50 percent of the total population in Darfur in 2003, one can estimate the size of the Fur, Masalit, and Zaghawa population at roughly 3.15 million. That would mean that at the start of the conflict in Darfur in 2003, the main civilian constituencies supporting the SLA and the JEM made up approximately 8.9 percent of Sudan's total population of 35.4 million.[16] With the Fur, Masalit, and Zaghawa populations being not only small in size, but also concentrated in the remote western region of the country, the Sudanese government likely calculated that it might be feasible to kill or displace a large portion of the rebel groups' civilian constituents. In contrast, when confronted with a separatist insurgency in Southern Sudan, launched by the Sudan People's Liberation Army (SPLA), the government adopted a strategy of terrorism, intended to make the war costly for civilians, but did not attempt to cleanse the separatist region of all SPLA sympathizers. Doing so would have been nearly impossible, given that the Southern Sudanese region encompassed 10 of the country's 25 states and possessed about 28 percent of the country's total population.[17]

---

[10] International Crisis Group 2005f; Flint and de Waal 2008.   [11] Flint 2007.
[12] International Crisis Group 2005f; International Crisis Group 2006b; Tanner and Tubiana 2007.
[13] Tanner and Tubiana 2007.   [14] Census results reported in Daly 2007, 179–180.
[15] United Nations 2005, 62.
[16] The estimate for Sudan's total population in 2003 is from the World Bank, *World Development Indicators*, available online at data.worldbank.org
[17] New Sudan Centre for Statistics and Evaluation, in association with UNICEF, May 2004, 32.

Counterinsurgency Operations in Darfur

In its attempt to defeat the insurgency in Darfur, the Sudanese government used extreme violence against civilians as part of a strategy of high-casualty cleansing, aimed at civilians from the Fur, Masalit, and Zaghawa ethnic groups. It has been widely debated whether the government's attacks on civilians constitute genocide of African ethnic groups in Darfur, with some arguing that acts seeking to destroy a significant part of an ethnic or religious group should qualify as genocide and others claiming that the term "genocide" should be applied only to cases in which the intent is to eliminate a group in its entirety.[18] Most experts on the conflict agree that, at a minimum, the violence ought to be considered ethnic cleansing. Although the government does not appear to have intended to kill all members of the Fur, Masalit, and Zaghawa ethnic groups, its operations did seek to kill large numbers of civilians from these groups and to drive them from their homes by systematically bombing, burning, and destroying villages.

To carry out this strategy of high-casualty cleansing, Sudanese government forces operated in conjunction with local Arab militias, called Janjaweed, which the government had used previously in smaller-scale conflicts in Darfur as well as during its struggle against the SPLA in Southern Sudan. Although the government has denied links to the Janjaweed, attempting to distance itself from extreme Janjaweed violence against civilians, numerous reports have provided evidence showing extensive government support for these militias, including the provision of weapons, salaries, training, and supplies for the Janjaweed.[19] Government and Janjaweed forces regularly carried out joint military operations and many Janjaweed militias were incorporated into the government's military command structure through the Popular Defense Forces and the Border Intelligence Guard, both of which are organized paramilitary units designed to support the regular armed forces.[20]

The pattern of government and Janjaweed attacks, which began in mid-2003, was similar throughout Darfur.[21] Although government forces did seek

---

[18] Prunier 2005; Straus 2005.

[19] International Crisis Group 2004a; Human Rights Watch 2005; International Crisis Group 2005b; Prunier 2005; United Nations 2005.

[20] Some have argued that governments outsource brutal counterinsurgent violence to militias, thus allowing the government to deny responsibility for abuses (e.g., Mitchell, Carey, and Butler 2014; Carey, Colaresi, and Mitchell 2015). In an analysis of all civil wars involving pro-government militias from 1989 to 2010, however, Stanton (2015) finds little evidence that governments outsource violence to militias; instead, in conflicts involving high levels of violence against civilians, both regular government forces and militia forces commit abuses.

[21] This section draws on multiple reports on Sudanese government operations in Darfur, including Amnesty International 2004b; Amnesty International 2004c; Human Rights Watch 2004a; Human Rights Watch 2004b; International Crisis Group 2004a; U.S. Department of State, the

to destroy JEM and SLA bases, most of the government's attacks deliberately targeted Fur, Masalit, and Zaghawa villages, and in most cases, the villages attacked were not located near rebel group bases or military operations. Attacks often began with aerial bombardment and artillery fire on a village, using improvised bombs made of barrels filled with explosives and small pieces of metal, dropped from the open bays of the government's Antonov transport planes, or using helicopters to target villages with rockets and machine gun fire. Aerial attacks focused on destroying village infrastructure such as schools, health centers, and water wells. Sudanese military forces and Janjaweed forces, operating in conjunction with one another, or in some cases operating alone, would then surround the village, firing on civilians using machine guns and rifles, burning homes and crops, looting any remaining property, and frequently raping girls and women. In many cases, villages were attacked repeatedly over the course of several days, weeks, or months, with government or Janjaweed forces returning to the village to kill or displace those who had returned.

Human rights organizations and international fact-finding missions have interviewed thousands of individuals affected by the violence, publishing eyewitness testimonies that help to illustrate the nature of government counterinsurgency operations. In an interview with Amnesty International, one witness recounted a government attack on the village of Murli in July 2003, explaining, "It was early in the morning, people were sleeping. About 400 armed people cordoned the village, with military uniforms, the same ones worn by the army, with vehicles and guns. A plane came later, to see if the operation was successful. At least 82 people were killed during the first attack. Some were shot and others, such as children and elderly, were burnt alive in their houses."[22] Another witness detailed a similar attack in the Abu Gamra region, near the town of Tina, in 2003:

The Arabs and the government forces arrived on both sides of the village, with vehicles, on horseback and on camels, and armed with big weapons. I hid in order to see how many they were. The Arabs cordoned the village with more than 1,000 horses. There was also a helicopter and an Antonov plane. They shelled the town with more than 200 shells. We counted 119 persons who were killed by the shelling. Then the Arabs burnt all our houses, took all the goods from the market. A bulldozer destroyed houses. Cars belonging to the merchants were burnt and generators were stolen. They said they wanted to conquer the whole territory and that the Blacks did not have a right to remain in the region.[23]

A witness interviewed by Human Rights Watch described a February 7, 2004, attack on the Masalit village of Tunfuka, saying that after several hours of

---

Bureau of Democracy, Human Rights, and Labor and the Bureau of Intelligence and Research 2004; Prunier 2005; United Nations 2005.
[22] Amnesty International 2004c, 14. [23] Ibid, 20.

bombing by Antonov planes, "Then seven army Land Cruisers came. The Janjaweed arrived an hour later. They burned the village, rounded up the cattle and shot people who were running away. They killed eighteen people. Then the Janjaweed left with the cattle followed by the government. The Janjaweed were shouting: 'Kill the Nuba!'"[24]

In July and August 2004, the U.S. State Department sent a team of independent experts to Chad to survey Sudanese refugees, to gauge the scale of the violence.[25] The team interviewed a random sample of Sudanese refugees from 19 different formal and informal camps in Chad, totaling 1,136 individuals. Their report concluded that the Sudanese government and Janjaweed forces were responsible for extensive violence against civilians, with half of all respondents saying that the attacks on their villages had been carried out jointly by government and Janjaweed forces and the other half saying that government or Janjaweed forces had acted alone in attacking their villages. Among those interviewed, 61 percent said that they had witnessed the killing of at least one family member; 67 percent said they had witnessed the killing of at least one nonfamily member; and 16 percent said they had witnessed rape. The report noted that physical violence against civilians was likely underreported in the survey, since the most severe attacks would not have left many survivors. Eighty-one percent reported witnessing the destruction of a village, 80 percent the theft of livestock, and 67 percent aerial bombardment, while 33 percent said they heard racial epithets during the attacks, such as "We have orders to kill all blacks" or "We kill all blacks and even kill our cattle when they have black calves."[26]

In response to mounting evidence of severe violence against civilians in Darfur, the UN Security Council, on September 14, 2004, passed a resolution calling for the creation of a formal commission of inquiry to investigate. After examining existing documentation on the conflict and conducting extensive interviews with refugees, internally displaced persons, local leaders in Darfur, rebel group leaders, and Sudanese government officials, the commission concluded:

The Government of the Sudan and the Janjaweed are responsible for serious violations of international human rights and humanitarian law amounting to crimes under international law. In particular, the Commission found that Government forces and militias conducted indiscriminate attacks, including killing of civilians, torture, enforced disappearances, destruction of villages, rape and other forms of sexual violence, pillaging and forced displacement, throughout Darfur. These acts were conducted on a widespread and systematic basis, and therefore may amount to crimes against humanity.[27]

---

[24] Human Rights Watch 2004a, 18.
[25] U.S. Department of State, the Bureau of Democracy, Human Rights, and Labor and the Bureau of Intelligence and Research 2004.
[26] Ibid.   [27] United Nations 2005, 3.

As in most civil wars, estimating the scale of the devastation is difficult. In its January 2005 report, the UN commission suggested that between 700 and 2,000 villages had been burned or otherwise destroyed in Darfur since the start of the conflict in 2003.[28] The United Nations reported in November 2004 that 1.65 million people had been internally displaced as a result of the violence in Darfur, while an additional 627,000 people in Darfur, though not displaced, were "conflict affected" and heavily reliant on international humanitarian aid. Another 200,000 had fled to Chad, bringing the total number of persons displaced or severely affected by the conflict to nearly 2.5 million, almost 40 percent of Darfur's prewar population of 6.3 million.[29] In addition, many thousands of civilians have been killed during the conflict. Based primarily on extrapolation from mortality surveys conducted by the World Health Organization (WHO) and Médecins Sans Frontières (MSF), two sociologists, who published their results in the September 2006 issue of *Science* magazine, estimated that between 170,000 and 255,000 civilians had died from November 2003 to May 2006.[30] This estimate included deaths resulting from violence as well as from conflict-related disease and malnutrition, but the authors suggested that their numbers likely underestimated deaths resulting from violence. Another Darfur scholar estimated that from the time the conflict began in February 2003 until April 2006, the total number of violent deaths was between 220,000 and 270,000, while the number of deaths from conflict-related disease and malnutrition was approximately 260,000.[31]

The Absence of Domestic Constraints on Violence

Sudan's repressive political institutions left almost no space for domestic political opposition that might encourage the government to restrain its use of violence against the Darfur rebellion. Although led by Bashir, most believe that the 1989 coup that overthrew Sudan's democratically elected government was organized by the National Islamic Front (NIF) and its leader, Hasan al-Turabi; Bashir and members of the Revolutionary Command Council, which served as the main governing body following the coup, swore allegiance to al-Turabi shortly after taking power.[32] In line with the NIF's ideological agenda, Bashir installed an Islamic form of government in Sudan and engaged in systematic repression of the Sudanese population, eliminating any possibility of political opposition; several experts have described the Sudanese government as totalitarian during this time period.[33] The new government "outlawed all political parties, professional organizations, trade unions, and civil society organizations"[34] and purged state institutions of anyone hostile to the NIF, firing thousands of individuals from the bureaucracy, the court system, and the

---

[28] Ibid., 63.   [29] Ibid., 62.   [30] Hagan and Palloni 2006.   [31] Reeves 2006.
[32] Collins 2008; Gallab 2008; Natsios 2012.   [33] Daly 2007; Gallab 2008.
[34] Gallab 2008, 113.

diplomatic corps, as well as from the military and police forces.[35] Although the new government did establish a Transitional National Council (TNC) to take the place of the ousted parliament, the TNC did not possess significant power, serving mainly to rubber stamp government policies; power in the Sudanese state was highly concentrated in the executive.[36]

In addition to removing all political opposition from within formal government institutions, Bashir also eliminated the space for opposition within civil society by imposing a state of emergency; instituting a curfew; banning almost all nonreligious organizations; shutting down all newspapers, apart from the armed forces newspaper; and taking control of radio and television.[37] Individuals suspected of opposition to the government were detained, imprisoned, and tortured, often in informal prisons or "ghost houses."[38] Opposition to Islam was punishable by death.[39]

Sudan did try to improve its image in the mid-1990s, holding elections for a newly established National Assembly and for the presidency, but this did little to change the structure of power within the state. About half of the members of the National Assembly were appointed by Bashir and although the others were elected, voting was manipulated to keep the NIF in power.[40] Bashir was elected president with more than 75 percent of the vote, while the NIF's leader, Turabi, became speaker of the National Assembly.[41] The Assembly created a new constitution, approved in a referendum, which further increased the power of the executive and formalized shari'a law.[42] With Turabi seeking more power in the Sudanese government, Bashir dissolved the National Assembly in December 1999, removed Turabi from power and later imprisoned him, purged the government of Turabi supporters, reestablished his control over state institutions, and implemented even more stringent restrictions on Sudanese civil society.[43] Further expanding the power of the executive during this period was a dramatic increase in oil exports and revenues, as a result of a newly built pipeline, which gave Bashir additional resources for use in patronage to secure his rule.[44]

Apart from the ongoing civil war with the SPLA in Southern Sudan, the only significant political opposition to the government came from the National Democratic Alliance (NDA), a group including representatives from 13 political parties, 56 trade unions, and a variety of other individuals banned from participating in politics under Bashir's regime.[45] The NDA, however, largely operated in exile, with an office in Eritrea, and was unable to take serious action against the Sudanese government.[46] A 2005 peace agreement between

---

[35] Daly 2007, 248; Collins 2008; Gallab 2008.   [36] Collins 2008.
[37] UN Commission on Human Rights 1994a; Collins 2008; Gallab 2008.
[38] UN General Assembly 1993; Daly 2007; Collins 2008; Gallab 2008.
[39] UN Commission on Human Rights 1993a; Gallab 2008.   [40] Collins 2008.
[41] Ibid., 222; Daly 2007.   [42] Collins 2008.   [43] International Crisis Group 2002b.
[44] Natsios 2012, 108–109.   [45] International Crisis Group 2002b; Collins 2008.
[46] Collins 2008.

the SPLA and Bashir's government, ending the conflict in Southern Sudan, created an interim power-sharing government, which was scheduled to remain in place until national elections in 2009, but Bashir resisted implementation of key components of the peace agreement and retained control over the central government.[47] The lack of serious political opposition or space for domestic public criticism as well as the extreme control Bashir and his advisors maintained over Sudanese political institutions meant that the government had a narrow domestic constituency and little incentive to be responsive to the wider Sudanese public. The government thus faced low domestic costs to engaging in violence against civilians in Darfur.

The Absence of International Constraints

The government also lacked incentives to seek support from a Western international constituency; the international costs of violence were low. Following the 1989 coup, Sudan became increasingly unpopular internationally, and by the time the Darfur conflict broke out, more than a decade into Bashir's rule, the government had little left to lose internationally. The United States had suspended its bilateral economic and military aid to Sudan in 1988 in response to Sudan's failure to keep up with loan repayments, but in response to the 1989 coup, the United States extended this suspension of aid.[48] The EU halted its development aid to Sudan in 1990 in response to human rights abuses; other major donors ended their development assistance programs in 1990 and 1991, only maintaining their humanitarian aid programs.[49] According to a World Bank assessment of Sudan's economy, although Sudan had received significant foreign assistance during the 1980s, following the coup, Sudan experienced "strained access to foreign finance and aid."[50] The decline in foreign aid was sharp, dropping from US$2 billion in 1985 to only US$127 million in 1993–1994.[51] The World Bank stopped paying out Sudan's loans in 1993, while the IMF threatened to throw Sudan out of the organization and suspended Sudan's voting rights for much of the 1990s.[52]

The rift between Sudan and a number of foreign governments widened in 1990 when Sudan refused to oppose Iraq's invasion of Kuwait. When the Arab League denounced the invasion, Sudan did not vote in favor of this condemnation; Sudan was one of only five members to abstain from a vote by the 45-member Islamic Conference Organization (ICO) to affirm its recognition of the Kuwaiti government and condemn the Iraqi invasion.[53] Saudi Arabia

---

[47] On obstacles to implementing the 2005 peace agreement between the government and the SPLA, see International Crisis Group 2008; International Crisis Group 2009.

[48] O'Sullivan 2003.　　[49] Barltrop 2010, 119, 212.　　[50] World Bank 2003, 43.

[51] Daly 2007, 256.　　[52] Ibid., 255.

[53] Tony Walker and Lamis Andoni, "Iraqi Occupation of Kuwait: Distaste for Gulf Rulers Prompts Muted Support for Invasion – Arab World," *Financial Times*, 4 August 1990; "Islamic Ministers

responded by cutting off aid to Sudan,[54] while the Gulf Cooperation Council also said it would block aid to countries that failed to oppose the Iraqi invasion.[55]

The relationship between Sudan and a number of Western, Arab, and African governments further soured in the mid-1990s as it became clear that Sudan was providing support to terrorist groups. In 1991, Turabi formed the Popular Arab and Islamic Congress (PAIC) and organized the group's first meeting in Khartoum; the group met in Khartoum again in 1993 and for a third time in 1995. PAIC was intended to serve as a coordinating body for a variety of extremist Islamist groups, including Islamic terrorist groups such as Hizbullah, Hamas, Islamic Jihad, al-Qaeda, Algeria's FIS and GIA, Egypt's al-Gamaa al-Islamiyya, and Indonesia's Abu Sayyaf Group.[56] The Sudanese government also allowed Islamic extremist groups to use Sudanese territory as a safe haven for conducting military training and other activities; Osama bin Laden directed al-Qaeda's operations from his base in Sudan throughout the early 1990s.[57] During that period, Sudan also aided Islamist groups in Somalia, who were fighting against the U.S. intervention, and Sudanese diplomats were involved in aiding the 1993 al-Qaeda attack on the World Trade Center.[58]

In response to this support for Islamic terrorist groups, the United States, in August 1993, added Sudan to its list of state sponsors of terrorism, which meant a ban on arms exports to Sudan as well as U.S. opposition to any aid or loans to Sudan from international financial institutions.[59] The EU banned arms exports to Sudan in March 1994; this embargo remained in effect during the Darfur conflict.[60] When evidence emerged that Sudan was involved in an al-Gamaa al-Islamiyya assassination attempt on Egyptian President Hosni Mubarak in 1995, the UN Security Council passed a series of resolutions calling on Sudan to "desist from engaging in activities of assisting, supporting and facilitating terrorist activities and from giving shelter and sanctuaries to terrorist elements" and to turn over the individuals suspected of involvement in the assassination attempt; when Sudan refused, the UN imposed diplomatic sanctions[61] and the United States expanded its sanctions to bar Sudanese officials from entering the United States.[62] Following the attack on Mubarak,

---

Condemn Iraq, Demand Withdrawal," *Reuters News*, 4 August 1990. See also Barltrop 2010; Natsios 2012.

[54] Peter Ford, "Saudis Direct Vast Wealth toward 'New Arab Order', Riyadh Expected to Aid States on the Basis of Loyalties during Gulf War," *Christian Science Monitor*, 15 March 1991.

[55] Eric Hall, "Saudi King Threatens Iraq Friends with Aid Cut-Off," *Reuters News*, 25 December 1990.

[56] Collins 2008; Natsios 2012.   [57] Natsios 2012.   [58] Collins 2008.   [59] O'Sullivan 2003.

[60] EU Council Decision 94/165/CFSP, 15 March 1994.

[61] UN Security Council Resolution 1044 (1996), 31 January 1996; UN Security Council Resolution 1054 (1996), 26 April 1996; UN Security Council Resolution 1070 (1996), 16 August 1996. A number of states – most notably Russia and China – did not comply with the UN sanctions against Sudan.

[62] O'Sullivan 2003; Collins 2008.

the Sudanese government also faced growing opposition from Arab and African states, including Egypt, Eritrea, Ethiopia, Kenya, and Uganda.[63] The United States again expanded its sanctions against Sudan in 1997, prohibiting all economic relations with Sudan and freezing all Sudanese assets in the United States.[64]

Sudan continued to support Islamic extremist groups throughout the late 1990s. Several of the al-Qaeda members involved in the attacks on the U.S. embassies in Kenya and Tanzania in 1998 had Sudanese passports or had previously conducted activities in Sudan. The United States retaliated by launching an attack on a pharmaceutical plant near Khartoum, which the United States believed was involved in producing chemical weapons.[65] Sudan was also believed to have been involved in the al-Qaeda attack on the USS Cole in October 2000.[66]

Also contributing to the perception of Sudan as a rogue state was Sudan's atrocious record on human rights. In 1993, the UN Commission on Human Rights appointed a special rapporteur for Sudan, who issued regular reports to the Commission and to the General Assembly on human rights abuses in the northern part of Sudan as well as abuses committed in the context of ongoing counterinsurgency operations in Southern Sudan; these reports detailed patterns of extrajudicial killing, summary executions, arbitrary detention, torture, slavery, forced displacement, and restrictions on political and religious freedom.[67] As Bashir's government escalated the war against the SPLA in Southern Sudan, human rights organizations reported that Sudanese government forces were responsible for extreme violations of human rights and humanitarian law, including indiscriminate bombing of villages and towns, the burning and destruction of civilian homes and crops, extrajudicial killing of individuals suspected of aiding the insurgency, enslavement of civilians, and forced displacement of civilians.[68]

As the costs of international isolation mounted, Sudan did begin to make efforts at improving relations with the United States and other foreign governments. In 1996, for example, Sudan arranged to have bin Laden and his operations moved to Afghanistan.[69] And after the September 11 attacks, Sudan offered to cooperate with the United States on counterterrorism efforts, leading the United States to permit the lifting of UN sanctions on Sudan; the United States, however, maintained its own bilateral sanctions regime, citing ongoing human rights abuses, and kept Sudan on its list of state sponsors of terrorism.[70]

---

[63] Collins 2008. [64] O'Sullivan 2003; Collins 2008.
[65] O'Sullivan 2003; Collins 2008; Natsios 2012. [66] Natsios 2012, 114.
[67] See, for example, UN General Assembly 1993; UN Commission on Human Rights 1994a; UN General Assembly 1994; UN Commission on Human Rights 1995; UN General Assembly 1995; UN Commission on Human Rights 1996.
[68] Human Rights Watch/Africa 1994; International Crisis Group 2002b. [69] Natsios 2012.
[70] International Crisis Group 2002b; O'Sullivan 2003.

In 2002, the Sudanese government agreed to participate in peace negotiations with the SPLA, coordinated by the Intergovernmental Authority on Development (IGAD), a regional East African group, and supported by three observer states: the United States, the United Kingdom, and Norway.[71]

Several countries began allowing limited development assistance to Sudan, but most assistance took the form of humanitarian aid, provided directly to NGOs or multilateral organizations.[72] Evidence suggests that donors avoided funneling assistance through Sudanese government agencies. Until 2004, the OECD did not publish data on the channel of aid delivery – whether foreign aid was being sent directly to the recipient government or was being channeled through NGOs or multilateral organizations. But data for 2004 provide a good estimate of the extent of foreign assistance flowing to the Sudanese government in the years leading up to the Darfur conflict, as international sanctions in response to abuses in Darfur did not take effect until mid-2004 and 2005.[73] In 2004, foreign governments and multilateral organizations disbursed US$377.3 million of official development assistance to Sudan, but only US$5 million of that aid was channeled through the Sudanese government.[74]

Thus, despite the minor improvements in Sudanese relations with foreign governments in the years after September 11, Sudan still had little to lose internationally when it launched its counterinsurgency in Darfur. For years, the Sudanese government had been receiving almost no foreign aid from either Western or Arab governments or multilateral organizations. The Sudanese government remained on the U.S. list of state sponsors of terrorism and had been subject to U.S. and EU sanctions since the mid-1990s. Furthermore, the United States and other international actors were hesitant to take any action in response to escalating violence in Darfur because they were concerned that doing so might lead to the unraveling of the ongoing IGAD-sponsored peace negotiations between the Sudanese government and the SPLA.[75] According to an International Crisis Group report, the Sudanese government was aware of international actors' unwillingness to risk the IGAD peace process by pressing the government on Darfur; the report noted that "until recently, the [Sudanese] government has essentially had a free hand in Darfur, able to support attacks against civilians suspected of backing the rebellion while calculating correctly that the international focus would remain on the incomplete IGAD process."[76]

[71] International Crisis Group 2002a; Natsios 2012.
[72] International Crisis Group 2002b; Barltrop 2010, 121.
[73] UN Security Council Resolution 1556 (2004), 30 July 2004; UN Security Council Resolution 1591 (2005), 29 March 2005; EU Council Regulation (EC) No 131/2004, 26 January 2004; EU Council Regulation (EC) No 1184/2005, 18 July 2005.
[74] Organisation for Economic Co-operation and Development (OECD), Creditor Reporting System. Available online at http://stats.oecd.org.
[75] Barltrop 2010.   [76] International Crisis Group 2004a, 2.

TURKEY'S STRATEGY OF LOW-CASUALTY CLEANSING AND TERRORISM

The PKK and Its Political Constituents

The PKK began to organize resistance to the Turkish government in the late 1970s and early 1980s, launching its first armed attacks against Turkish military targets on August 15, 1984. The PKK insurgency is based in the eastern and southeastern regions of Turkey, where the majority of the Kurdish population in Turkey is concentrated; in 1990, it was estimated that approximately 65 percent of the population in southeastern Turkey was Kurdish, while Kurds made up about 42 percent of the population in the eastern region of Turkey.[77] Estimating the extent of popular support for the PKK is difficult, in light of the legal restrictions on expressing support for Kurdish autonomy.[78] Until 1991, the use of the Kurdish language in public was prohibited, and significant restrictions on the use of Kurdish in government, education, and media persisted after 1991.[79] In addition, Turkey's Anti-Terrorism Law, passed in 1991, has been used to prosecute journalists, politicians, human rights activists, and others who have written about or spoken in favor of Kurdish rights or autonomy.[80] But sources suggest that support for the PKK was high among Kurds living in the eastern and southeastern regions of Turkey and, as one study has argued, "even Kurds who dislike its [the PKK's] methods or its leadership style recognize that the reality of PKK operations, more than any other single activity, has raised the Kurdish issue at the international level, focused attention upon the problem, and created pressures – so far not yet decisive – upon the Turkish state to reconsider its policies."[81] According to a Turkish journalist who has written extensively on the PKK, Turkish military officials estimated in 1994 that the PKK had more than 400,000 "active supporters and sympathizers in the Turkish Southeast."[82] In a survey taken in the southeast region in the mid-1990s, only 35 percent of respondents were willing to answer a question about their ties to members of the PKK, but of the 35 percent who responded, 42 percent said that at least one family member was part of the PKK.[83]

The PKK maintained a complex organizational structure, through which Kurdish constituents were able to participate to some degree in group decision making. Beneath its leader, Abdullah Öcalan, the PKK established a leadership council and a larger central committee, which served as the main decision-making bodies within the organization. Any major changes to the party's

---

[77] Kirişci and Winrow 1997, 120.   [78] Imset 1995.
[79] Human Rights Watch 1999; Human Rights Watch 2002b; International Crisis Group 2012.
[80] *The Law to Fight against Terrorism*, no. 3713, 12 April 1991. For an English translation of the law, see Alexander, Brenner, and Krause 2008, 117–124. On prosecutions under this law, see, for example, Human Rights Watch 1999; Human Rights Watch 2002b.
[81] Barkey and Fuller 1998, 46.   [82] Imset 1995.   [83] Barkey and Fuller 1998, 47.

political program had to be discussed and approved by the congress of party members, which met every several years during the 1980s and 1990s; however, Öcalan's influence over these congresses increased considerably over time, limiting the potential for open discussion or dissent.[84] The PKK also held several national conferences, which provided opportunities for members to discuss major issues confronting the group.[85] Although the party functioned as the group's main political institution, the PKK also created a popular front organization called the Kurdistan National Liberation Front (ERNK), responsible for recruiting new members, disseminating propaganda, and collecting money to support the group's operations.[86] The PKK also discussed forming governance structures in its territorial strongholds – regions along Turkey's borders with Iran, Iraq, and Syria.[87] In 1993, for example, the group said it planned to create a Parliament of Kurdistan in one of these regions.[88] In addition to these politically oriented institutions, the PKK established a separate armed wing responsible for military operations, referred to for much of the conflict as the People's Liberation Army of Kurdistan (Artêşa Rizgariya Gelê Kurdistan, ARGK);[89] Cemil Bayik led the armed wing for much of the group's early existence.[90]

The PKK's organizational structure – in particular, the activities of the popular front organization and the party's regular congresses – created incentives for the PKK to be responsive to its Kurdish supporters. In the late 1980s and early 1990s, for example, the PKK made a number of changes to its policies in response to criticism from Kurdish civilians. At its 1986 congress, the PKK decided to implement a policy of forced military conscription of young Kurdish men, but the policy led to civilian backlash, encouraging many to join government-sponsored village militias.[91] The PKK responded with attacks on village militias, in some cases killing Kurdish civilians who were not militia members during these attacks.[92] As Kurdish opposition to these actions grew, the PKK announced a policy reversal. At the PKK's second national conference in 1990, PKK members decided to end forced conscription; the PKK's fourth congress, which met a few months later, confirmed this decision.[93] Also at the fourth congress, PKK members "expressed their opposition to attacks on civilians," leading to fewer such attacks over the next few years.[94] As one expert on the conflict observed, "the PKK's willingness to take into account the demands and criticisms of the people it wanted to represent was an important factor in the group's growing popularity. . . . What seemed to matter was the PKK's public attempt to respect the wishes of its support base."[95] The PKK thus demonstrated early on in the conflict its desire to be responsive to its Kurdish constituents. The PKK's relationship with its civilian

---

[84] Imset 1995; Gunter 1997; White 2000; Marcus 2007.   [85] Marcus 2007.
[86] Gunter 1997, 35–37.   [87] Jongerden 2007; Aydin and Emrence 2015.
[88] Jongerden 2007, 63.   [89] Van Bruinessen 1988; White 2000.   [90] Gunter 1997, 34–40.
[91] Marcus 2007, 111–119.   [92] Ibid.   [93] Ibid., 119.   [94] Ibid., 118.   [95] Ibid., 119.

constituents likely created incentives for the Turkish government to use terrorism against Kurdish civilians.

Counterinsurgency Operations

Despite evidence that civilians in eastern and southeastern Turkey were aiding the insurgency, the Turkish government did not carry out large-scale attacks against Kurdish civilians. The Turkish air force was well equipped and played an important role in counterinsurgency operations, bombing PKK bases in Northern Iraq and providing aerial support for ground operations in remote, mountainous regions of eastern Turkey. However, the government did not use its aerial superiority to target Kurdish villages.[96] In fact, before using aerial bombardment in support of ground operations the Turkish military evacuated civilians from nearby villages.

Instead, the Turkish government used a more restrained form of coercion, pressuring civilians to join village defense militias as a way of proving their loyalty to the government and forcibly evacuating and destroying villages that refused to participate in the militia program. In 1993, Amnesty International estimated that over the previous several years, Turkish security forces had evacuated and destroyed hundreds of Kurdish villages.[97] In one incident reported in June 1993, which appears to be representative of the pattern of Turkish counterinsurgency operations, Turkish military forces entered a Kurdish village following a PKK attack on a nearby army unit, gathered all of the civilians into a central area of the village, and then burned shops, food stores, and all but one of the houses in the village. The Turkish forces did not, however, beat or physically harm the civilian inhabitants of the village.[98] In some cases, Turkish forces did harass civilians believed to be aiding the insurgency; later that same month, for example, Turkish security forces targeted a village that had refused to form a civil defense militia, rounding up civilians in the village, forcing them to lie face down on the ground, and beating them, though not killing any of the civilians.[99]

Turkish human rights organizations estimated in 1994 that Turkish security forces had forcibly evacuated 1,900 Kurdish villages – approximately 16 percent of the 12,000 villages in the region – many of which were then burned after being evacuated.[100] In 1995, the Turkish government admitted to having evacuated 978 villages and 1,676 hamlets in the Kurdish region, displacing a total of 310,000 civilians.[101] According to independent reports published in

---

[96] Teimourian 1993; Panico 1995.   [97] Amnesty International 1993b, 4.

[98] Ibid, 4–5.   [99] Ibid, 5.

[100] Aliza Marcus, "Turkish Army Targets Kurdish Villages," *Reuters News*, 25 November 1994. Panico 1995 provides a similar estimate, citing 1,400 villages evacuated and many of those villages burned.

[101] Celestine Bohlen, "War on Rebel Kurds Puts Turkey's Ideals to Test," *New York Times*, 16 July 1995.

1995, government forces had evacuated more than 1,000 villages and also had destroyed somewhere between 1,500 and 2,500 Kurdish villages since the conflict began.[102] Several years later, in 1998, a Turkish parliamentary commission released a report acknowledging that 905 villages and 2,523 hamlets had been evacuated by government and PKK forces, displacing 378,335 individuals.[103] Most of the internally displaced population did not receive any government assistance and were left on their own, often migrating to nearby towns or urban areas to stay with friends or family.[104] Rural populations declined considerably in the southeastern part of Turkey, decreasing by more than 50 percent in the two most heavily hit districts.[105]

Members of the Turkish government and the military described the forced evacuation of thousands of rural, Kurdish communities as a strategy aimed at isolating the PKK from its civilian base of support. Turkish President Turgut Özal laid this out in a 1993 letter he wrote to the prime minister, and in doing so noted that the size of the Kurdish population to be relocated was small enough to make cleansing possible:

Starting with the most troubled zones, villages and hamlets in the mountains of the region should be gradually evacuated. With this group of PKK (outlawed Kurdistan Workers' Party) supporters, in number no more than 150,000 to 200,000, being resettled in the Western parts of the country according to a careful plan, logistical support for the PKK will have been cut off and their standard of living will have improved.[106]

The government did not seek to control Kurdish civilians, or to deter other civilians from providing assistance to the PKK. Rather, the goal was to remove the PKK's civilian base of support entirely from the contested territory. In 1994, the Turkish Chief of Staff, Doğan Gures, confirmed this, saying, "We have changed the concept. We are now implementing area domination. There is no advancing on terrorists.... We now apply 'let them stay without logistical support – go hungry and surrender strategy.'"[107]

Some scholars see the government's forced evacuation strategy as a form of collective punishment[108] – a logic similar to that of terrorism – in which the goal is to impose severe costs on the rebel group through attacks on its constituents. And indeed members of the political opposition expressed a similar view when information became public about the nature of government counter-insurgency operations. A parliamentary representative from the Tunceli region, Sinan Yerlikaya, denounced the security force actions as terrorism: "If the PKK's raiding villages and killing people constitutes terror, then is the army's

---

[102] John Darnton, "Rights Violations in Turkey Said to Rise," *New York Times*, 6 March 1995.
[103] Turkish Parliament 1998.   [104] Ayata and Yükseker 2005, 16.
[105] Kocher 2002, 133–135. See also Jongerden 2007, 85–89.   [106] Quoted in ibid., 46.
[107] "Turkish Forces Change Tactics against Kurd Rebels," *Reuters News*, 30 July 1994.
[108] U.S. Committee on Refugees 1999; Kurban 2012.

burning of villages and forests not terror?"[109] The Turkish Minister for Human Rights, Azimet Koyluoglu, also referred to the evacuations as "state terrorism."[110]

Domestic Constraints on Violence

Although a 1980 military coup briefly suspended Turkey's democratic political system, democratic institutions were restored quickly with the creation of a new constitution in 1982, which received overwhelming support in a popular referendum, and the holding of parliamentary elections in November 1983. The Polity IV Project marks November 7, 1983 – the day following parliamentary elections – as the date of Turkey's return to democracy; the country's polity score increased from –5 to 7, qualifying Turkey as a full democracy under the Polity IV criteria.[111] The newly elected parliament, which replaced the military dictatorship, continued to expand political participation, allowing several parties and political leaders whom the military dictatorship had prohibited from participating in the 1983 elections to contest elections in 1984 and 1986. Although the military continues to influence Turkish politics, since 1983 Turkey has remained a full democracy – with polity scores ranging between 7 and 9 – holding regular local and national parliamentary elections and allowing the participation of a wide range of political parties.[112]

Despite its consolidated democratic political institutions, Turkey's political system remains exclusionary. According to the Ethnic Power Relations (EPR) data set, the Turkish ethnic group possesses monopoly control over political institutions, discriminating against the two main minority ethnic groups, the Kurds and the Roma. As one scholar has described the character of Turkey's government, "This state is based on a conception of 'nation-building' that calls for standardizing the citizenry to make them Turkish in language and nationality, secular in orientation, and obedient to the state."[113] Although several pro-Kurdish parties have participated in Turkish politics, these parties have faced significant restrictions on their activities and have been repeatedly closed down, accused of encouraging separatism in the Kurdish region. The first of Turkey's pro-Kurdish parties, the People's Labor Party (Halkın Emek Partisi, HEP), won 22 seats in parliament in the November 1991 elections by forming a coalition with the Social Democratic People's Party (Sosyaldemokrat Halk Partisi, SHP)

---

[109] Jonathan Lyons, "Investigation Ordered into Turkish Army Tactics," *Reuters News*, 6 October 1994.

[110] "Minister Accuses Turkey of 'State Terrorism,'" *Reuters News*, 11 October 1994.

[111] Marshall and Jaggers 2009.

[112] For conflicts that began prior to 1989, such as the conflict in Turkey, regime instability is measured in 1989; as of that date Turkey's democratic institutions had been in place for more than five years and thus the regime qualifies as a stable regime.

[113] Ergil 2000, 123.

as a means of reaching the threshold (10 percent of the total votes) required in order to gain representation in parliament.[114] In July 1993, however, the Constitutional Court banned the HEP, accusing the party of "becoming a focus of illegal political activities and engaging in activities against the indivisible unit of the state with its country and people."[115] Former HEP members got around these restrictions by forming a new pro-Kurdish party, the Democratic Party (Demokrasi Partisi, DEP), but the DEP was also closed down not long after its creation.[116] The Turkish parliament voted to rescind the parliamentary immunity that protected DEP members against prosecution in Turkish courts; with the lifting of their immunity, several DEP members were arrested, tried, and found guilty of membership in the PKK.[117] Again, members formed another pro-Kurdish party to replace the DEP, the People's Democratic Party (Halkın Demokrasi Partisi, HADEP); HADEP participated in the 1995 parliamentary elections, but did not receive enough votes to meet the threshold required for parliamentary representation.[118]

Turkey's exclusionary political system severely restricted the ability of Kurds to gain political representation or hold positions of political power, limiting the need for the government to appeal to individuals outside of its Turkish constituency. This political system likely created space for the government to use violent counterinsurgency strategies against Kurdish civilians without risking a loss of support among the wider population. Because the Turkish government was democratic, however, Kurdish citizens and others opposed to the government's treatment of Kurdish populations did have some avenues through which to express their dissent, leading to rising domestic pressure and rising domestic costs to violence.

Although the Turkish government sought to avoid inflicting civilian casualties during its forcible evacuation of Kurdish villages, the government's counterinsurgency strategy still involved severe human rights abuses, which prompted significant domestic criticism. In late 1994, reports that security forces had evacuated and burned 30 villages in Tunceli province led to widespread public concern. Deputy Speaker of the Turkish parliament, Kamer Genç, representing the Tunceli region, criticized the security forces publicly, saying, "First they empty the villages, and then they burn them so the PKK cannot seek refuge in them. This way the security forces are seen to be doing something. The PKK attacks and runs away, the people end up suffering."[119] As already mentioned, other representatives from the region characterized the government's actions as terrorism against Kurds, publicly denouncing the government in speeches to the parliament.[120] The Turkish Minister for Human Rights,

---

[114] Watts 1999; Ergil 2000.   [115] Watts 1999, 639. See also Watts 2010.
[116] Watts 1999; Ergil 2000.   [117] Watts 2010.   [118] Watts 1999; Ergil 2000.
[119] Jonathan Lyons, "Investigation Ordered into Turkish Army Tactics," *Reuters News*, 6 October 1994.
[120] Ibid.

Azimet Koyluoglu, issued a similar public condemnation: "In Tunceli it is the state that is evacuating, burning villages. In the southeast there are two million people left homeless. . . . Acts of terrorism in other regions are done by the PKK. In Tunceli it is state terrorism."[121] In his statement, Koyluoglu also urged a change in counterinsurgency operations, arguing that "Security forces should avoid the psychology of burning and destroying while in their relentless fight against terrorism. The evacuated villages must be given food and shelter. We can't even give them Red Crescent tents."[122]

Several weeks later, the Turkish parliament organized an investigation of the forced evacuations and destruction of villages in Tunceli.[123] A group of civil society leaders formed their own commission, made up of representatives from 36 different trade unions and voluntary organizations, to investigate as well; both the parliamentary group and the civil society group, however, reportedly had difficulty gaining access to the region to carry out their investigations.[124] Several Turkish human rights organizations regularly issued their own reports documenting security force abuses committed in the context of counterinsurgency operations against the PKK. Beginning in 1994, the Human Rights Association (İnsan Hakları Derneği, IHD) published annual tables documenting human rights violations such as extrajudicial executions, torture of detainees, attacks against civilians, and burning of villages.[125] The Human Rights Foundation of Turkey (Türkiye İnsan Hakları Vakfı, TIHV) began publishing annual reports on human rights in Turkey in 1993; these reports included lengthy discussions of the government's counterinsurgency practices, including the evacuation and burning of Kurdish villages.[126] Other Turkish nongovernmental organizations active in pressuring the government on human rights violations in the context of counterinsurgency operations included the Association for Human Rights and Solidarity for the Oppressed (İnsan Hakları ve Mazlumlar için Dayanışma Derneği, MAZLUMDER) and the Migrants' Association for Social Cooperation and Culture (Göç Edenler Sosyal Yardımlaşma ve Kültür Derneği, GÖÇ-DER).[127]

The Turkish government, however, continued to deny responsibility for committing human rights abuses, in particular for the widespread destruction of Kurdish villages.[128] During the October 1994 discussion in parliament

---

[121] "Minister Accuses Turkey of 'State Terrorism,'" *Reuters News*, 11 October 1994.　　[122] Ibid.

[123] Suna Erdem, "Turkish Rights Team to Check if Villages Burnt," *Reuters News*, 20 October 1994.

[124] Suna Erdem, "Turkish Army Hinders Deputy PM's Fact-Finding Tour," *Reuters News*, 7 October 1994; Nadire Mater and Sisira Wijesinghe, "Turkey – Human Rights: Government Bars Activists from Pillaged City," *Inter Press Service*, 10 November 1994.

[125] Summary tables available on IHD website at www.ihd.org.tr.

[126] See, for example, Human Rights Foundation of Turkey 1995.

[127] Ayata and Yükseker 2005.

[128] Jonathan Lyons, "Investigation Ordered into Turkish Army Tactics," *Reuters News*, 6 October 1994; Jonathan Lyons, "Tunceli Refugees Flee Turkish Security Sweep," *Reuters News*,

regarding the burning of villages in Tunceli, the Interior Minister, Nahit Mentese, refused to admit government involvement in the destruction and instead blamed the PKK: "Terrorists, trapped during assaults, may have burned the forests and the villages to save themselves or to begin a campaign against the forces of the state."[129] Turkish Prime Minister, Tansu Ciller, similarly denied government responsibility for the destruction of villages and, like the Interior Minister, suggested that PKK members were carrying out the attacks:

A lot of it is theater, in the sense that we have found – and I've seen official documentation – of the terrorists wearing the clothes of the soldiers, attacking the villages and burning them. This is not to say that there has been nothing wrong on the side of this fight against terrorism. It's very hard sometimes to discriminate. There is a lot of bombing or fire coming out of the houses and villages and for the military approaching it's very hard to tell who the terrorist is and who the villager is.[130]

In addition to issuing public denials of responsibility, the government also brought charges against senior members of the Turkish Human Rights Association (IHD) and the Human Rights Foundation of Turkey (TIHV) in response to their reports on security force abuses of human rights; the charges alleged that the human rights activists were supporting separatism, in violation of Article 8 of Turkey's Anti-Terrorism Law.[131] The activists were later acquitted or released.[132]

Despite the government's denials of responsibility for abuses, domestic pressure on the Turkish government to improve its treatment of Kurdish civilians mounted. In 1995, the Human Rights Ministry Advisory Council produced a report alleging that security forces had tortured detainees during counterinsurgency operations; when the government blocked publication of the report, one of the members of the Council resigned in protest.[133] In 1997, the Turkish parliament formed a commission, made up of 13 members of parliament representing several different political parties, to investigate the displacement of individuals from villages in the southeastern part of the country.[134] When the commission released its report in May 1998, it sparked extensive

---

12 October 1994; Suna Erdem, "Turkish Rights Team to Check if Villages Burnt," *Reuters News*, 20 October 1994.

[129] Jonathan Lyons, "Investigation Ordered into Turkish Army Tactics," *Reuters News*, 6 October 1994.

[130] John Darnton, "Rights Violations in Turkey Said to Rise," *New York Times*, 6 March 1995. See also Aliza Marcus, "Turkish Army Targets Kurdish Villages," *Reuters News*, 25 November 1994; Alan Cowell, "War on Kurds Hurts Turks in U.S. Eyes," *New York Times*, 17 November 1994.

[131] "Security Court Acquits Turkish Rights Activists," *Agence France-Presse*, 11 January 1995. See also Amnesty International Urgent Action 450/94, 22 December 1994.

[132] "Turkey: Human Rights Defenders Acquitted," Amnesty International News Service 10/95, 12 January 1995.

[133] "Turk Rights Adviser Resigns over Torture Report," *Reuters News*, 23 February 1995.

[134] Ayata and Yükseker 2005; Yükseker 2007.

debate in parliament.[135] The report estimated that government and PKK forces had been responsible for the evacuation of 378,335 individuals from 905 villages and 2,523 hamlets[136] and harshly criticized the security forces' involvement in the evacuation of Kurdish villages as "de facto action carried out by the security forces [that] was unlawful."[137] As the report detailed, under Turkish law, the State of Emergency that had been declared in conflict-affected provinces gave governors of these provinces the power to evacuate or relocate villages, but the governors of State of Emergency provinces had never formally issued evacuation orders.[138] The report concluded that the village evacuations violated Turkish constitutional law, as well as the Universal Declaration of Human Rights and the European Convention on Human Rights. More generally, the report criticized the government for failing to consider "democratic rights, the rule of law, equality, identity, culture and socio-economic development"[139] in its response to the PKK insurgency. That same year, one of Turkey's main political parties, the Republican People's Party (Cumhuriyet Halk Partisi, CHP), issued its own working group report, also admonishing the security forces for their evacuation and burning of villages in the southeastern part of the country.[140]

International Constraints on Violence

In addition to domestic criticism, the Turkish government faced strong international criticism of its counterinsurgency operations and their impact on Kurdish civilians. The Council of Europe and the EU were the organizations most actively pressuring Turkey on human rights issues. Turkey joined the Council of Europe in 1949 and in 1954 ratified the Council's Convention for the Protection of Human Rights and Fundamental Freedoms; as a Council member and a party to the Convention, Turkey is subject to the jurisdiction of the European Court of Human Rights. Turkey has sought membership in the EU since 1987 when it submitted an application for full membership in what was then the European Economic Community.[141]

Although both European organizations had raised concerns about human rights in Turkey previously, they stepped up their appeals as Turkey's counterinsurgency operations – and accompanying human rights abuses – intensified in the early 1990s. The Parliamentary Assembly of the Council of Europe passed a resolution in June 1992, raising concerns about human rights violations in the southeast region and announcing that it "condemns terrorist attacks ... as well as certain actions by the security forces and recalls that, in a democratic state,

---

[135] "Identity Debate in Parliament," *Turkish Probe*, 7 June 1998.
[136] Turkish Parliament 1998.   [137] Quoted in Yükseker 2007, 114.
[138] Human Rights Watch 2002a; Yükseker 2007.   [139] Yükseker 2007, 148.   [140] Ibid., 150.
[141] For an overview of Turkey's interactions with both institutions on issues related to human rights, see Çelik 2005.

any reply to terrorist provocation must remain within the rule of law."[142] As human rights violations continued, the Parliamentary Assembly took a stronger stance. A recommendation passed in April 1995 noted that "The Assembly is deeply concerned about human rights violations in Turkey – notably in the south-east of the country, following armed conflict between central government forces, the PKK and Kurdish nationalists" and recommended that the Council of Europe's Committee of Ministers consider suspending Turkey's membership if Turkey did not put a halt to its military offensive against PKK bases in Iraq, "seek a peaceful solution to the Kurdish problem," and "bring its Constitution and legislation in line with the principles and standards of the Council of Europe."[143] As one diplomat involved in the decision argued, "The Council cannot allow Turkey to remain a member while there are clear indications that human rights are seriously violated in Turkey."[144]

The EU made a similar threat in 1995, when it said it might block Turkey from joining the customs union – a key step in Turkey's bid to eventual EU membership – because of concern about human rights abuses.[145] In order for the customs union to take effect, the European Parliament would have to vote in favor. In a February 1995 resolution, the European Parliament made clear that its consent was conditional on improvements in Turkey's human rights record, stating "that the Human Rights situation in Turkey is too serious to allow the formation of the proposed customs union at present" and calling for additional reforms.[146] Several months later, at a Forum Europe event in April 1995, Hans van den Broek, one of the members of the European Commission involved in negotiations with Turkey, spoke about the need for Turkey to improve its human rights performance in advance of admission to the customs union:

But even more important than these technical measures, is progress on human rights in Turkey. At the last two Association Councils in December 1994 and March this year, the Union expressed its apprehension at the human rights situation and appealed to Turkey to make improvements in this area. Indeed, the alignment of our two systems involves not only economic and trade questions but also the need for guarantees of the fundamental rights of the individual, which citizens in the Union take for granted.[147]

A few months later, in a report to the European Parliament, the European Commission raised concerns about human rights in Turkey – in particular,

---

[142] Parliamentary Assembly of the Council of Europe, Resolution 985 (1992), 30 June 1992.
[143] Parliamentary Assembly of the Council of Europe, Recommendation 1266, 26 April 1995.
[144] Quoted in "Turkey – Human Rights: Council of Europe Warns Ankara to Shape up," *Inter Press Service*, 26 April 1995. See also "Council of Europe to Vote on Suspending Turkey," *Reuters News*, 26 April 1995.
[145] Çelik 2005, 989.
[146] European Parliament, Minutes of 16/02/1995 meeting. Available online at www.europarl .europa.eu.
[147] Hans van den Broek, "Turkey and the EU: The Challenge of the Customs Union," speech at Forum Europe, 24 April 1995, SPEECH /95/72. Available online at www.europa.eu.

about "lack of respect for the individual, such as illegal executions, unsolved cases of disappearance, and the expulsion of villagers in the south-east"[148] – and cited reform as essential to the prospects for Turkey's admission to the customs union.

The Turkish government finally bowed to this growing international pressure, amending its constitution to broaden political participation in July 1995[149] and altering its Anti-Terrorism Law,[150] which had been used to prosecute individuals who took pro-Kurdish stances or were critical of the government's operations against the PKK. Although the European Parliament acknowledged these improvements and ultimately voted in favor of the customs union in December 1996, it said that additional improvements in human rights performance and democracy were still essential.[151]

Indeed, pressure from the Council of Europe and the EU continued even after these reforms. In a 1997 report on the prospects for enlargement, the EU cited continuing concerns about human rights in Turkey, particularly in regard to the conduct of counterinsurgency operations:

In combating terrorism in the south east, Turkey needs to exercise restraint, to make greater efforts to uphold the rule of law and human rights and to find a civil and not a military solution. Persistent cases of torture, disappearances and extra-judicial executions, notwithstanding repeated official statements of the government's commitment to ending such practices, put into question the extent to which the authorities are able to monitor and control the activities of the security forces.[152]

The Council of Europe also continued to criticize Turkey's human rights record. In 1998, the Parliamentary Assembly of the Council of Europe's Committee on Migration, Refugees, and Demography published a report on internal displacement in Turkey, raising concerns about the involvement of Turkish security forces in the evacuation and burning of Kurdish villages. In response to the report, the Parliamentary Assembly issued a recommendation expressing its disapproval of the Turkish government's policies, saying, "The Assembly also condemns the evacuation and burning of villages by the Turkish armed forces."[153] Other international bodies raised similar concerns about the plight of displaced populations, pressing the Turkish government to address these issues.[154]

---

[148] "EU Report Decries Human Rights in Turkey," *Reuters News*, 10 July 1995.

[149] John Barham, "Turkey Reforms Laws to Please Strasbourg," *Financial Times*, 24 July 1995; Alistair Bell, "Turkey Constitution Changes Help EU Trade Pact," *Reuters News*, 24 July 1995.

[150] Aliza Marcus, "Turkish Rights Monitors Slam Freedom of Speech Law," *Reuters News*, 29 October 1995.

[151] Mark Lawrence, "EU-Turkey Customs Union Approved Despite Human Rights Worries," *Associated Press*, 13 December 1995; Celestine Bohlen, "European Parliament Admits Turkey to Its New Customs Union," *New York Times*, 14 December 1995. See also European Parliament, Resolution on the Human Rights situation in Turkey, 13 December 1995.

[152] European Commission 1997, 56.

[153] Parliamentary Assembly of the Council of Europe 1998.

[154] UN Commission on Human Rights 2002; Council of Europe, Commissioner for Human Rights 2009.

In addition, throughout the 1990s and 2000s, thousands of Kurdish civilians petitioned to bring cases against the Turkish government in the European Court of Human Rights, alleging violations of the Convention for the Protection of Human Rights and Fundamental Freedoms, such as extrajudicial killing, torture, and destruction of property; many of these petitions involved Kurds who had been forcibly evacuated from their homes by Turkish security forces.[155] The Court took up a number of these cases, issuing a series of judgments in which it found that Turkey's forcible evacuation and destruction of civilian homes in the context of counterinsurgency operations violated the Convention for the Protection of Human Rights and Fundamental Freedoms. In one of its earliest such judgments, issued on September 16, 1996, in *Akdivar and Others v. Turkey*, the Court found that the Turkish government had violated Article 8 of the Convention, on the right to respect for private and family life, and Article 1 of Protocol No. 1, on the right to peaceful enjoyment of one's possessions:

> The Court is of the opinion that there can be no doubt that the deliberate burning of the applicants' homes and their contents constitutes at the same time a serious interference with the right to respect for their family lives and homes and with the peaceful enjoyment of their possessions. No justification for these interferences having been proffered by the respondent Government – which have confined their response to denying involvement of the security forces in the incident – the Court must conclude that there has been a violation of both Article 8 of the Convention (art. 8) and Article 1 of Protocol No. 1 (P1-1).[156]

As of 2004, the Court had issued more than 30 similar judgments in cases involving forced evacuation and destruction of villages.[157] But these judgments applied only to individual cases; it was not until 2004 that the Council of Europe's Committee of Ministers passed a resolution allowing the Court to identify "an underlying systemic problem and the source of this problem, in particular when it is likely to give rise to numerous applications."[158] Just several weeks later, on June 29, the Court issued a judgment in *Doğan and Others v. Turkey*, in which it identified the forced evacuation and destruction of villages at the hands of Turkish security forces as a systemic problem:

> The Court has also found in numerous similar cases that security forces deliberately destroyed the homes and property of the respective applicants, depriving them of their livelihoods and forcing them to leave their villages in the state of emergency region of

---

[155] Ayata and Yükseker 2005; Kurban, Erozden, and Gulalp 2008.

[156] European Court of Human Rights (Grand Chamber), *Akdivar and Others v. Turkey*, Application no. 21893/93, 16 September 1996, para. 88.

[157] Kurban, Erozden, and Gulalp 2008, 14.

[158] Council of Europe, Resolution of the Committee of Ministers on Judgments Revealing an Underlying Systemic Problem, Res (2004)3, 12 May 2004.

Turkey (see, among many others, Akdivar and Others, Selçuk and Asker, Menteş and Others, Yöyler, İpek, judgments cited above; Bilgin v. Turkey, no. 23819/94, 16 November 2000, and Dulaş v. Turkey, no. 25801/94, 30 January 2001).[159]

The Turkish Government's Response

In response to domestic and international pressure, the Turkish government implemented a number of policy changes. As noted, in response to international pressure in the lead-up to the European Parliament's vote on Turkey's membership in the customs union in 1995, the Turkish government amended its constitution to broaden political participation,[160] as well as made changes to an antiterrorism law,[161] which had been used to prosecute members of the political opposition, journalists, human rights activists, and others who publicly criticized the Turkish government's stance on Kurdish issues or the Turkish government's counterinsurgency operations. Throughout the late 1990s and early 2000s, the Turkish government continued to make changes to its constitution and to pass legislation relevant to improving respect for human rights in the context of counterinsurgency operations. In March 1997, for example, the government passed a law amending the Code of Criminal Procedure to reduce the detention periods permitted for individuals arrested and accused of criminal activity, including crimes related to the separatist conflict.[162] The following month, the government established a Human Rights Coordinating High Committee, made up of representatives from various government ministries, tasked with monitoring the implementation of measures aimed at improving human rights.[163] In 1999, the government amended the penal code to increase sentences for members of the security forces found guilty of torture and adopted laws altering the structure of State Security Courts, which hear cases involving crimes related to the separatist insurgency, to eliminate the involvement of military judges in these courts.[164]

Just one month after the European Court of Human Rights' ruling in *Doğan and Others v. Turkey*, which found that Turkey had deliberately destroyed

---

[159] European Court of Human Rights (Third Section), *Doğan and Others v. Turkey*, Applications nos. 8803–8811/02, 8813/02 and 8815–8819/02, 29 June 2004, para. 142. On the significance of this ruling, see Kurban 2007; Kurban, Erozden, and Gulalp 2008.

[160] John Barham, "Turkey Reforms Laws to Please Strasbourg," *Financial Times*, 24 July 1995. Alistair Bell, "Turkey Constitution Changes Help EU Trade Pact," *Reuters News*, 24 July 1995. For an English translation of the text of these amendments, see Alexander, Brenner, and Krause 2008, 268–273.

[161] Aliza Marcus, "Turkish Rights Monitors Slam Freedom of Speech Law," *Reuters News*, 29 October 1995. For an English translation and discussion of these amendments, see Alexander, Brenner, and Krause 2008, 274–278.

[162] For an English translation of the new law, see Alexander, Brenner, and Krause 2008, 321–322.

[163] European Commission 1998; Senol 1998.   [164] European Commission 1999, 9–11.

civilian homes during counterinsurgency operations and had failed to provide adequate compensation to displaced individuals, the Turkish government passed the Law on Compensation for Losses Arising From Terrorism and the Fight Against Terrorism. The law established a procedure for compensating individuals who had been displaced as a result of the government's counter-insurgency operations.[165]

Turkish military and government leaders admitted that the pressure to prove Turkey's commitment to democracy was constraining the government's counterinsurgency operations. Highlighting the tension between the desire to uphold democratic principles and the need to carry out an effective counterinsurgency campaign, the Deputy Chief of the Turkish Armed Forces, General Ahmet Corekci, expressed his frustration with the constraints on military operations and said, "We'll finish terrorism soon but we're being held back by democracy and human rights."[166] President Demirel, in response to the general's remarks, emphasized that military operations were constrained by a desire to avoid excessive attacks on civilian populations and admitted that the military was having difficulty designing counterinsurgency strategies that would limit the use of violence against civilians while still being militarily effective. The president urged the public to view General Corekci's comments in a positive light, saying, "Don't read too much into this. He's not saying the army is treading on human rights. He's saying it has problems because it is not treading on human rights."[167] As a democracy, the Turkish government was under pressure from domestic and international audiences to prove that both military and civilian leaders were committed to behaving in accordance with democratic principles and respect for human rights. And yet, as a government facing an insurgency with a clearly defined civilian base of support in the southeastern part of the country, it also faced strong incentives to target civilians; Turkey, therefore, adopted a form of low-casualty cleansing and terrorism that depopulated regions of high support for the rebellion and inflicted costs on the insurgency's Kurdish civilian constituents while limiting the number of casualties.

ASSESSING THE ALTERNATIVE ARGUMENTS

One of the main alternative arguments for government violence emphasizes the military context, positing that the relative strength of the belligerents is the most important determinant of government strategy. When a government is

---

[165] Law on Compensation for Losses Arising from Terrorism and the Fight against Terrorism, No. 5233, 17 July 2004. See also the discussion in the Report by Thomas Hammarberg, Commissioner for Human Rights at the Council of Europe, following his visit to Turkey on 28 June–3 July 2009, Strasbourg, 1 October 2009, para. 111. Available online at www.coe.int. See also Kurban, Erozden, and Gulalp 2008.

[166] Alistair Bell, "Turkish General Attacks Democracy Reforms," *Reuters News*, 1 July 1995.

[167] Ibid.

militarily weak or is faced with a particularly strong insurgency, it is more likely to target civilians; similar arguments contend that armed groups are more likely to target civilians following military losses. Both governments discussed in this chapter, however, have large, strong militaries that had significant numerical and technological advantages over their rebel opponents. The Sudan Armed Forces had 104,500 troops at the start of the Darfur conflict, supported by an additional 10,000–20,000 paramilitary troops in the Popular Defence Forces[168] and at least 20,000 Janjaweed militia forces.[169] Estimates place the number of government troops active in Darfur at between 40,000 and 45,000 regular troops and 10,000 and 20,000 Janjaweed troops.[170] Rebel forces, in contrast, numbered about 10,000.[171] Some might argue that the Sudanese government's ongoing operations against the SPLA in Southern Sudan weakened the military's capabilities in Darfur, but during the early years of the conflict in Darfur when government targeting of civilians was at its most extreme, military operations in Southern Sudan were limited while negotiations with the SPLA were ongoing. Turkish forces had an even greater advantage over the PKK. At the height of the counterinsurgency, in 1993, Turkish armed forces numbered 480,000.[172] Approximately 185,000 of these troops were deployed to Turkey's southeastern region to fight against the PKK; the total number of government forces involved in counterinsurgency operations – including military troops, village guards, police, and special forces – was between 300,000 and 365,000.[173] Meanwhile, PKK strength was about 15,000–20,000 troops.[174]

Some might contend that measuring military strength by troop strength does not capture adequately a military's capacity for confronting a domestic insurgency, which depends on the military's level of training and expertise in counterinsurgency. It is certainly true that both governments faced challenges in adapting their militaries for counterinsurgency operations, but this cannot explain why the Sudanese and Turkish governments pursued such different counterinsurgency strategies. In addition, the Sudanese government had recent counterinsurgency experience, having fought against the SPLA in Southern Sudan since 1983. Despite having more recent experience with counterinsurgency operations than the Turkish government, however, it was the Sudanese government that directed the most severe violence against civilians during the campaigns in Darfur.

A second alternative hypothesis, also emphasizing the military context, suggests that targeting civilians is a strategy of last resort for most governments. Governments are likely to use violence against civilians only when the costs of

[168] The International Institute for Strategic Studies (IISS) 2003, 2004.
[169] Human Rights Watch 2004b.   [170] Bellamy, Williams, and Griffin 2010, 209.
[171] Stockholm International Peace Research Institute (SIPRI) 2005.
[172] The International Institute for Strategic Studies (IISS) multiple years.
[173] Jongerden 2007, 64.   [174] Ibid., 51.

conflict have risen precipitously, to unacceptable levels. However, in Sudan, government forces and Janjaweed militias attacked Fur, Masalit, and Zaghawa villages from the first weeks of the insurgency; the most intense and destructive government and Janjaweed attacks on Darfur villages occurred in the first year of the conflict. In Turkey, the government's campaign to evacuate and destroy Kurdish villages was most intense during the early to mid-1990s. Some argue that this depopulation strategy was a response to PKK gains and the realization that the prior counterinsurgency strategies had not been effective. Sources do not, however, indicate that government losses were particularly severe or that the government had become desperate; rather, the government's emphasis on maintaining defensive positions was not well matched to the task of counter-insurgency, allowing the PKK to operate with some freedom in rural areas and at night.[175]

The evidence from these cases also challenges alternative arguments tying civilian targeting to contestation over territory. These arguments claim that government and rebel group violence against civilians is likely to escalate during periods of high contestation, as governments and rebel groups compete for control over civilians and territory. In Darfur, however, the government began mobilizing Janjaweed militias almost immediately after the first rebel attacks in early 2003; government violence against civilians was extreme from the early days of the conflict, before contestation escalated.

The pattern of government violence in Turkey, at first glance, seems consist-ent with the hypothesis about contestation and its emphasis on the targeting of particular individuals and villages for punishment in order to deter civilians from aiding the opponent. Turkish government forces did direct violence against specific villages – in particular, villages that refused to form pro-government militias or that were suspected of sympathizing with the PKK – but while contestation arguments would expect Turkish forces to use these attacks on villages as a means of extending their control over civilians and territory, Turkish forces did not seek to establish a government presence in the Kurdish villages they targeted. Instead, Turkish forces evacuated and burned thousands of villages; the intent was not to deter civilians from providing intelligence to the PKK, but to deny the PKK access to its civilian base by removing these civilians from the territory in dispute. Similarly, the PKK did not attempt to establish physical control over the Kurdish region; it operated primarily out of bases in Northern Iraq, sending units to carry out guerrilla attacks on Turkish government and civilian targets and then retreating back into its safe haven across the border. Because the PKK did not attempt to hold territory in the separatist region, the conflict did not involve heavy contestation between ground forces aimed at establishing zones of government and rebel group control.

---

[175] Jongerden 2007.

Arguments focusing on the ratification of international legal agreements also fall short in accounting for patterns of violence against civilians in these cases. Turkey and Sudan ratified the 1949 Geneva Conventions during the 1950s, well before the conflicts discussed in this chapter began. And yet both governments engaged in forms of violence against civilians that are clear violations of the Geneva Convention prohibition on targeting noncombatants. Defenders of arguments emphasizing the power of international legal commitments might draw attention to more recent international humanitarian law agreements – the 1977 Second Additional Protocol to the Geneva Conventions and the 1998 Rome Statute of the International Criminal Court. But variation in the ratification of these international legal instruments cannot account for variation in government behavior either. As of 2015 Turkey had not ratified the Second Additional Protocol, but Sudan ratified the Second Additional Protocol in 2006, while the conflict in Darfur was ongoing. And although the most intense period of Sudanese government attacks on civilians did occur prior to ratification, the government continued to attack civilian targets after 2006.[176] As some human rights scholars have pointed out, abusive governments may sign onto international human rights treaties in an attempt to deflect criticism of their human rights violations.[177] Finally, some might argue that because neither Turkey nor Sudan had ratified the Rome Statute, these governments lacked constraints on their use of violence. While Rome Statute ratification may encourage limits on government violence in the future, Rome Statute ratifications have taken place too recently to be able to account for variation in patterns of government violence and restraint over the past two decades. Among governments fighting insurgencies from 1989 to 2010, only one ratified the Rome Statute prior to the civil war, and only six ratified the Rome Statute while conflict was ongoing.

CONCLUSION

The insurgencies in Turkey and Sudan share several characteristics in common. Both insurgencies had clearly identifiable civilian constituencies concentrated in a particular geographic region of the country – civilian constituencies that were an easy target for government attack. And in Turkey, the insurgency developed political institutions that may have generated incentives for rebel group leaders to be responsive to violence against these civilian constituents. Both governments, thus, had strong incentives to target civilians – as part of a strategy of cleansing or terrorism.

Where these cases diverge, however, is in the extent to which each government faced domestic and international costs to engaging in violence. As a full

---

[176] See, for example, Human Rights Watch 2008; Human Rights Watch 2011.
[177] Hathaway 2002; Hafner-Burton and Tsutsui 2007.

democracy seeking admission to the EU, the Turkish government was highly constrained in its ability to direct violence against civilians; the Turkish government thus chose a strategy of low-casualty cleansing and terrorism, destroying thousands of civilian homes, but avoiding high civilian casualties during these counterinsurgency operations. As an entrenched autocracy that was already isolated internationally, the Sudanese government had almost no domestic or international constraints on its behavior in Darfur. The low domestic and international costs of violence made it possible for the Sudanese government to pursue an extreme strategy of high-casualty cleansing.

7

Variation in Rebel Group Violence against Civilians: Turkey, El Salvador, and Azerbaijan

As the statistical analyses in Chapter 3 show, when rebel groups possess narrow domestic and international constituencies, the costs of violence are low, increasing the likelihood of attacks against civilians. This chapter and the chapter that follows together examine variation in rebel group violence, analyzing differences in rebel group strategies of violence across cases of civil war. Just as governments evaluate the benefits of violence based on an assessment of the rebel group's relationship to its civilian constituents, rebel groups, too, consider carefully their government opponent and its domestic constituents in selecting strategies of violence. When civilian support for the government is high, rebel groups have strong incentives to use violence as a means of controlling or eliminating this government constituency as part of a strategy of control or cleansing. In most cases, the government's constituency is too large or too dispersed geographically for the rebel group to be able to eliminate this base of support. In some separatist conflicts, however, a small group of government supporters is concentrated within the separatist region, making it possible for the rebel group to use cleansing as a means of removing these outsider civilians from the disputed territory.

The majority of rebel groups, unable to eliminate the government's base of civilian support, instead weigh the benefits of a strategy of terrorism. In deciding whether to use terrorism, rebel groups consider the likelihood that the government will respond to violence by making concessions, an assessment influenced heavily by the government's regime type. Because democratic institutions create incentives for governments to be responsive to the domestic public, rebel groups tend to perceive democratic governments as more sensitive to civilian losses and, therefore, more vulnerable to a strategy of terrorism. The more democratic the government, therefore, the more likely it is that the rebel group will use terrorism. Although all rebel groups have incentives to use terrorism when fighting democratic opponents, rebel groups weigh the costs of terrorist violence differently, depending on their political objectives. Rebel groups competing with the government to build a broad base of civilian support are likely to be concerned about popular backlash in response to terrorist violence and, therefore, select targets that impose costs without inflicting high civilian casualties.

The statistical findings provide evidence in support of these arguments, showing that separatist rebel groups are likely to use cleansing when a group of government constituents is living in a concentrated area of the separatist region. In addition, the findings show that rebel groups fighting against democratic governments are more likely to use terrorism and that rebel groups with inclusive political systems select lower-casualty targets for their terrorist attacks. The statistical analyses, however, tell us little about the motivations driving rebel group behavior.

The two case studies of rebel group terrorism in this chapter allow for an examination of the causal mechanisms driving patterns of rebel group behavior. Both of the rebel groups I examine are fighting against democratic opponents, but the two groups have different types of domestic constituencies. The Kurdistan Workers' Party (Partiya Karkerên Kurdistanê, PKK) in Turkey is an exclusionary group fighting for the autonomy of the Kurdish ethnic group, while the Farabundo Martí National Liberation Front (Frente Farabundo Martí para la Liberación Nacional, FMLN) in El Salvador is an inclusive group fighting for control of the central government. Consistent with the argument of this book, the PKK, a separatist insurgency with a narrow, geographically concentrated base of civilian support, had greater flexibility in its ability to use violence against civilians; the group adopted a strategy of high-casualty terrorism, regularly bombing populated civilian targets. In contrast, the FMLN, a revolutionary insurgency seeking to build a broad base of support among Salvadoran civilians, bombed economic and infrastructure targets such as power stations and factories, inflicting few civilian casualties.

The FMLN's intensification of its strategy of low-casualty terrorism coincides with the shift toward a more democratic form of government in El Salvador. However, other major changes in government counterinsurgency operations also took place during this period and likely explain the *initial* FMLN decision to step up its attacks on economic and infrastructure targets as part of a shift toward a more traditional guerrilla warfare strategy. Yet the evidence also shows that the process of democratization did influence FMLN strategy in the mid- to late 1980s. From the FMLN's perspective, democratization placed increased pressure on the government to maintain popular support in advance of elections and thus made the government more vulnerable to the civilian costs of the conflict; this thinking contributed to the FMLN's decision to escalate its strategy of low-casualty terrorism in the late 1980s and to expand attacks to the capital city, where violence would be most visible and impactful.

The third case study in this chapter examines rebel group cleansing. Only 10 rebel groups engaged in civil war since 1989 have adopted strategies of high-casualty cleansing and four of these 10 cases of rebel group cleansing occurred in the Balkans. In the Balkans, it appears that armed groups behaved in ways consistent with the argument of this book. The warring parties were aware that the international community favored holding popular votes to determine the status of contested territories; one of the motivations for cleansing was to homogenize particular segments of territory in advance of any popular consultation, in an effort to secure the preferred national boundary.[1] Because the Balkan cases have been documented extensively elsewhere, in this chapter I examine a lesser-known case of high-casualty cleansing, in the conflict over the territory of Nagorno-Karabakh in Azerbaijan. In this case, too, the logic of violence is consistent with the predictions of this book; Karabakh Armenian rebels used a strategy of high-casualty cleansing to expel the small, geographically concentrated population of Azeris, in an effort to stake a stronger claim to the disputed territory.

HIGH-CASUALTY TERRORISM: THE PKK IN TURKEY

As detailed in Chapter 6, the PKK, led by Abdullah Öcalan, began advocating in the late 1970s for the creation of an independent, socialist, Kurdish state in Turkey's eastern and southeastern regions, citing a long history of regional inequality and government discrimination against the Kurdish population.[2] Unlike other Kurdish nationalist groups active at the time, the PKK insisted that armed rebellion was the best means of obtaining independence from Turkey. The PKK launched its first armed assaults against the Turkish government on August 15, 1984, attacking military and police barracks in two towns in southeastern Turkey and distributing leaflets announcing the start of the insurgency.[3]

The Domestic and International Context

The domestic and international context created strong incentives for the PKK to adopt a strategy of terrorism. Faced with a democratic opponent likely to be sensitive to civilian losses, a strategy of terrorism offered a means of increasing domestic pressure on the government to make concessions. Although a 1980 military coup had briefly suspended the functioning of democratic institutions in Turkey, democracy was reestablished before the PKK launched its insurgency; this transition back to democracy was marked by the creation of a new constitution in 1982, the holding of parliamentary elections in 1983, and the expansion of political participation prior to elections in 1984 and 1986.

---

[1] Woodward 1995, 242–244.
[2] Economic and social indicators show significant regional disparities in levels of economic development. See Kirişci and Winrow 1997, 122–126.
[3] On these and other early PKK attacks, see Marcus 2007.

In addition to having strong incentives to use terrorism against its democratic opponent, the international context gave the PKK few available alternatives for generating pressure on the government to make concessions. Turkey's strong relationships with Western governments and intergovernmental organizations meant that PKK appeals to this international constituency for support were unlikely to be effective. As discussed in Chapter 6, the Council of Europe and the EU were deeply involved in encouraging the consolidation of democracy in Turkey throughout the 1980s and 1990s. And although European actors did criticize the Turkish government for human rights violations committed in the context of counterinsurgency operations, they did so while advising and engaging with the Turkish government in an effort to strengthen democratic institutions in the country. They also did not question the Turkish government's right to use military force to confront the challenge to its territorial integrity; public statements often began with affirmations of Turkey's rights as a sovereign state. The Parliamentary Assembly of the Council of Europe, for example, in an April 1995 recommendation expressing its concern over human rights abuses, began by stating that "The Assembly underlines the right of Turkey, as of any other country, to fight – within the limits of international law and in particular the European Convention on Human Rights – against terrorism."[4]

The PKK's Political Constituency

As a separatist group fighting for autonomy for Turkey's Kurdish minority, the PKK drew support primarily from the Kurdish population, which was concentrated in the eastern and southeastern region of the country. In 1990, it was estimated that Kurds accounted for about 12.6 percent of Turkey's total population, but that approximately 65 percent of the population in southeastern Turkey was Kurdish, while Kurds made up about 42 percent of the population in the eastern regions of Turkey.[5] When asked in a 1992 television interview if he considered himself to be the leader of the Kurdish people, Öcalan replied, "The leader of the overwhelming majority, yes. We have created their unity. They will obey us. I am talking freely and candidly now: No one can oppose us easily."[6] Several years later, an interviewer asked "Whom does the PKK represent?" Öcalan's response was: "Clearly, the PKK speaks for Turkey's Kurds. If anyone doubts this, let them have fair, democratic elections and see what happens."[7]

---

[4] Parliamentary Assembly of the Council of Europe, Recommendation 1266, 26 April 1995.
[5] Kirişci and Winrow 1997, 120.
[6] "PKK Leader Ocalan Interviewed on Policy, Goals," Ankara Show Television, 18 May 1992, as published in Foreign Broadcast Information Service – West Europe, 19 May 1992.
[7] Gunter 1998.

The PKK's primary political demand was autonomy for Turkey's Kurdish population and although many interpreted this to mean that the PKK sought the creation of an independent Kurdish state, Öcalan insisted in interviews that the PKK was open to a resolution involving autonomy within the existing borders of the Turkish state. In a 1995 interview, Öcalan claimed, "We are not insisting on a 'separate state' under any condition. What we are calling for very openly is a state model where a people's basic economic, cultural, social, and political rights are guaranteed. These rights could be used in a single state structure or in a separate state."[8] In other interviews, Öcalan even more explicitly called for the creation of a federal state:

I accept the current Turkish borders. Nobody wants Turkey to be divided. This is *very* important! I want to negotiate a just, democratic solution to this twenty-year-old struggle. The Turks must accept the Kurdish identity. They should say in the constitution that there are other people in Turkey and accept a federal system, as in the United States, Germany, Switzerland, Belgium, and Spain.[9]

Even as the PKK moderated its demands, claiming it would accept autonomy within Turkey, the PKK still envisioned itself as the primary governing authority within a future autonomous Kurdish state. In response to a question about the role the PKK would play if the conflict were to reach a negotiated settlement, Öcalan responded, "We can play an active role. If there is a federal state, we will want to run it. The PKK is the voice of the [Kurdish] people."[10] The PKK thus saw itself as representing a particular civilian constituency within Turkey – the Kurdish minority – and the PKK's goal was to govern these constituents within an autonomous region. Because the PKK's civilian constituency was narrow and geographically concentrated in the eastern and southeastern regions of Turkey, and because the PKK did not seek to govern individuals outside of this constituency or region, the PKK had few constraints on its ability to use violence against individuals outside of the Kurdish region. By attacking civilian targets in Istanbul or other major cities in the western part of Turkey, where most of the casualties were likely to be Turks or foreigners, the PKK could impose costs on the government and its constituents, while still retaining support from Kurds in the eastern and southeastern regions.

PKK Strategy

In its early years, the PKK directed its violence primarily at military and police targets – ambushing police or military units on patrol, attacking police and military bases, raiding government weapons supplies, and harassing local pro-government militias in southeastern Turkey.[11] During attacks on pro-

---

[8] "PKK Leader on Party Ideology, U.S. Policy," *Serxwebun* (Cologne), 1 April 1995, as published in Foreign Broadcast Information Service – West Europe, 27 June 1995.
[9] Gunter 1998.   [10] Ibid.   [11] Gunter 1997; Kirişci and Winrow 1997; Marcus 2007.

government militias, the PKK occasionally killed civilians in the villages that had organized the militias – a strategy of control, aimed at deterring civilians from joining these militias and collaborating with the government. Once it became clear, however, that these attacks were leading to increased opposition to the PKK, the group made more concerted efforts to avoid killing Kurdish civilians.[12] The PKK also killed civilians believed to be collaborating with the government, including many teachers, who were seen as supporting a government-run education system that marginalized Kurdish history and culture.[13] It was not until 1993, however, that the PKK turned its violence more deliberately against Turkish civilian populations in Istanbul and other major cities.

At a press conference held in mid-March 1993, Öcalan announced a unilateral ceasefire and indicated that the PKK was willing to negotiate, perhaps even willing to accept some form of autonomy short of full independence. Öcalan offered that "This ceasefire will be a test period which, I hope, will allow the start of political negotiations with the Turkish state. We want to renounce violence and open the way to a new era of peace between the Kurdish and Turkish people. For now we do not want separation from Turkey with which we have economic and historical ties."[14] Despite Öcalan's extension of the ceasefire into May and public calls for negotiations, the government failed to reciprocate the ceasefire and refused to enter into negotiations.[15] The PKK finally revoked the ceasefire in June 1993, vowing to intensify its armed struggle until the government consented to negotiations. Öcalan made clear that the group's strategy was one of terrorism, the aim being to use violence against civilian targets as a means of increasing the economic and political costs of the conflict for the Turkish government. At a press conference announcing an end to the ceasefire, Öcalan warned "We are going to wage an all-out war against it [Turkey] until it agrees to negotiate. The Turkish state must understand once and for all it cannot annihilate us and that the only solution is to negotiate. Turkey will have a bloody summer if the army continues its campaign against us. We will hit economic and tourist interests throughout Turkey."[16] Following this announcement, the PKK began to attack civilian targets more deliberately, particularly civilian targets in Istanbul and other major tourist cities.[17]

---

[12] Marcus 2007.   [13] Aydin and Emrence 2015.

[14] "Turkish Separatists Announce Ceasefire," *Agence France-Presse*, 17 March 1993; Nadim Ladki, "Kurdish Chief Calls New Year Ceasefire with Turkey," *Reuters News*, 17 March 1993.

[15] Ertugrul Kurkcu, "Turkey: Government Firm against PKK Declaration of War," *Inter Press Service*, 9 June 1993.

[16] "Turkish Separatists End Ceasefire: Threaten All-Out War, Tourism," *Agence France-Presse*, 8 June 1993.

[17] See annual reports on Turkey published by Amnesty International and Human Rights Watch for an overview of PKK violence in each year.

Several weeks after announcing an end to the ceasefire, the PKK exploded three bombs at two different hotels and a central shopping area in Antalya, a popular tourist destination on Turkey's Mediterranean coast; 26 people were injured in the attacks, including several tourists.[18] The following day, on June 28, a PKK unit fired on a passenger train, injuring another six civilians,[19] and in July, the PKK carried out a bomb attack in the coastal city of Kusadasi, injuring 18 civilians, including six tourists.[20] PKK attacks on civilian targets continued into 1994, with a series of bombings reported during December 1993 and January 1994 in Diyarbakir, a major city in southeastern Turkey; targets included a university, a night club, newspaper offices, and several government buildings.[21] Also in January, the group exploded bombs on three buses that had originated in the Turkish capital of Ankara, killing three civilians and injuring 20.[22] With the government still intent on resolving the conflict through military means, the PKK again warned that it would intensify violence, announcing at its third conference, held in early March 1994, that the group would "stage all-out revolutionary war in response to the enemy's all-out war of destruction" and insisting that "It is inevitable that we escalate our struggle.... All economic, political, military, social and cultural organizations, institutions, formations – and those who serve in them – have become targets. The entire country has become the battlefield."[23]

The PKK followed through with its threats. Almost immediately after the conclusion of the PKK conference, the group set off bombs at two tourist sites in Istanbul, injuring seven civilians.[24] Just one week later, the PKK killed two civilians and injured 14 when it exploded a bomb at a historic market in Istanbul.[25] The group set off three more bombs at tourist sites in Istanbul during May; carried out a series of bombings of tourist areas on the Mediterranean coast in June; and, in August, bombed an Istanbul bus station.[26] Although

---

[18] "Terrorist Bombs Injure 22 in Turkish Resort," *Associated Press*, 27 June 1993; "Bombs in Turkish Resort Injure 22 Including Tourists," *Reuters News*, 27 June 1993; "26 Injured in Bomb Blast at Turkish Resort," *Reuters News*, 28 June 1993.

[19] Rasit Gurdilek, "Twenty-Six Injured in Bomb Attacks," *Associated Press*, 28 June 1993.

[20] Rasit Gurdilek, "Kurdish Rebels in Turkey to Free Six Foreign Hostages: Go-between Says," *Associated Press*, 30 July 1993.

[21] "Kurdish Guerrillas Bomb Targets in Major Southeastern City," *Associated Press*, 2 January 1994.

[22] "Kurdish Rebels Claim Fatal Bus Bombs in Turkey," *Reuters News*, 17 January 1994.

[23] Cited in Gunter 1997, 49.

[24] "Separatist PKK Says It Carried Out Tourist Bomb Blast," *Agence France-Presse*, 27 March 1994; "Bombing Injures Three Tourists at St. Sophia," *Associated Press*, 27 March 1994.

[25] "Bomb Kills Two, Wounds 14 at Istanbul Bazaar," *Agence France-Presse*, 2 April 1994; Metin Demirsar, "Bomb Kills Two in Istanbul Bazaar, Kurds Suspected," *Reuters News*, 2 April 1994.

[26] "Three Bombs Explode in Istanbul Tourist Areas," *Reuters News*, 7 May 1994; Suna Erdem, "Bombs Wound 18 People in Turkish Tourist Resorts," *Reuters News*, 22 June 1994; "Istanbul Bomb Wounds Six Turks: Three Foreigners," *Reuters News*, 12 August 1994.

fewer PKK attacks were reported in 1995, the PKK exploded three bombs in Istanbul in August – at a restaurant and on a street popular with tourists – killing two civilians and injuring 40.[27]

As the 1996 tourist season approached, Öcalan made repeated threats against civilian targets, announcing in March that "If there is no ceasefire on the part of Turkey then we will have all out war and all weapons will be used. The tourist locations are for us the most important war zones."[28] In May, Öcalan made even more specific threats, warning that the group would target areas along Turkey's Mediterranean coast, saying, "Some of our fighters have set off for the south and they are going to start operations. The south, that means Antalya, the tourist region. I don't know what exactly they are going to do. I have told my people to concentrate on economic targets. ... Our most important goal is to hurt the Turkish economy."[29] Despite these warnings, the PKK did not carry out any major bombings in 1996. It appears that several PKK units had gathered bomb-making equipment in preparation for attacks, but were discovered in police raids in Antalya and Izmir, both major cities on the Mediterranean.[30] It was not until several years later – in 1998 – that the PKK again staged successful bombings of civilian targets. An April 1998 attack near a tourist landmark in Istanbul injured nine civilians, while a July 1998 attack on a historic Istanbul market inflicted more civilian casualties than any other previous PKK attack, killing seven and injuring 118.[31]

PKK violence slowed following the February 1999 arrest and trial of PKK leader Abdullah Öcalan, who was sentenced to death and later, after Turkey revoked its death penalty, to life in prison.[32] Öcalan, still commanding the PKK from prison, ordered the PKK to suspend its armed struggle and withdraw into Northern Iraq, in an effort to pursue negotiations with the Turkish government. For several years, PKK violence remained low as the group sought a political resolution to the conflict. After December 1999 when the EU accepted Turkey as a candidate for future membership, the government began making minor concessions to Kurds in an effort to bring its human rights performance in line with EU standards, including reducing restrictions on the use of the

---

[27] "Three Bombs Mark End of Peaceful Summer," *Agence France-Presse*, 28 August 1995.

[28] "PKK Says Will Bomb Turkish Tourist Targets," *Reuters News*, 11 March 1996.

[29] "Kurdish Leader Warns Tourists of Attacks in Turkey," *Reuters News*, 5 May 1996.

[30] "Turkish Police Detain Rebel Kurds in Resort Town," *Reuters News*, 8 July 1996; "Turkish Police Detain Kurd Rebels in Western City," *Reuters News*, 9 July 1996.

[31] "Nine Injured in Istanbul Bomb Blast," *Agence France-Presse*, 10 April 1998; "Turkey Arrests Nine Kurds over Istanbul Bombing," *Agence France-Presse*, 15 April 1998; " Turkish Police Arrest Four Kurds for Deadly Istanbul Bombing," *Agence France-Presse*, 18 August 1998; "Turkish Police Say Rebels Planted July Bazaar Bomb," *Reuters News*, 18 August 1998.

[32] One major bombing was reported in the weeks after Öcalan's arrest – at an Istanbul shopping mall in March 1999 – seen as a protest against Öcalan's capture. See "Bomb Attacks in Turkey over the Past 20 Years," *Agence France-Presse*, 20 November 2003; "Kurdish Group Claims Responsibility for Istanbul Inferno," *Agence France-Presse*, 14 March 1999.

Kurdish language in media and education and lifting the state of emergency that had been declared in the Kurdish region.[33] Disappointed with the slow pace of government reforms, Öcalan announced an end to the PKK ceasefire in June 2004. The PKK again targeted civilians and tourist areas, with a series of bombings in Istanbul and Mediterranean cities reported in early 2006.[34]

The characteristics of PKK terrorism are consistent in several respects with the arguments of this book. First, the PKK decision to bomb civilian targets was a deliberate strategic choice. After lifting its ceasefire in June 1993, the PKK made clear through public statements its intention to attack civilian targets, particularly tourist sites in Istanbul and along Turkey's coast. Second, the strategic logic driving this violence was coercion. The fact that the PKK did not bomb civilian targets until after the Turkish government refused to negotiate in 1993 demonstrates that the shift in PKK tactics was a direct response to government behavior. As Öcalan stated publicly, if attacks on military and police targets could not force the government to negotiate, then perhaps attacks on civilian targets would. Throughout the 1990s, even as the PKK escalated its attacks on civilian targets, Öcalan repeatedly expressed his willingness to negotiate with the Turkish government and his willingness to consider options short of an independent Kurdish state, emphasizing that the group's intensification of violence had a deliberate political aim. Third, the decision to attack civilian targets, as opposed to military targets, was linked to a perception by the PKK that such attacks would impose different kinds of costs on the Turkish government. Öcalan cited specifically the group's intention to impose costs on the economy and on the tourism industry. Fourth, although it is difficult to prove that the PKK attacked civilian targets because it believed that *democracy* made the government sensitive to civilian losses, it is clear from PKK statements that the PKK believed that the government would be sensitive to civilian losses and the resultant costs to tourism and the economy. And finally, the PKK drew support primarily from the Kurdish population, which was concentrated in the eastern and southeastern region of the country. This narrow, geographically concentrated civilian constituency made it possible for the PKK to attack high-casualty civilian targets outside of the separatist region without risking significant backlash from its civilian base; the PKK primarily attacked public sites in western Turkey where most of the civilian casualties were likely to be Turks or foreigners.

LOW-CASUALTY TERRORISM: THE FMLN IN EL SALVADOR

Opposition to the Salvadoran government developed during the 1970s, as leftist groups organized peasant resistance to the country's repressive economic

---

[33] See Amnesty International Annual Reports, 2001–2007. See also Marcus 2007.
[34] Marcus 2007; Amnesty International Annual Report 2007.

and political system in which access to land, economic opportunity, and political power was restricted to a small class of landowners and military leaders. Five major leftist opposition groups began collaborating with one another in 1979, announcing publicly the formation of a new unified rebel group – the FMLN – in 1980.

The Domestic and International Context

Incentives for terrorism were low during the early years of the conflict, when the FMLN faced an autocratic opponent insulated from domestic pressure. Several years after the start of the rebellion, however, El Salvador announced plans to democratize the government, increasing incentives for the FMLN to target civilians as a means of eliciting concessions from the government. The government held elections in March 1982 to form a Constituent Assembly, which designed a new constitution; presidential and legislative elections followed in 1984 and 1985, installing José Napoleón Duarte, of the Christian Democratic Party (Partido Demócrata Cristiano, PDC), as president.[35] The successful transfer of power between political parties, with the election of National Republican Alliance (Alianza Republicana Nacionalista, ARENA) candidate Alfredo Cristiani to the presidency in 1989, further consolidated El Salvador's democratic system. El Salvador's nascent democracy was not without flaws; Cristiana's ARENA party had links to pro-government death squads that had committed some of the most severe atrocities of the conflict, and the new civilian government largely failed to hold military leaders accountable for past human rights abuses. Yet El Salvador continued to hold regular free and fair presidential and legislative elections throughout the 1980s, and the military did make gradual improvements in its respect for human rights, under pressure from El Salvador's main foreign backer, the United States. Related to efforts to reduce human rights violations, the military also began placing greater emphasis on social programs designed to win the hearts and minds of the civilian population.

The international context limited the options available to the FMLN, particularly as the government continued to implement democratic reforms. The United States backed the Salvadoran government, providing extensive military and economic aid throughout the conflict, as well as stationing military advisors in the country. Prior to the conflict, U.S. aid to El Salvador was relatively low, never exceeding US$14 million in any year from 1965 to 1979.[36] U.S. aid increased dramatically with the start of the war, peaking at US$574 million in total economic and military aid in 1987.[37] From 1979 to 1990, U.S. economic and military aid to El Salvador totaled more than US$3.9

---

[35] See Wood 2000 for a discussion of El Salvador's transition to democracy.
[36] McClintock 1998, 221.   [37] Ibid., 204.

billion, making El Salvador the fifth largest recipient of aid from the United States during the 1980s.[38] Military support for the Salvadoran government led to significant increases in the size of the Salvadoran military, as well as improvements in the quality of the military's equipment; while economic aid allowed the government to continue making its debt payments and to fulfill other economic obligations, such as rebuilding damaged infrastructure and providing food aid to the population.[39] Beginning in 1981, the United States made its assistance conditional on moves toward democracy and greater respect for human rights, stepping up this pressure in 1983 with a visit from Vice President George H. W. Bush, who pressed the Salvadoran government on human rights issues, including the government's use of death squads.[40] After the holding of presidential elections in 1984, however, the United States removed most of its conditions on military assistance and further increased its economic and military aid.[41]

The FMLN received support from a number of different governments in Latin America and elsewhere, as well as from non-governmental solidarity organizations throughout the world, but relied most heavily on support from the Cuban and Nicaraguan governments, which provided training, supplied financing, and funneled arms from the Soviet Union and other Soviet-allied countries.[42] In the early years of the insurgency, the FMLN also appealed to foreign governments outside of the Soviet sphere of influence; in 1981, for example, the FMLN won recognition from France and Mexico, which referred to the group as a "representative political force."[43]

As the Salvadoran government democratized in the mid-1980s, however, it became increasingly difficult for the FMLN to make appeals to international actors, who came to view the Salvadoran government as legitimate.[44] A July 1984 *New York Times* headline – "Duarte Winning Support Abroad, Using His Democratic Credentials" – announced this shift in international opinion and reported that the newly elected Salvadoran president was spending significant time abroad during his first weeks in office, traveling to the United States and Europe to mobilize support for his government. The French president met with Duarte, pulling back from its previous expressed support for the insurgency; while the West German government promised increased aid.[45]

---

[38] Ibid., 204, 221.   [39] McClintock 1998.

[40] McClintock 1998; Peceny and Stanley 2010. See also Lydia Chavez, "U.S. Envoy Is Facing Hard Tests," *New York Times*, 1 January 1984.

[41] McClintock 1998. See also Robert S. Greenberger, "Reagan's Central American Policies Post Victory in House: Defeat in World Court," *Wall Street Journal*, 11 May 1984.

[42] McClintock 1998. Declassified U.S. government documents provide information on American assessments of FMLN financing; see, for example, U.S. Embassy in San Salvador 1986; Central Intelligence Agency Director of Central Intelligence 1989.

[43] Byrne 1996, 90.   [44] Byrne 1996.

[45] James LeMoyne and Lydia Chavez, "Duarte Winning Support Abroad: Using His Democratic Credentials," *New York Times*, 25 July 1984.

Even members of the FMLN admitted the difficulty in winning international support following the 1984 elections. As one FMLN leader explained, in the period following the elections, "The diplomatic plane, considered by the FMLN as vital for the triumph of the revolution, had weakened enormously. The strongest thing they had was the French-Mexican support, which had weakened because both countries had resumed relations with the Government of El Salvador. The categorical conclusion of the Central Committee was that the Government had come out of the international isolation in which it had found itself."[46] In this international atmosphere – with the United States providing extensive military and economic aid to the Salvadoran government and with other foreign governments expressing their support for the newly elected Salvadoran leaders – the FMLN was unable to mobilize significant international pressure on the government. Instead, the FMLN had to find other means of generating pressure on the government to make concessions.

The FMLN's Political Constituency

As a revolutionary leftist rebellion seeking power within the central government, the FMLN had inclusive political objectives that demanded the maintenance of a broad base of domestic civilian support. Thus, although the FMLN faced increasing incentives to use terrorism as the Salvadoran government democratized, the FMLN was also constrained in its ability to use violence by its need to secure domestic support.

Central to the FMLN's political agenda was its desire to install a more representative form of government in El Salvador to replace what the group saw as an exclusionary and repressive economic and political system dominated by a small group of economic and military elites. In its platform published in 1980, for example, the group announced its intention to "carry out political, economic, and social reforms that will assure a just distribution of wealth, the enjoyment of culture and health and an effective exercise of the democratic rights of the majority."[47] One of the FMLN's leaders, Joaquín Villalobos, emphasized this point in a 1983 radio statement, saying, "The FMLN is struggling for a government of full participation, with representation from all the democratic political forces, including of course the FMLN-FDR.... The FMLN maintains that a government of full participation should guarantee freedom of expression and organization, respect for Human Rights, and truly free elections with participation by all parties and forces."[48] Several years later, in an article published in *Foreign Policy*, Villalobos again articulated the group's democratic agenda, saying, "In the new system there should be room for domestic political competition, with democratic elections and political

---

[46] Prisk 1991, 98.   [47] McClintock 1998, 57.   [48] Ibid., 58.

parties – thus permitting the masses to participate in decision making and in the political, economic, and social management of the country."[49]

The FMLN, as an organization, functioned democratically, with each of its five member organizations retaining their own organizational structure and leadership; leaders from each of the five organizations then coordinated their actions through a General Command and a Political–Diplomatic Commission, bodies that met regularly to discuss and plan FMLN strategy.[50] According to Salvador Samayoa, an FMLN spokesperson, the political leadership of the FMLN was the main decision-making body: "The party directs the armed forces, and not the reverse. Our military line, plans, and concrete actions are decided by the directorate of the party, not the armed units."[51]

The FMLN controlled territory to varying degrees throughout the war, exerting its greatest degree of control over regions in the northern and northeastern parts of the country, near the border with Honduras.[52] In the early 1980s, the FMLN controlled between 25 and 35 percent of the country's municipalities, with this percentage declining to about 15 percent of municipalities by 1989.[53] In zones of FMLN control, the group reportedly maintained a close relationship with its constituents; commanders interacted frequently with civilian supporters and even responded to criticism from supporters, in some cases promoting or demoting FMLN members in response to feedback from civilian communities.[54] The FMLN drew on a variety of civil society organizations, such as agricultural cooperatives, to develop its network of civilian support.[55] In a 1989 interview, Samayoa commented on the FMLN's relationship with the population, saying, "If the FMLN had a bad relationship with the people it would be very difficult to continue fighting the army. We could not survive, much less develop and grow, if we didn't have the support of the population. We could not mobilize troops and units of any type without being detected and denounced if the people were against us."[56] Although assessing the extent of popular support for the FMLN is difficult, observers have noted that the group received significant backing from civilians, who provided the group with intelligence and other forms of assistance;[57] one scholar estimates that approximately one-quarter of the population supported the FMLN.[58]

The FMLN was persistent in its claims that the group was pluralist, able to incorporate individuals from a variety of different political backgrounds. As Villalobos explained in his 1989 *Foreign Policy* article, "For revolutions are essentially democratic. They can and should be defended not only by a solid

[49] Villalobos 1989, 117.   [50] Byrne 1996, 77; McClintock 1998.
[51] Samayoa and Karl 1989, 341.   [52] Bracamonte and Spencer 1995; Wood 2003.
[53] McClintock 1998, 80. See also Wood 2003, 131. Wood estimates that the FMLN controlled approximately one-fifth of the country's territory in 1983.
[54] McClintock 1998.   [55] Byrne 1996; Wood 2003.   [56] Samayoa and Karl 1989, 342.
[57] Wood 2003; Peceny and Stanley 2010.   [58] McClintock 1998, 76–77.

correlation of forces but also by a flexible democratic program representative of broad sectors, tendencies, and realities, both internal and external. The aim is to create real democracy for the entire people in the economic and political arenas."[59] He went on to point out that the FMLN originated as a coalition of multiple opposition groups and remained so throughout the insurgency; he also emphasized the FMLN's alliance with the Democratic Revolutionary Front (Frente Democrático Revolucionario, FDR), a coalition of opposition political parties.[60] Although workers and peasants were an important base of support for the FMLN, Villalobos argued that the revolution "reaches to other sectors of society, including the middle class."[61]

FMLN Strategy

During the first few years of major armed conflict, before the government began its transition to democracy, the FMLN built a large army, capable of concentrating its forces to engage in conventional battles with the Salvadoran military; the FMLN carried out a series of military offensives, with the aim of achieving a decisive military victory. Although the group did attack infrastructure targets, its focus was on attacks on government troops, bases, and military equipment. During the early years of rebellion, the FMLN did not target civilians and made efforts to build international support, despite the fact that Cold War politics made this strategy challenging.

The dramatic increase in aid from the United States in the mid-1980s made it possible for the Salvadoran government to intensify its military operations against the FMLN, making greater use of air power to attack FMLN positions, and shifting from a focus on defending infrastructure to more frequent offensives against the FMLN.[62] The FMLN countered these changes in government strategy by altering its strategy as well, shifting from conventional to unconventional warfare – reducing the size and increasing the mobility of its units; launching smaller scale ambushes and surprise attacks on government forces; relying more heavily on landmines to impede government mobility and inflict casualties; and initiating a major campaign of economic sabotage, in which the group attacked bridges, electric plants, and other infrastructure targets, as well

---

[59] Villalobos 1989, 112.   [60] Ibid., 113–114.   [61] Ibid., 116.

[62] Byrne 1996; McClintock 1998. The Chief of Operations of the Combined General Staff of the Salvadoran Armed Forces, Colonel René Emilio Ponce, describes these changes in an interview recorded in Manwaring and Prisk 1988, 293–297. See also "The Army and Rebels Have Both Stepped Up Their Offensive in El Salvador," *Latin American Mexico and NAFTA Report*, 30 November 1984; Charles J. Hanley, "The One Sure Fact: 'The People Are Suffering,'" *Associated Press*, 17 July 1985. Declassified U.S. government documents also detail changes in U.S. support to the Salvadoran military, and the resultant changes in the Salvadoran military's strategy. See, for example, Central Intelligence Agency Directorate of Intelligence 1986.

as major export crops and their processing facilities.[63] In public statements and interviews with foreign journalists, FMLN commanders made clear that this shift in strategy was deliberate.[64]

FMLN attacks on economic and infrastructure targets caused an estimated $263.9 million worth of damage in 1984.[65] The following year, the sabotage campaign was even more destructive; according to FMLN estimates, the group carried out 50 attacks on major power lines, 700 attacks on other utility posts, and 12 attacks on coffee processing facilities, destroying more than eight million pounds of coffee, El Salvador's primary export.[66] In its assessment of this economic sabotage campaign, the U.S. Central Intelligence Agency (CIA) estimated that "during the first six months of 1985 such operations increased more than 550 percent over the same period in 1984," leading to significant disruption to the economy, including "lengthy blackouts" in the capital and the eastern region of the country.[67] In addition to disrupting coffee production and electric, water, and sewage service throughout the country, the FMLN also staged frequent transportation stoppages (an average of seven per year, lasting about a week each);[68] during stoppages, the group announced a prohibition on all vehicle traffic and stationed units along major roadways, forcibly stopping and disabling any vehicle that attempted to pass.

The FMLN expanded its sabotage campaign throughout the late 1980s, carrying out 120 sabotage attacks in western regions of the country in 1986, up from 70 in 1985, and increasing attacks on infrastructure targets in the capital of San Salvador from 54 attacks in 1985 to 73 in 1986.[69] In 1987 and 1988, the FMLN escalated attacks in urban areas – in particular, in the capital city; in a February 1989 Special National Intelligence Estimate, the CIA reported that the number of FMLN incidents in San Salvador tripled between 1986 and 1988.[70] The CIA also noted that the FMLN was using "high-visibility, low-risk operations" and was carrying out sabotage attacks in spurts in order to "enhance impact."[71] By the time

---

[63] Byrne 1996; Wood 2003. See also John Carlin, "The War That Soldiers Cannot Win: Second of Two Articles on Power Struggle in El Salvador – Economy the New Battleground," *Times*, 13 August 1985; "The Army and Rebels Have Both Stepped Up Their Offensive in El Salvador," *Latin American Mexico and NAFTA Report*, 30 November 1984.

[64] Edward Cody, "Salvadoran Rebels Change Tactics: Leaders Say Small-Unit Attacks Employed in War of Attrition," *Washington Post*, 17 May 1985; James LeMoyne, "Salvador Rebel Vows to Spread War," *New York Times*, 7 July 1985; James LeMoyne, "Salvadoran Rebels Draw a Bead on the Economy," *New York Times*, 14 July 1985.

[65] Byrne 1996, 149.

[66] Byrne 1996, 149; "Continuing Salvadoran War Exacts Huge Economic and Human Cost," *Latin American Weekly Report*, 10 January 1986.

[67] Central Intelligence Agency Directorate of Intelligence 1986, 16.

[68] Byrne 1996, 150. See also "Rebels Paralyze Highway Traffic," *Associated Press*, 19 August 1985.

[69] Byrne 1996, 150. See also "FMLN Steps Up Attacks/Fighting in El Salvador," *Financial Times*, 21 January 1986.

[70] Central Intelligence Agency Director of Central Intelligence 1989, 10.   [71] Ibid., 12.

the war ended, the United States estimated that the total damage from the FMLN's sabotage campaign had exceeded $2 billion.[72]

The FMLN's aim in attacking economic and infrastructure targets was to disrupt and weaken the country's economy, reducing the resources available to the government for prosecuting the war as well as undermining support for the newly elected government by making the government seem incapable of providing basic services such as electricity, sanitation, and a functioning economy.[73] As one study of FMLN strategy described the sabotage campaign, "The destruction of the economy and the infrastructure would have a profound impact on the social conditions of the population. The people would blame their new social problems on the government. Mass organizations would publicly and visibly protest against the government in an attempt to radicalize the masses."[74] Economic sabotage was also aimed at imposing high costs on one of the government's key constituencies: the economic elite.[75] As the economic costs of the conflict rose and as economic elites became increasingly dissatisfied with these losses, the FMLN hoped that the government would face increasing pressure to make concessions.

Since many of the FMLN's own constituents lived in rural areas, where access to electricity was scarce, attacking the country's economic infrastructure had a greater impact on the government's constituents than on the FMLN's constituents.[76] Still, the FMLN was concerned about the impact that their economic sabotage campaign would have on their ability to maintain popular support and tried to mitigate backlash by emphasizing that economic elites were the main targets. One FMLN commander described how the FMLN justified its attacks to its constituents: "When one explained sabotage to them, it was necessary to make the population see that the sabotage was against the economy of the bourgeoisie and against the government; you said to them, of course, this was war, and war was going to affect them in some way, but that these weren't actions against them, but against the bourgeoisie, against private enterprise, against the Government."[77]

Villalobos, in a written statement published in September 1986, explained the shift to a campaign of economic sabotage as a "destabilisation plan, the objective of which is to destroy the foundations of the war economy while preventing the fulfilment of the [government's] project of capitalist modernisation aimed at reactivating the economy and securing the system's survival."[78] According to another FMLN commander, Miguel Castellanos, the FMLN

[72] Byrne 1996, 159; Douglas Farah, "Salvador: The Last Puzzle: This Central American Problem May Be Our Toughest," *Washington Post*, 4 March 1990.

[73] LeMoyne 1989; Bracamonte and Spencer 1995; Byrne 1996.

[74] Bracamonte and Spencer 1995, 27.   [75] Byrne 1996, 106–107.   [76] Ibid.

[77] Prisk 1991, 78.

[78] "El Salvador: FMLN Says Analysts Have Got It Wrong," *Latin American Mexico and NAFTA Report*, 25 September 1986.

believed that the declining economy had fomented popular discontent, while democratization had made the government more vulnerable to public opposition; if the FMLN could, through its attacks on economic and infrastructure targets, drive the economy into further decline, thus intensifying dissatisfaction with the government's performance, this might be fatal for the new democracy. Castellanos described the logic at length in an interview with a journalist:

We knew that the institutional political project was continuing and that they were finishing the electoral law for the presidential elections of 1984; in that sense the FMLN could see that the regime was taking the country toward, let us say, constitutionality. Also one could see an effort to reduce international isolation and the unpopularity of the Armed Forces.... Here it is very important to point out that the general framework in which all of this was happening was that of a continually deepening economic crisis.

This economic crisis should always be kept in the forefront because it became a serious encumbrance for the opening that the democratic process provided. This crisis was a fundamental limitation in being able to win over the masses. The FMLN analyzed this situation and intensified economic sabotage.

The FMLN pointed out that the national economy works to maintain the war and the system; therefore, it must be attacked – the crisis must be sharpened. Economic sabotage is fundamentally the destruction of the economic infrastructure – sabotage of the electric plants, telephone lines, and transport, and destruction of the most important crops, such as cotton and coffee. The purpose is to intensify the crisis and make the regime collapse economically. This will have repercussions because of the discontent of the masses, and if possible, in the short or long term, because of a popular uprising supported by the organizations that control the FMLN.[79]

Captured FMLN documents confirm that in making strategic decisions the group was taking into consideration the impact that democratization and the holding of regular elections would have on the government's incentive structure. For example, a series of FMLN documents written by Villalobos that were captured in February 1988 indicated that the FMLN thought it could take advantage of the 1988 and 1989 election campaigns, which were scheduled to coincide with the harvest seasons. This timing, Villalobos argued, gave "the FMLN an opportunity to exploit the GOES' [Government of El Salvador's] political and military weakness";[80] by sabotaging the harvest of agricultural export products, the FMLN could undermine political support for the government.[81]

Even the United States, in its internal communications, acknowledged that the sabotage campaign had the potential to undermine the democratic government in El Salvador. A 1986 CIA Intelligence Assessment noted that while the FMLN shift to increased use of urban terrorism and economic sabotage was unlikely to lead to the overthrow of the Duarte government, it could undermine the process of democratization: "prolonged urban terrorism and sabotage has

---

[79] Prisk 1991, 72–73.   [80] U.S. Secretary of State 1988, 2.
[81] U.S. Embassy in San Salvador 1988a, 4.

the potential to sap popular support for the government, sow dissension between the military and the civilian authorities, and undermine longer-term economic and administrative reform."[82] Similarly, in a 1988 telegram to the U.S. Secretary of State, the American Embassy in San Salvador warned that "the guerrillas have the tactical advantage because El Salvador's economy is the GOES' most vulnerable target, providing the ideal opportunity for destabilizing the government."[83]

FMLN commanders repeatedly emphasized that their campaign of economic sabotage was aimed at imposing costs on the government and its constituents without imposing significant casualties. In January 1985, the *Washington Post* reported that "Salvador Samayoa, a [FMLN] front leader, told Orme [a *Washington Post* correspondent] that sabotage is the guerrillas' only response to U.S. economic aid, which he said enables the Duarte government to pursue the war. Such attacks also can be effective without causing many casualties, he said."[84] In another interview, Samayoa defended the FMLN's use of bombs to attack economic targets in urban areas, but, again, emphasized the goal of avoiding civilian casualties:

Hundreds of people in the city think that the war is something that doesn't concern them, that the killing and terrorizing of peasants does not concern them at all. The initial idea of the car bombs was to make people in the city feel the war. Explosives have also been used in San Salvador as an instrument of sabotage against the property of certain economic sectors or against the military. For us, what is unjustifiable – what we have never done, not once, and I hope we won't ever do – is to put explosives where there are people. Personally, I believe that car bombs have little benefit and high political cost.[85]

FMLN Commander Villalobos made similar comments in his 1989 *Foreign Policy* article, saying, "The FMLN is not a terrorist organization. Its military practices seek to win the support of society, not to intentionally and premeditatedly cause civilian casualties."[86] Outside observers confirm that the FMLN's military operations did not inflict high civilian casualties, noting that the majority of those killed at the hands of the FMLN were individuals in the security forces.[87]

As the costs of the war mounted, representatives from the FMLN and the Salvadoran government met several times between October 1984 and October 1989, but these negotiations concluded without agreement; observers attributed the failure in negotiations to the fact that neither side was yet willing to compromise, both still believing that they could achieve military victory.[88] On November 11, 1989, the FMLN launched a major offensive in San Salvador, in

---

[82] Central Intelligence Agency Directorate of Intelligence 1986, 19.
[83] U.S. Embassy in San Salvador 1988b, 11.
[84] Edward Cody, "Salvadoran Talks at Impasse," *Washington Post*, 23 January 1985.
[85] Samayoa and Karl 1989, 346.   [86] Villalobos 1989, 107.   [87] McClintock 1998, 59.
[88] Byrne 1996.

the hope of sparking a popular revolt that would precipitate the government's collapse. The FMLN offensive was a powerful show of force, with the rebel group gaining control over large areas of San Salvador for several days; however, the popular insurrection the FMLN had hoped for never materialized and the FMLN was forced out of the capital city. Although the offensive failed to capture San Salvador, it demonstrated that the FMLN remained a significant military threat, increasing incentives for the government to enter into peace negotiations. Following the failed offensive, the FMLN, too, began to moderate its demands and seemed willing to accept a settlement short of revolution.[89] Peace negotiations, mediated by the United Nations, began in April 1990; the two sides signed a series of agreements in April, May, and July 1990, outlining the goals of the peace talks, and began discussing more substantive issues toward the end of 1990.

Despite participating in negotiations, the FMLN did not slow its campaign of economic sabotage. FMLN attacks on economic and infrastructure targets in 1990 continued at a pace similar to that of the late 1980s; the FMLN launched more than 1,000 attacks on electric lines and power stations in 1990, leading to an estimated $125 million in losses to the Salvadoran economy.[90] Public statements from FMLN leaders indicate that the FMLN was using attacks on economic targets as a means of extracting more significant concessions from the government during negotiations. Following the second round of peace talks, held in May 1990, the FMLN released a statement asserting its right to continue military operations until a formal ceasefire could be agreed upon: "The FMLN reiterates that as long as no cease-fire is agreed to through political accords, such as the end of military impunity and concrete commitments for the demilitarization of the country, we reserve the right to defend ourselves and also to launch offensives of any size when it is necessary."[91] In the days prior to a fifth round of negotiations, held in late August 1990, the FMLN carried out a series of attacks on the country's electric system, reducing energy supplies by 45 percent. According to the director of the state electricity company, "The destruction of the electricity transmission system by the FMLN on the eve of the fifth meeting is part of a policy of pressure."[92] An official at the U.S. Embassy in El Salvador described the FMLN's continued campaign of economic sabotage as demonstrating to the government that "even if the FMLN can't win, it can prevent the economic reactivization that the government wants."[93] As negotiations reached a

---

[89] Wood 2000, 82.   [90] U.S. Department of State 1992. Also cited in Byrne 1996, 185.

[91] "Diplomatic Progress in El Salvador," *San Francisco Chronicle*, 22 May 1990; see also Douglas Grant Mine, "Salvador Rebels Say They Reserve Right to Attacks," *Associated Press*, 21 May 1990.

[92] "Salvador Rebels Mount Sabotage Attacks Ahead of Talks," *Reuters News*, 16 August 1990.

[93] Chris Norton, "Salvadoran Factions Feel Growing Heat to Bring Halt to War," *Christian Science Monitor*, 4 May 1990.

stalemate over the issue of military reform, the FMLN again intensified its attacks on economic and military targets, making clear in a statement signed by the group's five senior commanders that this escalation of violence was intended to force the government to make concessions regarding the status of the military.[94]

The FMLN was right to calculate that attacks on economic targets would put pressure on the government to make concessions. Alfredo Cristiani, elected to the presidency in March 1989, came to power promising to resolve the conflict with the FMLN and to achieve economic progress through free market reforms.[95] Yet economic decline continued. In 1979, the year the conflict began, per capita GDP was $2325 (in constant 2000 US$), but by 1990 had dropped to $1638 (in constant 2000 US$).[96] The value of the country's exports, both in absolute terms and as a percentage of GDP, also declined throughout the decade of civil war, while external debt increased from 26 percent of gross national income in 1979 to 46 percent in 1990. Inflation, which hovered around 15 percent for much of the early 1980s, increased in the latter part of the decade and was estimated at 24 percent in 1990. This poor economic performance made it difficult for the government to maintain popular support. A public opinion poll conducted in September 1990 showed that the government was suffering from dismal public approval ratings; only a year and half after Cristiani had come to power with a clear majority of the vote in presidential elections, government approval ratings had dropped to just 25 percent.[97]

Ultimately, the government was forced to make significant concessions, which included allowing FMLN participation in elections, establishing an Ad Hoc Commission to investigate human rights abuses committed by senior members of the military as well as a Commission on the Truth to carry out broader human rights investigations, and agreeing to restructure the military. The FMLN, too, made concessions, agreeing to less extensive socioeconomic reforms than it had initially demanded. The two sides formalized these terms in the final peace agreement signed in Mexico City in January 1992.[98]

A number of aspects of the FMLN case are consistent with the arguments put forth in this book. First, as the statements of FMLN leaders show, the shift in the mid-1980s to increased reliance on a strategy of low-casualty

---

[94] Douglas Grant Mine, "Heavy Fighting Rocks El Salvador," *Associated Press*, 20 November 1990.

[95] See Cristiani's editorial, "In El Salvador: A New Arena Party," published in the *New York Times*, 15 March 1989.

[96] The economic statistics in this section are taken from the World Bank, *World Development Indicators*, multiple years, available online at data.worldbank.org

[97] Poll conducted by CID-Gallup, based in Costa Rica. Cited in "Economic Woes Fuel Salvador Government's Peace Bid," *Reuters News*, 10 September 1990.

[98] On peace negotiations, see Wood 2000.

terrorism – what the FMLN referred to as a campaign of economic sabotage involving attacks on economic and infrastructure targets – was intentional. Statements from FMLN leaders and external observers indicate that the initial FMLN decision to intensify its economic sabotage campaign was part of a larger strategic shift toward a traditional guerrilla warfare strategy in response to a new government counterinsurgency strategy, which involved a larger, better equipped military and increased use of air power to support ground operations.

Second, the FMLN's decision to attack infrastructure targets was motivated by a perception that such attacks would be costly to the government, in light of the country's ongoing economic difficulties. The FMLN believed that these costs were particularly problematic for the government because it had transitioned to democracy and, therefore, needed to maintain public support to remain in power. Thus, although the government's change in regime does not appear to have prompted the *initial* change in FMLN strategy, the evidence indicates that the character of the regime did enter into FMLN decision making in the mid- to late 1980s. The FMLN was aware of the pressure the newly democratic government faced to maintain popular support and the backing of economic elites. FMLN documents and public statements indicate that the group sought to exploit this political situation, intensifying its campaign of economic sabotage in the lead-up to elections and expanding its attacks into urban areas in an effort to achieve maximum public impact and visibility.

Third, although initially the FMLN's sabotage campaign was part of a strategy aimed at weakening the government enough to make overthrow possible, once it became clear that this was unlikely, the FMLN used attacks on infrastructure targets as a means of coercing the government into making concessions during peace negotiations. And finally, as a revolutionary rebellion competing with the government to build a national base of support, the FMLN avoided attacks on high-casualty targets that might have generated public backlash and instead focused its attacks on low-casualty infrastructure targets.

CLEANSING IN NAGORNO-KARABAKH

In 1923, the Soviet Union designated Nagorno-Karabakh – a region in the western part of Azerbaijan with a large Armenian majority – as an autonomous oblast within the Soviet Socialist Republic of Azerbaijan. Nagorno-Karabakh remained part of Azerbaijan throughout the Soviet period, despite multiple requests by the Soviet Socialist Republic of Armenia to transfer the region to Armenian control.[99] As Mikhail Gorbachev's policy of glasnost loosened restrictions on public expression in the late 1980s, demands for Nagorno-Karabakh's self-determination grew and the regional Soviet parliament in

---

[99] International Crisis Group 2005d, 4.

Nagorno-Karabakh announced the region's unilateral secession from Azerbaijan.[100] In January 1990, Moscow declared a state of emergency in Nagorno-Karabakh and sent in Soviet and Azerbaijani troops to put down the separatist movement.

With the collapse of the Soviet Union came the withdrawal of Soviet troops. Nagorno-Karabakh militias escalated their armed struggle, marking the start of the civil war between Nagorno-Karabakh and the newly independent Azerbaijani government. In the early months, the conflict was fought primarily between militias, but by the end of 1992 Armenia and Azerbaijan had both established national armies, while Nagorno-Karabakh had created a National Defense Council, which oversaw the Armed Forces of the Republic of Nagorno-Karabakh.[101]

The Domestic and International Context

Several characteristics of the Karabakh insurgency set it apart from the other insurgencies discussed in this book. First, unlike the insurgencies in El Salvador and Turkey, the Karabakh rebels did not face a democratic opponent, and thus did not have incentives to use a strategy of terrorism. After Azerbaijan declared its independence from the Soviet Union in 1991, the former communist leadership retained control over the Azerbaijani government;[102] the Polity IV Project assigned the new government a polity score of −3, placing it closer to autocracy than to democracy on the 21-point polity scale. Although presidential elections held in June 1992 led to a slight increase in Azerbaijan's polity score, the government was overthrown in a military coup the following year[103] and Azerbaijan's polity score dropped back to a −3, where it remained through the end of the conflict.

The second characteristic that distinguishes the Karabakh insurgency from the other insurgencies in this book is the rebel group's relationship with its primary international supporter. Most separatist insurgencies seek autonomy or independence, but Nagorno-Karabakh initially requested unification with Armenia. Armenia actively supported these demands, providing extensive military, financial, and diplomatic backing to Nagorno-Karabakh.[104] The Armenian government provided Karabakh forces with weapons and military equipment,[105] and although Armenia publicly denied any direct involvement of its troops,[106] numerous credible sources report that Armenian troops took part in military operations.[107] In 1993, Armenia began financing Nagorno-Karabakh's budget through low-interest loans, which Nagorno-Karabakh has yet to repay.[108] On the diplomatic front, the Armenian government took the

---

[100] Cornell 1999; Melander 2001; de Waal 2003; Zürcher 2007.   [101] Zürcher 2007.
[102] Cornell 2001; Kamrava 2001.   [103] Cornell 2001; Kamrava 2001.   [104] Melander 2001.
[105] Denber and Goldman 1992.   [106] Ibid.; Human Rights Watch/Helsinki 1994.
[107] Human Rights Watch/Helsinki 1994; Cornell 1999; de Waal 2003.
[108] Cornell 1999; International Crisis Group 2005d, 12. See also Tchilingirian 1999, who reports
    Armenian contributions to the 1997 budget in Nagorno-Karabakh.

lead in negotiations with the Azerbaijani government – particularly after 1997, when the Azerbaijani government began refusing to negotiate directly with the Karabakh Armenians.[109]

Thus, although other insurgencies confronting nondemocratic governments – such as the Timorese and Acehnese insurgencies in Indonesia – have sought to use international pressure as a means of forcing government concessions, from the start of the conflict, Karabakh insurgents had strong backing from the Armenian government and did not need to appeal for support from a wider international constituency. In addition, Armenia was able to shield the Karabakh insurgents from serious international criticism, lowering the international costs of violence. For example, pressure from Armenian diaspora groups, combined with a favorable image of the newly independent Armenian government as committed to democratization, led to significant restrictions on U.S. aid to Azerbaijan throughout the conflict.[110] Other international actors largely refrained from direct criticism of Armenian or Karabakh actions. The UN Security Council passed a series of resolutions on Nagorno-Karabakh in 1993,[111] in which it called for the withdrawal of Armenian forces from Azerbaijani territory outside of Nagorno-Karabakh, but these resolutions raised concerns about the displacement of civilians without holding either side responsible for this displacement. As one scholar noted about the Karabakh insurgency, "After having made themselves guilty of a number of violations of laws of war, carried out ethnic cleansing and a massacre on the civilian population of Khojaly, they received no clear-cut condemnation from any significant state or international organization."[112]

Karabakh Political Objectives and the Geography of Nagorno-Karabakh

The Nagorno-Karabakh insurgency, like other separatist insurgencies, has a narrow civilian constituency; the insurgents claim to represent and ultimately seek to govern a particular ethnic group: Karabakh Armenians. Thus, like other separatist insurgencies, the domestic costs of using violence against civilians outside of this narrow civilian constituency were low. In many separatist conflicts, however, the government's political constituents are too numerous or too dispersed geographically to make their removal from the separatist region possible. But in Nagorno-Karabakh, the Azeri population living inside the separatist region was small and geographically concentrated in particular

---

[109] Tchilingirian 1999; International Crisis Group 2005c; de Waal 2010.

[110] Paul 2000; Cornell 1999. See also FREEDOM Support Act, Section 907, 102nd Congress, 24 October 1992 (S.2532.ENR).

[111] UN Security Council Resolution 822 (1993), 30 April 1993 (S/RES/822); Resolution 853 (1993), 29 July 1993 (S/RES/853); Resolution 874 (1993), 14 October 1993 (S/RES/874); Resolution 884 (1993), 12 November 1993 (S/RES/884).

[112] Cornell 1999, 121.

cities and towns, creating strong incentives for Karabakh insurgents to adopt a strategy of cleansing, forcibly expelling these civilians from the separatist region in an attempt to solidify the Armenian majority's claim to the territory.

The demography of Nagorno-Karabakh is at the heart of Karabakh demands for autonomy. The last Soviet census, taken in 1989, counted the Armenian population in Nagorno-Karabakh at 145,500, constituting 76.9 percent of the total population of 189,085; the Azeri population in the region was estimated at 40,700, or 21.5 percent.[113] Nagorno-Karabakh sought unification with Armenia throughout the Soviet period, but since the Soviet collapse, public opinion in Nagorno-Karabakh has been split over whether to press for unification or independence.[114] If the region were to become independent, Karabakh leaders have stressed the importance of maintaining close ties with Armenia.[115] Meanwhile, the Armenian government has emphasized the region's right to self-determination.[116]

The geography of the region has complicated Nagorno-Karabakh's demand for a closer relationship with Armenia. Prior to the war, the narrow strip of Azerbaijani territory separating Nagorno-Karabakh from Armenia was populated primarily by Azeris; according to data from the 1989 census, the three districts in this territory were between 89.9 percent and 99.4 percent Azeri.[117] This territory has been a central issue of contention in the conflict, with the Karabakh insurgency demanding a settlement that secures this territorial link with Armenia.[118]

Within Nagorno-Karabakh, the Armenian and Azeri populations, for the most part, remained separate from one another prior to the war. Data from the 1989 census on 121 of Nagorno-Karabakh's localities show that "84 were 'localities with Armenian population domination' and 31 were 'with Azeri population domination,' while the remaining 6 (and generally the very largest) were 'mixed.'"[119] Nearly half of the Azeri population was concentrated in the city of Shusha and its surrounding region.[120] In addition to being geographically concentrated, a number of Azeri towns occupied strategically important territory within Nagorno-Karabakh. Shusha, for example, is situated at a high point within Nagorno-Karabakh and is also the nearest major town to the Lachin corridor, the point at which the Azeri territory dividing Nagorno-Karabakh from Armenia is at its narrowest.[121]

⸱

[113] International Crisis Group 2005d, 4.   [114] Ibid.   [115] Tchilingirian 1999.
[116] See, for example, Armenian President Levon Ter-Petrossian's September 1992 speech before the UN General Assembly: UN General Assembly, 47th Session, Provisional Verbatim Record of the 8th Meeting, New York, 23 September 1992 (A/47/PV.8).
[117] International Crisis Group 2005d, 7.
[118] International Crisis Group 2005c, 22–23; International Crisis Group 2007a, 5–6.
[119] Rowland 2008, 104.   [120] Ibid.   [121] Cornell 1999; de Waal 2003.

The Karabakh Insurgency's Strategy

A narrow domestic constituency of Karabakh Armenians and strong backing from the Armenian government meant that the Karabakh insurgency faced low domestic and international costs to targeting civilians, while the geographic concentration of Azeri populations within regions of strategic importance both inside and outside Nagorno-Karabakh created strong incentives to eliminate this opposing civilian constituency. Consistent with the theoretical expectations of this book, a key component of the Karabakh insurgency's strategy was the cleansing of Azeri civilians from towns and villages inside Nagorno-Karabakh and in the territories separating Nagorno-Karabakh from Armenia.

The conflict began in February 1992 with an Azerbaijani assault on Nagorno-Karabakh's capital of Stepanakert, where the separatist government was based. After a week of artillery fire and bombardment of the city, Karabakh militias fought back, capturing a series of Azeri villages in the surrounding region. As each town was captured, remaining Azeri civilians were forcibly expelled.[122] One of the most vicious expulsions took place during an attack on Khojali in February 1992, which was one of the largest remaining Azeri towns; Karabakh forces killed an estimated 485 Azeri civilians, many of whom were unarmed and were killed while fleeing across open territory.[123] After capturing Khojali, Karabakh forces captured Shusha and moved into Lachin, the main town within the corridor of Azerbaijani land separating Nagorno-Karabakh from Armenia. Like the other Azeri towns, Shusha and Lachin were cleansed of their Azeri inhabitants. Lachin had a prewar population of 47,400 Azeris, none of whom remained at the end of the conflict; they were replaced by 10,000 Armenian settlers.[124]

When Azerbaijani forces staged a major counteroffensive in late 1992, retaking much of the territory they had lost earlier in the year, they, too, engaged in expulsions, replacing the Armenian population with Azeri settlers and refugees. Karabakh and Armenian forces, however, launched a renewed offensive in 1993, gaining control over nearly all of Nagorno-Karabakh as well as the corridor of land separating the region from Armenia. During this second offensive, Karabakh and Armenian forces also expanded their reach into a zone of Azerbaijani territory to the east of Nagorno-Karabakh, purportedly to establish a more defensible border. Major Azeri towns in the region, such as Agdam, Kelbajar, Jebrail, and Fizuli, were looted, burned, and "systematically levelled so that only foundations remain"[125] and their Azeri populations were forcibly expelled.[126]

A 1994 ceasefire halted the fighting, but as of 2015, the parties to the conflict had yet to agree on a permanent resolution. Karabakh and Armenian forces

---

[122] See Croissant 1998; de Waal 2003; Zürcher 2007.
[123] Thomas Goltz, "A Town Betrayed; The Killing Ground in Karabakh," *Washington Post*, 8 March 1992. See also Croissant 1998; de Waal 2003; Zürcher 2007.
[124] International Crisis Group 2005d, 7.   [125] Ibid.
[126] Human Rights Watch/Helsinki 1994; International Crisis Group 2005d.

control most of the original territory of Nagorno-Karabakh as well as the Azerbaijani territory captured during the 1993 offensive. Armenian settlers occupy many of the Azeri villages and towns cleansed during the war.[127] Almost all of the Azeri population was expelled from Nagorno-Karabakh; a decade after the war, in 2005, it was estimated that 99.7 percent of Nagorno-Karabakh's population was Armenian.[128] The Azeri population was also displaced entirely from several districts surrounding Nagorno-Karabakh. According to the 1989 census, the total population in these districts was 424,900, with Azeris constituting between 89.9 and 99.6 percent of the population in each district.[129] Most major towns in these districts were destroyed; by the end of the conflict, it was estimated that no Azeri population remained.[130] In total, as a result of the conflict, an estimated 204,667 Azeris fled Armenia, while 247,000 Armenians left Azerbaijan. Another 604,000 Azeris were displaced within Azerbaijan, many of whom were forcibly expelled from Nagorno-Karabakh and the surrounding territories; in addition, 72,000 Armenians were displaced within Azerbaijan.[131] From 1988 to 1994, 2,500 Armenian civilians were killed, while deaths among Karabakh and Armenian forces numbered 6,000; Azeri military and civilian deaths totaled approximately 10,000.[132] More than 13 percent of Azerbaijan's prewar population of 7 million was, therefore, either killed or displaced by the conflict.

Publicly, the Armenian and Karabakh Armenian leadership claims that the displacement of Azeri civilians from the Azerbaijani territories surrounding Nagorno-Karabakh was necessary in order "to maintain security and protect [the] civilian population from shooting and bombing from the Azeri side, as experienced during the war."[133] Murad Petrosian, deputy commander of the Nagorno-Karabakh army, provided a similar justification in an interview with Human Rights Watch, saying that Nagorno-Karabakh did not have enough troops to be able to control a hostile Azeri civilian population and, therefore, was forced to expel these civilians from the occupied territories.[134] Armenian officials have made public statements echoing these concerns about security.[135] In addition to citing the need for protection against Azerbaijani shelling, Karabakh Armenian and Armenian officials also argued that the occupation

[127] International Crisis Group 2005d.   [128] Rowland 2008, 108.
[129] International Crisis Group 2005d, 7.
[130] International Crisis Group 2005d; Rowland 2008.
[131] Estimates are from Zürcher 2007, 180. International Crisis Group 2005d cites similar estimates.
[132] Zürcher 2007, 180.
[133] Officials in the Nagorno-Karabakh Ministry of Foreign Affairs, as quoted in International Crisis Group 2005d, 27.
[134] Human Rights Watch/Helsinki 1994, 103.
[135] Michael Specter, "Armenians Suffer Painfully in War: But with Pride and Determination," *New York Times*, 15 July 1994. See also statements on the website of the Embassy of Armenia to the United States of America, available online at http://usa.mfa.am/en/karabagh/.

of Azerbaijani territory and expulsion of civilians from this territory was necessary to create defensible borders for Nagorno-Karabakh.[136]

Outside observers, however, have questioned whether the displacement of Azeri civilians was motivated purely by security concerns.[137] Instead, they suggest that by cleansing Azeri populations from Nagorno-Karabakh and the corridor of Azerbaijani territory separating Nagorno-Karabakh from Armenia, the Karabakh insurgency likely sought to "make a fait accompli of its integration with Armenia."[138] As one expert on the conflict noted, the cleansing of the Azeri population from Nagorno-Karabakh served to solidify the control of the Karabakh Armenians, noting that "A key result of the war was the ethnic homogenization of Nagorny Karabakh through the removal of the Azeri population. This removed a key political cleavage, enabling a certain core consensus on the existence and purpose of the resulting de facto state."[139]

Although Nagorno-Karabakh officials have not admitted publicly that their intention was to create conditions on the ground that would establish unification with Armenia, Karabakh demands during peace negotiations hint at this logic. Karabakh and Armenian officials seem willing to transfer of most of the occupied territories outside of Nagorno-Karabakh back to Azerbaijan, but have been unwilling to give up their demand for a territorial connection to Armenia.[140] In addition, Karabakh officials have admitted that the settlement of Armenians in formerly Azerbaijani territory – in particular, in the region linking Nagorno-Karabakh to Armenia – is a deliberate policy, intended to establish Nagorno-Karabakh's de facto control over the disputed territory.[141] Nagorno-Karabakh's president from 1997 to 2007, Arkadi Ghoukasian, was quoted in an interview as saying, "It is in our interest that Lachin is inhabited, and this is based on the premise that.... Lachin and the Lachin corridor must remain under Nagorno-Karabakh's control."[142]

The evidence suggests that homogenizing the population by forcibly expelling Azeri civilians – a deliberate strategy of cleansing – was a central part of the effort by Karabakh insurgents to define the boundaries of a new de facto state, connected by land to the territory of neighboring Armenia. The Azeri population, at slightly more than 20 percent of Nagorno-Karabakh's total population and concentrated in particular towns within Nagorno-Karabakh and its surrounding regions, was large enough to constitute a military and political threat to the insurgency and yet concentrated enough to make expulsion possible, thus creating strong incentives for the rebel group to adopt a strategy of cleansing.

---

[136] De Waal 2003, 228; International Crisis Group 2005b, 27.
[137] Human Rights Watch/Helsinki 1994.   [138] Cornell 1999, 34.   [139] Broers 2005, 69.
[140] Cornell 1999; Baghdasarian 2005; International Crisis Group 2005c; International Crisis Group 2007a. See also Office of the Nagorno Karabakh Republic, Washington, D.C., "The NK Border Changes and Demografic [sic] Situation in the 20th Century," available online at: http://nkrusa.org/nk_conflict/references.shtml.
[141] Cornell 2001.   [142] International Crisis Group 2005c, 22.

ASSESSING THE ALTERNATIVE ARGUMENTS

All three rebel groups discussed in this chapter used violence against civilians strategically, with their leaders explicitly acknowledging this in public statements, interviews, and internal group documents. In none of these cases was violence the result of a lack of organizational control over members. I have argued that rebel groups make strategic choices regarding the use of violence based on an assessment of their opponent's civilian constituency, as well as an assessment of the domestic and international costs of violence. However, several alternative arguments posit that other factors might drive rebel group strategic choices.

One of the most common military context arguments posits that rebel groups are most likely to adopt strategies of terrorism when they are weak militarily and unable to confront government forces directly. The results of the statistical analyses in Chapter 3 show that although weak rebel groups are more likely to use terrorism, they are not any more likely to use high-casualty terrorism. The evidence from the terrorism case studies is broadly consistent with these quantitative findings. In the FMLN case, the evidence suggests that a decline in relative strength may have played a role in the FMLN's decision to adopt a strategy of terrorism, but it does not appear that considerations of relative strength were a key factor driving the PKK decision to adopt a strategy of high-casualty terrorism.

In comparison to other rebel groups, the FMLN is not weak; its troop strength relative to the Salvadoran government places the FMLN in the top 35 percent of rebel groups fighting in civil wars since 1989. The FMLN had a large and well-trained military force. And, in fact, during the early years of the conflict, the FMLN carried out a number of large-scale attacks on government military forces. In the mid-1980s, the Salvadoran government, with aid from the United States, made significant changes to its military structure, increasing the size of the military and improving the military's equipment – in particular, its heavy weaponry and air power. These changes made it possible for the military to alter its counterinsurgency strategy, making increased use of aerial bombardment to attack FMLN positions and launching more frequent offensives against rebel strongholds. The FMLN admitted that this new government counterinsurgency strategy had necessitated a change in FMLN strategy; the government's increased ability to provide air support to ground troops, for example, made it difficult for the FMLN to win conventional engagements with government forces. It is not clear, however, whether the FMLN's forces were weakened significantly by this new government counterinsurgency campaign.[143] The FMLN did shift from conventional to guerrilla attacks on government military forces, but the frequency of FMLN attacks on government forces did not change, even as the FMLN stepped up attacks on civilian infrastructure targets. From 1980 to 1984, the FMLN launched 821 attacks

[143] U.S. Embassy in San Salvador 1988b.

on government, police, and military targets; the pace of FMLN attacks continued in the latter half of the 1980s, with 1,082 attacks on government, police, and military targets from 1985 to 1991.[144] Furthermore, in November 1989, the FMLN launched perhaps its most devastating attack of the conflict, initiating a major offensive against the capital of San Salvador and gaining control over several neighborhoods. Thus, while it is possible to argue that the change in the government's counterinsurgency strategy put the FMLN at a military disadvantage in fighting conventional engagements, and that this ought to be viewed as a form of decline in the FMLN's strength relative to the government, the FMLN remained a robust fighting force, making it difficult to sustain the claim that the FMLN was so weak as to have few options left for confronting the government.

In absolute terms, the PKK is one of the strongest rebel groups to have launched an insurgency in the period from 1989 to 2010, but because the Turkish military is also large, the PKK falls slightly below the median in terms of its troop strength relative to the government. The PKK's military was organized and well trained. The group maintained multiple training camps in northern Iraq, possessed strong and consistent leadership in Abdullah Öcalan, and coordinated strategy through congresses of its members held throughout the insurgency. Although the PKK did engage in frequent attacks on civilian targets, particularly after 1993, there is no evidence to suggest that the PKK adopted this strategy because it was no longer able to confront Turkish military and police forces directly. In fact, from 1984 to 1999, the PKK launched 609 separate attacks on Turkish government, police, and military targets – more than five times the number of attacks (120) it carried out against public civilian targets during the same time period.[145]

Some might argue that cleansing, too, is driven by military weakness. Rebel groups that have difficulty confronting the government militarily may resort to cleansing as a means of ridding territory of the government's base of civilian support. The statistical analyses discussed in Chapter 3, however, find that the opposite is true; relative strength is *positively* associated with the likelihood of rebel group high-casualty cleansing, indicating that rebel groups that are strong in relation to their government opponents are more likely than weak rebel groups to adopt a strategy of cleansing. Consistent with these statistical findings, the Karabakh insurgency ranked among the top 20 percent of rebel groups fighting since 1989, in terms of its strength relative to the government; the Karabakh insurgents also had Armenian support, which meant not only thousands of additional troops, but also heavy weaponry left over from the Soviet

---

[144] National Consortium for the Study of Terrorism and Responses to Terrorism (START), Global Terrorism Database [Data file], available online at www.start.umd.edu/gtd.

[145] Ibid. The figures on rebel group attacks on government, police, and military targets cited throughout this section include assassinations, bombings, and other armed assaults on government and military targets, but do not include kidnappings or hijackings.

period. Apart from a brief Azerbaijani counteroffensive in late 1993, the Karabakh and Armenian forces dominated the war, capturing nearly all of Nagorno-Karabakh and extending their control into a swath of Azerbaijani territory surrounding the separatist region. Furthermore, cleansing of Azeri civilians took place not at a moment of military weakness, but at the height of the insurgency's power – as its offensive campaigns in early 1993 and 1994 overran a series of major Azeri villages and towns.

A second alternative explanation, like the first, focuses on the military context. This hypothesis posits that rebel groups are most likely to resort to civilian targeting when the costs of the conflict are rising, increasing the rebel group's desperation to win government concessions and to minimize its own losses. If this hypothesis is correct, one might expect to see a shift of rebel resources – away from attacks on heavily defended government and military targets and toward attacks on undefended civilian targets. Yet, as discussed earlier, in both conflicts analyzed in this chapter in which rebel groups adopted strategies of terrorism, the rebel groups carried out frequent attacks on government, police, and military targets, in addition to attacks on civilian targets. And in both of these conflicts, the total number of attacks on government, police, and military targets was greater than the number of attacks on civilian targets; the evidence shows little indication that these rebel groups engaged in civilian targeting as a means of conserving their military resources. Desperation does not appear to be the primary motivation for cleansing either; the Karabakh insurgency in Azerbaijan carried out expulsions of Azeri civilians not during periods when military defeat appeared imminent, but at times when they were faring well militarily.

A third alternative hypothesis suggests a different motivation for rebel group terrorism. Rather than attacking civilians as a means of obtaining concessions from the government, this hypothesis suggests that rebel groups use terrorist violence as a means of outbidding rival rebel factions. By carrying out dramatic attacks on public civilian targets such as buses, shopping districts, or hotels, this hypothesis suggests, rebel groups demonstrate to their civilian constituencies that they are committed to challenging the government and possess sufficient resolve to continue fighting until the government makes serious concessions.[146]

Neither the PKK nor the FMLN adopted terrorism as a means of outbidding rival rebel groups. The PKK formed during the 1970s, at a time when many different rightist, leftist, and Kurdish organizations were competing with one another for support;[147] during this period, terrorist bombings were common in Turkey, much as outbidding arguments would predict. This competition among rival groups, however, died out following the military coup in 1980. Although the PKK reemerged in the mid-1980s, most of the other groups did not renew their activities, leaving the PKK as the only significant rebel group fighting for

---

[146] Bloom 2005; Kydd and Walter 2006; Chenoweth 2010.
[147] Gunter 1997; Marcus 2007; Sayari 2010.

Kurdish autonomy. The outbidding argument cannot explain, therefore, why the PKK used terrorism in the context of the civil war that began in 1984, nor can the outbidding argument explain why PKK terrorism increased dramatically in the early 1990s, from fewer than 10 bombings per year in the late 1980s to more than 50 attacks per year in the early 1990s.

At the start of the conflict in El Salvador in the late 1970s, five different insurgent groups were active.[148] In 1978 and 1979, before these groups merged to form the FMLN, several groups bombed infrastructure targets, as the outbidding hypothesis would predict. What the outbidding argument cannot explain, however, is why bombings continued long after the five insurgent groups merged to form the FMLN or why the FMLN stepped up bombings of infrastructure targets in the mid- to late 1980s.

A final alternative hypothesis, also emphasizing the military context, claims that violence against civilians is associated with efforts to exert greater control over civilians during periods of high contestation over territory. In the early years of the conflict, the PKK did use violence as a means of controlling civilians, targeting villages where pro-government militias were active in an attempt to deter civilians from aiding the government, but these attacks were not driven by high contestation over territory. As noted in the previous chapter, the PKK did not attempt to hold significant portions of the disputed territory; instead, it mainly operated from bases along Turkey's borders with Iran, Iraq, and Syria. The FMLN, in contrast, did establish zones of insurgent-controlled territory, and contestation over territorial control did vary over time – increasing, for example, in the mid-1980s when the government improved its ability to provide air support to ground operations. Although the FMLN did alter its strategy during this period of increased contestation over territory – expanding its campaign of economic sabotage as part of a shift to greater reliance on guerrilla warfare – reports do not indicate that the FMLN increased its use of violence to control the civilian population. Contestation arguments, for example, would predict a greater incidence of targeted attacks on civilians or villages believed to be aiding the government, but reports suggest that the FMLN continued to refrain from such forms of violence against civilians, despite expanding its use of low-casualty terrorism. Finally, in Karabakh, although contestation over territory was high during the conflict, the evidence shows that the aim of violence was not to control Azeri civilians, but rather to expel them from disputed territory.

CONCLUSION

Existing studies group together all forms of wartime violence against civilians, labeling it as civilian targeting and largely ignoring variation in forms of violence against civilians. Yet rebel groups choose particular forms of violence

---

[148] Wood 2003.

deliberately, based on an assessment of the costs and benefits of different forms of violence. For all three of the rebel groups discussed in this chapter, the international costs of targeting civilians were low. The government of El Salvador had strong backing from the United States, while the government of Turkey received support from a variety of European governments and institutions, making it difficult for either the FMLN or the PKK insurgencies to use international pressure as a means of forcing government concessions. Although the Karabakh insurgents did not face similar obstacles to making international appeals, their close ties to Armenia meant they had less need to turn to international actors for support.

In addition to having few international constraints on their use of violence, the PKK and the Karabakh insurgents, as separatist insurgencies with narrow, ethnically based civilian constituencies, also had few domestic constraints on their use of violence. Both insurgencies were able to attack civilians outside their own Kurdish and Armenian constituencies without risking a loss of support. Although both insurgent groups used violence against civilians, the forms of violence they chose differed, based on their government opponent and its relationship with its *own* civilian constituents. Whereas the PKK faced a democratic opponent, likely to be sensitive to domestic public pressure, the Karabakh insurgents faced a nondemocratic opponent, unlikely to make concessions in response to rising civilian losses. The PKK, thus, had strong incentives to use terrorism as a means of imposing costs on the Turkish government; the Karabakh insurgency, in contrast, did not have strong incentives for terrorism.

The nature of the government constituencies in the two cases differs as well. In Turkey, the Kurdish population is barely a majority in the southern and southeastern regions of Turkey where the PKK has sought to establish an autonomous Kurdish state; the government's constituency – the Turkish population – is sizable. In Azerbaijan, however, the separatist region of Nagorno-Karabakh was overwhelmingly Armenian and the minority Azeri population was concentrated in particular regions. Because the government's constituency within the separatist region was small and concentrated geographically, the Karabakh insurgency had strong incentives to use cleansing as a means of asserting Armenian control over the disputed territory. In Turkey, cleansing was a less feasible option for the PKK.

In contrast to the PKK and Karabakh insurgents, the FMLN faced greater domestic constraints on its use of violence. Faced with a democratic opponent, the FMLN had incentives to engage in terrorism, but as a revolutionary insurgency seeking to build a broad civilian constituency, the FMLN was also afraid that violence would mean a loss of civilian support. The FMLN thus chose a strategy of terrorism that imposed high costs, but not high casualties – bombing primarily infrastructure targets as a means of weakening the economy and pressuring the government to make concessions.

8

Extreme Rebel Group Violence against Civilians: The Lord's Resistance Army in Uganda

On July 8, 2005, following a year-long formal investigation into the ongoing conflict in Northern Uganda, the International Criminal Court (ICC) issued arrest warrants for five senior leaders of the Lord's Resistance Army (LRA), an armed opposition group that had been embroiled in a civil war against the Ugandan government for nearly two decades.[1] According to the ICC arrest warrants, the "LRA has engaged in a cycle of violence and established a pattern of 'brutalization of civilians' by acts including murder, abduction, sexual enslavement, mutilation, as well as mass burnings of houses and looting of camp settlements."[2] One study found that from the start of the conflict in the late 1980s through 2006, the LRA abducted between 54,000 and 75,000 people, including between 25,000 and 38,000 children.[3] LRA forces abducted civilians to serve as porters, often transporting looted food and goods, or to fight as soldiers, while many of the abducted girls and women were forced to be wives for LRA soldiers and commanders. A majority of the LRA's troops were child soldiers, with some sources estimating that children accounted for as much as 80 percent of the LRA's troops.[4] The LRA also engaged in extreme brutality against civilians – killing, raping, torturing, and mutilating civilians. An estimated 90 to 95 percent of the population in Northern Uganda was displaced by the conflict, with over 1.6 million people living in camps for internally displaced persons as of June 2005.[5]

---

[1] For a critical perspective on the ICC investigations, see, for example, Hovil and Quinn 2005.

[2] International Criminal Court, Warrants of Arrest for Joseph Kony, Vincent Otti, Okot Odhiambo, Dominic Ongwen, and Raska Lukwiya, Issued 8 July 2005, available online at www.icc-cpi.int. Although all five arrest warrants were issued on July 8, 2005, the ICC did not make the warrants public until October 13, 2005.

[3] Pham, Vinck, and Stover 2008, 410. See also Blattman and Annan 2010, who provide a similar estimate of LRA abductions.

[4] Amnesty International 2004d.

[5] UN Office for the Coordination of Humanitarian Affairs (OCHA) 2005, 1.

Despite frequent claims in the media and by the Ugandan government that this violence was the brutality of a bizarre organization whose only aim was to inflict harm on civilians, this chapter shows that the LRA, like the other rebel groups examined in this book, used violence against civilians strategically. Where the LRA differs from the rebel groups discussed thus far, however, is in its relationship to its domestic civilian constituency. In most civil wars, a rebel group would require some civilian constituency – even if a very narrow one – in order to pose a significant military challenge to the government. And indeed, at its inception, the LRA did have a civilian constituency among the Acholi population in Northern Uganda, where opposition to Yoweri Museveni's rule was strong. As the conflict progressed, however, the LRA lost this base of domestic civilian support, leading the group to rely heavily on abduction to fill its ranks. The theoretical argument of this book does not anticipate a case such as this, in which the rebel group loses its civilian constituency, but studying this case provides an opportunity to consider whether and how the theoretical argument of this book might be extended.

At its core, this book argues that the relationships governments and rebel groups have with domestic and international constituencies influence incentives and disincentives for violence. And in fact the LRA's behavior toward civilians is in many ways consistent with this claim. Most rebel groups facing an autocratic government opponent, as the LRA did, would use guerrilla attacks on government and military targets to pressure the government militarily, while refraining from attacks on civilian targets and making international appeals to pressure the government diplomatically. But rebel groups are only able to make international appeals if they can convince international actors that the group's grievances are legitimate. Without a domestic base of support, it was difficult for the LRA to do this. In addition, Ugandan President Yoweri Museveni's strong relationships with international donors – who praised Museveni for bringing stability to Uganda after years of conflict and upheaval – further limited the potential for the LRA to win the sympathy of international actors.

Lacking either a domestic or an international constituency to which it could appeal for support, the LRA turned to an extreme combination of high-casualty control and terrorism in an attempt to punish civilians for failing to support the rebellion, while also creating massive instability in the northern region of the country – disrupting the economy and society, preventing the government from providing services to its citizens, and calling into question the government's claim to be able to maintain stability – in an effort to force government concessions.

While all of the other rebel groups discussed thus far have targeted their opponent's civilian constituency, the LRA did not attack civilians in the Ugandan capital or in the government's stronghold in the southern part of the country; rather, the LRA attacked civilians living in Northern Uganda. It is this appearance of violence against the LRA's "own" civilians that has led so many to declare the LRA's violence incomprehensible or insane. As I demonstrate in this chapter, however, by the time LRA violence against civilians escalated, civilians in Northern Uganda were no longer the LRA's civilian constituency; the LRA had lost its civilian base of support and, thus, had also lost any domestic constraints on its use of violence.

This chapter identifies two broad patterns in LRA violence – first, consistent attacks on government and military targets, in addition to attacks on civilian targets, and second, regular ambushes of civilian vehicles – which together provide evidence in support of the claim that the LRA used violence strategically, as a means of destabilizing the Ugandan government. While particular features of LRA violence remained consistent across time, the LRA shifted its use of violence at a number of points during the conflict. In the last section of the chapter I trace these shifts in LRA violence, arguing that the LRA stepped back from its strategy of terrorism at times when the group perceived that avenues for pressuring the government diplomatically might be available – in particular, when domestic and international mediators attempted to negotiate a resolution to the conflict.

This chapter incorporates evidence gathered in interviews I conducted in Uganda's capital of Kampala and the northern town of Gulu in July and August 2005. I interviewed Ugandan government and military officials, local and national politicians representing Northern Uganda, former LRA members, human rights activists, and nongovernmental organization (NGO) officials.[6] In addition, to trace patterns and shifts in LRA violence over time, I collected an original event-level data set on incidents of violence in Northern Uganda. The data set includes all reported incidents in which force was used by the government or rebel group, beginning in 1988, when the first incident was reported involving Joseph Kony's rebel group, and continuing through December 2003. Although the conflict continued after December 2003, its intensity decreased during a prolonged effort at mediation and a series of attempted negotiations. The data set also records all major reported political events relevant to the conflict – for example, attempts at peace negotiations, LRA statements to the public, and major speeches by President Museveni. I collected this information using the two Ugandan English-language newspapers, the *Monitor*, an independent paper, and *New Vision*, a government-owned paper;[7] Uganda's primary English-language radio station, Radio Uganda; and international news sources. In total, the news media reported 763 violent incidents and

---

[6] I identify interviewees by their affiliations. Although some of those I interviewed did not object to the use of their names, others would not have agreed to an interview or would not have been as frank in their replies if their names had been used.

[7] The *Monitor* and *New Vision* are available in electronic media archives (Factiva) beginning in 1997; for the period prior to 1997, I rely on international media sources. A comparison of Ugandan and international news coverage for the period after 1997 shows that, of the total number of reported incidents of violence, about 15–20 percent of incidents were reported in Ugandan sources, but not in international sources. This percentage is the same across types of violent incidents, such as abductions, ambushes, and battles. Thus, although the number of incidents of violence reported for the period prior to 1997 would likely be greater if Ugandan sources were available, the availability of domestic news sources would not likely alter the overall patterns of violence described here.

303 political events from 1988 to 2003 related to the conflict between the Ugandan government and the LRA.

THE EARLY YEARS OF THE LRA INSURGENCY

Yoweri Museveni and his National Resistance Movement/Army (NRM/A) came to power in Uganda in January 1986, following a violent insurgency. When the NRM/A, which drew heavily from Southern Uganda both for its leadership and for its popular support, overthrew the northern-dominated government, many government soldiers fled north. Fighting continued for several more months, ending in a military victory for Museveni's forces. Almost immediately, armed opposition to Museveni's rule developed in Northern Uganda, with the establishment of the Ugandan People's Democratic Army (UPDA) and the Holy Spirit Movement (HSM). The HSM was defeated in 1987 and the UPDA signed a peace agreement with the government in 1988. Many in the North, however, remained dissatisfied with Museveni's government and saw the peace agreement as providing individual benefits for senior members of the UPDA, without creating a comprehensive program to address northern grievances regarding regional disparities in levels of economic development and the exclusion of Northerners from political power.[8] Although the NRM claimed to be representative, it functioned as an autocracy (with a polity score of -7 for the first seven years of its rule), banning political parties and implementing a no-party system run by an unelected parliament and president.

The LRA insurgency emerged out of the remnants of these earlier insurgencies. Many civilians in Northern Uganda sympathized with the LRA initially, and in fact, former government soldiers, HSM and UPDA fighters, as well as others who opposed Museveni's government joined the LRA voluntarily during its early years.[9] As one local leader in Northern Uganda explained, if you believed it was necessary to oppose Museveni's government by force, the LRA was the only remaining option.[10] Like the rebellions that preceded it, the LRA originated in the northern districts of Gulu, Kitgum, and Lira and for many years confined its activity to these three districts. Together these districts comprise what is referred to in Uganda as "Acholiland," a reference to the largest ethnic group in the region. The LRA's leader, Joseph Kony, is Acholi, as

---

[8] Finnström 2008; Lamwaka 2002. See also the text of the Pece Peace Agreement, available online through the Conciliation Resources website at www.c-r.org. During interviews, local leaders in Northern Uganda emphasized the failure of the peace agreement to address the full range of Northern grievances.

[9] Finnström 2006. Interviews with international NGO official, Kampala, 17 July 2005; Ugandan government official, Kampala, 17 July 2005; Ugandan NGO official, Kampala, 19 July 2005; official from Uganda Human Rights Commission, Kampala, 20 July 2005; senior Ugandan government official, Kampala, 25 July 2005; local Ugandan government official, Gulu, 27 July 2005; former senior Ugandan government official, Gulu, 29 July 2005.

[10] Interview with Member of Parliament representing Northern Uganda, Kampala, 4 August 2005.

are most of the LRA soldiers, and most of the soldiers and leaders of the UPDA and HSM insurgencies.[11]

Initially, the LRA primarily attacked government targets,[12] launching a series of "daring attacks against the government troops in Gulu district in 1988–89" that led to "a series of minor but militarily significant setbacks" for the NRA.[13] The LRA relied on a guerrilla warfare strategy, developing highly mobile forces that launched surprise attacks and ambushes on government positions.[14] Although the LRA was responsible for abductions and abuses of civilians in the early years of its insurgency, these abuses were less frequent and took place on a much smaller scale than in the later years of the conflict. As one interviewee described it, the LRA was "among the population" at this point in the insurgency, receiving support from civilians and largely refraining from violence against civilians.[15]

The first mention of Joseph Kony in the international press was an attack on a local militia group in February 1988.[16] References to Kony and his rebel group, which at the time was still referred to as a faction of the HSM, were rare for the years from 1988 to 1990, with only 17 incidents reported over this period. Of these, one incident involved an ambush of a government vehicle, while 10 incidents were military engagements between government and Kony forces, including a series of battles in Gulu district in June and July of 1988 and a battle in Kitgum district in March 1989.[17] Four of the reported incidents were abductions of civilians; none of the abductions, however, involved the killing of civilians or destruction of civilian property and one was an attempt to exchange abducted civilians for medicine.[18] Two of the 17 incidents involved the killing of civilians – the looting of villages in Apac district in March 1989, during

---

[11] On Kony's early life, see Gersony 1997; Doom and Vlassenroot 1999. See also International Crisis Group 2004b, on the makeup of the LRA and other Northern Ugandan insurgencies.

[12] Lomo and Hovil 2004.   [13] O'Kadameri 2002, 34.

[14] On LRA military tactics, see International Crisis Group 2004b. Interviews with international NGO official, Kampala, 17 July 2005; U.S. government official, Kampala, 17 July 2005; Ugandan NGO official, Kampala, 21 July 2005; former senior LRA military commander, Gulu, 28 July 2005.

[15] Interview with international NGO official, Kampala, 17 July 2005.

[16] "Ugandan Rebels Kill 50 Civilians in North: Newspaper Says," *Reuters News*, 29 February 1988; Jonathan Wright, "Uganda's Religious Rebels Go on without Priestess Leader," *Reuters News*, 25 March 1988.

[17] "Eight Reported Killed in Rebel Ambush in Northern Uganda," *Reuters News*, 12 July 1988; "At Least 272 Rebels Said Killed in Clashes with Ugandan Troops," *Reuters News*, 16 August 1988; "Uganda: Holy Spirit Rebels Released," *BBC Summary of World Broadcasts*, 20 March 1989; "'Holy Spirit' Rebels Terrorize Villagers," *Associated Press*, 24 March 1989; "Uganda: Rebel Action in Gulu and Kitgum," *BBC Summary of World Broadcasts*, 11 August 1989.

[18] Jonathan Wright, "Uganda's Religious Rebels Go on without Priestess Leader," *Reuters News*, 25 March 1988; "Ugandan Rebels Abduct 120 Civilians," *Reuters News*, 7 April 1988; "Ugandan Rebels Kidnap Priests and Nuns: Newspaper Says," *Reuters News*, 5 July 1988; "Ugandan Rebels Release Two Journalists," *Xinhua News Agency*, 2 January 1991.

which an unknown number of civilians were killed, and an April 1990 attack on a village, in which 43 civilians were killed and many huts burned, reportedly as punishment for the village's failure to support the rebellion.[19]

Although the lack of reporting makes it difficult to obtain a complete picture of the rebel group's tactics, it does appear that attacks aimed deliberately at civilians were infrequent, suggesting that during the early years of the rebellion the LRA was relying on traditional tactics of guerrilla warfare. The few attacks on civilians that did occur appear to have been part of a strategy of high-casualty control, using collective punishment to target villages that did not support the rebellion as a means of coercing broader civilian cooperation with the insurgency. As one scholar who conducted field research in Northern Uganda during this time period explains:

> There was also an unspoken agreement that the struggle was directed primarily against the NRA [the government], and that as long as the populace did not support the NRA, it would be left more or less in peace. Since individual groups of NRA soldiers plundered, killed, and raped, thus behaving more violently towards the local inhabitants than the UPDCA [Kony] soldiers, at least in some areas Kony's troops could count on the silence and toleration, if not the support of the people.[20]

THE SHIFT TO A STRATEGY OF EXTREME TERRORISM

The LRA's behavior shifted dramatically in the early 1990s as the group escalated attacks against civilians. Three interrelated factors explain this shift in LRA behavior. First, the LRA failed to articulate a clear political agenda to justify its continuing rebellion. In the early years of the insurgency, the LRA could latch on to the grievances cited by earlier rebellions, but the LRA's failure to articulate its political objectives became increasingly problematic as the insurgency wore on, making it difficult for the LRA to build either domestic or international support. Second, the LRA responded violently to civilian participation in pro-government militias created during the government's 1991 counterinsurgency campaign, a strategy that backfired, contributing to a loss of civilian support for the LRA. Third, backing from Sudan – a government highly unpopular with Western actors – further limited the LRA's ability to win international sympathy, as did the fact that Museveni held a favored position among Western donors, who touted Uganda as a model for African development. With few alternatives available for challenging Museveni's rule, the LRA turned to violence against civilians on a much more extreme scale.

---

[19] "Uganda Sect Rebels Hack Villagers to Death," *Reuters News*, 11 April 1990; "43 Reported Killed in Attack by Holy Spirit Rebel Group," BBC Monitoring Service: Africa, 12 April 1990; Amnesty International 1999.

[20] Behrend 1999, 188.

The LRA's Failure to Articulate a Political Agenda

When the LRA emerged in the late 1980s, Kony appeared to be fighting for many of the same reasons as the northern insurgencies that had preceded him – to redress northern grievances against the NRA and ultimately to overthrow Museveni's government. Kony, however, never articulated these political objectives well, leading to debate over whether the LRA had a political agenda at all. The LRA did not establish a distinct political wing of its organization or appoint political representatives. Several Ugandans living abroad in London and Nairobi have claimed to be LRA spokespersons, but it has never been clear whether these individuals had the support of Joseph Kony or were simply using the existence of the LRA as an opportunity to express their opposition to Museveni's government.[21] Further confounding observers is the fact that the large majority of LRA attacks on civilians have targeted Northern Ugandans, the group the LRA claimed to represent. When asked about the LRA's political agenda, nearly everyone I interviewed acknowledged that the LRA does have political objectives similar to those motivating other insurgencies in the North, but said that the LRA was ineffective in communicating these objectives to the public.[22]

The Ugandan government argued that the LRA lacked clear political objectives, with a parliamentary committee report on the war in Northern Uganda stating that it was unable to determine why the LRA was fighting.[23] In an October 2003 editorial, the government-owned newspaper, *New Vision*, expressed what has become a common characterization of the LRA: "They [the LRA] have absolutely no political ideology. They have never espoused any social programmes. They hardly fight the army; they take no territory. Instead, they torment civilians to no end."[24] In his public speeches, President Museveni often expressed a similar viewpoint. In a 1996 speech broadcast nationally on radio and television, for example, Museveni stated:

There are those who say we should talk to bandits of Kony. I am personally opposed to this idea. … If the authors of mass murders are forgiven just because we are too lazy to apprehend them, what will prevent such horrors from reoccurring [?][25]

After September 11, 2001, the Ugandan government adopted the language of terrorism to characterize the LRA, successfully lobbying for identification of the

---

[21] See, for example, a series of press releases issued by Ladit Balgara in 1998. "Kony Warns on Aboke Rescue," *New Vision*, 25 May 1998; "LRA Rebels Blast Otunnu," *All Africa*, 19 June 1998; "Kony Wants Uganda Not Nile Republic," *All Africa*, 4 July 1998; "LRA Rejects Kacoke Madit," *New Vision*, 3 July 1998.

[22] Interviews in Kampala and Gulu, July–August 2005. See also Lomo and Hovil 2004.

[23] Doom and Vlassenroot 1999, 20.   [24] "Heed Final Call, LRA," *New Vision*, 10 October 2003.

[25] Edmond Kizito, "Ugandan Leader Vows to Crush Rebels: Nation Mourns," *Reuters News*, 15 March 1996. Museveni made similar statements in a June 3, 1996 national address, which was broadcast nationally on Radio Uganda. See "President Addresses Nation on Security Issues: Offers Amnesty," *BBC Monitoring Service: Africa*, 5 June 1996.

LRA as an international terrorist group, included on the U.S. Terrorist Exclusion List.[26] One senior military official I interviewed, for example, referred to the LRA as a "terror machine."[27]

Complicating attempts to understand the LRA's motivations is the fact that spiritualism played an important role in guiding the group. Kony, who is believed to be a cousin of Alice Auma Lakwena, the leader of the HSM, claims to have spiritual revelations and powers similar to Lakwena's. In the early years of the insurgency Kony called for the installation of a government based on the Ten Commandments.[28] Despite the disconnect between Kony's moral rhetoric and the LRA's abductions of children and deliberate killing of civilians, many LRA members believed that Kony possessed spiritual powers.[29] Most of the LRA's public attempts to justify the insurgency, however, focused more on a general opposition to Museveni's government than on the group's spiritual motivations; in fact, some have argued that the Ugandan government intentionally played up the religious dimension of the conflict in an effort to discredit the LRA.[30]

In contrast to government and media portrayals of the LRA as a group without a political agenda, a former LRA commander quickly listed a number of LRA aims when asked: to take revenge on the NRA for overthrowing the Obote regime and the Northerners who had occupied positions of power within his government; to restore the government the NRA had ousted; to defend the North against Museveni's government; and to create a government based on the Ten Commandments.[31] Even this former commander, however, after listing these political objectives, noted that Kony frequently changed his justification for fighting, making it difficult even for LRA members to gain a clear understanding of the group's aims.

LRA units and commanders have, from time to time, made attempts to convey political messages. One researcher who spent considerable time in Northern Uganda reported the existence of written LRA manifestos detailing the group's political objectives, which were distributed throughout the North in the 1990s; however, it is unclear how widely such political writings were circulated, as the Ugandan government made efforts to restrict the dissemination of LRA material.[32] In April 1996, LRA units entered several villages in Gulu district, rounding up civilians and encouraging them to vote for the

---

[26] "Uganda Pledges to Support USA in Combating Terrorism," BBC Monitoring Service: Africa, 12 December 2001.

[27] Interview with senior Ugandan military official, Kampala, 21 July 2005.

[28] "Ugandan Rebels Kill Three People: Abduct Official," *Agence France-Presse*, 16 March 1993; "Ugandan Rebels Want Ten Commandment Government," *Reuters News*, 2 April 1993

[29] Interview with former senior LRA military commander, Gulu, 28 July 2005. See also Lomo and Hovil 2004.

[30] Finnström 2008.

[31] Interview with former senior LRA military commander, Gulu, 28 July 2005.

[32] Finnström 2008.

opposition candidate, Paul Kawanga Ssemogerere, in the May 1996 presidential elections.[33] Occasionally, the LRA has released abducted civilians, sending with them letters addressed to government officials; for example, after the failure of peace negotiations in March 2003, the LRA abducted and later released a priest, sending with him a statement to be read on local radio stations, calling for peace talks with President Museveni.[34]

Rarely has Joseph Kony or one of his senior commanders spoken with the media directly; in the few attempts to make contact, LRA leaders have expressed a general opposition to Museveni's government without much elaboration. In his only live radio interview, Kony phoned into Gulu district's Mega FM radio on December 28, 2002, to express his support for peace negotiations. During the interview Kony explained that he began his rebellion because Museveni's NRA had killed Northern Ugandans during its operations in the northern part of the country in 1986, insisting that "We [the LRA] are not fighting Acholi but fighting the government."[35] One of the LRA's senior commanders, Vincent Otti, was reported to have contacted media outlets several times in 2003; in a call to the independent Ugandan newspaper, the *Monitor*, Otti claimed to be fighting to combat corruption, nepotism, and the marginalization of Northerners by the Museveni government.[36] Several times in 2003, Joseph Kony contacted a member of parliament representing the North to discuss the possibility of peace negotiations with the government. When asked why he was fighting, Kony replied that he was fighting for his "tribe" – that he did not want his tribe to be enslaved; Kony also insisted that the LRA's cause was just.[37]

Declining Civilian Support and a Strategy of High-Casualty Control

In March 1991, the government launched a major offensive military operation against the LRA, called Operation North. One of its key components was the creation of local militias, called Bow and Arrow Groups or simply Arrow Groups.[38] Because at least some recruitment into local militias was coerced by the government, it is difficult to assess the extent to which civilians had truly

[33] Edmond Kizito, "Uganda Rebels Urge Support for Opposition Candidate," *Reuters News*, 14 April 1996.

[34] "LRA Now Targets Catholic Church," *Monitor*, 9 June 2003. The LRA sent a similar letter with another local leader who was abducted and released in the Teso region in August 2003. See "Kony Wants Fresh Talks," *Monitor*, 11 August 2003.

[35] "Ugandan Officials Downplay Rebel Leader Kony's Offer of Peace Talks," BBC Monitoring Newsfile, 29 December 2002. See also "Infamous Ugandan Rebel Ends Years of Reclusion to Call for Talks," *Agence France-Presse*, 29 December 2002.

[36] Walakira Geofrey, "I Will Not Surrender: Lord's Resistance Army Deputy Commander Otti Says," *Monitor*, 14 November 2003.

[37] Interview with Member of Parliament representing Northern Uganda, Kampala, 4 August 2005.

[38] Gersony 1997; Branch 2005.

begun to turn away from the LRA, but the evidence suggests that the LRA perceived civilian participation in the local militias as a betrayal.[39] In response, the LRA launched a number of attacks directed at members of militia groups and their families – attacks that can be characterized as a strategy of control aimed at deterring civilians from joining Arrow Group militias.[40] One government official who was instrumental in forming the militias expressed regret at having mobilized civilians, saying that in retrospect, this "antagonized" the LRA and "aggravated the situation" by "drawing a rift between the people and the LRA" and making it seem as if the government was not committed to peace; the official argued that the formation of militias had contributed directly to an increase in LRA attacks on civilians.[41] In a 1991 report on the conflict in Northern Uganda, Amnesty International explained that LRA atrocities had increased significantly since April 1991 and corroborated this claim with details regarding specific LRA abuses, such as a May 20, 1991, attack on a village in Kitgum in which rebels forced 20 civilians into a hut and then burned the hut, killing 14.[42] In addition to increasing the scale of its killings, the LRA began mutilating civilians in 1991, with a series of incidents reported in Gulu district during June and July in which rebels cut off the hands, ears, lips, and noses of civilians – purportedly to deter other civilians from aiding the government.[43]

This violence succeeded in the short run; in response to repeated LRA attacks and the government's failure to provide adequate weapons and support to militia members, the Arrow Group militias demobilized.[44] In the long run, however, the LRA's strategy backfired, as civilians increasingly turned away from the rebel movement.[45] One local leader I interviewed went so far as to say that the war would have progressed much differently had the LRA not engaged in attacks on civilians following Operation North, suggesting that the LRA might have been able to mobilize the population politically against Museveni's government.[46]

---

[39] Interviews with Ugandan NGO official, Kampala, 21 July 2005; former politician from Northern Uganda, Gulu, 28 July 2005. See also Gersony 1997; Behrend 1999; O'Kadameri 2002.

[40] Amnesty International 1991d; Gersony 1997; Behrend 1999; O'Kadameri 2002; Lomo and Hovil 2004; Branch 2005. Interviews with Ugandan expert on the conflict in Northern Uganda, Kampala, 21 July 2005; Ugandan NGO official, Kampala, 21 July 2005; former senior LRA military commander, Gulu, 28 July 2005; former senior Ugandan government official, Gulu, 29 July 2005. See also Kalyvas 1999, who uses evidence from Algeria to demonstrate that the creation of pro-government militias can lead to an escalation in violence aimed at controlling civilians.

[41] Interview with former senior Ugandan government official, Gulu, 29 July 2005.

[42] Amnesty International 1991d, 19.   [43] Ibid.   [44] Branch 2005.

[45] Behrend 1999. Interviews with Ugandan government official, Kampala, 17 July 2005; Ugandan NGO official, Kampala, 19 July 2005; Ugandan NGO official, Kampala, 21 July 2005; local Ugandan government official, Gulu, 27 July 2005; former senior LRA military commander, Gulu, 28 July 2005; member of parliament representing Northern Uganda, Kampala, 4 August 2005.

[46] Interview with Ugandan human rights activist, Gulu, 26 July 2005.

With the conclusion of Operation North came a lull in fighting, and later, peace negotiations, led by the government's Minister for the North, Betty Bigombe, herself an Acholi from Gulu district. Negotiations ultimately broke down in February 1994 when Museveni issued an ultimatum, insisting on LRA surrender and refusing to offer political concessions.[47] Some argue that Kony saw the failed negotiations as an indication that he had lost the support of the Acholi community and the Acholi elders, who had participated in the peace negotiations.[48]

The Futility of International Appeals

The LRA's lack of a clear political agenda and violent response to local militias eroded the group's support among civilians in Northern Uganda. In addition, the LRA faced significant obstacles to making international appeals. First, the LRA received aid from Sudan, which was at the time an international pariah, criticized heavily for its support of international terrorist groups as detailed in Chapter 6. The Sudanese government backed the LRA as a means of destabilizing Southern Sudan and impeding the operations of the Sudan People's Liberation Army (SPLA), as well as retaliating against Museveni's government for its support of the SPLA.[49] Some sources speculate that contacts between the LRA and Sudan may have begun in late 1993, but after peace negotiations between the LRA and the Ugandan government failed in 1994, Sudan began providing the LRA with material supplies such as uniforms, shelter, and food as well as financing, training, weapons, and, perhaps most importantly, a safe haven in southern Sudanese territory.[50] For many years Sudan denied supporting the LRA, finally admitting its involvement in October 1998.[51] This external source of support deepened the divide between the LRA and the Acholi community; it also made it nearly impossible for the LRA to win sympathy from other international actors.

The second factor that contributed to the LRA's inability to seek support from a Western international constituency was Museveni's favorable image among international donors. Museveni was lauded internationally for his success in stabilizing Uganda after years of brutal dictatorship under Idi Amin, followed by conflict and upheaval after Amin's overthrow.[52] Museveni was able to secure significant financial and diplomatic backing from the international community. Foreign aid financed the majority of Uganda's central government expenditures throughout the late 1990s and early 2000s.[53] In 2000, Uganda was chosen by the

---

[47] O'Kadameri 2002.   [48] Doom and Vlassenroot 1999.   [49] Prunier 2004.
[50] Gersony 1997; Branch 2005.
[51] Simon Denyer, "Sudan Says Supporting Ugandan: Eritrean Rebels," *Reuters News*, 23 October 1998.
[52] On the dictatorship of Idi Amin, see Mamdani 1984.
[53] Data on government expenditures are from the World Bank, *World Development Indicators*, multiple years, available online at data.worldbank.org.

IMF and the World Bank as the first country to reach the "completion point" in their Heavily Indebted Poor Countries (HIPC) Initiative, meaning that Uganda had demonstrated its commitment to sound economic policies and, therefore, would receive full debt relief, totaling approximately US$2 billion.[54]

TRACING LRA BEHAVIOR: IS LRA VIOLENCE STRATEGIC?

Elsewhere in this book, I have argued that rebel groups facing autocratic governments have difficulty mobilizing enough domestic pressure to force government concessions and, thus, seek support from international actors to pressure the government into making concessions. The LRA, however, was unable to mobilize support from either domestic or international constituencies. The only strategy available to the LRA was to use military pressure to coerce the government into negotiating. Yet as the LRA had learned with the failure of peace negotiations in 1993–1994, traditional guerrilla tactics aimed at wearing down the military and police were unlikely to inflict enough damage on the government to force concessions. Within this domestic and international context, I argue that the LRA adopted a strategy of extreme terrorism, aiming to create a pervasive sense of insecurity throughout the country and to undermine the government's ability to provide services and security to its citizens.[55] A number of interviewees in Northern Uganda agreed that the LRA's violent attacks against civilians were part of a deliberate, strategic attempt to "discredit" or "humiliate" the government.[56] While popular accounts of the conflict in Northern Uganda claim that LRA violence is inexplicable and without logic, this section challenges this common conception, drawing on event-level data to present evidence of the strategic use of violence.

Identifying Broad Patterns in LRA Behavior

Two broad trends stand out in LRA violence from 1994 to 2003: first, the consistency of LRA attacks on Ugandan military and government targets, and second, the frequency of LRA ambushes of civilian and aid organization vehicles. As the first trend demonstrates, it is not the case, as the Ugandan government and the international media have claimed, that the LRA directed violence only at civilian targets. Even as the LRA shifted to a strategy of

---

[54] International Monetary Fund, "Debt Relief under the Heavily Indebted Poor Countries (HIPC) Initiative: A Factsheet," December 2007. International Monetary Fund, "IMF and World Bank Support Debt Relief for Uganda," Press Release No. 00/34, 2 May 2000.

[55] Hultman (2009) similarly argues that the Mozambique National Resistance (Resistência Nacional Moçambicana, RENAMO) used violence against civilians in an effort to destabilize the government in Mozambique.

[56] Interviews with Ugandan human rights activist, Gulu, 26 July 2005; Ugandan military official, Gulu, 27 July 2005; former senior LRA military commander, Gulu, 28 July 2005; former senior Ugandan government official, Gulu, 29 July 2005.

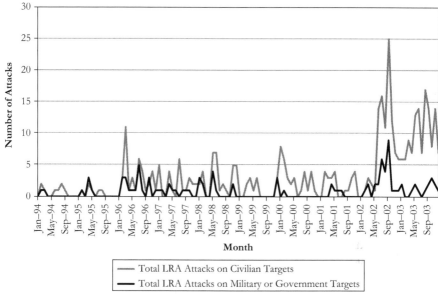

FIGURE 8.1 LRA Attacks on Military and Civilian Targets.

extreme terrorism after 1994, the group continued to attack military and government targets.

Figure 8.1 shows the total number of LRA attacks on civilian and government or military targets, by month, for the years 1994 to 2003. Attacks on *government or military targets* include LRA ambushes of government, military, or police vehicles; attacks on military or police units or bases; and attacks on government officials or buildings. Attacks on *civilian targets* include LRA ambushes of civilian or aid organization vehicles, incidents in which the LRA abducted or killed civilians, and incidents in which the LRA burned civilian homes or granaries.[57] As Figure 8.1 makes clear, LRA attacks on military targets did not end in 1994, as government and media accounts often suggest. One hundred LRA attacks on military or government targets were reported from 1994 to 2003, as compared with 398 LRA attacks on civilian targets; about 20 percent of the LRA's total attacks during this time period were on military or government targets. These numbers, however, likely underestimate the total number of LRA attacks on military targets, as newspapers often reported battles or military engagements between the government and LRA

[57] Many LRA attacks involved multiple forms of violence; the LRA might, for example, enter a village and abduct 20 civilians, kill several civilians, and burn civilian huts. If multiple forms of violence were used during an attack on a single village, this is coded as a single attack on a civilian target.

without specifying how the battle began; many incidents recorded as battles, therefore, likely began as LRA attacks on military units.

For the most part, during periods when LRA attacks on civilian targets increased, so did LRA attacks on military targets. The percentage of total LRA attacks that were directed against military and government targets did decline somewhat over time – with attacks on military and government targets accounting for 34 and 45 percent of LRA attacks in 1995 and 1996 and between 18 and 26 percent of attacks from 1997 to 2003 – but this pattern is consistent with the argument that incentives to target civilians grew as the LRA's domestic constituency disappeared. The only year in which the LRA did not carry out numerous attacks on government and military targets was 2000, a year in which only one of the LRA's 34 attacks was on a government or military target.

Nearly all LRA attacks on government or military targets led to deaths, but many LRA attacks on civilian targets did not. Of the 398 LRA attacks on civilian targets from 1994 to 2003, 259 involved the death of at least one civilian. Thus, the percentage of attacks directed at government or military targets is even higher when examining lethal attacks. Looking at lethal attacks, from 1995 to 1999 the LRA targeted the government or military between 36 and 56 percent of the time, with this percentage dropping to 23 percent in 2001 and 35 percent in 2002. The years 2000 and 2003 are anomalies, with particularly large numbers of lethal LRA attacks on civilians. Thus, for much of the conflict, the LRA regularly attacked government and military targets, indicating that the LRA *has* sought to challenge the Ugandan government militarily.

The second trend in LRA violence is the frequency of vehicle ambushes. Of the 398 total LRA attacks on civilian targets reported from 1994 to 2003, 119 attacks, or 30 percent, were ambushes of civilian or aid organization vehicles, with most attacks targeting civilian vehicles. In the large majority of ambushes, the LRA killed civilians and destroyed vehicles, but did not loot vehicles or abduct civilians. Although ambushes might conceivably be used to prevent access to a particular geographic area, thus serving as a means of controlling territory, the LRA does not appear to have used ambushes for this purpose. The LRA never attempted to hold territory during the conflict; the group entered Uganda periodically, attacking military and civilian targets and then withdrawing to Southern Sudan. LRA ambushes also do not appear to have been aimed at punishing civilians for collaborating with the government; unlike LRA attacks on villages, which on occasion were accompanied by messages indicating that the attack was punishment for some transgression, the LRA's ambushes took place on major roadways throughout Northern Uganda and do not appear to have been directed at any particular group of civilians.

Instead, ambushes of civilian vehicles appear to have been a means of generating instability in Northern Uganda. Ambushes slowed, and often prevented, the movement of individuals and goods within Northern Uganda; road traffic was often instructed to travel in convoys protected by military personnel

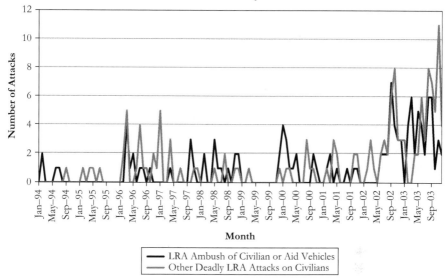

FIGURE 8.2 LRA Deadly Attacks on Civilians.

or was halted entirely on roadways subject to frequent LRA ambushes, contributing to the near shutdown of the Northern Ugandan economy.[58] In addition to weakening the region's economy, LRA ambushes contributed to the disruption of society and a pervasive sense of insecurity, demonstrating the failure of the Ugandan government to provide effective security.[59]

Figure 8.2 compares LRA ambushes of civilian and aid vehicles with other types of attacks in which the LRA killed civilians, most of which are attacks on civilians in villages or camps for internally displaced persons. As Figure 8.2 illustrates, ambushes outpaced other types of deadly attacks on civilians at numerous points during the conflict, particularly from late 1997 until early 2000; in several years, ambushes accounted for the majority of LRA attacks against civilians. When other types of lethal attacks on civilians increased sharply in late 2002 and 2003, ambushes of civilian vehicles increased substantially as well, to 23 reported ambushes on civilian vehicles in 2002 and 41 in 2003. Overall, ambushes of civilian and aid organization vehicles constituted 46 percent of the LRA's total deadly attacks on civilians from 1994 to 2003.

---

[58] "Northern Ugandan War Leaves Region's Economy in Shambles," *Agence France-Presse*, 27 August 2002.

[59] Interviews with international NGO official and expert on conflict in Northern Uganda, Kampala, 17 July 2005; Ugandan human rights activist, Gulu, 26 July 2005; former senior LRA military commander, Gulu, 28 July 2005.

The Impact of Mediation Attempts

Although attacks on government and military targets and ambushes of civilian vehicles were consistent patterns throughout the conflict, the LRA also altered its use of violence at several key points in time after 1994. If the argument of this chapter is correct – if the LRA adopted a strategy of extreme terrorism because it was unable to develop support from either domestic or international constituencies – then the LRA should have retreated from this strategy of terrorism when it saw an opportunity to attract sympathy from domestic or international actors. Attempts by domestic or international actors to mediate a resolution to the conflict, especially attempts to make direct contact with the LRA, therefore, should correspond with declines in LRA violence, while breakdowns in negotiations should correspond with increases in LRA violence.

Following the failure of the 1993–1994 peace talks, several years passed before the next attempt at negotiating a settlement, but efforts picked up thereafter, with seven major mediation attempts occurring between 1996 and 2003, in which domestic or international actors sought to secure a settlement. Figure 8.3 plots these mediation attempts, along with the number of incidents of lethal LRA violence against civilians (vehicle ambushes and killing) and nonlethal LRA violence against civilians (abductions and scorched earth incidents), in each month from 1994 to 2003. As Figure 8.3 shows, these mediation attempts correspond with marked declines in LRA violence.

The first attempt at renewing negotiations began in late December 1996, when Norbert Mao, a member of parliament representing Northern Uganda, announced that the LRA had contacted parliament, indicating a willingness to restart negotiations.[60] A few months later, in April 1997, several members of parliament met with LRA representatives in London for further discussions,[61] but Uganda's Foreign Minister announced publicly in mid-April that the government was unwilling to participate in formal negotiations.[62] LRA activity had been high throughout 1996, with 37 attacks on civilian targets reported from February through mid-December 1996, but LRA activity then dropped substantially, with only four LRA attacks against civilian targets during the period of contact between the LRA and members of parliament. Following the government's announcement that it would not pursue further talks, LRA attacks on civilians resumed; the next week, the LRA ambushed a

---

[60] "MP Says Kony Rebels Ready for Peace Talks if Mediator Available," BBC Monitoring Service: Africa, 20 December 1996.

[61] Moyiga Nduru, "Parliamentarians Hold Talks with Rebels in London," *Inter Press Service*, 10 April 1997; "Lord's Resistance Army Said Ready for Peace Talks with Government," BBC Monitoring Service: Africa, 16 April 1997.

[62] "Ugandan Government Refuses to Negotiate with Rebels," *Agence France-Presse*, 16 April 1997.

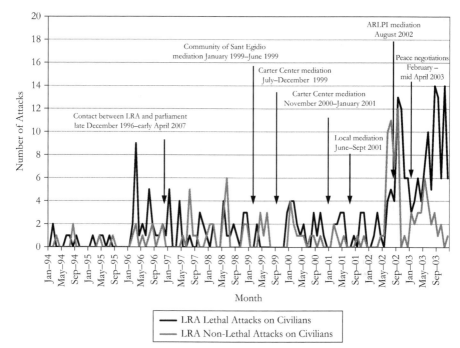

FIGURE 8.3 LRA Attacks on Civilians and the Timing of Peace Negotiations.

civilian vehicle and attacked two villages, abducting civilians, burning huts, and killing civilians.[63]

The next attempt at negotiations came in January 1999, mediated by the Community of Sant Egidio, a Catholic organization based in Rome.[64] Although the LRA had carried out a number of attacks on civilian targets in the months prior to mediation, once mediation had begun, the LRA halted its attacks on civilian targets. No LRA attacks on civilian targets were reported for January or February 1999, and only two were reported in March; both were small-scale attacks involving only a handful of rebels.

In June 1999, in response to the Community of Sant Egidio's continued mediation efforts, President Museveni announced an amnesty program for LRA members who surrendered. Later that month, local leaders from Northern Uganda traveled to Southern Sudan to meet with LRA leaders.[65] Several

[63] "Ugandan Rebels Kill 15 in Attack in Northern Uganda," *Agence France-Presse*, 22 April 1997; "Rebels Kill Four in Northern Uganda," *Agence France-Presse*, 26 April 1997.
[64] "Catholic Church Said to Be Mediating between Government and LRA Rebels," BBC Monitoring Africa, 24 May 1999.
[65] "Ugandan President Museveni Offers Amnesty to Rebels," *Agence France-Presse*, 2 June 1999; "Catholics Brokered Museveni-Kony Truce," *EastAfrican*, 2 June 1999; "Leaders on Peace Mission to Southern Sudan for Talks with Rebels," BBC Monitoring Africa, 21 June 1999.

months later, United States-based NGO the Carter Center launched a third major attempt at mediation.[66] During this period – from July 1999 to November 1999 – the LRA did not engage in any attacks on civilian or military targets.

Meanwhile, on December 8, 1999, Uganda and Sudan signed a peace agreement, in which they each promised to stop aiding rebel groups in the other country.[67] Negotiations between the Ugandan government and the LRA broke down almost immediately, precipitating a sharp increase in LRA violence. After five months without attacking either civilian or military targets, in late December, the LRA carried out two ambushes of civilian vehicles, an attack on a camp for internally displaced persons in Kitgum district, two ambushes of military vehicles, and an attack on several homes of government and military officials in Gulu district.[68] LRA violence continued in January and February 2000, with 14 LRA attacks on civilian targets.

In November 2000, the Carter Center launched a renewed peace initiative – the fourth major attempt noted in Figure 8.3.[69] Again, LRA violence was low during the period of mediation, with only one LRA attack on civilians reported from November 2000 to January 2001. Several months later, in June 2001, local government officials in Northern Uganda initiated a fifth attempt at peace negotiations, meeting with LRA representatives in Gulu district.[70] Peace talks continued through early September 2001, but collapsed following the September 11, 2001, attacks on the United States, as the Ugandan government characterized the fight against the LRA as Uganda's own fight against terrorism and announced it would no longer participate in negotiations.[71] The LRA carried

---

[66] "Uganda, USA Reportedly Seeking Home for Sudanese Based Ugandan Rebel," BBC Monitoring Africa, 27 November 1999; "U.S. Organizations Continue Talks with Rebels on Ending Conflict in North," BBC Monitoring Africa, 8 January 2000.

[67] Simon Denyer, "Uganda, Sudan Agree on Ending Rebel Activity," *Reuters News*, 8 December 1999; Judith Achieng, "Politics – Uganda/Sudan: A Glimmer of Hope in the Volatile Region," *Inter Press Service*, 9 December 1999.

[68] "Northern Ugandan Roads Closed after Rebel Ambush on Army Convoy," *Agence France-Presse*, 28 December 1999; "10 UPDF Hurt in LRA Ambush," *Monitor*, 28 December 1999; "LRA Rebels Stage Ambushes Again," *Monitor*, 29 December 1999; "LRA Rebels Kill 10 in Attack on Northern Town of Gulu," *Agence France-Presse*, 1 January 2000; "Rebels Kill Five: Burn 40 Thatched Houses in North," BBC Monitoring Africa, 2 January 2000.

[69] Paul Busharizi, "Uganda, Sudan to Talk Peace with Rebels," *Reuters News*, 22 November 2000; "Carter Center Willing to Meet Uganda Rebel Leader," *Reuters News*, 1 February 2001.

[70] "Officials in 'Historic' Meeting with Rebel Commanders in North," BBC Monitoring Africa, 5 June 2001; "Gulu Boss Holds Talks with Kony Chief," *New Vision*, 12 June 2001; "Government to Continue Peace Talks with Lord's Resistance Army Rebels," BBC Monitoring Africa, 30 June 2001.

[71] In a September 12 statement responding to the attacks, Museveni referred to the LRA and another Ugandan rebel group, the Allied Democratic Forces (ADF), as terrorist groups. See "Uganda Leader Condemns U.S. Attacks, Noting 'Sudan and Other Terrorist Networks'," BBC Monitoring Africa, 12 September 2001; "LRA, ADF on American Terrorist List," *All Africa*, 7 December 2001; "Uganda Pledges to Support USA in Combating Terrorism," BBC Monitoring Africa, 12 December 2001.

out only two attacks on civilian targets during the peace negotiations, but in the two months following the government's withdrawal from talks, the LRA launched seven attacks against civilians.

Under pressure from the U.S. government to end its support for foreign terrorist organizations, Sudan agreed in March 2002 to allow Uganda to conduct military operations against LRA bases in Southern Sudan.[72] The LRA responded with a series of attacks on Sudanese army units and villages in government-controlled areas of Southern Sudan; more than 470 civilians are believed to have been killed in the village attacks and many homes burned, in what many have interpreted as attacks aimed at punishing Sudan for its cooperation with Uganda.[73] Soon, however, the LRA returned its attention to Uganda, requesting a renewal of peace negotiations in early June 2002; but the government refused.[74] The following week, one of the larger LRA units, commanded by Vincent Otti, released 100 women and children (who had presumably been abducted); Otti sent a letter with those released, stating his willingness to negotiate.[75] The following day, Museveni reiterated the government's refusal.[76] After more than two months without attacking civilians in Northern Uganda, the LRA carried out 13 attacks on civilians during the last two weeks in June 2002, with attacks spread geographically across several districts in Northern Uganda.[77]

[72] Paul Busharizi, "Sudan Allows Uganda Cross-Border Strike at Rebels," *Reuters News*, 13 March 2002; "Uganda, Sudan Issue Joint Statement on Pursuit of Rebels to UN," BBC Monitoring Africa, 22 March 2002; "Ugandan Troops Overrun Rebel Camp in Sudan," *Agence France-Presse*, 29 March 2002; Paul Busharizi, "Uganda Army Says Flushes Rebels Out of Sudan Camps," *Reuters News*, 30 March 2002; "Ugandan Army Seizes Arms in Anti-Rebel Offensive in Sudan," *Agence France-Presse*, 30 March 2002. See also Human Rights and Peace Centre (HURIPEC) 2003 for a discussion of Sudan-Uganda relations post–September 11th.

[73] "Ugandan LRA Rebels Attack Khartoum Forces Inside Sudan," *Agence France-Presse*, 21 March 2002; "Ugandan Rebels Said to Have Killed 22 Sudanese Troops," BBC Monitoring Middle East, 25 March 2002; "Ugandan Rebels Shoot 60 Mourners Dead Inside Sudan," *Agence France-Presse*, 28 April 2002; "Ugandan Rebels Kill 470 in Brutal Sudan Attacks," *Agence France-Presse*, 11 May 2002. .

[74] "Ugandan Rebels in Sudan Told to Surrender or Be Killed," BBC Monitoring Africa, 3 June 2002.

[75] "Some 100 Freed from LRA Captivity," *New Vision*, 14 June 2002; "Rebel Leader Renews Call for Peace Talks with Government," BBC Monitoring Africa, 21 June 2002.

[76] "Museveni Rules Out Talking With Kony," *New Vision*, 14 June 2002.

[77] "Kony Rebels Attack Gulu UPDF Detach," *Monitor*, 20 June 2002; Henry Wasswa, "Rebels Attack Village in Northern Uganda, Abduct More Than 20 People," *Associated Press*, 21 June 2002; "Rebels Kill Three Civilians in North Uganda," *Agence France-Presse*, 25 June 2002; "LRA Rebels Reportedly Abduct 14 People in Northern District," BBC Monitoring Africa, 25 June 2002; "LRA Rebels Reportedly Kill Four in Northern Town," BBC Monitoring Newsfile, 26 June 2002; "Rebels Kill Two in Another Attack in North Uganda," *Agence France-Presse*, 26 June 2002; "Rebels Attack Aswa," *Monitor*, 27 June 2002; "Ugandan Rebels Attack Civilian Camp: Torch Shelters for 6,000," *Agence France-Presse*, 28 June 2002; "Rebels Kill 10: Abduct 50 in North Uganda," *Agence France-Presse*, 30 June 2002.

Following this spike in LRA violence, a group of religious leaders in Northern Uganda organized the Acholi Religious Leaders Peace Initiative (ARLPI) and began meeting with the LRA in the sixth major mediation attempt shown in Figure 8.3.[78] Museveni agreed to a ceasefire, saying that public pressure was forcing him to the negotiating table.[79] The LRA also agreed to a ceasefire, but negotiations broke down over government demands that the LRA withdraw to government-designated sites in Southern Sudan.[80] LRA attacks on civilians slowed during July and August, but once it was clear that it would not be possible to reach agreement on the terms of a ceasefire, LRA attacks on civilians increased, reaching their highest ever level in September 2002, with 25 attacks, including seven ambushes of civilian vehicles and 18 attacks on villages. LRA violence remained high for several months, with 19 attacks on civilian targets in October and November.

The seventh attempt at negotiations came in early 2003, following LRA efforts to reach out to the government. Kony expressed support for negotiations during a telephone interview with Radio FM in Gulu;[81] reached out to Member of Parliament Norbert Mao to reiterate his desire to restart talks, this time with an international mediator; and declared a unilateral ceasefire.[82] As pressure from foreign donors mounted, the government consented to a temporary ceasefire in a designated area of Pader district and to further talks.[83] Although government and LRA representatives met several times, negotiations fell apart when the LRA demanded that the government extend the ceasefire to all regions of Northern Uganda.[84] Ignoring calls from the Ugandan parliament, Ugandan NGOs, the Ugandan Human Rights Commissioner, the LRA, key donor governments, and even the Pope, Museveni ended the ceasefire on April 19,

[78] "Ugandan Paper Details Series of Lord's Resistance Army Rebels Peace Talks," BBC Monitoring Africa, 14 August 2002; "Archbishop Odama Mediates with LRA Commanders," *New Vision*, 13 August 2002.

[79] "Museveni Writes to Kony," *New Vision*, 13 August 2002.

[80] "LRA Rebels Declare Temporary Ceasefire in Northern Uganda," *Agence France-Presse*, 25 August 2002; "Ugandan Army to Guarantee Rebels Safe Passage," *Agence France-Presse*, 26 August 2002; "Rebels Fear Ebola in Cease-Fire Zones," *Monitor*, 28 August 2002.

[81] Quoted in "Infamous Ugandan Rebel Ends Years of Reclusion to Call for Talks," *Agence France-Presse*, 29 December 2002. A local government official, who once knew Kony personally, was in the radio studio at the time of the call and confirmed that the caller was Joseph Kony.

[82] "LRA Rebel Leader's Conversation With Northern MP Norbert Mao," BBC Monitoring Africa, 13 January 2003. The LRA requested an international mediator again in January. See "Ugandan Rebels Offer to Talk Peace, with International Involvement," *Agence France-Presse*, 4 February 2003.

[83] "President Rejects Kony's Ceasefire," *Monitor*, 5 March 2003; "No Ceasefire, Says Museveni," *New Vision*, 6 March 2003; Henry Wasswa, "Ugandan President Calls Cease-Fire in Certain Areas of Northern Uganda in Bid to Hold Peace Talks with Rebels," *Associated Press*, 10 March 2003.

[84] "LRA Reportedly Demands Unconditional Ceasefire," UN IRIN, 10 April 2003; "Acholi Deaths to Continue – LRA," *New Vision*, 13 April 2003.

refusing to return to peace negotiations and intensifying military operations.[85] During the period of peace negotiations in February and March 2003, LRA violence dropped dramatically, from a high of 37 total attacks on civilian targets during the months of September and October 2002 to 15 total attacks on civilian targets in February and March 2003. The LRA did not carry out any attacks on military or government targets during the months of February and March. After the government retracted its ceasefire and resumed military operations in mid-April, LRA violence spiked, with 13 LRA attacks on civilian targets in May 2003 and 14 attacks in June.

Some might argue that the decline in LRA attacks on civilians during periods of peace negotiations is not surprising; at points in time when the LRA was weakened militarily, the group was simply unable to carry out attacks on military and civilian targets and was forced to plead for peace. Throughout the conflict, however, the LRA was much weaker militarily than the Ugandan government; even at the height of LRA military strength in the mid-1990s, the group had only an estimated 2,000 troops, as compared with the government's approximately 50,000 troops.[86] Furthermore, the rapid increases in LRA violence immediately following government refusals to make concessions suggest that the LRA was capable of carrying out violence against civilian targets during periods of peace negotiations, but chose not to.

ASSESSING THE ALTERNATIVE ARGUMENTS

Alternative hypotheses have difficulty accounting for the patterns of LRA violence described in this chapter. The first alternative hypothesis emphasizes organizational control, arguing that rebel groups that lack effective control over their members are more likely to engage in high levels of violence against civilians. In Jeremy Weinstein's articulation of this argument, rebel groups that receive support from external actors, as the LRA did from Sudan, use the promise of short-term material rewards to recruit members; these groups have difficulty controlling violence among their low-commitment members. The broad correlation that Weinstein predicts – between external support and civilian abuse – exists in the LRA case. But as one scholar notes, the LRA does not fit easily into either of Weinstein's two categories of rebel group organization – it is not a rebellion organized primarily around members' commitment to political principles, nor is it a rebellion organized around the provision of material benefits for members.[87] Many of the individuals who joined the LRA at the start of the insurgency were motivated by political grievances against Museveni's government; during this period of "high commitment" membership, LRA abuses of civilians were low, as Weinstein would predict. Contrary

---

[85] "Ugandan Army Ordered to Resume Operations against LRA Rebels," *Agence France-Presse*, 19 April 2003.
[86] The International Institute for Strategic Studies (IISS) 1996. [87] Bevan 2007.

to Weinstein's model, however, when the LRA began receiving aid from Sudan, it did not recruit members based on offers of material rewards; instead, the LRA's main method of recruitment became abduction.

LRA violence did increase in the period after the group began receiving external assistance, as Weinstein would predict, but this violence was not a result of individual members or units acting outside the command of their leaders. Instead, LRA violence against civilians was deliberate. The LRA maintained a complex military organizational structure and many of its core members had military training, through their participation in the Ugandan military under previous governments.[88] Abduction – of young children in particular – served as a method of better controlling the group's membership, as young children could be indoctrinated, trained, and frightened into carrying out high levels of violence.[89] In addition, the rapid changes in LRA violence in response to repeated attempts at negotiations provide further evidence of the group's ability to control the use of violence. A group that is unable to control its members would not be able to orchestrate such rapid changes in violence; the fact that these changes correspond with clear government behaviors suggests that violence, in the LRA case, was used strategically.

Some would argue that the LRA targeted civilians out of military weakness or in response to mounting conflict losses.[90] This hypothesis seems plausible initially. The first increase in LRA attacks on civilians, in 1991 and 1992, followed the government's major counterinsurgency efforts during Operation North. It is likely that the government's counterinsurgency operations weakened the LRA, reducing the size of its forces and restricting its movement. But although this first period of increased attacks on civilians does coincide with a decline in LRA military strength, the second and more significant increase in LRA abuses, in 1994, does not. In fact, this second escalation of LRA attacks on civilians took place at a point in time when the LRA was growing stronger militarily, not weaker. Following the failure of peace negotiations in 1994, Sudan began to funnel significant amounts of weapons, material supplies, and money to the LRA, in addition to providing the group with military training and a safe haven in Southern Sudan. For similar reasons, military context arguments that emphasize the costs of conflict cannot account for the patterns in LRA violence against civilians. Although the LRA did face high conflict costs in the early 1990s, when it first began targeting civilians, the LRA was not facing particularly high conflict costs by the mid-1990s, when the group launched more substantial attacks on civilians.

---

[88] Interviews with international NGO official, Kampala, 17 July 2005; international NGO official, Kampala, 20 July 2005; Ugandan expert on the conflict in Northern Uganda, Kampala, 21 July 2005; former senior LRA military commander, Gulu, 28 July 2005.

[89] Interviews with international NGO official, Kampala, 17 July 2005; former senior LRA military commander, Gulu, 28 July 2005.

[90] See, for example, Wood 2014a.

Finally, it is worth considering whether LRA violence was, in fact, a form of terrorism or whether most of the violence ought to be categorized as a strategy of high-casualty control. The evidence from Uganda indicates that the LRA did, at times, use violence as part of a strategy of control – as a means of punishing particular individuals or villages that were believed to be aiding the government. But the conflict in Northern Uganda was never a traditional territorial civil war, in which the government and the rebel group each seeks to extend its zone of physical control over territory. In fact, the LRA never tried to control or hold territory in Northern Uganda, instead staging rapid incursions into Northern Uganda to attack government, military, or civilian targets, before withdrawing across the border into Southern Sudan. If the LRA was using violence for the purpose of controlling civilians and territory, one would expect to see changes in LRA violence in response to civilian actions supporting or opposing the government. As the evidence presented in the previous section on peace negotiations demonstrates, however, the character of LRA violence has shifted primarily in response to government actions, not civilian actions.

CONCLUSION

The media and the Ugandan government have often portrayed LRA violence as having no discernible logic, but this chapter has presented evidence demonstrating that LRA violence was, in fact, driven by strategic calculations. Because the LRA was fighting an autocratic government, coercing the government into making concessions was difficult. Although attacks on police and military targets or limited attacks on civilians might generate public calls for the government to negotiate an end to the conflict, Uganda's political institutions protected the government from public criticism. Rebel groups fighting autocratic opponents thus often turn to Western international actors for support, in the hopes that international diplomatic pressure might force the government to negotiate. For several reasons, however, the LRA was unable to make such appeals. Most crucially, the LRA failed to articulate a clear political agenda; without a clear justification for waging war, international actors were unlikely to be sympathetic. Second, the Ugandan government has long held a favored position among international donors. Finally, the fact that the LRA's main source of external support was the government of Sudan, a government shunned internationally for its support of terrorist groups, further eroded the LRA's legitimacy. Without any prospect for building either a domestic or an international constituency in support of its rebellion, but still intent on challenging the government, the LRA adopted a strategy of extreme terrorism, using violence against both military and civilian targets in an effort to undermine the government's ability to provide services, to establish rule of law, and to govern effectively.

Using evidence from a new data set on incidents of government and LRA violence from 1988 to 2003, the analysis in this chapter shows that the LRA began its insurgency with small-scale guerrilla attacks on government and military targets. However, once the government made clear, with its withdrawal from peace negotiations in February 1994, that it would not be coerced easily, the LRA shifted to a strategy of extreme terrorism. The LRA carried out regular attacks on government and military targets throughout the conflict, indicating that the government was, in fact, the intended target of coercion. Approximately 30 percent of the group's attacks on civilians took the form of ambushes of civilian vehicles, a tactic aimed at generating a sense of instability and insecurity throughout the northern region of the country. The LRA only retreated from its strategy of extreme terrorism at times when it seemed as if diplomatic coercion of the Ugandan government might be feasible, at times when domestic and international mediators seemed to take the LRA and its grievances seriously. During periods of mediation, LRA attacks on civilians declined sharply, only to increase again each time that government officials signaled their unwillingness to make concessions.

This pattern continued after 2003. Following the failed peace talks in February and March 2003, the next serious attempt at negotiations came after months of mediation by Betty Bigombe, a former member of Museveni's cabinet who had been involved in previous negotiation attempts. LRA violence remained low during the negotiations, spiking again when the government backed out.[91] LRA violence declined during the latter half of 2005, as Bigombe again tried to bring the two sides to the negotiating table.[92] This mediation came to a halt, however, in October 2005 when the ICC unsealed its arrest warrants, making public its indictments of five senior LRA leaders; LRA violence again increased dramatically.[93]

In response, Riek Machar, the Vice President of Southern Sudan, offered to mediate, leading to the most successful peace talks since the conflict began in 1987. These negotiations achieved the signing of a series of agreements – a 2006 cessation of hostilities agreement; agreements in 2007 on comprehensive solutions to the conflict and on reconciliation and accountability;[94] and finally, in 2008, an agreement on provisions for a permanent ceasefire as well as disarmament, demobilization, and rehabilitation of LRA members. While negotiations were ongoing, LRA violence declined;[95] the group appeared to be taking advantage of the public arena of negotiations and the presence of international mediators to outline a clearer set of political grievances and to generate diplomatic pressure on the Ugandan government. In November 2008, however, Joseph Kony failed to sign the agreements that had been negotiated earlier in the year, precipitating a complete breakdown in the peace process. A few weeks later, the Ugandan government, with the consent of neighboring

---

[91] International Crisis Group 2005e.   [92] International Crisis Group 2005a.
[93] International Crisis Group 2006a.
[94] International Crisis Group 2007b; International Crisis Group 2007c.
[95] Atkinson 2009; Human Rights Watch 2010.

governments and logistical assistance from the United States, launched a military offensive against LRA bases in the Democratic Republic of Congo. Unsurprisingly, given the pattern of LRA attacks described in this chapter, the LRA responded with a series of violent attacks against civilians in the Democratic Republic of Congo and Southern Sudan, killing more than 865 civilians over the course of only a few weeks; evidence suggests that the attacks were organized and planned in advance, coordinated by LRA leadership.[96]

[96] Human Rights Watch 2009; Human Rights Watch 2010.

9

Conclusion

Not all civil wars are fought in similar ways. As the evidence presented in this book makes clear, governments and rebel groups vary widely in their use of violence during civil war – in particular, their use of violence against civilians. Some governments and rebel groups commit horrific atrocities against civilians – deliberately bombing or shelling civilian residential areas, shooting or beating to death groups of civilians in village massacres, burning and destroying civilian homes and crops – while other governments and rebel groups largely avoid attacks on civilians, directing their violence primarily at military targets. Atrocities against civilians tend to dominate both popular reporting and scholarly research on civil wars, often giving the impression that civil wars are characterized by brutal behavior on all sides. In fact, as the original data presented in this book make clear, restraint is not uncommon in civil war. From 1989 to 2010 more than 40 percent of governments and rebel groups engaged in civil war largely avoided deliberate attacks against civilians and, in so doing, behaved in ways consistent with international human rights and humanitarian legal standards prohibiting civilian abuse. What can explain this variation in government and rebel group behavior? Why do some governments and rebel groups deliberately attack civilians during civil war, while other governments and rebel groups do not?

Other studies of wartime violence have emphasized the local context within which acts of violence occur, but this book takes as its starting point the international context within which civil wars take place. Although the major instruments of international human rights and humanitarian law were codified at the conclusion of World War II, the Cold War struggle between the United States and the Soviet Union distracted attention from these efforts throughout much of the second half of the twentieth century. In the early 1990s, however, international actors began holding individuals accountable for violations of international human rights and humanitarian law – establishing ad hoc tribunals to address crimes committed in the context of the wars in Yugoslavia, Rwanda, Sierra Leone, and Cambodia, and, later, institutionalizing the enforcement of international human rights and humanitarian law through the creation of the International Criminal Court (ICC) – what Kathryn Sikkink refers to as a "justice cascade."[1]

The growing strength and institutionalization of international human rights and humanitarian law has had important implications for the behavior of governments and rebel groups fighting in civil wars. The stronger international humanitarian legal regime has not created a situation in which all belligerents engaged in civil war comply with international legal standards, as the cases explored in this book make clear. This international legal framework, however, has set standards of appropriate behavior during wartime, clearly articulating the prohibition on targeting civilians during interstate and civil wars. Although the enforcement of international legal standards is inconsistent, violations of international human rights and humanitarian law are costly, at a minimum inviting international condemnation or the severing of diplomatic ties, but often also leading to the imposition of economic sanctions or arms embargoes and, in some cases, even prompting military intervention or investigation by the ICC. This international context has important implications for the way that governments and rebel groups weigh the costs and benefits of engaging in violence.

RESTRAINT AS A DELIBERATE STRATEGIC CHOICE

Although all governments and rebel groups face an international context in which abuses of civilians and violations of international law are likely to invite criticism, if not stronger action, how governments and rebel groups weigh the costs of violence depends on their relationships with their own domestic and international constituents. For governments and rebel groups that need support from broad domestic and international constituencies, the domestic and international costs of violence are high, increasing incentives for restraint. These governments and rebel groups often use restraint strategically – deliberately limiting their use of violence against civilians and framing their behavior as comporting with international humanitarian legal standards as a means of appealing to domestic and international audiences for support.

Belligerents weigh the *domestic* costs of violence by evaluating the extent to which they need to build support from a broad *domestic* constituency. Governments and rebel groups with broad domestic constituencies as well as institutional incentives to be responsive to these constituencies face the highest domestic costs to violence and, thus, the strongest incentives to use restraint. Three key characteristics shape belligerent relationships with their domestic

---

[1] Sikkink 2011.

constituents: (1) the extent to which institutions compel leaders to be responsive to their constituents, (2) the inclusiveness of the political system, and (3) the consolidation of political power.

Belligerents weigh the *international* costs of violence by evaluating the extent to which they need to secure support from a broad *international* constituency – in particular, a Western international constituency. The governments most in need of international support and, therefore, most likely to adopt a strategy of restraint, are governments with unstable regimes. Struggling to maintain fragile political institutions, these governments cannot afford to risk losing international support by engaging in abuses of civilians. Like governments, the rebel groups most in need of international support are those that are most vulnerable domestically: rebel groups facing autocratic government opponents. Autocratic governments have a greater capacity to withstand military and civilian losses, making it difficult for rebel groups to generate enough pressure on the government to force concessions. Instead, these rebel groups seek to leverage international pressure on their autocratic opponents and often use restraint as a means of winning international support.

The statistical evidence supports the claim that governments and rebel groups with broader domestic and international constituencies – and institutional incentives to respond to these constituencies – have strong incentives for restraint. Governments with democratic, inclusive, and unstable regimes are, indeed, the governments most likely to exercise restraint in their fighting. The likelihood of restraint is between 1.5 and 6.1 times greater among governments with democratic regimes than among governments with autocratic regimes. For example, the most autocratic government in the data set – a government equivalent to Saddam Hussein's exclusionary dictatorship in Iraq – has only a 6.6 percent likelihood of exercising restraint, but a democratic government fighting in a similar civil war has a 40 percent likelihood of exercising restraint. For governments with inclusive regimes, the likelihood of restraint is between 1.2 and 3.4 times greater than for governments with exclusionary regimes; for governments with unstable regimes, the likelihood of restraint is between 1.3 and 4.6 times greater, as compared to governments with stable regimes.

The case studies lend further weight to these statistical findings. Following the collapse of Suharto's autocratic rule and the transition to democracy in Indonesia, the government was under heavy pressure to prove that it intended to strike a path different from that of Suharto. Anxious to secure domestic and international support during the uncertain regime transition, the government made significant changes in its policies toward Aceh and East Timor, making efforts to improve its treatment of civilians and consenting to greater political freedoms for both regions.

The statistical evidence shows that rebel groups, too, are more likely to exercise restraint when they need to build support from broad domestic and international constituencies. Rebel groups fighting autocratic opponents, rebel groups with governance structures that encourage accountability to civilian constituents, and rebel groups with inclusive political objectives are more likely to exercise restraint. The likelihood that a rebel group will adopt a strategy of restraint is between 2.4 and 8.3 times higher when fighting an autocratic opponent than when fighting a democratic opponent, while for rebel groups that establish governance structures, the likelihood of restraint is between 1.2 and 2.5 times greater than for rebel groups lacking governance structures. And for rebel groups with inclusive political objectives, the likelihood of restraint is between 1.3 and 3.8 times greater than for rebel groups with exclusionary political objectives.

In their attempt to confront Suharto's autocratic government, the Acehnese and Timorese insurgencies in Indonesia, both of which possessed well-developed political structures encouraging responsiveness to their constituents, sought to use their good behavior as a means of appealing to international actors for support. But as these two cases demonstrate, even though rebel groups fighting autocratic governments are likely to exercise restraint and to seek support from international actors, they will not necessarily be successful in obtaining that support. The Free Aceh Movement (Gerakan Aceh Merdeka, GAM) miscalculated its ability to draw comparisons between Aceh and East Timor, not recognizing that the international community would view these two demands for self-determination differently because of the different circumstances under which each region was incorporated into Indonesia. For the international community, the fact that East Timor had been annexed by force in the 1970s, while Aceh had joined Indonesia voluntarily at independence, justified a stronger international response in support of East Timor's demands for autonomy.

VARIATION IN VIOLENCE

Although restraint is common in civil war – and much more common than news media sources often suggest – violence against civilians is common as well. Civilians are crucial sources of support for governments and rebel groups, providing recruits, supplies, and intelligence; civilians are also political constituents, individuals on whose behalf governments and rebel groups fight. Eroding this base of civilian support and targeting civilian constituents as a means of ratcheting up the costs of a conflict are often key components of wartime strategy. As human rights and humanitarian norms have grown in strength, however, domestic and international actors have become less willing to accept that civilians are legitimate targets during war. Thus, only those governments and rebel groups with little need for domestic and international support – governments and rebel groups for whom the domestic and international costs of engaging in violence are low – are likely to target civilians.

Violence against civilians is not identical across cases of civil war. Wartime violence varies not only in scale, but also in form, as the data presented in Chapters 2 and 3 make clear. The second half of this book's theoretical argument focused on three strategies of violence in particular: control, cleansing, and terrorism. Strategies of control target specific individuals believed to be aiding the opponent; the aim is to deter other civilians from collaborating with the opponent, thereby expanding control over civilians and the territory they inhabit. Rather than seeking to control the civilian population within contested territory, some belligerents seek to eliminate entirely the opposing side's civilian base of support, using a strategy of cleansing to kill and displace large numbers of civilians. Whereas strategies of control and cleansing direct violence against civilians in an effort to alter the behavior of *civilians themselves*, strategies of terrorism use violence against civilians in an attempt to alter the behavior of the *opponent*. By targeting the opponent's civilian constituents, strategies of terrorism aim to increase the costs of the conflict for the opponent, thus forcing concessions.

While governments and rebel groups weigh the *costs* of violence based on their relationship with *their own* domestic and international constituencies, governments and rebel groups weigh the *benefits* of violence based on an assessment of *their opponent's* relationship with its constituents. The greater the civilian support for the opponent, the stronger the incentives for a government or rebel group to sever these ties between the opponent and its constituents and, thus, the stronger the incentives to use a strategy of control or cleansing. This argument is difficult to test statistically. Doing so would require data on the extent of popular support for each belligerent within contested territory, something that is difficult to measure. Evidence of variation in the use of strategies of control, however, is apparent in the case studies. Faced with hostile populations in East Timor and Aceh, the Indonesian government under Suharto used strategies of high-casualty control – detaining, torturing, and killing large numbers of civilians suspected of aiding the insurgents. The two rebel groups, in contrast, had significant support among civilians and thus had little incentive to engage in strategies of high-casualty control against Acehnese or Timorese civilians. Perhaps the most telling case is that of the LRA in Uganda, where it is possible to observe a shift over time in LRA strategy. In response to civilian participation in pro-government militias – signaling greater support for the government within Northern Uganda – the LRA began attacking families and villages associated with the militias.

Many belligerents might prefer to sever the ties between the opponent and its civilian constituents more permanently, by removing the opponent's civilian supporters from contested territory through a strategy of cleansing; but in most cases, the opponent's base of support is too large or too dispersed geographically for cleansing to be feasible. When the opponent's civilian constituency is small and geographically concentrated, however, the incentives to adopt a strategy of cleansing are greater. For rebel groups, access to government constituents poses an additional challenge. Even if the government draws support from a geographically concentrated constituency, the rebel group may not have the resources to reach this group. In some separatist conflicts, however, rebel groups do have both strong incentives to rid the separatist region of government constituents – "outsiders" who may call into question the legitimacy of the separatist group's claim to the contested territory – and the capacity to remove these individuals from the region.

As this argument would predict, high-casualty cleansing is rare in civil war, with less than 13 percent of governments and less than 10 percent of rebel groups adopting a strategy of high-casualty cleansing. Consistent with the argument of this book, the statistical results show that the likelihood of government high-casualty cleansing is 2.7 times greater for an autocratic government confronting a rebel group whose supporters are regionally concentrated than for an autocratic government confronting a rebel group without a regionally concentrated base of civilian support. The Darfur case study illustrates this relationship. The three ethnic groups supporting the rebellion in Darfur – the Fur, Masalit, and Zaghawa – were small in number, constituting less than 10 percent of the total population of Sudan, and geographically concentrated in the western region of the country, creating incentives for the Sudanese government to use a strategy of cleansing. Furthermore, as an autocracy that derived support primarily from northern ethnic groups and was unpopular internationally, the Sudanese government had few constraints on its use of violence. The Sudanese government thus used extreme violence against civilians in Darfur, killing tens of thousands of civilians, burning homes and crops, and displacing more than 1.8 million people.

The statistical analyses also show that when the government has a small, concentrated constituency living within the separatist region, the likelihood that the rebel group will use high-casualty cleansing is more than 30 percentage points higher than when the government does not possess a concentrated constituency. In Nagorno-Karabakh, the Azeri population was a significant minority at 20 percent of the population – large enough to threaten the Armenian rebels' claim to the separatist region and yet small enough to make their expulsion possible. The Karabakh insurgents adopted a strategy of high-casualty cleansing, expelling Azeris from the separatist region and surrounding territories to consolidate their hold over Karabakh and establish a de facto territorial link with Armenia.

Unlike strategies of control and cleansing, which aim to weaken the opponent by cutting off its source of civilian support, strategies of terrorism use violence against the opponent's civilian constituents as a means of ratcheting up the costs of the conflict for the opponent, with the aim of forcing greater concessions. In deciding whether to use terrorism, governments and rebel groups assess whether their opponent is likely to be sensitive to civilian losses, based in large part on the extent to which the opponent's political institutions encourage accountability to its civilian constituents. Rebel groups perceive democratic governments to be more vulnerable to domestic public pressure and, therefore, more likely to make concessions in an effort to halt civilian losses; the more democratic the government, the more likely it is that the rebel group will use terrorism. Similarly, governments facing rebel groups with governance institutions perceive these groups as vulnerable to pressure from their civilian constituents; these governments have stronger incentives to use terrorism as a means of pressuring the rebel group to make concessions.

The form that terrorism takes, however, depends on the constraints a government or rebel group faces from its own domestic constituency. Governments and rebel groups that need to maintain support from a broad domestic constituency tend to be wary of imposing high civilian casualties; these governments and rebel groups choose strategies of terrorism that inflict costs on the opponent's civilian constituents – through destruction of property or infrastructure, for example – without imposing high casualties. Governments and rebel groups with narrower civilian constituencies have greater leeway to use high-casualty strategies of terrorism.

The statistical results provide strong support for the arguments regarding government strategies of terrorism. Governments facing rebel groups that possess governance institutions are between 3.4 and 9.8 times more likely to adopt strategies of high-casualty terrorism than governments facing rebel groups without such institutions. And, as predicted, the likelihood of high-casualty terrorism is greatest among governments with narrow political constituencies – exclusionary governments. The likelihood of high-casualty terrorism is between 1.8 and 3.8 times greater for exclusionary governments as compared with inclusive governments.

Case study evidence from Turkey captures the nuance in government strategies of terrorism. The Turkish government had a narrow civilian constituency – among ethnic Turks. And it confronted a rebel group receiving strong support from Kurdish civilians in the eastern and southeastern regions of the country and perceived to be sensitive to losses among these Kurdish constituents. Government incentives for both terrorism and cleansing were strong. As a democratic government seeking entry into the EU, however, Turkey faced domestic and international constraints on its behavior, leading the government to adopt a strategy of low-casualty cleansing and terrorism. The Turkish government destroyed thousands of Kurdish villages, but sought to avoid inflicting casualties, evacuating villages before burning them.

The empirical findings on rebel group terrorism also provide strong support for the theoretical arguments. When facing an autocratic opponent, the likelihood that a rebel group will pursue a strategy of terrorism is low, at 7.4 percent; when facing a democratic opponent, however, the likelihood that a rebel group will pursue a strategy of terrorism increases dramatically, to 80.5 percent. Although all rebel groups facing democratic opponents have incentives to use terrorism, the statistical results also show that inclusive rebel groups – rebel groups with broad civilian constituencies – are likely to adopt strategies of terrorism that inflict costs on civilians without imposing high casualties. For a rebel group fighting a democratic government, the likelihood of high-casualty terrorism is 32.9 percentage points higher if the rebel group is exclusionary than if the rebel group is inclusive.

Case study evidence from conflicts in Turkey and El Salvador demonstrates that rebel group bombings of civilian targets are often deliberate and strategic. The Turkish government was democratic from the start of the Kurdish rebellion, but it was not until the government made clear its unwillingness to negotiate with the PKK that the rebel group began launching attacks on buses, shopping centers, and tourist sites in Istanbul and along the Mediterranean coast as part of a strategy of high-casualty terrorism. PKK leader Abdullah Öcalan stated publicly that the group's goal in carrying out these bombings was to increase the costs of the conflict, in an attempt to force the government to the negotiating table. In El Salvador, the FMLN focused its attacks primarily on government and military targets in the early years of the conflict, but intensified its economic sabotage campaign – a strategy of low-casualty terrorism – in the mid-1980s, in the hopes that this would further weaken the Salvadoran economy and undermine domestic support for the government, particularly in advance of democratic elections. Both rebel groups used terrorism against their democratic opponents, but as a revolutionary insurgency seeking to build a broad base of domestic support, the FMLN was more constrained than the separatist PKK. Unwilling to risk losing its national base of civilian support by inflicting high civilian casualties, the FMLN adopted a form of low-casualty terrorism that focused on economic and infrastructure targets such as power lines, bridges, and coffee-processing facilities.

As the examination of the LRA conflict in Northern Uganda illustrates, even in this most extreme case of rebel group violence, strategic motivations drove rebel group violence. The rest of the book demonstrates that belligerents with narrow domestic civilian constituencies face lower domestic costs to violence and, therefore, are more likely to use violence, but the LRA case takes this argument to its extreme, showing how a rebel group behaves when it has lost its domestic civilian constituency almost entirely. Unable to articulate a clear political agenda and confronting a government favored by powerful international donors, the LRA was unable to build either a domestic or an international constituency of supporters. Still intent on challenging the government, the LRA embarked on a strategy of extreme terrorism, aimed at undermining the Ugandan government's ability to function effectively. Event-level data on violent incidents in Northern Uganda show that a large portion of the LRA's attacks on civilians took the form of ambushes of civilian vehicles on major roadways throughout Northern Uganda, aimed at generating a broad sense of insecurity in Northern Uganda and undermining support for the government. The event-level data also show that the LRA stepped back from its attacks on civilians at moments when domestic and international mediators intervened, only to return to violence each time the government refused to negotiate.

IMPLICATIONS FOR FUTURE CONFLICTS

As the international context evolves, so too should belligerent behavior. Although it is difficult to predict the trajectory of change in the international system, if international human rights and humanitarian norms continue to gain strength, belligerents in need of domestic and international support should face even greater pressure to comply with international norms as a basis for claiming legitimacy. Governments and rebel groups that are insulated from domestic and international pressure, however, will ignore international humanitarian law, targeting civilians with violence. This book has focused on conflicts occurring from 1989 to 2010, but these patterns of government and rebel group behavior have continued to play out in recent conflicts, such as the 2011 civil war between Muammar el-Qaddafi's government and Libyan insurgents.

In comparison to the other conflicts explored in this book, the Libyan conflict is unusual in that violence against civilians began prior to the development of an organized, armed opposition. When antigovernment protests spread in mid-February 2011, Libyan forces responded with repression – arresting thousands of civilians; torturing and, in some cases, executing detainees; and firing on protesters, killing an estimated 500 to 700 civilians by the end of February.[2] As protests continued, Qaddafi threatened greater violence, announcing on Libyan National Television that he would lead "millions to purge Libya inch by inch, house by house, household by household, alley by alley, and individual by individual until I purify this land."[3] In its arrest warrant for Qaddafi, the ICC stated that "there are reasonable grounds to believe" that these abuses constituted a deliberate government policy aimed at "deterring and quelling, by any means, including by the use of lethal force, the demonstrations of civilians against Gaddafi's regime," amounting to crimes against humanity.[4]

Numerous intergovernmental organizations, including the EU, the General Secretariat of the Organization of the Islamic Conference, the Peace and Security Council of the African Union, and the UN Security Council, condemned the violence in Libya.[5] On February 25, the UN Human Rights Council adopted a resolution condemning "the recent gross and systematic human rights

---

[2] Amnesty International 2011b; International Crisis Group 2011b; UN Human Rights Council 2011; Human Rights Watch World Report 2012; UN Human Rights Council 2012.

[3] UN Human Rights Council 2011, 3.

[4] International Criminal Court, Warrant of Arrest for Muammar Mohammed Abu Minyar Gaddafi, 27 June 2011, available online at www.icc-cpi.int.

[5] "Declaration by the High Representative, Catherine Ashton, on behalf of the European Union on Events in Libya," Brussels, 20 February 2011 (6795/1/11, PRESSE 33), available online at http://eeas .europa.eu/statements/behalf/; "OIC General Secretariat Condemns Strongly the Excessive Use of Force against Civilians in the Libyan Jamahiriya," OIC, 22 February 2011, available online at www .oic-oci.org; "Communique," Peace and Security Council of the African Union, 261st Meeting, Addis Ababa, Ethiopia, 23 February 2011, available online at www.peaceau.org; UN Security Council Press Statement on Libya, 22 February 2011 (SC/1080).

violations" in Libya and ordering an investigation;[6] the following day, the UN Security Council passed a resolution referring the case to the ICC and imposing sanctions on Libya.[7] Thus, by the time armed opposition began – with the establishment of the Interim National Transitional Council (NTC) in early March 2011 – the Libyan government already faced significant international pressure to moderate its behavior.

The Libyan case, however, is consistent with the arguments made in this book. As a long-standing autocratic government with an exclusionary political system and a history of tensions with Western international actors, Qaddafi's government had few domestic or international incentives to exercise restraint. After gaining power through a military coup in 1969, Qaddafi ruled Libya for more than four decades, establishing an autocratic government (with a polity score of −7) that concentrated power in the executive, prohibited political parties and other civil society organizations, and severely repressed political opposition.[8] Many international actors viewed Libya as a rogue state. Libya provided aid to insurgent groups known to use terrorist tactics; was implicated in several major terrorist attacks, including the 1988 bombing of Pan Am Flight 103; and pursued the development of nuclear and chemical weapons. In response, the United States designated Libya as a state sponsor of terrorism; both the United States and the United Nations imposed diplomatic and economic sanctions on Libya.[9] Although Libya made efforts to repair its foreign relations by agreeing in 2003 to dismantle its nuclear and chemical weapons programs and to compensate the families of the Pan Am Flight 103 victims,[10] this process of rehabilitation was slow.

In addition to having few domestic or international incentives for restraint, Qaddafi's government had strong incentives to use violence against the revolution's popular base of support. Although the NTC did not establish a formal organizational structure until March 5, the opposition had popular origins, with local councils playing an important role in the organization of protests and the formation of the rebel group.[11] In public statements, the NTC announced its commitment to establishing a democratic government, with the group's chairman, Mohammed Abdul Jalil, insisting, "We are looking for a civil, republican, democratic state that respects all international treaties and international law and that respects human rights and denounces terrorism."[12]

[6] UN Human Rights Council, 15th Special Session, Resolution S-15/1, 25 February 2011 (A/HRC/RES/S-15/1).

[7] UN Security Council, Resolution 1970 (2011), 26 February 2011 (S/RES/1970 (2011)).

[8] International Crisis Group 2011b; UN Human Rights Council 2012.

[9] Takeyh 2001; Jentleson and Whytock 2006.   [10] Ibid.

[11] International Crisis Group 2011b.

[12] "Soft-Spoken Rebel Heard Across Libya," *Financial Times*, 13 March 2011. See also, "Founding Statement of the Interim Transitional National Council," Benghazi, Libya, 5 March 2011, available online at www.ntclibya.org/.

Qaddafi's government thus adopted a strategy of terrorism, using heavy artillery, including rockets, mortars, and cluster bombs, to attack towns and cities, without discriminating between civilian and military targets.[13] The pattern of government abuses that had begun during protests, including arbitrary arrests and detentions, torture and killing of detainees, and disappearances, continued as the armed conflict developed.[14]

The NTC, in contrast, largely avoided attacks on civilians, as the argument of this book would predict. As a revolutionary rebel group that sought to establish a more inclusive, democratic government in Libya, the NTC faced high domestic costs to violence against civilians. Confronted with an autocratic government unlikely to make concessions in response to domestic public pressure, the NTC needed international support to oust Qaddafi, thus the international costs of engaging in violence were also high. On several occasions, NTC forces abused civilians in communities perceived to be sympathetic to Qaddafi, but reports indicate these were isolated incidents rather than a policy directed by the group leadership.[15]

From its inception, the NTC lobbied international actors to increase pressure on Qaddafi. Just days after formally establishing the NTC, members of the council traveled to Europe to appeal to European policy makers. Following meetings between the French President, Nicolas Sarkozy, and NTC representatives, France officially recognized the NTC.[16] In a speech to members of the European Parliament, Mahmoud Jibril, chairman of the NTC executive board and head of international affairs,[17] stated explicitly that "the purpose of this Council for the time being, in the interim period, is trying to mobilize the support of the world community whether from world public opinion or from governments of the world to support the resistance of the Libyan people and help their cause get through and establish their own future."[18] In late March, NTC representatives met with leaders attending the London Conference on Libya, including U.S. Secretary of State Hillary Clinton and British Foreign Secretary William Hague;[19] when the international contact group met again in Qatar in mid-April, NTC leaders were invited to address the meeting.[20]

---

[13] Amnesty International 2011a; Amnesty International 2011b; Human Rights Watch World Report 2012; UN Human Rights Council 2012.

[14] UN Human Rights Council 2012.   [15] Ibid.; Amnesty International 2011b.

[16] Arnaud Bouvier, "Libyan Opposition Demands EU Recognition at Euro Parliament," *Agence France-Presse*, 8 March 2011; "Europe Meets the Arab Awakening," *Financial Times*, 9 March 2011; "France, Germany Urge EU to Dialogue with Libyan Opposition," *Agence France-Presse*, 10 March 2011.

[17] International Crisis Group 2011b, 24.

[18] Mahmoud Jibril, speech given to the Alliance of Liberals and Democrats for Europe (ALDE), 9 March 2011. Video footage of speech available at www.ntclibya.org/english/2011/03/09/alde-group-meeting-with-inc/.

[19] "Clinton Meets Libyan Opposition in London: Official," *Agence France-Presse*, 29 March 2011.

[20] Marc Burleigh, "All Eyes on Doha as Libya Contact Group Meets," *Agence France-Presse*, 12 April 2011.

In lobbying international actors, NTC leaders emphasized their commitment to democracy, human rights, and international law, portraying themselves as the legitimate representatives of the Libyan people. On its website, the NTC promised to "respect all international and regional agreements signed by the former Libyan government,"[21] while a NTC statement released in advance of the London Conference emphasized, "We have learnt from the struggles of our past during the dark days of dictatorship that there is no alternative to building a free and democratic society and ensuring the supremacy of international humanitarian law and human rights declarations."[22] NTC leaders also contrasted their commitment to the rule of law with Qaddafi's abuses. In his speech to members of the European Parliament, Jibril reminded his audience that "the killing machine of the regime is still inflicting, as of the moment we speak right now, inflicting heavy casualties on our people in different cities of our beloved country."[23]

These lobbying efforts were successful in getting international actors to exert greater pressure on Qaddafi's government. On March 17, the UN Security Council passed a second resolution on Libya, in which it authorized member states "to take all necessary measures … to protect civilians and civilian populated areas under threat of attack in the Libyan Arab Jamahiriya" and established a no-fly zone over Libya.[24] Within days, international coalition forces led by Britain, France, and the United States launched air strikes against Libyan military targets, later turning the intervention effort over to NATO.[25] Although it took several months, ultimately the international intervention was successful in aiding efforts to overthrow Qaddafi.[26]

IMPLICATIONS FOR POLICY

Can this book tell us anything about how to halt atrocities once they have begun or how to prevent wartime abuse of civilians all together? As the conflicts in Sudan and Libya illustrate, when a government is insulated from both domestic and international pressure, it is extremely difficult to prevent atrocities against civilians or to halt abuses once they have begun. Public condemnations, arms embargoes, diplomatic punishments, and even economic sanctions are unlikely to produce significant changes in government behavior. Governments

---

[21] "Introducing the Council," accessed 1 September 2014, available on the NTC's website at www.ntclibya.org/english/about/.

[22] "Libyan Opposition Vow Free and Fair Elections," *Agence France-Presse*, 29 March 2011.

[23] Mahmoud Jibril, speech given to the Alliance of Liberals and Democrats for Europe (ALDE), 9 March 2011. Video footage of speech available online at www.ntclibya.org/english/2011/03/09/alde-group-meeting-with-inc/.

[24] UN Security Council, Resolution 1973 (2011), 17 March 2011 (S/RES/1973 (2011)).

[25] David D. Kirkpatrick, Steven Erlanger, and Elisabeth Bumiller, "Allies Open Air Assault on Qaddafi's Forces," *New York Times*, 20 March 2011; Elisabeth Bumiller and David D. Kirkpatrick, "NATO to Assume New Role in Libya," *New York Times*, 25 March 2011.

[26] International Crisis Group 2011a.

that embark on a path of civilian abuse have already calculated that they have little need for the assistance or approval of Western international actors. In such cases, little can be done in the short run to force changes in government behavior, unless international actors are willing to intervene militarily – as in Libya – to forcibly remove the abusive government from power. Military intervention, however, may not be a feasible or desirable policy option for a variety of other reasons. In Sudan, for example, international actors waited to send the joint African Union–United Nations peacekeeping mission until they had the Sudanese government's consent, which was after the most severe violence against civilians had already taken place. And in Libya, although international intervention helped to remove Qaddafi from power, conflict has persisted in the years since his overthrow.

In the longer term, however, international actors do have other options for preventing government atrocities. Although international actors are unlikely to be able to remove government incentives for violence by altering the characteristics of an insurgency – the extent of popular support for the insurgency, the degree to which insurgent supporters are geographically concentrated, or the nature of an insurgency's ties to its civilian constituents – international actors can increase the domestic and international costs to engaging in violence. By encouraging governments to move in the direction of political liberalization – by broadening their civilian constituencies and reforming political institutions in ways that increase leaders' accountability to their constituents – international actors can increase domestic constraints on government behavior. Convincing an autocratic government to liberalize certainly is not an easy task and would require intense international pressure, perhaps combined with positive inducements. And encouraging democratization without fomenting even greater domestic unrest would require careful attention to the sequencing of political reforms and a focus on building strong civic institutions before rushing forward with elections.[27] But as the Indonesia case demonstrates, moves toward a more open political system may significantly influence how a government weighs the domestic costs of engaging in violence.

International actors can also influence how governments weigh the international costs of civilian targeting. While it might seem, at first glance, as if the most effective way of increasing the international costs of violence would be to step up international punishment of abusive governments – for example, by strengthening the threat of ICC prosecution or by strengthening UN peace enforcement missions – the cases in this book suggest that the threat of stronger punishment is unlikely to prevent government abuse. Most governments willing to engage in atrocities have already calculated that they can withstand significant international condemnation and even can withstand most international

---

[27] For the argument that democratization can lead to an increased risk of war, see Mansfield and Snyder 1995; Mansfield and Snyder 2005. For a discussion of ways in which democratization can be managed to minimize the risk of conflict, see Snyder 2000.

punishments. And for many governments, the threat of more serious punishment, such as military action, will ring hollow.

The governments most likely to exercise restraint are the governments that view continued international support as crucial, governments that are afraid of losing access to valuable international benefits. Rather than devising stronger punishment for transgressions of international human rights and humanitarian law, international actors should thus look for ways of creating positive inducements that can be withdrawn in the event of serious violence. In Indonesia, for example, the newly installed government struggling to maintain power following the fall of Suharto was highly dependent on aid from the IMF and other international donors; unwilling to risk losing this key source of support, the government made efforts to rein in the military's counterinsurgency operations in East Timor and Aceh. In Turkey, the government calculated that high-casualty violence against civilians was not worth the risk of jeopardizing the country's application for EU membership. This is not to say that international actors should strive to create dependency among states that are prone to insurgency, but international actors may be able to find ways to create significant material benefits for governments that integrate themselves into the international community and to establish concrete procedures for suspending these benefits in the event of government abuse.

The conflicts in Sudan and Libya illustrate the challenges of halting government violence once it has begun, but international actors may have greater leverage over rebel groups. Much rebel group violence against civilians takes the form of terrorism, violence aimed at forcing the government to the negotiating table by increasing the costs of the conflict. International actors may be able to halt this type of violence – and even prevent it – by pressuring governments to take rebel group grievances and political demands seriously. As with governments, it is the promise of significant gain that is most likely to encourage respect for international norms of wartime conduct. The PKK, for example, might not have begun attacking Turkish tourist sites in 1993 had the Turkish government been willing to reciprocate the PKK's unilateral ceasefire and enter into negotiations. Even limited government concessions, such as allowing the use of the Kurdish language in schools, might have signaled the government's willingness to take seriously the PKK's demands. Reaching agreement on even minor issues likely would have been a lengthy process, but the evidence presented in this book shows that rebel groups are often willing to suspend attacks on civilians during negotiations; engaging the PKK in dialogue might have prevented the group from attacking civilian targets, at least in the short run. In the Ugandan case, the evidence suggests that engagement with the LRA encouraged the group to step back from its attacks on civilians.

Certainly engaging in dialogue with groups that have committed heinous crimes is distasteful and, in many cases, difficult to justify to a public outraged by a long history of violence against civilians. Some might argue that negotiating with "terrorists" or those who have targeted civilians only rewards their use of violence. Defeating an insurgent group in an outright military victory, however, is nearly impossible. Even the most powerful militaries have difficulty penetrating peripheral regions; with the advantage of being able to blend into the local population, rebellions may persist for years with few members and few resources, carrying out occasional but deadly attacks on civilian targets. As objectionable as it may be to negotiate with such an opponent, governments have little choice. The evidence presented in this book shows that the rebel groups most likely to exercise restraint are those groups that believe they can make appeals for domestic and international support. And as the case of the LRA in Northern Uganda demonstrates, even the most violent rebel groups, the groups whose objectives seem most obscure, use violence for strategic purposes and are often willing to forego attacks on civilians if they perceive the opportunity to be treated as legitimate actors with legitimate demands. Forcing governments not only to agree to negotiations but also to accept significant concessions may require concerted domestic and international pressure over a long period of time. And it is true that peace negotiations may break down, leading to a return to violence, as seen again and again in Uganda, but if domestic and international actors can keep both sides engaged in a peace process, even if this peace process is drawn out over many years, it may be possible to encourage rebel groups to weigh the costs of violence more heavily.

IMPLICATIONS FOR RESEARCH

The empirical findings of this book suggest the need to refine existing arguments regarding the causes of wartime violence against civilians. Although a lack of organizational control likely accounts for some of the violent attacks on civilians that occur during civil war, the evidence in this book shows that much of the violence that occurs during civil war is deliberate violence, perpetrated by governments and rebel groups that perceive benefits to targeting their opponent's civilian constituents. The evidence does show, however, that organizational characteristics may impact a government or rebel group's ability to implement a strategy of restraint. In Indonesia, for example, although the new civilian leadership wanted to pursue a new, more restrained counterinsurgency strategy in Aceh and East Timor, these new leaders struggled to assert control over the powerful Indonesian military, presenting challenges for the implementation of a strategy of restraint.

The findings in this book also show that governments and rebel groups weigh the costs and benefits of violence based not only on the military context, but also on the wider strategic context, which is shaped by belligerent relationships with their domestic and international constituencies. The statistical results do indicate that, in some cases, violence may be a weapon of the weak – showing that weaker rebel groups are more likely to use strategies of terrorism and weaker governments are more likely to use strategies of high-casualty cleansing – but the relative strength of the belligerents does not influence significantly the likelihood of government or rebel group restraint. Strong governments and rebel groups are no more likely than weak governments and rebel groups to avoid attacks on civilian targets. And although governments fighting in interstate wars may use civilian targeting as a desperate attempt to stave off rising conflict costs, the same is not true of civil wars – perhaps because the domestic costs of attacking civilians are higher in civil wars.

Furthermore, the case study evidence indicates that neither declining military strength nor rising conflict costs can account for variation over time in government or rebel group violence. The Indonesian, Sudanese, and Turkish governments – and more recently, the Libyan government – all directed violence against civilians from the earliest days of the conflict, when their militaries had not yet incurred significant losses. And although the Indonesian government faced rising costs in Aceh as the insurgency grew in the late 1990s, it did not increase its use of violence against civilians, but rather shifted to a strategy of restraint. Similarly, among rebel groups, neither the PKK in Turkey, nor the FMLN in El Salvador, nor the LRA in Uganda began attacking civilians at moments of military weakness or rising conflict costs. In each of these cases, the rebel group launched frequent attacks on government, military, and police targets throughout the conflict and continued to do so even after beginning to target civilians; little evidence exists to support the contention that these groups were driven to use violence against civilians because of an inability to confront the government militarily.

To be clear, this is not to say that characteristics of the military context are irrelevant; rather, the military context is only one component of the larger strategic context governments and rebel groups face. Even if some of the most common military context variables cannot account for variation in government and rebel group behavior *across* conflicts, these factors may still help to account for shifts in government and rebel group behavior during a conflict. In fact, this may offer a means of reconciling the seemingly contradictory findings of cross-national and subnational research on civil war violence.

The evidence presented in this book shows little evidence that reciprocity motivates compliance with international law during civil war. The relationship between government and rebel group restraint, though positive, is not statistically significant in any of the analyses. And the case study evidence suggests that a very different dynamic may be at work. Rather than belligerents matching one another's violence, the cases indicate that when one belligerent engages in high levels of violence against civilians, the opposing side often responds not with violence but with restraint. In Indonesia, for example, Suharto's government directed extreme violence against civilians in Aceh and East Timor, while the rebel groups in each of these separatist regions respected the immunity of noncombatants, drawing attention to Indonesia's abuses as a means of winning international support. In Uganda, it was the government that refrained from using large-scale violence against civilians, while the LRA was responsible for severe atrocities. Other cases reveal that patterns of government and rebel group violence are not always such extreme contrasts. In Turkey, for example, the government adopted a strategy of low-casualty cleansing and terrorism, destroying Kurdish villages without imposing high casualties, while the PKK used high-casualty terrorism, carrying out frequent bombings of tourist sites and other civilian targets.

Existing theoretical arguments are unable to account for variation in government and rebel group violence against civilians across conflicts for two main reasons. First, they do not provide a complete assessment of the domestic and international costs that governments and rebel groups face in using violence against civilians. Second, perhaps because of this failure to weigh accurately the domestic and international costs of violence, they also fail to recognize that governments and rebel groups often deliberately exercise restraint in their fighting, in an attempt to build domestic and international legitimacy. In fact, more than 40 percent of all governments and rebel groups fighting in civil wars since 1989 avoided attacks on civilian populations, focusing their violence primarily on their opponent's military forces and bases. And as the statistical and case study evidence confirms, this restraint is driven, in part, by international pressure. Yet conventional ways of measuring a country's vulnerability to international influence – measures of economic or political interdependence – do not capture the causal mechanism at work. Governments do not exercise restraint because they fear a decline in trade or a loss of international stature, but because they fear losing power domestically and need domestic and international support to secure their rule.

These findings have important implications not only for the study of civil war and political violence, but also for the study of international law. International law does not have a direct impact on government and rebel group behavior in civil war; statistically, ratifying an instrument of international humanitarian law does not make it any more likely that a government will abide by the provisions of that agreement. This is consistent with much of the recent research on international human rights law. Scholars have examined a variety of international human rights treaties, and have found little evidence that treaty ratification is associated with better human rights performance.[28] This does not, however, mean that international law has no impact. International law creates a framework of appropriate behavior, to which governments as well as rebel groups make reference in trying to build domestic and international support. This is most evident in the Indonesia and Libya case studies, where the rebel groups made frequent appeals to international audiences for support, drawing particular attention to the contrast between the government's abuse of civilians and their own respect for international standards of conduct. Similarly, the Indonesian and Turkish governments, anxious

---

[28] Hathaway 2002; Neumayer 2005; Hafner-Burton and Tsutsui 2007; Hafner-Burton, Tsutsui, and Meyer 2008; Vreeland 2008. Democracies may be an exception; Neumayer 2005 finds that ratification is associated with better human rights performance in democracies.

to secure backing from Western actors, asserted their commitment to abide by international human rights and humanitarian law in confronting domestic insurgencies; both governments signaled this commitment through changes in government policy and counterinsurgency strategy. Furthermore, the evidence presented here contributes to understanding of the conditions under which governments and rebel groups are likely to comply with international law. The prospect of positive rewards – in the form of domestic and international support – does appear to create incentives for government and rebel group compliance, but only when governments and rebel groups view increased support as necessary to the achievement of their political objectives. Even in times of war, having a set of institutions that defines appropriate conduct and rewards individuals for abiding by these standards of conduct can have an important impact on government and rebel group behavior.

References

Alexander, Yonah, Edgar H. Brenner, and Serhat Tutuncuoglu Krause. 2008. *Turkey: Terrorism, Civil Rights, and the European Union.* New York: Routledge.

Amnesty International. 1985. *East Timor Violations of Human Rights: Extrajudicial Executions, "Disappearances," Torture and Political Imprisonment.* London: Amnesty International Publications.

——— 1989–2011. *Amnesty International Annual Report.* London: Amnesty International Publications.

——— 1991a. "East Timor: After the Massacre." *Amnesty International Report.*

——— 1991b. "East Timor: Amnesty International Statement to the United Nations Special Committee on Decolonization, August 1991." *Amnesty International Report.*

——— 1991c. "East Timor: The Santa Cruz Massacre." *Amnesty International Report.*

——— 1991d. "Uganda: Human Rights Violations by the National Resistance Army." *Amnesty International Report.*

——— 1993a. "Indonesia: 'Shock Therapy': Restoring Order in Aceh 1989–1993." *Amnesty International Report.*

——— 1993b. "Turkey: Escalation of Human Rights Abuses against Kurdish Villagers." *Amnesty International Report.*

——— 1994. "Indonesia/East Timor: Fact and Fiction: Implementing the Recommendations of the UN Commission on Human Rights." *Amnesty International Report.*

——— 1999. "Uganda: Breaking the Circle: Protecting Human Rights in the Northern War Zone." *Amnesty International Report.*

——— 2003. "Indonesia: Protecting the Protectors: Human Rights Defenders and Humanitarian Workers in Nanggroe Aceh Darussalam." *Amnesty International Report.*

——— 2004a. "Indonesia: New Military Operations, Old Patterns of Human Rights Abuses in Aceh (Nanggroe Aceh Darussalam, NAD)," *Amnesty International Report.*

——— 2004b. "Sudan: At the Mercy of Killers – Destruction of Villages in Darfur." *Amnesty International Report.*

——— 2004c. "Sudan: Darfur – 'Too Many People Killed for No Reason.'" *Amnesty International Report.*

——— 2004d. "Uganda: Stop the Slaughter." *Amnesty International Issue Brief.*

2011a. "Libya: The Battle for Libya: Killings, Disappearances and Torture." *Amnesty International Report.*

2011b. "Libya: Misratah – Under Siege and Under Fire." *Amnesty International Report.*

Arjona, Ana. 2014. "Wartime Institutions: A Research Agenda." *Journal of Conflict Resolution* 58 (8): 1360–1389.

Asia Watch. 1992. *Political Control, Human Rights, and the UN Mission in Cambodia.* New York and Washington, DC: Asia Watch, a Division of Human Rights Watch.

Aspinall, Edward. 2002. "Sovereignty, the Successor State, and Universal Human Rights: History and the International Structuring of Acehnese Nationalism." *Indonesia* 73: 1–24.

2005. *Opposing Suharto: Compromise, Resistance, and Regime Change in Indonesia.* Stanford: Stanford University Press.

2006. "Violence and Identity Formation in Aceh under Indonesian Rule." In *Verandah of Violence: The Background to the Aceh Problem*, edited by Anthony Reid. Seattle: Singapore University Press in association with University of Washington Press.

2007a. "The Construction of Grievance: Natural Resources and Identity in a Separatist Conflict." *Journal of Conflict Resolution* 51 (6): 950–972.

2007b. "From Islamism to Nationalism in Aceh, Indonesia." *Nations and Nationalism* 13 (2): 245–263.

2008. "Place and Displacement in the Aceh Conflict." In *Conflict, Violence, and Displacement in Indonesia*, edited by Eva-Lotta E. Hedman. Ithaca: Cornell Southeast Asia Program Publications.

2009. *Islam and Nation: Separatist Rebellion in Aceh, Indonesia.* Stanford: Stanford University Press.

Aspinall, Edward, and Harold Crouch. 2003. *The Aceh Peace Process: Why It Failed.* Policy Studies 1. Washington, DC: East-West Center.

Atkinson, Ronald R. 2009. *From Uganda to the Congo and Beyond: Pursuing the Lord's Resistance Army.* New York: International Peace Institute.

Ayata, Bilgin, and Deniz Yükseker. 2005. "A Belated Awakening: National and International Responses to the Internal Displacement of Kurds in Turkey." *New Perspectives on Turkey* 32: 5–42.

Aydin, Aysegul, and Cem Emrence. 2015. *Zones of Rebellion: Kurdish Insurgents and the Turkish State.* Ithaca: Cornell University Press.

Azam, Jean-Paul. 2002. "Looting and Conflict between Ethnoregional Groups: Lessons for State Formation in Africa." *Journal of Conflict Resolution* 46 (1): 131–153.

2006. "On Thugs and Heroes: Why Warlords Victimize Their Own Civilians." *Economics of Governance* 7 (1): 53–73.

Azam, Jean-Paul, and Anke Hoeffler. 2002. "Violence against Civilians in Civil Wars: Looting or Terror?" *Journal of Peace Research* 39 (4): 461–485.

Badan Pusat Statistik – Statistics Indonesia. 2011. *Statistik Indonesia: Statistical Yearbook of Indonesia 2011.* Jakarta: BPS – Statistics Indonesia.

Baghdasarian, Gegham. 2005. "A Karabakh Armenian Perspective." In *The Limits of Leadership: Elites and Societies in the Nagorny Karabakh Peace Process*, edited by Laurence Broers. Accord 17. London: Conciliation Resources.

Balcells, Laia. 2010. "Rivalry and Revenge: Violence against Civilians in Conventional Civil Wars." *International Studies Quarterly* 54 (2): 291–313.

2011. "Continuation of Politics by Two Means: Direct and Indirect Violence in Civil War." *Journal of Conflict Resolution* 55 (3): 397–422.

Barkey, Henri J., and Graham E. Fuller. 1998. *Turkey's Kurdish Question*. Lanham: Rowman & Littlefield Publishers.

Barltrop, Richard. 2010. *Darfur and the International Community: The Challenges of Conflict Resolution in Sudan*. New York: I.B.Tauris & Co.

Barnett, Michael. 2003. *Eyewitness to a Genocide: The United Nations and Rwanda*. Ithaca: Cornell University Press.

Bass, Gary Jonathan. 2000. *Stay the Hand of Vengeance: The Politics of War Crimes Tribunals*. Princeton: Princeton University Press.

Behrend, Heike. 1999. *Alice Lakwena and the Holy Spirits: War in Northern Uganda, 1985–1997*. Athens: Ohio University Press.

Bellamy, Alex J., Paul D. Williams, and Stuart Griffin. 2010. *Understanding Peacekeeping, Second Edition*. Cambridge: Polity.

Berrebi, Claude, and Esteban F. Klor. 2006. "On Terrorism and Electoral Outcomes: Theory and Evidence from the Israeli-Palestinian Conflict." *Journal of Conflict Resolution* 50 (6): 899–925.

2008. "Are Voters Sensitive to Terrorism? Direct Evidence from the Israeli Electorate." *American Political Science Review* 102 (3): 279–301.

Best, Geoffrey. 1994. *War and Law Since 1945*. New York: Clarendon Press.

Bevan, James. 2007. "The Myth of Madness: Cold Rationality and 'Resource' Plunder by the Lord's Resistance Army." *Civil Wars* 9 (4): 343–358.

Blair, Graeme, Kosuke Imai, and Jason Lyall. 2014. "Comparing and Combining List and Endorsement Experiments: Evidence from Afghanistan." *American Journal of Political Science* 58 (4): 1043–1063.

Blandy, Charles W. 2003. "Military Aspects of the Two Russo–Chechen Conflicts in Recent Times." *Central Asian Survey* 22 (4): 421–432.

Blattman, Christopher and Jeannie Annan. 2010. "On the Nature and Causes of LRA Abduction: What the Abductees Say." In *The Lord's Resistance Army: Myth and Reality*, edited by Tim Allen and Koen Vlassenroot. London: Zed Books.

Bloom, Mia. 2005. *Dying to Kill: The Allure of Suicide Terror*. New York: Columbia University Press.

Bob, Clifford. 2005. *The Marketing of Rebellion: Insurgents, Media, and International Activism*. Cambridge: Cambridge University Press.

Bracamonte, José Angel Moroni, and David E. Spencer. 1995. *Strategy and Tactics of the Salvadoran FMLN Guerrillas: Last Battle of the Cold War, Blueprint for Future Conflicts*. Westport: Praeger Publishers.

Branch, Adam. 2005. "Neither Peace Nor Justice: Political Violence and the Peasantry in Northern Uganda, 1986–1998." *African Studies Quarterly* 8 (2): 1–31.

Broers, Laurence. 2005. "The Politics of Non-Recognition and Democratisation." In *The Limits of Leadership: Elites and Societies in the Nagorny Karabakh Peace Process*, edited by Laurence Broers. Accord 17. London: Conciliation Resources.

Bueno de Mesquita, Bruce, Alastair Smith, Randolph M. Siverson, and James D. Morrow. 2003. *The Logic of Political Survival*. Cambridge: The MIT Press.

Bueno de Mesquita, Bruce, James D. Morrow, Randolph M. Siverson, and Alastair Smith. 1999. "An Institutional Explanation of the Democratic Peace." *American Political Science Review* 93 (4): 791–807.

Burley, Anne-Marie. 1992. "Law among Liberal States: Liberal Internationalism and the Act of State Doctrine." *Columbia Law Review* 92 (8): 1907–1996.

Byrne, Hugh. 1996. *El Salvador's Civil War: A Study of Revolution*. Boulder: Lynne Rienner Publishers.

Carey, Sabine C., Michael P. Colaresi, and Neil J. Mitchell. 2015. "Governments, Informal Links to Militias, and Accountability." *Journal of Conflict Resolution* 59 (5): 850–876.

Cederman, Lars-Erik, and Kristian Skrede Gleditsch. 2009. "Introduction to Special Issue on 'Disaggregating Civil War.'" *Journal of Conflict Resolution* 53 (4): 487–495.

Çelik, Ayşa Betül. 2005. "Transnationalization of Human Rights Norms and Its Impact on Internally Displaced Kurds." *Human Rights Quarterly* 27 (3): 969–997.

Central Intelligence Agency Directorate of Intelligence. 1986. "El Salvador: A Net Assessment of the War, An Intelligence Assessment." Central Intelligence Agency Freedom of Information Act Electronic Reading Room. Available from www.cia.gov/library/readingroom/.

Central Intelligence Agency Director of Central Intelligence. 1989. "El Salvador: Government and Insurgent Prospects, Special National Intelligence Estimate." Central Intelligence Agency Freedom of Information Act Electronic Reading Room. Available from www.cia.gov/library/readingroom/.

Chandra, Siddharth, and Douglas Kammen. 2002. "Generating Reforms and Reforming Generations: Military Politics in Indonesia's Democratic Transition and Consolidation." *World Politics* 55 (1): 96–136.

Chayes, Abram, and Antonia Handler Chayes. 1993. "On Compliance." *International Organization* 47 (2): 175–205.

Chenoweth, Erica. 2010. "Democratic Competition and Terrorist Activity." *The Journal of Politics* 72 (1): 16–30.

Cohen, Dara Kay. 2013. "Explaining Rape during Civil War: Cross-National Evidence (1980–2009)." *American Political Science Review* 107 (3): 461–477.

Collins, Robert O. 2008. *A History of Modern Sudan*. Cambridge: Cambridge University Press.

Commission for Reception, Truth and Reconciliation in East Timor (CAVR). 2005. *Chega! The Report of the Commission for Reception, Truth and Reconciliation in Timor-Leste (CAVR)*. Dili.

Cornell, Svante E. 1999. *The Nagorno-Karabakh Conflict*. Report No. 46. Department of East European Studies, Uppsala University.

2001. "Democratization Falters in Azerbaijan." *Journal of Democracy* 12 (2): 118–131.

Council of Europe, Commissioner for Human Rights. 2009. Report by Thomas Hammarberg, Commissioner for Human Rights of the Council of Europe, following his visit to Turkey on 28 June–3 July 2009. Available from www.coe.int.

Crawford, Timothy W. 2006. "Moral Hazard, Intervention and Internal War: A Conceptual Analysis." In *Gambling on Humanitarian Intervention: Moral Hazard, Rebellion and Civil War*, edited by Timothy W. Crawford and Alan J. Kuperman. New York: Routledge.

Crenshaw, Martha. 1981. "The Causes of Terrorism." *Comparative Politics* 13 (4): 379–399.

ed. 1995. *Terrorism in Context*. University Park: The Pennsylvania State University Press.

Croissant, Michael P. 1998. *The Armenia-Azerbaijan Conflict: Causes and Implications*. Westport: Praeger Publishers.

Cunningham, David E., Kristian Skrede Gleditsch, and Idean Salehyan. 2009. "It Takes Two: A Dyadic Analysis of Civil War Duration and Outcome." *Journal of Conflict Resolution* 53 (4): 570–597.

Dai, Xinyuan. 2005. "Why Comply? The Domestic Constituency Mechanism." *International Organization* 59 (2): 363–398.

Daly, M. W. 2007. *Darfur's Sorrow: A History of Destruction and Genocide.* Cambridge: Cambridge University Press.

Davies, Matt. 2006. *Indonesia's War over Aceh: Last Stand on Mecca's Porch.* New York: Routledge.

de Waal, Alex. 2007. "Sudan: The Turbulent State." In *War in Darfur and the Search for Peace,* edited by Alex de Waal. Global Equality Initiative, Harvard University and Justice Africa.

de Waal, Thomas. 2003. *Black Garden: Armenia and Azerbaijan through Peace and War.* New York: NYU Press.

2010. "Remaking the Nagorno-Karabakh Peace Process." *Survival* 52 (4): 159–176.

Denber, Rachel, and Robert K. Goldman. 1992. *Bloodshed in the Caucasus: Escalation of the Armed Conflict in Nagorno Karabakh.* New York: Human Rights Watch/Helsinki.

DeRouen, Karl R., and David Sobek. 2004. "The Dynamics of Civil War Duration and Outcome." *Journal of Peace Research* 41 (3): 303–320.

Des Forges, Alison. 1999. *"Leave None to Tell the Story": Genocide in Rwanda.* New York: Human Rights Watch.

di Tiro, Hasan M. 1980. "The Legal Status of Acheh Sumatra under International Law," National Liberation Front Acheh-Sumatra. Available from asnlf.org.

1984. *The Price of Freedom: The Unfinished Diary of Tengku Hasan di Tiro.* Aceh: Ministry of Education and Information, National Liberation Front of Acheh Sumatra.

Doom, Ruddy and Koen Vlassenroot. 1999. "Kony's Message: A New Koine? The Lord's Resistance Army in Northern Uganda." *African Affairs* 98 (390): 5–36.

Downes, Alexander B. 2006. "Desperate Times, Desperate Measures: The Causes of Civilian Victimization in War." *International Security* 30 (4): 152–195.

2007. "Draining the Sea by Filling the Graves: Investigating the Effectiveness of Indiscriminate Violence as a Counterinsurgency Strategy." *Civil Wars* 9 (4): 420–444.

2008. *Targeting Civilians in War.* Ithaca: Cornell University Press.

Doyle, Michael W. 1986. "Liberalism and World Politics." *American Political Science Review* 80 (4): 1151–1169.

Doyle, Michael W., and Nicholas Sambanis. 2006. *Making War and Building Peace: United Nations Peace Operations.* Princeton: Princeton University Press.

Dunn, James. 1996. *Timor: A People Betrayed.* Sydney: ABC Books.

Eck, Kristine, and Lisa Hultman. 2007. "One-Sided Violence against Civilians in War: Insights from New Fatality Data." *Journal of Peace Research* 44 (2): 233–246.

Ergil, Dogu. 2000. "The Kurdish Question in Turkey." *Journal of Democracy* 11 (3): 122–135.

European Commission. 1997. *Agenda 2000: For a Stronger and Wider Union.* Bulletin of the European Union. Luxembourg: Office for Official Publications of the European Communities.

1998. "Regular Report from the Commission on Turkey's Progress towards Accession, 1998." European Commission of the European Union.

1999. "Regular Report from the Commission on Turkey's Progress towards Accession, 1999." European Commission of the European Union.

Fearon, James D. 2004. "Why Do Some Civil Wars Last So Much Longer than Others?" *Journal of Peace Research* 41 (3): 275–301.

Fearon, James D., and David D. Laitin. 2003. "Ethnicity, Insurgency, and Civil War." *American Political Science Review* 97 (1): 75–90.

Finnemore, Martha, and Kathryn Sikkink. 1998. "International Norm Dynamics and Political Change." *International Organization* 52 (4): 887–917.

Finnström, Sverker. 2006. "Wars of the Past and War in the Present: The Lord's Resistance Movement/Army in Uganda." *Africa: The Journal of the International African Institute* 76 (2): 200–220.

———. 2008. *Living with Bad Surroundings: War, History, and Everyday Moments in Northern Uganda*. Durham: Duke University Press.

Flint, Julie. 2007. "Darfur's Armed Movements." In *War in Darfur and the Search for Peace*. Global Equality Initiative, Harvard University and Justice Africa.

Flint, Julie, and Alex de Waal. 2008. *Darfur: A New History of a Long War*. 2nd ed. London: Zed Books.

Fortna, Virginia Page. 2008. *Does Peacekeeping Work? Shaping Belligerents' Choices after Civil War*. Princeton: Princeton University Press.

Fujii, Lee Ann. 2009. *Killing Neighbors: Webs of Violence in Rwanda*. Ithaca: Cornell University Press.

Gallab, Abdullahi A. 2008. *The First Islamist Republic: Development and Disintegration of Islamism in the Sudan*. Hampshire: Ashgate Publishing.

Gandhi, Jennifer. 2008. *Political Institutions under Dictatorship*. Cambridge: Cambridge University Press.

Gandhi, Jennifer, and Ellen Lust-Okar. 2009. "Elections under Authoritarianism." *Annual Review of Political Science* 12 (1): 403–422.

Gartner, Scott Sigmund, and Gary M. Segura. 1998. "War, Casualties, and Public Opinion." *Journal of Conflict Resolution* 42 (3): 278 –300.

Gates, Scott, and Håvard Strand. 2006. "Modeling the Duration of Civil Wars: Measurement and Estimation Issues." Working Paper. PRIO: Centre for the Study of Civil War.

Geddes, Barbara. 1999. "What Do We Know about Democratization after Twenty Years?" *Annual Review of Political Science* 2 (1): 115–144.

Gersony, Robert. 1997. "The Anguish of Northern Uganda: Results of a Field-Based Assessment of the Civil Conflicts in Northern Uganda." *Report submitted to the US Embassy and USAID Mission, Kampala*.

Gleditsch, Kristian Skrede. 2002. "Expanded Trade and GDP Data." *Journal of Conflict Resolution* 46 (5): 712–724.

Gleditsch, Kristian S., and Michael D. Ward. 2001. "Measuring Space: A Minimum-Distance Database and Applications to International Studies." *Journal of Peace Research* 38 (6): 739–758.

Gleditsch, Nils Petter, Peter Wallensteen, Mikael Eriksson, Margareta Sollenberg, and Håvard Strand. 2002. "Armed Conflict 1946–2001: A New Dataset." *Journal of Peace Research* 39 (5): 615–637.

Goodman, Ryan, and Derek Jinks. 2004. "How to Influence States: Socialization and International Human Rights Law." *Duke Law Journal* 54 (3): 621–703.

Greenhill, Kelly M. 2010. *Weapons of Mass Migration: Forced Displacement, Coercion, and Foreign Policy*. Ithaca: Cornell University Press.

Grewal, Sharanbir, and Erik Voeten. 2015. "Are New Democracies Better Human Rights Compliers?" *International Organization* 69 (2): 497–518.

Gunter, Michael M. 1997. *The Kurds and the Future of Turkey.* New York: Palgrave Macmillan.

1998. "Abdullah Öcalan: 'We Are Fighting Turks Everywhere.'" *Middle East Quarterly* 5 (2). Available from www.meforum.org/399/abdullah-ocalan-we-are-fighting-turks-everywhere.

Gutiérrez Sanín, Francisco, and Elisabeth Jean Wood. 2014. "Ideology in Civil War: Instrumental Adoption and Beyond." *Journal of Peace Research* 51 (2): 213–226.

Hafner-Burton, Emilie M. 2005. "Trading Human Rights: How Preferential Trade Agreements Influence Government Repression." *International Organization* 59 (3): 593–629.

2008. "Sticks and Stones: Naming and Shaming the Human Rights Enforcement Problem." *International Organization* 62 (4): 689–716.

Hafner-Burton, Emilie M., and Kiyoteru Tsutsui. 2005. "Human Rights in a Globalizing World: The Paradox of Empty Promises." *American Journal of Sociology* 110 (5): 1373–1411.

2007. "Justice Lost! The Failure of International Human Rights Law to Matter Where Needed Most." *Journal of Peace Research* 44 (4): 407–425.

Hafner-Burton, Emilie M., Kiyoteru Tsutsui, and John W. Meyer. 2008. "International Human Rights Law and the Politics of Legitimation: Repressive States and Human Rights Treaties." *International Sociology* 23 (1): 115–141.

Hagan, John, and Alberto Palloni. 2006. "Death in Darfur." *Science* 313 (5793): 1578.

Hajek, John. 2000. "Towards a Language History of East Timor." *Quaderni del Dipartimento di Linguistica – Università di Firenze* 10: 213–227.

Harff, Barbara. 2003. "No Lessons Learned from the Holocaust? Assessing Risks of Genocide and Political Mass Murder since 1955." *American Political Science Review* 97 (1): 57–73.

Hathaway, Oona A. 2002. "Do Human Rights Treaties Make a Difference." *Yale Law Journal* 111: 1935–2042.

2007. "Why Do Countries Commit to Human Rights Treaties?" *Journal of Conflict Resolution* 51 (4): 588–621.

Henckaerts, Jean-Marie, and Louise Doswald-Beck. 2005. *Customary International Humanitarian Law, Volume 1: Rules.* Cambridge: Cambridge University Press.

Hill, Helen M. 2002. *Stirrings of Nationalism in East Timor, Fretilin 1974–1978: The Origins, Ideologies and Strategies of a Nationalist Movement.* Sydney: Otford Press.

Hoffman, Bruce. 2006. *Inside Terrorism.* New York: Columbia University Press.

Hoover Green, Amelia. 2011. *Repertoires of Violence against Noncombatants: The Role of Armed Group Institutions and Ideologies.* Ph.D. Dissertation. Yale University.

Hovil, Lucy, and Eric Werker. 2005. "Portrait of a Failed Rebellion: An Account of Rational, Sub-Optimal Violence in Western Uganda." *Rationality and Society* 17 (1): 5–34.

Hovil, Lucy and Joanna R. Quinn. 2005. *Peace First, Justice Later: Traditional Justice in Northern Uganda.* Refugee Law Project Working Paper No. 17. Kampala: Refugee Law Project.

Huber, Konrad. 2004. *The HDC in Aceh: Promises and Pitfalls of NGO Mediation and Implementation.* Policy Studies 9. Washington, D.C.: East-West Center.

Hultman, Lisa. 2007. "Battle Losses and Rebel Violence: Raising the Costs for Fighting." *Terrorism and Political Violence* 19 (2): 205–222.

2009. "The Power to Hurt in Civil War: The Strategic Aim of RENAMO Violence." *Journal of Southern African Studies* 35 (4): 821–834.

2012. "Attacks on Civilians in Civil War: Targeting the Achilles Heel of Democratic Governments." *International Interactions* 38 (2): 164–181.

Human Rights and Peace Centre (HURIPEC). 2003. *The Hidden War: The Forgotten People, War in Acholiland and Its Ramifications for Peace and Security in Uganda.* Kampala: Human Rights and Peace Centre, Makerere University Faculty of Law and Liu Institute for Global Issues.

Human Rights Foundation of Turkey. 1995. *Turkey Human Rights Report 1994.* Ankara: Human Rights Foundation of Turkey.

Human Rights Watch. 1989–2012. *Human Rights Watch World Report.* New York: Human Rights Watch.

1990. "Indonesia: Human Rights Abuses in Aceh." *Human Rights Watch Report* 2 (16).

1991a. "East Timor: The November 12 Massacre and Its Aftermath." *Human Rights Watch Report* 3 (26).

1991b. "Indonesia: Continuing Human Rights Violations in Aceh." *Human Rights Watch Report* 3 (16).

1992. "Indonesia: Commission of Inquiry Needed for Aceh." *Human Rights Watch Report* 4 (5).

1999. "Turkey: Violations of Free Expression in Turkey." *Human Rights Watch Report.*

2001. "Indonesia: The War in Aceh." *Human Rights Watch Report* 13 (4).

2002a. "Displaced and Disregarded: Turkey's Failing Village Return Program." *Human Rights Watch Report* 14 (7).

2002b. "Questions and Answers: Freedom of Expression and Language Rights in Turkey." *Human Rights Watch Report.*

2003. "Aceh under Martial Law: Inside the Secret War." *Human Rights Watch Report* 15 (10).

2004a. "Darfur Destroyed: Ethnic Cleansing by Government and Militia Forces in Western Sudan." *Human Rights Watch Report* 16 (6).

2004b. "Darfur in Flames: Atrocities in Western Sudan." *Human Rights Watch Report* 16 (5).

2005. "Entrenching Impunity: Government Responsibility for International Crimes in Darfur." *Human Rights Watch Report* 17 (17).

2008. "'They Shot at Us as We Fled': Government Attacks on Civilians in West Darfur in February 2008." *Human Rights Watch Report.*

2009. "The Christmas Massacres: LRA Attacks on Civilians in Northern Congo." *Human Rights Watch Report.*

2010. "Trail of Death: LRA Atrocities in Northeastern Congo." *Human Rights Watch Report.*

2011. "Darfur in the Shadows: The Sudanese Government's Ongoing Attacks on Civilians and Human Rights." *Human Rights Watch Report.*

Human Rights Watch/Africa. 1994. *Civilian Devastation: Abuses by All Parties in the War in Southern Sudan.* New York: Human Rights Watch.

Human Rights Watch/Asia. 1994. *The Limits of Openness: Human Rights in Indonesia and East Timor.* New York: Human Rights Watch.

Human Rights Watch/Helsinki. 1994. *Azerbaijan: Seven Years of Conflict in Nagorno-Karabakh.* New York: Human Rights Watch.

Humphreys, Macartan, and Jeremy M. Weinstein. 2006. "Handling and Manhandling Civilians in Civil War." *American Political Science Review* 100 (3): 429–447.

Huxley, Tim. 2002. *Disintegrating Indonesia? Implications for Regional Security.* Adelphi Paper 349. New York: Oxford University Press for the International Institute for Strategic Studies.

Imset, Ismet G. 1995. "The PKK: Freedom Fighters or Terrorists?" *American Kurdish Information Network (AKIN).* Available from www.kurdistan.org/work/commentary/the-pkk-freedom-fighters-or-terrorists/.

International Criminal Court. 2007a. *Warrant of Arrest for Ahmad Harun.* The Hague. Available from www.icc-cpi.int.

2007b. *Warrant of Arrest for Ali Kushayb.* The Hague. Available from www.icc-cpi.int.

2009. *Warrant of Arrest for Omar Hassan Ahmad Al Bashir.* The Hague. Available from www.icc-cpi.int.

2010. *Second Warrant of Arrest for Omar Hassan Ahmad Al Bashir.* The Hague. Available from www.icc-cpi.int.

International Crisis Group. 2000a. "Aceh: Escalating Tension." *ICG Asia Briefing* 4.

2000b. "Indonesia: Keeping the Military under Control." *ICG Asia Report* 9.

2001a. "Aceh: Can Autonomy Stem the Conflict?" *ICG Asia Report* 18.

2001b. "Indonesia: Impunity Versus Accountability for Gross Human Rights Violations." *ICG Asia Report* 12.

2002a. "Dialogue or Destruction? Organising for Peace as the War in Sudan Escalates." *ICG Africa Report* 48.

2002b. "God, Oil and Country: Changing the Logic of War in Sudan." *ICG Africa Report* 39.

2003a. "Aceh: How Not to Win Hearts and Minds." *ICG Asia Briefing* 27.

2003b. "Sudan's Other Wars." *ICG Africa Briefing* 14.

2004a. "Darfur Rising: Sudan's New Crisis." *ICG Africa Report* 76.

2004b. "Northern Uganda: Understanding and Solving the Conflict." *ICG Africa Report* 77.

2005a. "Building a Comprehensive Peace Strategy for Northern Uganda." *ICG Africa Briefing* 27.

2005b. "Darfur: The Failure to Protect." *ICG Africa Report* 89.

2005c. "Nagorno-Karabakh: A Plan for Peace." *ICG Europe Report* 167.

2005d. "Nagorno-Karabakh: Viewing the Conflict from the Ground." *ICG Europe Report* 166.

2005e. "Shock Therapy for Northern Uganda's Peace Process." *ICG Africa Briefing* 23.

2005f. "Unifying Darfur's Rebels: A Prerequisite for Peace." *ICG Africa Briefing* 32.

2006a. "A Strategy for Ending Northern Uganda's Crisis." *ICG Africa Briefing* 35.

2006b. "Darfur's Fragile Peace Agreement." *ICG Africa Briefing* 39.

2007a. "Nagorno-Karabakh: Risking War." *ICG Europe Report* 187.

2007b. "Northern Uganda Peace Process: The Need to Maintain Momentum." *ICG Africa Briefing* 46.

2007c. "Northern Uganda: Seizing the Opportunity for Peace." *ICG Africa Report* 124.

2008. "Sudan's Comprehensive Peace Agreement: Beyond the Crisis." *ICG Africa Briefing* 50.

2009. "Sudan: Preventing Implosion." *ICG Africa Briefing* 68.

2011a. "Holding Libya Together: Security Challenges after Qadhafi." *ICG Middle East/North Africa Report* 115.

2011b. "Popular Protest in North Africa and the Middle East (V): Making Sense of Libya." *ICG Middle East/North Africa Report* 107.

2012. "Turkey's Kurdish Impasse: The View from Diyarbakir." *ICG Europe Report* 222.

International Foundation for Election Systems (IFES). 2002. "Final Report: National Public Opinion Survey 2002, Republic of Indonesia." International Foundation for Election Systems. Available from www.ifes.org.

2003. "National Public Opinion Survey 2003, Republic of Indonesia." International Foundation for Election Systems. Available from www.ifes.org.

The International Institute for Strategic Studies (IISS). 1989–2010. *The Military Balance*. London: The International Institute for Strategic Studies.

Jemadu, Aleksius. 2006. "Democratisation, the Indonesian Armed Forces and the Resolving of the Aceh Conflict." In *Verandah of Violence: The Background to the Aceh Problem*, edited by Anthony Reid. Seattle: Singapore University Press in association with University of Washington Press.

Jentleson, Bruce W., and Christopher A. Whytock. 2006. "Who 'Won' Libya? The Force-Diplomacy Debate and Its Implications for Theory and Policy." *International Security* 30 (3): 47–86.

Jo, Hyeran. 2015. *Compliant Rebels: Rebel Groups and International Law in World Politics*. New York: Cambridge University Press.

Jo, Hyeran, and Catarina P. Thomson. 2014. "Legitimacy and Compliance with International Law: Access to Detainees in Civil Conflicts, 1991–2006." *British Journal of Political Science* 44 (2): 323–355.

Johanson, Vanessa. 1999. "The Sultan Will Be Dr Hasan Tiro." *Inside Indonesia* (60): 10.

Jolliffe, Jill. 1978. *East Timor: Nationalism and Colonialism*. Brisbane: University of Queensland Press.

2009. *Balibo*. Melbourne: Scribe.

Jongerden, Joost. 2007. *The Settlement Issue in Turkey and the Kurds: An Analysis of Spatical Policies, Modernity and War*. Leiden, The Netherlands: Brill.

Jumbert, Maria Gabrielsen, and David Lanz. 2013. "Globalised Rebellion: The Darfur Insurgents and the World." *The Journal of Modern African Studies* 51 (2): 193–217.

Kalyvas, Stathis N. 1999. "Wanton and Senseless?: The Logic of Massacres in Algeria." *Rationality and Society* 11 (3): 243–285.

2001. "'New' and 'Old' Civil Wars: A Valid Distinction?" *World Politics* 54 (1): 99–118.

2004. "The Paradox of Terrorism in Civil War." *The Journal of Ethics* 8 (1): 97–138.

2006. *The Logic of Violence in Civil War*. Cambridge: Cambridge University Press.

2008. "Promises and Pitfalls of an Emerging Research Program: The Microdynamics of Civil War." In *Order, Conflict, and Violence*, edited by Stathis N. Kalyvas, Ian Shapiro, and Tarek Masoud. Cambridge: Cambridge University Press.

Kalyvas, Stathis N., and Laia Balcells. 2010. "International System and Technologies of Rebellion: How the End of the Cold War Shaped Internal Conflict." *American Political Science Review* 104 (3): 415–429.

Kalyvas, Stathis N., and Matthew Adam Kocher. 2007. "How 'Free' Is Free Riding in Civil Wars? Violence, Insurgency, and the Collective Action Problem." *World Politics* 59 (2): 177–216.

Kamrava, Mehran. 2001. "State-Building in Azerbaijan: The Search for Consolidation." *Middle East Journal* 55 (2): 216–236.

Kant, Immanuel. 2003. *To Perpetual Peace: A Philosophical Sketch.* Translated by Ted Humphrey. Indianapolis: Hackett Publishing.

Keck, Margaret E., and Kathryn Sikkink. 1998. *Activists beyond Borders: Advocacy Networks in International Politics.* Ithaca: Cornell University Press.

Keith, Linda Camp, C. Neal Tate, and Steven C. Poe. 2009. "Is The Law a Mere Parchment Barrier to Human Rights Abuse?" *The Journal of Politics* 71 (2): 644–660.

Kennedy, Kerry. 2000. *Speak Truth to Power: Human Rights Defenders Who Are Changing Our World.* Edited by Nan Richardson. New York: Umbrage Editions.

Kiernan, Ben. 2003. "The Demography of Genocide in Southeast Asia: The Death Tolls in Cambodia, 1975–79, and East Timor, 1975–80." *Critical Asian Studies* 35 (4): 585–597.

King, Gary, Michael Tomz, and Jason Wittenberg. 2000. "Making the Most of Statistical Analyses: Improving Interpretation and Presentation." *American Journal of Political Science* 44 (2): 347–361.

Kingsbury, Damien. 2003. *Power Politics and the Indonesian Military.* New York: RoutledgeCurzon.

Kirişci, Kemal, and Gareth M. Winrow. 1997. *The Kurdish Question and Turkey: An Example of a Trans-State Ethnic Conflict.* Portland: Frank Cass.

Kocher, Matthew. 2002. "The Decline of PKK and the Viability of a One-state Solution in Turkey." *International Journal on Multicultural Studies* 4 (1): 128–147.

Koh, Harold Hongju. 1997. "Why Do Nations Obey International Law?" *Yale Law Journal* 106 (8): 2599–2659.

   1998. "The 1998 Frankel Lecture: Bringing International Law Home." *Houston Law Review* 35: 623–681.

KPP HAM. 2000. *Full Report of the Investigative Commission into Human Rights Violations in East Timor.* Jakarta: KPP HAM. Reprinted in *Masters of Terror: Indonesia's Military and Violence in East Timor*, edited by Richard Tanter, Desmond Ball, and Gerry van Klinken. New York: Rowman & Littlefield Publishers, 2006.

Krueger, Alan B., and David D. Laitin. 2008. "Kto Kogo?: A Cross-Country Study of the Origins and Targets of Terrorism." In *Terrorism, Economic Development, and Political Openness*, edited by Philip Keefer and Norman Loayza, 148–173. Cambridge: Cambridge University Press.

Kuperman, Alan J. 2006. "Suicidal Rebellions and the Moral Hazard of Humanitarian Intervention." In *Gambling on Humanitarian Intervention: Moral Hazard, Rebellion and Civil War*, edited by Timothy W. Crawford and Alan J. Kuperman. New York: Routledge.

Kurban, Dilek. 2007. "Human Rights Watch, Kurdish Human Rights Project, and the European Court of Human Rights on Internal Displacement in Turkey." In *Coming to Terms with Forced Migration: Post-Displacement Restitution of Citizenship Rights in Turkey*, 119–144. Istanbul: Turkish Economic and Social Studies Foundation (TESEV) Publications.

   2012. *Reparations and Displacement in Turkey: Lessons Learned from the Compensation Law.* Case Studies on Transitional Justice and Displacement. International Center for Transitional Justice (ICTJ) and the Brookings-LSE Project on Internal Displacement.

Kurban, Dilek, Ozan Erözden, and Haldun Gülalp. 2008. *Supranational Rights Litigation, Implementation and the Domestic Impact of Strasbourg Court Jurisprudence: A Case Study of Turkey*. Case Study Report. JURISTRAS.

Kydd, Andrew H., and Barbara F. Walter. 2006. "The Strategies of Terrorism." *International Security* 31 (1): 49–80.

Lacina, Bethany, and Nils Petter Gleditsch. 2005. "Monitoring Trends in Global Combat: A New Dataset of Battle Deaths." *European Journal of Population* 21 (2): 145–166.

Lamwaka, Caroline. 2002. "The Peace Process in Northern Uganda 1986–1990." In *Protracted Conflict, Elusive Peace: Initiatives to End the Violence in Northern Uganda*, edited by Okello Lucima. Conciliation Resources, Accord Programme.

Lawrence, T.E. 1929. "Science of Guerrilla Warfare." *The Encyclopædia Britannica*. New York: Encyclopædia Britannica.

Leeds, Brett Ashley, Jeffrey M. Ritter, Sara McLaughlin Mitchell, and Andrew G. Long. 2002. "Alliance Treaty Obligations and Provisions, 1815–1944." *International Interactions* 28 (3): 237–260.

LeMoyne, James. 1989. "El Salvador's Forgotten War." *Foreign Affairs* 68 (3): 105.

Li, Quan. 2005. "Does Democracy Promote or Reduce Transnational Terrorist Incidents?" *Journal of Conflict Resolution* 49 (2): 278–297.

Liddle, R. William. 1996. "Indonesia: Suharto's Tightening Grip." *Journal of Democracy* 7 (4): 58–72.

Lijphart, Arend. 2007. *Thinking about Democracy: Power Sharing and Majority Rule in Theory and Practice*. New York: Routledge.

Lomo, Zachary, and Lucy Hovil. 2004. "Behind the Violence: Causes, Consequences and the Search for Solutions to the War in Northern Uganda." *Refugee Law Project Working Paper* 11. Kampala, Uganda: Refugee Law Project.

Lupu, Yonatan. 2013. "Best Evidence: The Role of Information in Domestic Judicial Enforcement of International Human Rights Agreements." *International Organization* 67 (3): 469–503.

Lyall, Jason. 2009. "Does Indiscriminate Violence Incite Insurgent Attacks? Evidence from Chechnya." *Journal of Conflict Resolution* 53 (3): 331–362.

———. 2010. "Are Coethnics More Effective Counterinsurgents? Evidence from the Second Chechen War." *American Political Science Review* 104 (1): 1–20.

Lyall, Jason, Graeme Blair, and Kosuke Imai. 2013. "Explaining Support for Combatants during Wartime: A Survey Experiment in Afghanistan." *American Political Science Review* 107 (4): 679–705.

Malone, Margaret Mary. 2004. *Regulation of Lobbyists in Developed Countries: Current Rules and Practices*. Dublin: Institute of Public Administration, National University of Ireland.

Mamdani, Mahmood. 1984. *Imperialism and Fascism in Uganda*. Africa World Press.

———. 2001. *When Victims Become Killers: Colonialism, Nativism, and the Genocide in Rwanda*. Princeton: Princeton University Press.

Mampilly, Zachariah Cherian. 2011. *Rebel Rulers: Insurgent Governance and Civilian Life during War*. Ithaca: Cornell University Press.

Manekin, Devorah. 2013. "Violence Against Civilians in the Second Intifada: The Moderating Effect of Armed Group Structure on Opportunistic Violence." *Comparative Political Studies* 46 (10): 1273–1300.

Mansfield, Edward D., and Jack Snyder. 1995. "Democratization and the Danger of War." *International Security* 20 (1): 5–38.

2005. *Electing to Fight: Why Emerging Democracies Go to War*. Cambridge: The MIT Press.

Mansfield, Edward D., and Jon C. Pevehouse. 2006. "Democratization and International Organizations." *International Organization* 60 (1): 137–167.

Manwaring, Max G., and Court Prisk, eds. 1988. *El Salvador at War: An Oral History of Conflict from the 1979 Insurrection to the Present*. Washington, D.C.: National Defense University Press.

Mao, Zedong. 1961. *On Guerrilla Warfare*. Translated by Samuel B Griffith. New York: Praeger Publishers.

Marcus, Aliza. 2007. *Blood and Belief: The PKK and the Kurdish Fight for Independence*. New York: NYU Press.

Marshall, Monty G., and Donna Ramsey Marshall. 2014. "Coup D'Etat Events, 1946–2013: Codebook." Center for Systemic Peace. Available from www.system icpeace.org.

Marshall, Monty G., and Keith Jaggers. 2009. "Polity IV Project: Political Regime Characteristics and Transitions, 1800–2007." Center for Systemic Peace.

Mathews, Jessica T. 1997. "Power Shift." *Foreign Affairs* 76 (1): 50–66.

McClintock, Cynthia. 1998. *Revolutionary Movements in Latin America: El Salvador's FMLN and Peru's Shining Path*. Washington, D.C.: United States Institute of Peace Press.

Melander, Erik. 2001. "The Nagorno-Karabakh Conflict Revisited: Was the War Inevitable?" *Journal of Cold War Studies* 3 (2): 48–75.

Merom, Gil. 2003. *How Democracies Lose Small Wars: State, Society, and the Failures of France in Algeria, Israel in Lebanon, and the United States in Vietnam*. Cambridge: Cambridge University Press.

Mietzner, Marcus. 2006. *The Politics of Military Reform in Post-Suharto Indonesia: Elite Conflict, Nationalism, and Institutional Resistance*. Policy Studies 23. Washington, D.C.: East-West Center.

2009a. *Military Politics, Islam, and the State in Indonesia: From Turbulent Transition to Democratic Consolidation*. Singapore: Institute of Southeast Asian Studies.

2009b. "Political Opinion Polling in Post-Authoritarian Indonesia: Catalyst or Obstacle to Democratic Consolidation?" *Journal of the Humanities and Social Sciences of Southeast Asia and Oceania* 165 (1): 95–126.

Miller, Michelle Ann. 2006. "What's So Special About Special Autonomy in Aceh?" In *Verandah of Violence: The Background to the Aceh Problem*, edited by Anthony Reid. Seattle: Singapore University Press in association with University of Washington Press.

Minorities at Risk Project. 2007. *Minorities at Risk (MAR) Codebook Version 2/2009*. College Park: Center for International Development and Conflict Management.

Mitchell, Neil J., Sabine C. Carey, and Christopher K. Butler. 2014. "The Impact of Pro-Government Militias on Human Rights Violations." *International Interactions* 40 (5): 812–836.

Moravcsik, Andrew. 2000. "The Origins of Human Rights Regimes: Democratic Delegation in Postwar Europe." *International Organization* 54 (2): 217–252.

Morgan, T. Clifton, Navin Bapat, and Valentin Krustev. 2009. "The Threat and Imposition of Economic Sanctions, 1971–2000." *Conflict Management and Peace Science* 26 (1): 92–110.

Morrow, James D. 2007. "When Do States Follow the Laws of War?" *American Political Science Review* 101 (3): 559–572.

2014. *Order within Anarchy: The Laws of War as an International Institution.* New York: Cambridge University Press.

Morrow, James D., and Hyeran Jo. 2006. "Compliance with the Laws of War: Dataset and Coding Rules." *Conflict Management and Peace Science* 23 (1): 91–113.

Mueller, John. 1973. *War, Presidents and Public Opinion.* New York: John Wiley & Sons Inc.

2005. "The Iraq Syndrome." *Foreign Affairs* 84 (6): 44–54.

Murphy, Ann Marie. 2010. "U.S. Rapprochement with Indonesia: From Problem State to Partner." *Contemporary Southeast Asia* 32 (3): 362–387.

Natsios, Andrew S. 2012. *Sudan, South Sudan, and Darfur: What Everyone Needs to Know.* New York: Oxford University Press.

Nessen, William. 2006. "Sentiments Made Visible: The Rise and Reason of Aceh's National Liberation Movement." In *Verandah of Violence: Background to the Aceh Problem,* edited by Anthony Reid. Seattle: Singapore University Press in association with University of Washington Press.

Neumayer, Eric. 2005. "Do International Human Rights Treaties Improve Respect for Human Rights?" *Journal of Conflict Resolution* 49 (6): 925–953.

Nicol, Bill. 2002. *Timor: A Nation Reborn.* Jakarta: Equinox Publishing.

Niner, Sarah. 2001. "A Long Journey of Resistance: The Origins and Struggle of CNRT." In *Bitter Flowers, Sweet Flowers: East Timor, Indonesia, and the World Community,* edited by Richard Tanter, Mark Selden, and Stephen R. Shalom. New York: Rowman & Littlefield.

OECD. 2009. *Lobbyists, Governments and Public Trust, Volume 1.* OECD Publishing. Available from www.oecd.org.

2012. *Lobbyists, Governments and Public Trust, Volume 2.* OECD Publishing. Available from www.oecd.org.

O'Kadameri, Billie. 2002. "LRA and Government Negotiations, 1993–1994." In *Protracted Conflict, Elusive Peace: Initiatives to End the Violence in Northern Uganda.* London: Conciliation Resources, Accord Program.

Oneal, John, and Bruce Russett. 2001. *Triangulating Peace: Democracy, Interdependence, and International Organizations.* New York: W. W. Norton & Company.

O'Sullivan, Meghan L. 2003. *Shrewd Sanctions: Statecraft and State Sponsors of Terrorism.* Washington, D.C.: Brookings Institution Press.

Panico, Christopher. 1995. "Turkey's Kurdish Conflict." *Jane's Intelligence Review* 7 (4).

Pape, Robert A. 1996. *Bombing to Win: Air Power and Coercion in War.* Ithaca: Cornell University Press.

2003. "The Strategic Logic of Suicide Terrorism." *American Political Science Review* 97 (3): 343–361.

Parliamentary Assembly of the Council of Europe. 1998. *Humanitarian Situation of the Kurdish Refugees and Displaced Persons in South-East Turkey and North Iraq.* Report of the Committee on Migration, Refugees and Demography, 3 June, Doc. 8131.

Paul, Rachel Anderson. 2000. "Grassroots Mobilization and Diaspora Politics: Armenian Interest Groups and the Role of Collective Memory." *Nationalism and Ethnic Politics* 6 (1): 24–47.

Peceny, Mark, and William D. Stanley. 2010. "Counterinsurgency in El Salvador." *Politics & Society* 38 (1): 67–94.

Pham, Phuong, Patrick Vinck, and Eric Stover. 2008. "The Lord's Resistance Army and Forced Conscription in Northern Uganda." *Human Rights Quarterly* 30: 404–411.

Pinto, Constâncio, and Matthew Jardine. 1997. *Inside the East Timor Resistance.* Toronto: James Lorimer & Company.

Powell, Emilia Justyna, and Jeffrey K. Staton. 2009. "Domestic Judicial Institutions and Human Rights Treaty Violation." *International Studies Quarterly* 53 (1): 149–174.

Powell, Jonathan M., and Clayton L. Thyne. 2011. "Global Instances of Coups from 1950 to 2010: A New Dataset." *Journal of Peace Research* 48 (2): 249–259.

Power, Samantha. 2002. *A Problem from Hell: America and the Age of Genocide.* New York: Harper Perennial.

Prisk, Courtney E. 1991. *The Comandante Speaks: Memoirs of an El Salvadoran Guerrilla Leader.* Boulder: Westview Press.

Prunier, Gérard. 1995. *The Rwanda Crisis: History of a Genocide.* New York: Columbia University Press.

2004. "Rebel Movements and Proxy Warfare: Uganda, Sudan and the Congo (1986–99)." *African Affairs* 103 (412): 359–383.

2005. *Darfur: The Ambiguous Genocide.* Ithaca: Cornell University Press.

Ramos-Horta, José. 1987. *Funu: The Unfinished Saga of East Timor.* The Red Sea Press.

Reeves, Eric. 2006. "Quantifying Genocide in Darfur." Available from www.sudanreeves.org.

Regan, Patrick M., Richard W. Frank, and Aysegul Aydin. 2009. "Diplomatic Interventions and Civil War: A New Dataset." *Journal of Peace Research* 46 (1): 135–146.

Reid, Anthony. 2004. "War, Peace and the Burden of History in Aceh." *Asian Ethnicity* 5 (3): 301–314.

Reiter, Dan, and Allan C. Stam. 2002. *Democracies at War.* Princeton: Princeton University Press.

Risse, Thomas, and Kathryn Sikkink. 1999. "The Socialization of International Human Rights Norms into Domestic Practices: Introduction." In *The Power of Human Rights: International Norms and Domestic Change,* edited by Thomas Risse, Stephen C. Ropp, and Kathryn Sikkink, 1–38. New York: Cambridge University Press.

Risse, Thomas, Stephen C. Ropp, and Kathryn Sikkink, eds. 2013. *The Persistent Power of Human Rights: From Commitment to Compliance.* Cambridge: Cambridge University Press.

Robertson, Geoffrey. 1999. *Crimes Against Humanity: The Struggle for Global Justice.* New York: Allen Lane, The Penguin Press.

Robinson, Geoffrey. 1998. "*Rawan* Is as *Rawan* Does: The Origins of Disorder in New Order Aceh." *Indonesia* 66: 127–156.

Rowland, Richard. 2008. "Population Trends in a Contested Pseudo-State: The Case of Nagorno-Karabakh." *Eurasian Geography and Economics* 49 (1): 99–111.

Rummel, R.J. 1994. *Death by Government.* New Brunswick: Transaction Publishers.

1997. *Power Kills: Democracy as a Method of Nonviolence.* New Brunswick: Transaction Publishers.

Russett, Bruce. 1994. *Grasping the Democratic Peace: Principles for a Post-Cold War World.* Princeton: Princeton University Press.

Saideman, Stephen M. 2001. *The Ties That Divide: Ethnic Politics, Foreign Policy, and International Conflict.* New York: Columbia University Press.

Salehyan, Idean, David Siroky, and Reed M. Wood. 2014. "External Rebel Sponsorship and Civilian Abuse: A Principal-Agent Analysis of Wartime Atrocities." *International Organization* 68 (3): 633–661.

Samayoa, Salvador, and Terry Karl. 1989. "Negotiations or Total War." *World Policy Journal* 6 (2): 321–355.

Sayari, Sabri. 2010. "Political Violence and Terrorism in Turkey, 1976–80: A Retrospective Analysis." *Terrorism and Political Violence* 22 (2): 198–215.

Schulze, Kirsten E. 2003. "The Struggle for an Independent Aceh: The Ideology, Capacity, and Strategy of GAM." *Studies in Conflict & Terrorism* 26 (4): 241–271.

——— 2004. *The Free Aceh Movement (GAM): Anatomy of a Separatist Organization.* Policy Studies 2. Washington, D.C.: East-West Center.

——— 2006. "Insurgency and Counter-Insurgency: Strategy and the Aceh Conflict, October 1976–May 2004." In *Verandah of Violence: The Background to the Aceh Problem,* edited by Anthony Reid. Seattle: Singapore University Press in association with University of Washington Press.

Senol, Mesut. 1998. "Latest Developments Regarding Human Rights in Turkey." *Perceptions: Journal of International Affairs (Center for Strategic Research, Republic of Turkey, Ministry of Foreign Affairs)* 3 (4).

Shah, Saubhagya. 2008. *Civil Society in Uncivil Places: Soft State and Regime Change in Nepal.* Policy Studies 48. Washington, D.C.: East-West Center.

Sikkink, Kathryn. 2011. *The Justice Cascade: How Human Rights Prosecutions Are Changing World Politics.* New York: W. W. Norton & Company.

Silva, Romesh, and Patrick Ball. 2006. "The Profile of Human Rights Violations in Timor-Leste, 1974–1999: A Report by the Benetech Human Rights Data Analysis Group to the Commission on Reception, Truth and Reconciliation of Timor-Leste." The Benetech Initiative.

Simmons, Beth A. 2000. "International Law and State Behavior: Commitment and Compliance in International Monetary Affairs." *American Political Science Review* 94 (4): 819–835.

——— 2009. *Mobilizing for Human Rights: International Law in Domestic Politics.* Cambridge: Cambridge University Press.

Slaughter, Anne-Marie. 1995. "International Law in a World of Liberal States." *European Journal of International Law* 6 (1): 503–538.

Slaughter, Anne-Marie, and William Burke-White. 2006. "The Future of International Law Is Domestic (or, the European Way of Law)." *Harvard International Law Journal* 47 (2): 327–352.

Smith, Anthony L. 2003. "A Glass Half Full: Indonesia–U.S. Relations in the Age of Terror." *Contemporary Southeast Asia* 25 (3): 449–472.

Smith, Sebastian. 1998. *Allah's Mountains: The Battle for Chechnya.* New York: I. B. Tauris Publishers.

Snyder, Jack L. 2000. *From Voting to Violence: Democratization and Nationalist Conflict.* New York: W. W. Norton & Company.

Stanton, Jessica A. 2013. "Terrorism in the Context of Civil War." *The Journal of Politics* 75 (4): 1009–1022.

——— 2015. "Regulating Militias: Governments, Militias, and Civilian Targeting in Civil War." *Journal of Conflict Resolution* 59 (5): 899–923.

Staveteig, Sarah. 2007. "How Many Persons in East Timor Went 'Missing' during the Indonesian Occupation?: Results from Indirect Estimates." *Interim Report* IR-07-003. Laxenburg, Austria: International Institute for Applied Systems Analysis.

Steele, Abbey. 2009. "Seeking Safety: Avoiding Displacement and Choosing Destinations in Civil Wars." *Journal of Peace Research* 46 (3): 419–429.

2011. "Electing Displacement: Political Cleansing in Apartadó, Colombia." *Journal of Conflict Resolution* 55 (3): 423–445.

Stockholm International Peace Research Institute (SIPRI). 1989–2010. *SIPRI Yearbook: Armaments, Disarmament and International Security.* New York: Oxford University Press.

Straus, Scott. 2005. "Darfur and the Genocide Debate." *Foreign Affairs* 84 (1): 123–133.

2006. *The Order of Genocide: Race, Power, and War in Rwanda.* Ithaca: Cornell University Press.

2012. "Retreating from the Brink: Theorizing Mass Violence and the Dynamics of Restraint." *Perspectives on Politics* 10 (2): 343–362.

Sukma, Rizal. 2001. "The Acehnese Rebellion: Secessionist Movement in Post-Suharto Indonesia." In *Non-Traditional Security Issues in Southeast Asia,* edited by Andrew T.H. Tan and J.D. Kenneth Boutin. Singapore: Select Publishing for Institute of Defence and Strategic Studies.

2004. *Security Operations in Aceh: Goals, Consequences, and Lessons.* Policy Studies 3. Washington, D.C.: East-West Center.

Sulaiman, M. Isa. 2006. "From Autonomy to Periphery: A Critical Evaluation of the Acehnese Nationalist Movement." In *Verandah of Violence: The Background to the Aceh Problem,* edited by Anthony Reid. Seattle: Singapore University Press in association with University of Washington Press.

Svensson, Isak. 2007. "Bargaining, Bias and Peace Brokers: How Rebels Commit to Peace." *Journal of Peace Research* 44 (2): 177–194.

Takeyh, Ray. 2001. "The Rogue Who Came in from the Cold." *Foreign Affairs* 80 (3): 62–72.

Tanner, Victor, and Jerome Tubiana. 2007. *Divided They Fall: The Fragmentation of Darfur's Rebel Groups.* Geneva: Small Arms Survey, Graduate Institute of International Studies.

Taylor, John G. 1999a. "East Timor: Forced Resettlement." *Forced Migration Review* (5): 31–33.

1999b. *East Timor: The Price Of Freedom.* New York: Zed Books.

Tchilingirian, Hratch. 1999. "Nagorno Karabagh: Transition and the Elite." *Central Asian Survey* 18 (4): 435–461.

Teimourian, Hazhir. 1993. "The Challenge of the Kurdistan Workers' Party." *Jane's Intelligence Review* 5 (1).

Teitel, Ruti G. 2011. *Humanity's Law.* Oxford: Oxford University Press.

Toft, Monica Duffy. 2009. *Securing the Peace: The Durable Settlement of Civil Wars.* Princeton: Princeton University Press.

Tubiana, Jérôme. 2007. "Darfur: A War for Land?" In *War in Darfur and the Search for Peace,* edited by Alex de Waal. Global Equality Initiative, Harvard University and Justice Africa.

Turkish Parliament. 1998. *Doğu Ve Güneydoğu Anadolu'da Boşaltılan Yerleşim Birimleri Nedeniyle Göç Eden Yurttaşlarımızın Sorunlarının Araştırılarak Alınması Gereken Tedbirlerin Tespit Edilmesi Amacıyla Kurulan Meclis Araştırma Komisyonu Raporu.* Available from www.tbmm.gov.tr/sirasayi/donem20/yil01/ss532.pdf.

UN Commission on Human Rights. 1992. 48th Session, Report of the Special Rapporteur Mr. P. Kooiimans, pursuant to Commission on Human Rights resolution 1991/38, Addendum, Visit by the Special Rapporteur to Indonesia and East Timor (E/CN.4/1992/17/Add.1).

1993a. 49th Session, Implementation of the Declaration on the Elimination of All Forms of Intolerance and of Discrimination Based on Religion or Belief: Report Submitted by Mr. Angelo Vidal d'Almeida Ribeiro, Special Rapporteur Appointed in Accordance with Commission on Human Rights Resolution 1986/20 of 10 March 1986 (E/CN.4/1993/62).

1993b. 49th Session, Summary Record of the 52nd Meeting, Second Part, held 3 March 1993 (E/CN.4/1993/SR.52/Add.1).

1994a. 50th Session, Situation of Human Rights in the Sudan: Report of the Special Rapporteur (E/CN.4/1994/48).

1994b. 51st Session, Report by the Special Rapporteur, Mr. Bacre Waly Ndiaye, on his mission to Indonesia and East Timor from 3 to 13 July 1994 (E/CN.4/1995/61/Add.1).

1995. 51st Session, Situation of Human Rights in the Sudan: Report of the Special Rapporteur (E/CN.4/1995/58).

1996. 52nd Session, Situation of Human Rights in the Sudan: Report of the Special Rapporteur (E/CN.4/1996/62).

2002. 59th Session, Report of the Representative of the Secretary-General on Internally Displaced Persons, Mr. Francis Deng, submitted pursuant to Commission on Human Rights Resolution 2002/56, Addendum, Profiles in Displacement: Turkey (E/CN.4/2003/86/Add.2).

UN Commission on Human Rights, Sub-Commission on Prevention of Discrimination and Protection of Minorities. 1992. 44th Session, Summary Record of the 23rd Meeting, Second Part, held 19 August 1992 (EN/CN.4/Sub.2/1992/SR.23/Add.1).

1993. 45th Session, Summary Record of the 13th Meeting, held 11 August 1993 (EN/CN.4/Sub.2/1993/SR.13).

1994. 46th Session, Summary Record of the 15th Meeting, held 11 August 1994 (EN/CN.4/Sub.2/1994/SR.15).

UN General Assembly. 1993. 48th Session, Situation of Human Rights in the Sudan (A/48/601).

1994. 49th Session, Situation of Human Rights in the Sudan (A/49/539).

1995. 50th Session, Situation of Human Rights in the Sudan (A/50/569).

1999. 54th Session, Situation of Human Rights in East Timor (A/54/660).

UN Human Rights Council. 2011. 17th Session, Report of the High Commissioner under Human Rights Council Resolution S-15/1 (A/HRC/17/45).

2012. 19th Session, Report of the International Commission of Inquiry on Libya (A/HRC/19/68).

United Nations. 2005. *Report of the International Commission of Inquiry on Darfur to the United Nations Secretary-General*. Geneva.

UN Office for the Coordination of Humanitarian Affairs (OCHA). 2005. *Consolidated Appeal for Uganda 2005, Mid-Year Review*. New York: UN Office for the Coordination of Humanitarian Affairs.

Unrepresented Nations and Peoples Organization. 1997. *Unrepresented Nations and Peoples Organization: Yearbook 1996*. The Hague: Kluwer Law International.

U.S. Committee on Refugees. 1999. *The Wall of Denial: Internal Displacement in Turkey*. Washington, D.C.: U.S. Committee for Refugees.

U.S. Department of State. 1992. Report on El Salvador Required under the Foreign Assistance Appropriations Act of 1991. United States Declassified Documents. Available from http://foia.state.gov.

U.S. Department of State, the Bureau of Democracy, Human Rights, and Labor and the Bureau of Intelligence and Research. 2004. *Documenting Atrocities in Darfur.* State Publication 11182. Washington, D.C.: U.S. Department of State.

U.S. Embassy in Jakarta. 2008a. "Telegram 14397 from U.S. Embassy Jakarta to State Department, Subject: [Deleted] Views on East Timor Developments, September 9, 1983." In *Suharto: A Declassified Documentary Orbit,* edited by Brad Simpson. National Security Archive Electronic Briefing Book No. 242. Washington, D.C. Available from www2.gwu.edu/~nsarchiv/NSAEBB/NSAEBB242/index.htm.

2008b. "Telegram 15303 from U.S. Embassy Jakarta to State Department, Subject: Current Developments in East Timor, September 23, 1983." In *Suharto: A Declassified Documentary Orbit,* edited by Brad Simpson. National Security Archive Electronic Briefing Book No. 242. Washington, D.C. Available from www2.gwu.edu/~nsarchiv/NSAEBB/NSAEBB242/index.htm.

U.S. Embassy in San Salvador. 1986. "Text of Telegram from U.S. Embassy in San Salvador to the U.S. Secretary of State regarding Guerrilla Finances – 'Where Does the Money Come From?'" U.S. Department of State, Freedom of Information Act Virtual Reading Room. Available from http://foia.state.gov.

1988a. "Telegram from U.S. Embassy in San Salvador to U.S. Secretary of State regarding FMLN Captured Documents – 'Discredit the Electoral Farce.'" U.S. Department of State, Freedom of Information Act Virtual Reading Room. Available from http://foia.state.gov.

1988b. "Text of Telegram from the U.S. Embassy in San Salvador to the U.S. Secretary of State." U.S. Department of State, Freedom of Information Act Virtual Reading Room. Available from http://foia.state.gov.

U.S. Secretary of State. 1988. "Telegram from U.S. Secretary of State, Washington, DC, to all OECD Capitals regarding FMLN Captured Documents: 'Political Work Needed to Foment General Insurrection.'" U.S. Department of State, Freedom of Information Act Virtual Reading Room. Available from http://foia.state.gov.

Valentino, Benjamin A. 2000. "Final Solutions: The Causes of Mass Killing and Genocide." *Security Studies* 9 (3): 1–59.

2004. *Final Solutions: Mass Killing and Genocide in the Twentieth Century.* Ithaca: Cornell University Press.

Valentino, Benjamin A., Paul Huth, and Dylan Balch-Lindsay. 2004. "'Draining the Sea': Mass Killing and Guerrilla Warfare." *International Organization* 58 (2): 375–407.

Valentino, Benjamin A., Paul K. Huth, and Sarah Croco. 2006. "Covenants without the Sword: International Law and the Protection of Civilians in Times of War." *World Politics* 58 (3): 339–377.

2010. "Bear Any Burden? How Democracies Minimize the Costs of War." *The Journal of Politics* 72 (2): 528–544.

van Bruinessen, Martin. 1988. "Between Guerrilla War and Political Murder: The Workers' Party of Kurdistan." *Middle East Report* (153): 40.

Verwimp, Philip. 2003. "Testing the Double-Genocide Thesis for Central and Southern Rwanda." *Journal of Conflict Resolution* 47 (4): 423–442.

2005. "An Economic Profile of Peasant Perpetrators of Genocide: Micro-Level Evidence from Rwanda." *Journal of Development Economics* 77 (2): 297–323.

Villalobos, Joaquín. 1989. "A Democratic Revolution for El Salvador." *Foreign Policy* (74): 103.

Vinjamuri, Leslie, and Aaron Boesenecker. 2007. *Accountability and Peace Agreements: Mapping Trends from 1980–2006.* HD Report. Geneva: Henry Dunant Centre for Humanitarian Dialogue.

Vreeland, James Raymond. 2008. "Political Institutions and Human Rights: Why Dictatorships Enter into the United Nations Convention against Torture." *International Organization* 62 (1): 65–101.

Wagner, Steven. 1999. "Summary of Public Opinion Preceding the Parliamentary Elections in Indonesia – June 1999." The International Foundation for Election Systems (IFES).

Walter, Barbara F. 2009. *Reputation and Civil War: Why Separatist Conflicts Are So Violent.* Cambridge: Cambridge University Press.

Watts, Nicole F. 1999. "Allies and Enemies: Pro-Kurdish Parties in Turkish Politics, 1990–94." *International Journal of Middle East Studies* 31 (4): 631–656.

2010. *Activists in Office: Kurdish Politics and Protest in Turkey.* Seattle: University of Washington Press.

Weeks, Jessica L. 2008. "Autocratic Audience Costs: Regime Type and Signaling Resolve." *International Organization* 62 (1): 35–64.

Weinberg, Leonard, Ami Pedahzur, and Sivan Hirsch-Hoefler. 2004. "The Challenges of Conceptualizing Terrorism." *Terrorism and Political Violence* 16 (4): 1–18.

Weinstein, Jeremy M. 2005. "Resources and the Information Problem in Rebel Recruitment." *Journal of Conflict Resolution* 49 (4): 598–624.

2007. *Inside Rebellion: The Politics of Insurgent Violence.* Cambridge: Cambridge University Press.

White, Paul J. 2000. *Primitive Rebels Or Revolutionary Modernizers?: The Kurdish National Movement in Turkey.* London: Zed Books.

Widjajanto, Bambang, and Douglas Kammen. 1999. "The Structure of Military Abuse." *Inside Indonesia* (62).

Wimmer, Andreas, Lars-Erik Cederman, and Brian Min. 2009. "Ethnic Politics and Armed Conflict: A Configurational Analysis of a New Global Data Set," *American Sociological Review* 74 (2): 316–337.

Wood, Elisabeth Jean. 2000. *Forging Democracy from Below: Insurgent Transitions in South Africa and El Salvador.* Cambridge: Cambridge University Press.

2003. *Insurgent Collective Action and Civil War in El Salvador.* Cambridge: Cambridge University Press.

2006. "Variation in Sexual Violence during War." *Politics & Society* 34 (3): 307–342.

2009. "Armed Groups and Sexual Violence: When Is Wartime Rape Rare?" *Politics & Society* 37 (1): 131–161.

Wood, Reed M. 2010. "Rebel Capability and Strategic Violence against Civilians." *Journal of Peace Research* 47 (5): 601–614.

2014a. "From Loss to Looting? Battlefield Costs and Rebel Incentives for Violence." *International Organization* 68 (4): 979–999.

2014b. "Opportunities to Kill or Incentives for Restraint? Rebel Capabilities, the Origins of Support, and Civilian Victimization in Civil War." *Conflict Management and Peace Science* 31 (5): 461–480.

Wood, Reed M., Jacob D. Kathman, and Stephen E. Gent. 2012. "Armed Intervention and Civilian Victimization in Intrastate Conflicts." *Journal of Peace Research* 49 (5): 647–660.

Woodward, Susan L. 1995. *Balkan Tragedy: Chaos and Dissolution after the Cold War.* Washington, D.C.: Brookings Institution Press.

World Bank. 2003. "Sudan – Stabilization and Reconstruction: Country Economic Memorandum (Vol. 1 of 2): Main Text." Washington, D.C.: World Bank. Available from documents.worldbank.org.

Wucherpfennig, Julian, Nils W. Metternich, Lars-Erik Cederman, and Kristian Skrede Gleditsch. 2012. "Ethnicity, the State, and the Duration of Civil War." *World Politics* 64 (1): 79–115.

Yükseker, Deniz. 2007. "Research Findings on Internal Displacement in Turkey: National Reports." In *Coming to Terms with Forced Migration: Post-Displacement Restitution of Citizenship Rights in Turkey*, 145–157. Istanbul: Turkish Economic and Social Studies Foundation (TESEV) Publications.

Zürcher, Christoph. 2007. *The Post-Soviet Wars: Rebellion, Ethnic Conflict, and Nationhood in the Caucasus.* New York: NYU Press.

Index

Made in the USA
Middletown, DE
27 August 2021